Women in Law

# Women in Law

## A BIO-BIBLIOGRAPHICAL SOURCEBOOK

Edited by
**Rebecca Mae Salokar and**
**Mary L. Volcansek**

Greenwood Press

Westport, Connecticut
London

**Library of Congress Cataloging-in-Publication Data**

Women in law : a bio-bibliographical sourcebook / edited by Rebecca Mae Salokar and Mary L. Volcansek.
p. cm.
Includes bibliographical references and index.
ISBN 0–313–29410–0 (alk. paper)
1. Women lawyers—Biography. 2. Women judges—Biography. 3. Women law teachers—Biography. 4. Women political activists—Biography. 5. Women in politics—Biography. 6. Law—Bio-bibliography. I. Salokar, Rebecca Mae. II. Volcansek, Mary L., 1948– .
K170.W66 1996
016.34'0082—dc20 96–10747

British Library Cataloguing in Publication Data is available.



Library of Congress Catalog Card Number: 96–10747
ISBN: 0–313–29410–0

First published in 1996

Greenwood Press, 88 Post Road West, Westport, CT 06881
An imprint of Greenwood Publishing Group, Inc.

Printed in the United States of America

The paper used in this book complies with the Permanent Paper Standard issued by the National Information Standards Organization (Z39.48–1984).

10 9 8 7 6 5 4 3 2 1

*Dedicated to our mothers*

*Leota L. Matthews*
*Aileen R. Salokar*

# CONTENTS

# Women in Law

# INTRODUCTION

Women were largely excluded from public life until the twentieth century, and still the extent of their access to political and legal prominence varies according to geography, culture, religion, and tradition. Few now in the Western world would deny that women have assumed their places in a variety of significant professions and public positions. In this book we seek to highlight the accomplishments of some 43 women who, through the vehicle of law, have made a difference. Some were trained as lawyers, whereas others used the law to attain other political goals. Often the political agendas they championed were not restricted to issues related to their sex; some sought broader social change. Like the male of the species, some women have achieved infamy, while others found fame. Those whom we have chosen to feature in this book are, in our opinion, of the heroic variety.

Although our scope was restricted to nations in the Western legal tradition, that did not prove to be very limiting. Because the reach of European colonialism was wide, its legal tradition was transported to Asia, Africa, Australia, and the Americas. Only those parts of the world dominated by Marxist legal doctrine, some parts of Asia, and sections of Islamic Asia are beyond our scope. The women selected are disproportionately from some countries because, in part, of the differential progress made by women in certain nations. The disparity also reflects our inability to locate or interest specialists from some regions. This is particularly true of South Asia, South and Central America, Australia and New Zealand, the Mediterranean, and Scandinavia.

A male friend of mine, when wishing to provoke a polite argument, will ask me: "Why were there never any great women composers, painters, writers, sculptors, etc.?" Even if he is referring to eras preceding this century, his premise is flawed. There were women who contributed to the arts: Artemisia Gentileschi and Judith Leyster (painters), Clara Wieck (composer), and Mary Wollstonecraft, Jane Austen, the Brontës, and Elizabeth Barrett (writers), to mention but a few. That their numbers were small, however, is not disputed. Where women were clearly absent was public and political life. There is no simple answer as to why this was the case, nor is there one explanation for why it changed in this century. Instead, a constellation of reasons converged in different patterns and at different times from country to country and culture to culture to limit females' horizons. Women's lives have been affected by region, period, personality, and circumstance.[1]

Women were prohibited from even the most basic participation in political life—voting—until only recently. New Zealand was the first to grant the franchise to women late in the last century (1893); Finland and Norway joined after the turn of the century; Britain and the United States followed after World War I. Belgium, France, Greece, and Italy extended voting rights to women after World War II; Portugal, Spain, and Switzerland did not grant the right to vote to women until the 1970s; and one canton in Switzerland did not give women full political rights until 1991.[2] Even now, Bahrain, Kuwait, and the United Arab Emirates deny women the right to vote and to stand for elective office.[3] In the case of some nations of sub-Saharan Africa as well as other places, the franchise was, even if granted, irrelevant if no elections were held. Some of the women chronicled in this collection were active participants in civil life, and others contributed as educators and lawyers before being allowed to vote.

The literature on gender is vast. This introduction is not intended to survey all that has been written by or about women in law. Rather, it aims to set a backdrop against which the achievements of the women whose biographies follow can be set and perhaps better appreciated. It also addresses some of the specific problems that inhere in writing about women.

## PUBLIC AND PRIVATE SPHERES

Traditionally, life and work have been divided into the public and the private, and men occupied, at least historically, the public aspects of political and commercial activity. Women were relegated to the private, domestic side. This distinction was often maintained in Europe and North America on religious and philosophical grounds and was frequently translated into law. There were, however, always exceptions. Wives worked with husbands or acted as their agents, and widows had considerable latitude in the public sphere.[4] There was no parity between the two, even though women were generally quite powerful in the home. But the outside world, man's world, was (and is) treated as more important.[5] The public/private dichotomy is not and never was totally rigid, and there is considerable historical uncertainty about how many women worked in the public world. It is clear, however, that few women before the twentieth century obtained positions of public importance.[6]

In Africa, the situation was different. Women had always participated in commerce beyond the household and had a collective voice in community affairs. That situation was only altered by the arrival of the modern state that attempted to introduce the public/private divide. "Work" became not labor, but wage labor, and that shift devalued domestic or other productive activities that were coincidentally typically female pursuits. In the sub-Saharan regions during colonial rule, the same priorities and distinctions that prevailed in Europe and North America were pushed: the vote, where it was given, was given to men; political representation, where it existed, was exclusively for men. The modern state in Africa has, in other words, "diminished women's voice and power" by artificially imposing the division.[7]

The separation of life into public and private meant not only that women were excluded from certain jobs, but also that they were not participants in the civil or political life of the country. Where they entered the workforce, it was in the nurturing professions like medicine or education, where the roles were regarded as compatible with those of wife or mother. Their abilities to participate in community affairs were circumscribed and limited. They could not affect the law, but rather were limited by it.

Religion has often provided the foundation for prescriptions for purely domestic roles for women. All of the major Western religions—Catholicism, Judaism, Islam, and Protestantism—have been invoked to justify differential roles for men and women in society. Religion served as a basis for extending and systematizing patterns of male domination in Europe, and early successes in obtaining political rights for women were largely in the Protestant countries—Britain and the Nordic countries. These countries also exhibited political moderation, guaranteed civil liberties, developed middle classes tied to a liberal political ideology, and gave increasing powers to legislative assemblies. Not surprisingly, they provided a fertile ground for a bourgeois feminist movement.[8]

Notably, however, Protestantism had also provided the basis for upholding the strictly domestic role for women. That argument is stated perhaps most clearly in the decision of the United States Supreme Court to uphold the validity of an Illinois law that prevented women from practicing law. Justice Joseph Bradley, in that 1873 decision, had cited the "law of the Creator" as precedent for his pronouncement that "the natural and proper timidity and delicacy which belongs to the female sex evidently unfits it for many of the occupations of civil life [for] the paramount destiny and mission of woman are to fulfill the noble and benign offices of wife and mother."[9]

The Roman Catholic Church's doctrines also restricted women's roles narrowly to those of wife and mother.[10] The Islamic Koran was revolutionary in its time for liberating women, but it, nevertheless, placed women in a subordinated position, for "men have authority over women by virtue of the preference God has accorded men over them."[11] Islamic prescriptions for gender relationships have been translated differently in the Arab-Muslim world than in Asia, where social hierarchies are recognized as part of customary norms and have typically been even more oppressive to females.[12]

Religion melts into culture, history, and tradition, though, and forms a different pattern in every country. Structural changes in society have clearly altered how each of these influences has impacted the role of women. Industrialization in Europe and later in Africa as well as the rise of capitalism changed the face of production from the family unit to a larger collective. Domestic duties shifted from centrality to the periphery as outside employment became essential for survival; the economic unit was transformed.[13]

Women were not, however, universally disadvantaged in any cultural milieu. Class has clearly been an equalizing force, and those with "more education, money and land" are advantaged regardless of gender.[14] The link between class and achievement is clear among many of the women featured in this collection. Most were from solid bourgeois or even semi-aristocratic families, with resources and access traditionally denied to their less fortunate sisters. Indeed, efforts by women to breach barriers to careers were typically tied to their increased education and were pursued by those with the resources to engage in employment and political activity. In the United States, after the Civil War, women began to seek access to the bar; this agitation for expanded venues was coterminous with increased education for females. Consequently, the number of women lawyers more than doubled from 75 in 1880 to 208 in 1890 in the United States.

If class was one defining element for women's access, race and ethnicity were another. Women from the dominant racial groups undoubtedly had more resources at their disposal but may have confronted family resistance. Deborah Rhode says that the euphemism often used for the absence of a daughter who was in graduate or professional school was that she was "south for the winter." Interestingly, women of color in the United States did not face that dilemma, for their families were anxious to support a child who might supplement income in ways that unskilled labor could not. Charlotte Ray was the first black woman to graduate from law school, graduating from Howard University in 1873. The number of African American women lawyers remained constant, however, at about 25 for the next century. Even so, proportionately more women than men of color were completing college than was the case for whites. That pattern was equally true of other ethnic minorities in the United States.[15]

## LEGAL OBSTACLES

Although women of a certain class and a certain generation gained entry into some professions, there remained legal barriers to women's participation in civil and political life. All of the great rights proclaimed in the name of liberal democracy in the late eighteenth century—the Declaration of Independence, the U.S. Constitution, and the Declaration of the Rights of Man and Citizen—were clearly addressed to *men*, not to humanity as a whole. Even the U.S. Supreme Court made that distinction clear in a 1874 decision in which it stated that the privileges and immunities clause of the Fourteenth Amendment allowed states to extend the right to vote, as a privilege of citizenship, to men alone.[16] A similar prohibition continued in France through the 150 years that followed the revolution of 1789 that established the rights of *man* and citizen.[17]

Legal barriers to women's participation in civil life and in the professions were erected across Europe and in North America, often with religious foundations or for the "protection" of women. Roman law-based codes addressed private issues and in France, institutionalized woman's subordination to her husband by compelling a wife to live where her husband chose, forfeiting her personal income to her husband, and relinquishing her rights to her children in the event of a divorce. Scandinavian countries practiced a form of customary law that was also private in nature. Early women's rights advocates there often sought rights that the law or local customs had not even granted to men, making their task doubly difficult.[18]

Great Britain, as a common law nation, had a more public law system, and the impediments to women under it were embodied in statute and in case law. Parallel to the U.S. Supreme Court's decision regarding the legal status of women, an English Court in 1872 held that a married woman had no legal status, that is, was not a person in the eyes of the law, separate from that of her husband.[19] (Wives were shortly thereafter granted control of their own property by statute.[20]) Legal disabilities were imposed and perpetuated in various jurisdictions, and in some states of the United States were not repealed until after the middle of the twentieth century.

Though women had been denied many of the rights of men granted by the great liberal charters, most of the early feminist groups embraced liberalism as their vehicle and focused also on the theme of individual rights and the rights of self-development. The so-called rights discourse, or rights rhetoric, was necessary to dismantle the legal disabilities, but did not, in the view of many feminists, go far enough in truly achieving equality. The attitudes of families, not to mention the absence of resources, inhibited many women. Often those who broke the barriers did so out of necessity. Takie Lebra found that Japanese women usually found themselves in professions because of circumstances, even when the prevailing norms dictated that women receive education only as a fallback position in the event of spinsterhood or widowhood.[21]

Many of the legal barriers to access were eventually broken. The right to vote, as noted earlier, was extended across much of the world steeped in the Western legal tradition by the middle of this century. Late in the nineteenth century, as the apprentice system was being replaced by formal education, law schools in the United States began opening their doors to female students. Washington University in St. Louis and the University of Iowa were the first, in 1869. The University of Michigan's law school admitted women in 1870, and its medical school was also the first to admit them.[22] When Harvard Law finally admitted women in 1950, then dean Erwin Griswold remarked that the change was not significant: "Most of us have seen women from time to time in our lives and have managed to survive the shock."[23] By 1972, all U.S. law schools were coeducational. Great Britain opened its doors to female legal practitioners in 1919, with the Sex Disqualification (Removal) Act,[24] but most other European countries were slower to remove the prohibitions.

## INFORMAL BARRIERS

Legal barriers to access fell, but other, often more invidious, obstacles remained. Women were excluded from positions in public life by a phenomenon called Putnam's law or the Law of Increasing Disproportions—as one ascends the political hierarchy, the advantages of maleness, education, high socioeconomic status, and elite background increases disproportionately; elites try to reproduce themselves in recruiting newcomers.[25] That "law" was formulated with reference to Europe, but the same patterns can be found around the globe. Small differences in behavior can doom one's chances of moving up the ladder in public life, and stereotypical perceptions of women tend to magnify whatever variations there may be. Women are viewed, according to Lee Epstein, as (1) incapable of assertiveness and dominance, (2) inclined toward the family sphere, (3) hampered in public pursuits by demands of wife and mother, (4) socialized away from masculine professions, (5) uninitiated in the male (economic, political, and professional worlds) culture, (6) limited in their areas of expertise to so-called women's concerns, and (7) discriminated against if they enter the elite ranks.[26]

Therefore, even though women were given access to education in the middle of the nineteenth century and to higher education and the professions during the twentieth, they were largely barred from the policy-making functions of the polity. Women don't "fit in" and lack the informal networks on which career success depends.[27] How these informal prejudices can block women almost needs no retelling. Most people are familiar with the story of how U.S. Supreme Court Justice Sandra Day O'Connor and now Chief Justice William Rehnquist both graduated from Stanford Law School in 1952; he was number one in the class and she was number three. Rehnquist took a position as law clerk in the Supreme Court, while O'Connor was unable to locate a job as an attorney with a law firm. She was offered a legal secretary position instead and ended up as a deputy county attorney in California.[28]

Similar stories can be told about women in every profession. In the United States, until about 1950, women earned about half of the college degrees and about one-third of the graduate degrees granted, but accounted for only about 7 percent of those practicing in the professions of law, medicine, engineering, and scientific research. As recently as 1965, there were only three women partners in Wall Street firms and seven federal judges; there were no women of color in either capacity.[29] In 1991, an American Bar Association survey of young lawyers found that men were twice as likely to achieve partnership status than were women with similar backgrounds.[30] Outside North America (the Canadians have far outdistanced the United States in promoting women in public positions), the record is more disappointing.

## THE WALLS BREACHED

The major shift in women's opportunities and hence their entrance into positions of influence occurred in the late 1960s. In France, the changes are tied to the "Events of May, 1968,"[31] and in the United States, to a less clearly marked time somewhere between 1969 and 1973. Women have entered the labor force in substantial numbers. Among the European democracies in 1991, more than half of all women participated in jobs outside the home. The highest level of female participation can be found in Sweden (80.3 percent), but even where it is the lowest (Spain, Greece, Czech Republic, Slovakia, and Hungary), the percentage approaches half.[32] For the legal profession, where the presence of women in the United States increased from a mere 1.1 percent in 1910 to 12 percent in 1980,[33] the numbers continue to rise. Since 1973, all growth in U.S. law school enrollments has been caused by the entrance of women.[34] Even more staggering increases have occurred in insurance, advertising, banking, and financial services.[35]

As more and more women left the domestic sphere, they entered the political one, where law is crafted, negotiated, and passed. Parties of the left were generally more conscientious in attending to women's issues and women's concerns, but women did not necessarily support them at the ballot box. Shortly after the Second World War, the majority of the women in France cast their ballots for the conservative parties.[36] Similarly, in Italy it was the Communist party that as early as 1921 tried to place the *questione femminile* at the top of their agenda and after World War II advocated liberating women workers,[37] but there, too, women initially voted for the conservatives. Those trends have now altered, but women have found that while the left may present solid programs on women's issues, they continue sexist practices by acting on stereotypes—the "male/female model characteristic of the rest of society."[38]

Women have achieved more representation in legislative assemblies, particularly where some version of proportional representation is used, but they do not necessarily rise in the political hierarchy. There are the Indira Gandhis, Golda Meirs, and Violetta Chamorras, but they, like the Margaret Thatchers, are the exceptions, and they rose, in the view of some, by acting like men. That Mrs. Thatcher's success did nothing to further other women politicians is best demonstrated by the very low proportion of women in the British House of Commons as of 1993—only 9.2 percent. The average for the 19 nations of Western Europe is almost 19 percent, and only France, Greece, Italy, Malta, and Portugal have fewer female representatives. The Nordic countries of Denmark, Norway, and Sweden have the largest proportions of female parliamentarians.[39] The figures are slightly lower for Eastern European countries: 7.3 percent in Hungary, 10 percent in the Czech Republic, 13 percent in Poland, and 18.1 percent in the Slovak Republic.[40] Women's numbers are higher proportionately, 16 to 17 percent, in other parts of the world (Rwanda, Uganda, Mozambique, Argentina, and Nicaragua).[41]

Another political arena in which women have made inroads is the judiciary. Prior to the 1970s there were very few women judges in any country, but that has now changed, at least in the United States, France, Italy, Germany, and Canada. Studies of women legislators have demonstrated that they tend to be more strongly supportive of gender equality issues than are men. However, judges are institutionally limited in the advocacy role they can play, and even among legislators, support for women's causes does not necessarily translate into acting in the legislative forum to further those interests.[42] Particularly in the context of this volume, many women have been most successful and have made the greatest difference when painting on a larger canvas than that of women's concerns. As more women become political and judicial players, their views and their agendas will likely continue to expand beyond the more narrow, albeit important, question of women's rights. Indeed, most of those featured here did not focus exclusively on whatever discrimination had been hurled in their direction, but on what goals they intended to accomplish.

## ACHIEVING WOMEN

The limitations placed on women over the centuries, whether legal or informal, nevertheless allowed some to rise. Of those, the women who chose the vehicle of the law to achieve are the focus of this book. Almost all entered the public world as legal practitioners, scholars, and educators, or as political activists before attitudes toward women in the professions and in the political sphere began to soften some 20 years ago. What set these women apart and both equipped and motivated them to excel?

These women are typically not those who focused on the discrimination they themselves faced. A 1967 study of lawyers in the United States found that nearly half of the women surveyed felt they had been the objects of professional discrimination. That, of course, meant that half did not see themselves as victims of bias. "Discrimination is perceived differently," according to Cynthia Fuchs Epstein, "and discrimination is dispensed differently."[43] The consequences of both legal and informal biases against women and other issues of concern primarily for women formed the core of interests for many of the women we feature. Irene Cortes of the Philippines Supreme Court, Italian politician Nilde Iotti, Canadian Justice Claire L'Heureux-Dubé, British High Court Judge Brenda Hale, Irish President Mary Robinson, Canadian lawyer Helen Kinnear, and pre-Nazi era German feminists Anita Augsburg and Helene Stöcker, to name but a few, devoted much of their energy to issues of the family, divorce, illegitimate offspring, adoption, procreation and abortion, and gender equality. Florence Allen, the first woman to serve on the United States Court of Appeals, was a champion of the women's suffrage movement, and Wiltraut Rupp-von Brünneck worked during the Nazi regime in Germany to protect the positions of women academics and lawyers.

These women were often, however, engaged in many other social issues.

Judge L'Heureux-Dubé explicitly asked to take cases beyond those involving family law, because she did not want to be ghettoized into strictly domestic matters. Von Brünneck and Iotti spent time on these questions, but were also involved in such tasks as writing their respective nations' postwar constitutions—Iotti as a delegate and von Brünneck as an aide. Flerida Romero had worked on reforming the family code but also participated in writing the 1987 constitution for the Philippines. Florence Allen, once on the bench, was a proponent of the New Deal and racial desegregation.

The range of causes championed by the women we have chosen to include is wide, and the common element is the intention to make the society in which they lived a better place for all people. Some, such as Sadako Ogata, have defined their society globally, and she assists displaced people around the world in her position as United Nations High Commissioner for Refugees. Her sister citizen of Japan, Takako Doi, served as the first woman to head a political party in Japan and also as the first to serve as speaker of the lower house of the Japanese Parliament. Doi is a staunch opponent of Japanese militarism and an advocate for environmental protection, as well as a spokesperson for the rights of women and children. Sylvie Kanigi, first woman prime minister of Burundi, sought ethnic reconciliation and economic development within her country.

Israelis Tamar Pelleg-Sryck and Leah Tsemel each fashioned entire legal practices and careers around defense of the rights of Palestinians in the Israeli-held territories. Judge Simone Rozès sought to improve the French judiciary, Helen Suzman was a lone advocate for the end of apartheid in South Africa, and Canada's first woman magistrate, Emily Murphy, was an activist on behalf of the poor. Cecilia Muñoz Palma used her position on the Philippine Supreme Court to oppose human rights abuses by the Marcos government and to defend the poor, while Canadian law professor Margaret Somerville sought to bring together multiple approaches to the legal and ethical dilemmas posed by innovations in medical technology. German Constitutional Court Judge Jutta Limbach is concerned with many questions of women's rights, but she is also strongly associated with the quest for justice in the former East Germany after unification in 1989. These are hardly unidimensional women, and their concerns for social justice extend beyond those of their own gender.

Much of the literature on women in professional and political roles has found that the women who rose in their careers were typically advantaged by their family circumstances. Certainly, that is largely the case with the women we treat. Myra Bradwell, whom the U.S. Supreme Court propelled into history by upholding a state law prohibiting women from the practice of law, was from a comfortable family. The same can be said of Mary Robinson, first woman U.S. District Judge Burnita Matthews, Sadako Ogata, British Judge Mary Arden, Takako Doi, Leah Tsemel, and Philippine Supreme Court Justice Irene Cortes.

Others had to overcome their circumstances. The first woman Rwandan prime minister, Agathe Uwilingiyiana, was born to a Tutsi family of peasant farmers. She achieved much from those humble beginnings, only to be brutally assassinated at age 41. Nilde Iotti was also from a working-class family. Her background combined strong commitments to socialism and Catholicism and led her to the Italian Communist party where she eventually achieved political prominence. U.S. congressional representative and law professor Barbara Jordan also came from relatively humble origins in Houston. Bertha Wilson, who rose to be the first woman on the Canadian Supreme Court, was born in Scotland, married a minister, and only emigrated to Canada when she was 26. Soia Mentschikoff's family, aristocratic White Russians, had fled the Russian Revolution when she was two and immigrated to New York to start anew.

Conditions in Europe at the time many of these women were growing up created dire circumstances for them to overcome. Miriam Ben-Porat, the first woman to serve on the Israeli Supreme Court, was born to a wealthy Lithuanian family and fortunately decided to go to Israel in 1936; most of her family later perished at the hands of the Germans. Similarly, Jutta Limbach, the first woman president of the German Constitutional Court, had a father who was a successful engineer but was barred from working by the Nazis. Anita Augsburg and Helene Stöcker had to flee Germany in 1933, and Elisabeth Selbert's husband was imprisoned there by the Gestapo. Wiltraut Rupp-von Brünneck's lineage was quite aristocratic, and she survived the war, but family lands were expropriated and she was removed from her judgeship in the Soviet Occupation Zone of Germany in the war's aftermath. Tamar Pelleg-Sryck hailed from a wealthy family in a Jewish enclave of what had been Poland, but was deported to Kazakhastan and had a long odyssey before arriving in Palestine in 1943. Perhaps the most tragic, however, was the background of young Simone Veil; as a young Jewish girl in France, she survived the Auschwitz and Bergen-Belsen concentration camps. Each overcame the disturbing events of wartime to excel and to choose law as a means of combatting social injustice.

Much of the literature on successful women also notes the prominence of a mentor in their lives. This was true for some of the women we profile but is not a prominent feature for all. Takako Doi was nurtured and encouraged by her law professor, with whom she later collaborated. Helen Kinnear joined her father's law firm, and Florence Allen, Suzanne Bastid, and Mary Arden followed their fathers' leads into the legal field. Soia Mentschikoff married her law professor, Karl Llewelyn, and collaborated with him in drafting the Uniform Commercial Code.

Most had strong family support, and that was particularly true of those who had husbands. James Bradwell, for example, served as his wife Myra's mentor and teacher. Janet Reno, the first woman to be U.S. attorney general, had an almost overpowering role model in her mother, a professional journalist who allegedly once wrestled an alligator. And Nilde Iotti was mentored by her lover, Palmiro Togliatti, who was the leader of the Italian Communist party but whom she could not marry because of the Italian law prohibiting divorce. Others, such as Burnita Shelton Matthews, were actively discouraged by their parents; she was sent, despite her desire to study law, to a music conservatory. Florence

Allen, incidentally, spent two years in Berlin studying to be a concert musician before she studied law, but her family was apparently supportive of both career choices. Constance Baker Motley, the first African-American woman to serve in the U.S. judiciary, was financially supported through college and law school by a white benefactor, Clarence Blakeslee.

Some of our outstanding women also faced other difficulties. Mary Robinson, a Catholic, has what is known in Ireland as a "mixed marriage," for her husband is Protestant. Even more difficult was Sylvie Kanigi's choice of a husband; the Tutsi woman who would become Burundi's first woman prime minister married a Hutu man. Both Robinson and Kanigi aimed for reconciliation of opposing groups, those of their heritage and the ones of their husbands, whose rivalries had spilled so much blood and created such divides.

This book's title carries the term *bio-bibliography*. Some of the women we feature have been scholars and have made significant contributions to the study of law. Others were lawyers, judges, or political activists. At least one, anti-apartheid advocate Helen Suzman, never finished college. Those who chose the academic route, however, made major contributions. Beverly Blair Cook is recognized as the woman political scientist who made the study of women in the law respectable, but she also made substantial contributions to our understanding of judicial socialization and the influence of public opinion on judicial decision making. Irene Cortes was a law professor at the University of the Philippines and rose to be dean of the College of Law, vice president for Academic Affairs, and executive vice president of the University. Soia Mentschikoff was the first woman professor at Harvard Law School, before women were even permitted as students, and was later the dean of the University of Miami School of Law. Margaret Somerville, who began her professional life first as a pharmacist, became the first woman in Canada to hold a university chair in law. Her research on medicolegal ethics and bioethics has been path breaking. Sadako Ogata was a professor of international relations at Sophia University in Tokyo and eventually held virtually every administrative position in the university before serving full time with the United Nations. Jutta Limbach, before entering the German judiciary, held the position of distinguished professor of law at Free University in Berlin, Rosalyn Higgins is an internationally recognized professor of international law at the London School of Economics, and Suzanne Bastid-Basdevant broke French gender barriers as a renowned professor of public international law.

## WRITING ABOUT WOMEN'S LIVES

There are difficulties that inhere in writing any biography, but particularly when writing women's biographies. The most common adjective used, for example, to describe the women in this volume is "first"—the first woman ______. Some of the women we have chosen to highlight might not seem to be *that* outstanding if their accomplishments are measured against those of men. After all, we hail Sandra Day O'Connor as the *first* woman to serve on the U.S. Supreme Court and Janet Reno as the *first* woman to be Attorney General of the United States, but who remembers who was the first man to hold either office?

The contributions attributed to a woman subject may seem, at times, magnified. Indeed, a different kind of person is being profiled when she is female, for not all "achieved the kind of celebrity or lasting fame that many male biographical subjects enjoyed."[44] Since women were largely prohibited from public pursuits or marginalized when they entered them, the more circumscribed scope of their accomplishments is hardly surprising. They lacked the resources essential to obtaining fame—educations, professions, and supportive wives.[45]

Biography has evolved as the most common form for chronicling women's lives and history, and it is often criticized for being unrepresentative, for singling out women whose stories tell us little about how most women made their way.[46] The same applies, of course, to accounts of the lives of men. Biographies of both men and women share as well the difficulty of separating the subject from the author: "On the trail of another man, the biographer must put up with finding himself at every turn; any biography uneasily shelters an autobiography within."[47] What appears worthy of report may often reflect the writer as much or more than the subject.

Writing about women inevitably becomes, moreover, a gender-oriented process, for "when the subject is female, gender moves to the center of the analysis."[48] This is partly, according to some feminist writers, because women's lives have differed so profoundly from men's. One element that is inevitably highlighted, and correctly so, in retelling an accomplished woman's life is how she managed to excel and to rise above the limitations that her gender placed on her—the role or attitude of her husband or parents, the balance between motherhood and career, the problems of commutes, or interruptions of careers for childbearing. Even some of the seemingly mundane concerns of women would not merit mention when writing about men. For example, Virginia Drachman describes the considerable discussion among women lawyers in the United States at the close of the nineteenth century about the propriety of wearing a bonnet in the courtroom, for which there was no consensus.[49] The parallel question near the close of the twentieth century was whether or not women should wear trousers in court, and the decision by the lord chief justice in England to permit that attire was front-page news in Britain.[50] Despite the considerable gains of women over the last century, some of their concerns are quite specific to their sex. Gender defines both self-identity and the relationship of that self to society.[51]

There are some difficulties in writing biographies that are generic and others that are more specifically associated with writing about women. The first difficulty, the temptation to become obsessed with the subject and to find only positive attributes, is shared by all biographers. Carol Sanger charges that there is also an inclination, particularly when writing about women, to fall into "the commemorative Victorian tradition,'' in which the woman and her life are retouched to make the best presentation.[52] The life and achievements are retold with uncritical adoration. The second problem is ideology, since the author's rigorous effort to be true to the cause may interfere with objectivity. Commitment to feminism, for example, may color how one writes about women, and other subjects may be shaded by a writer's ideological leanings.

## SUBJECTS AND AUTHORS

In the profiles that follow, we have attempted to avoid some of the pitfalls of biographical writing. Whereas most such works on women are typically written by other women, we are fortunate to have a healthy mix of both men and women among our authors. That perhaps leads to the question of how the women whom we feature were selected and their biographers found. Obviously, the possibilities for women who meet our criteria—having made a significant contribution through the law, either as a legal practitioner or as one who has used the law to achieve social change—is a broad net; the Western legal tradition did not prove to provide much of a limiting parameter.

We organized an editorial advisory panel for this book, eight scholars from the United States, Canada, and Europe. They were chosen for their known expertise in women's issues or for their work on legal subjects in various parts of the world. The editorial advisory board was invited to nominate women for inclusion and to justify their selections. Once all were collected, the list was circulated for additional names or for comments and suggestions on the first round of names. Some were eliminated and others added. Geographical gaps and disproportionate representation of, for example, women from the United States, were then addressed and we contacted various specialists on those regions and asked for their nominations. A final register was then compiled.

The Appendix is a listing of the women subjects included in this work by their professional contributions to law as practicing attorneys or judges, educators and scholars, and political officeholders and activists. That many of these women's names appear on more than one list is not surprising. Like their male cohorts, women have made use of multiple professions in order to effect social and legal change. It is also not surprising that several of our subjects either knew each other or served as role models for other women who are included in this text. In order to privide a cross-reference for the reader, we have identified those who have their own entry with an asterick where they are mentioned in the context of another's biographical sketch.

## NOTES

1. Carol Sanger, ''Curriculum Vitae (Feminae): Biography and Early American Women Lawyers,'' 46 *Stanford Law Review* (May, 1994): 1257.

2. Michael Gallagher, Michael Laver, and Peter Mair, *Representative Government in Modern Europe* (New York: McGraw-Hill, 1995), 272.

3. Victoria Brittain, ''Poor Nations Shame Rich in UNICEF Rankings,'' *Manchester Guardian Weekly* (June 18, 1995): 5.

4. Deborah L. Rhode, *Justice and Gender: Sex Discrimination and the Law* (Cambridge, Mass.: Harvard University Press, 1989), 9–10.

5. Claire Duchen, *Women's Rights and Women's Lives in France, 1944–1968* (London: Routledge, 1994), 95.

6. Deborah L. Rhode, ''Perspectives on Professional Women,'' 40 *Stanford Law Review* (May, 1988): 1164–65.

7. Kathleen Staudt, ''Women's Politics, the State, and Capitalist Transformation in Africa,'' in Irving Leonard Markovitz (ed.), *Studies in Power and Class in Africa* (New York: Oxford University Press, 1987), 193–97.

8. Joni Lovenduski, *Women and European Politics: Contemporary Feminism and Public Policy* (Amherst: University of Massachusetts Press, 1986), 20.

9. *Bradwell v. Illinois*, 83 U.S. 130 (1873).

10. Judith Adler Hellman, *Journeys Among Women: Feminism in Five Italian Cities* (New York: Oxford University Press, 1987), 27.

11. As quoted in Anne Lippert, ''Algerian Women's Access to Power: 1962–1985,'' in Irving Leonard Markovitz (ed.), *Studies in Power and Class in Africa* (New York: Oxford University Press, 1987), 214.

12. Wazir Jahan Karim, *Women and Culture: Between Malay Adat and Islam* (Boulder, Colo.: Westview Press, 1992), 14–16.

13. Lovenduski, 16–17.

14. Staudt, 203.

15. Rhode, ''Perspectives on Professional Women,'' 1169–70.

16. *Minor v. Happersett*, 88 U.S. 162 (1874).

17. Duchen, 2–3.

18. Lovenduski, 15–16.

19. *R. v. Harrald*, (1872) 7 QB 361.

20. The Married Women's Property Acts of 1882 and 1893, as cited in O. F. Robinson, T. D. Fergus, and W. M. Gordon, *European Legal History: Sources and Institutions* (London: Butterworths, 1994), 296.

21. Takie Sugiyama Lebra, *Japanese Women: Constraint and Fulfillment* (Honolulu: University of Hawaii Press, 1984), 231.

22. Virginia G. Drachman, *Women Lawyers and the Origins of Professional Identity in America* (Ann Arbor: University of Michigan Press, 1993), 4.

23. As quoted in Deborah L. Rhode, ''Gender and Professional Roles,'' 63 *Fordham Law Review* (October, 1994): 39.

24. Robinson, et al., 297.

25. Lovenduski, 206.

26. As quoted in ibid., 210–11.

27. Rhode, ''Professional Women,'' 1190.

28. Sue Davis, ''The Voice of Sandra Day O'Connor,'' 77 *Judicature* (November–December, 1993): 135.

29. Rhode, ''Professional Women,'' 1173–74.

30. Rhode, ''Gender Roles,'' 60.

31. Duchen, 5. The ''Events of May, 1968,'' refers to a series of incidents in France

that started with student demonstrations in Paris and led to a general national strike. In response to the evidence of widespread discontent, the government of France changed a number of policies, and the events sparked the genesis of DeGaulle's resignation a year later.

32. Gallagher, et al., 290.

33. Cynthia Fuchs Epstein, *Women in Law* (New York: Basic Books, 1981), 4.

34. Richard L. Abel, *American Lawyers* (New York: Oxford University Press, 1989), 91.

35. Ibid., 92.

36. Duchen, 39–40.

37. Hellman, 31.

38. Ibid., 45.

39. Gallagher, et al., 290.

40. Ibid., 295.

41. Brittain, 5.

42. Elaine Martin, ''The Representative Role of Women Judges,'' 77 *Judicature* (November–December, 1993): 172.

43. Epstein, 80.

44. ''Introduction,'' in Sara Alpern, Joyce Antler, Elisabeth Israels Perry, and Ingrid Winther Scobie (eds.), *The Challenge of Feminist Biography: Writing the Lives of Modern American Women* (Urbana: University of Illinois Press, 1992), 6.

45. Sanger, 1250.

46. Elizabeth Windschuttle, ''Introduction,'' in Elizabeth Windschuttle (ed.), *Women, Class and History: Feminist Perspectives on Australia, 1788–1978* (Auckland: Fontana/Collins, 1980), 23.

47. Paul Murray Kendall, *The Art of Biography* (New York: W.W. Norton, Inc., 1965), x.

48. Alpern, et al., 7.

49. Drachman, 30–31.

50. Frances Gibb and Michael Hornell, ''Women Lawyers Freed to Wear Trousers in Court,'' *The Times* (May 17, 1995): 1.

51. The Personal Narratives Group, ''Truth,'' in Personal Narratives Group, *Interpreting Women's Lives: Feminist Theory and Personal Narratives* (Bloomington: Indiana University Press, 1989), 263.

52. Sanger, 1269.

## REFERENCES

Abel, Richard L. *American Lawyers*. New York: Oxford University Press, 1989.

Alpern, Sara, Joyce Antler, Elisabeth Israels Perry, and Ingrid Winther Scobie, eds. *The Challenge of Feminist Biography: Writing the Lives of Modern American Women*. Urbana: University of Illinois Press, 1992.

Davis, Sue. ''The Voice of Sandra Day O'Connor.'' *Judicature* 77 (November–December, 1993): 134–39.

Drachman, Virginia G. *Women Lawyers and the Origins of Professional Identity in America*. Ann Arbor: University of Michigan Press, 1993.

Duchen, Claire. *Women's Rights and Women's Lives in France, 1944–1968*. London: Routledge, 1994.

Epstein, Cynthia Fuchs. *Women in Law*. New York: Basic Books, 1981.

Gallagher, Michael, Michael Laver, and Peter Mair. *Representative Government in Modern Europe*. New York: McGraw-Hill, 1995.

Gibb, Frances, and Michael Hornell. ''Women Lawyers Freed to Wear Trousers in Court.'' *The Times* (May 17, 1995): 1.

Hellman, Judith Adler. *Journeys Among Women: Feminism in Five Italian Cities*. New York: Oxford University Press, 1987.

Karim, Wazir Jahan. *Women and Culture: Between Malay Adat and Islam*. Boulder, Colo.: Westview Press, 1992.

Kendall, Paul Murray. *The Art of Biography*. New York: W. W. Norton, 1965.

Lebra, Takie Sugiyama. *Japanese Women: Constraint and Fulfillment*. Honolulu: University of Hawaii Press, 1984.

Lippert, Anne. ''Algerian Women's Access to Power: 1962–1985,'' In *Studies in Power and Class in Africa*. Ed. Irving Leonard Markovitz. New York: Oxford University Press, 1987, 209–32.

Lovenduski, Joni. *Women and European Politics: Contemporary Feminism and Public Policy*. Amherst: University of Massachusetts Press, 1986.

Martin, Elaine. ''The Representative Role of Women Judges,'' *Judicature* 77 (November–December, 1993): 172–73.

Personal Narratives Group. *Interpreting Women's Lives: Feminist Theory and Personal Narratives*. Bloomington: Indiana University Press, 1989.

Rhode, Deborah L. ''Gender and Professional Roles.'' *Fordham Law Review* 63 (October, 1994): 39–72.

Rhode, Deborah L. *Justice and Gender: Sex Discrimination and the Law*. Cambridge, Mass.: Harvard University Press, 1989.

Rhode, Deborah L. ''Perspectives on Professional Women.'' *Stanford Law Review* 40 (May, 1988): 1163–1207.

Robinson, O. F., T. D. Fergus, and W. M. Gordon. *European Legal History: Sources and Institutions*. London: Butterworths, 1994.

Sanger, Carol. ''Curriculum Vitae (Feminae): Biography and Early American Women Lawyers.'' *Stanford Law Review* 46 (May, 1994): 1245–81.

Staudt, Kathleen. ''Women's Politics, the State, and Capitalist Transformation in Africa.'' In *Studies in Power and Class in Africa*. Ed. Irving Leonard Markovitz. New York: Oxford University Press, 1987, 193–208.

Windschuttle, Elizabeth, (ed.). *Women, Class and History: Feminist Perspectives on Australia, 1788–1978*. Auckland: Fontana/Collins, 1980.

*MARY L. VOLCANSEK*

# FLORENCE ELLINWOOD ALLEN (1884–1966)

Florence Ellinwood Allen, appointed by President Roosevelt to the United States Court of Appeals for the Sixth Circuit in 1934, was the first woman in the United States to serve on a federal court of appeals.[1] Prior to her appointment to the federal judiciary, she was the first woman elected to a state court of last resort (Supreme Court of Ohio, 1922–1934) and the first woman to sit on a trial court of general jurisdiction (Court of Common Pleas for Cuyahoga County, 1920–1922). Allen's legal career spanned the years between the early twentieth-century women's movement's successful battle for the vote to the emergence of the "second wave" of feminist political activity in the 1960s. Her life reflects the inroads made by women in the legal profession during the postsuffrage era, as well as the persistence of gender barriers to judicial appointment to the nation's highest court. Despite an intense campaign to nominate Allen to the Supreme Court of the United States during the Roosevelt, Truman, and Eisenhower administrations, Allen's prediction that a Supreme Court appointment "will never happen to a woman while I am living" ultimately proved to be true.[2] Indeed, Florence Allen remained the only woman appointed to a judgeship on the United States courts of appeals during her lifetime.[3] Not until the two decades following her judicial retirement in 1959, when women's rights activity was again on the rise, were women appointed in larger numbers to the federal judiciary.

## FAMILY BACKGROUND AND EDUCATION

Born on March 23, 1884 in Salt Lake City, Utah, to Clarence Emir Allen and Corinne Anne Marie Tuckerman Allen, Florence Allen was the third daughter in a family of seven children. In choosing a legal career, Allen followed in the professional footsteps of her father, Clarence Emir Allen, a classics professor turned attorney who served in the Utah legislature from 1888 to 1894, and was elected to the United States Congress on a populist platform in 1895. As a state legislator, Clarence Allen incorporated into Utah's laws several innovative labor practices he had instituted while managing a Utah mining company in the mid-1880s, including workmen's compensation, an eight-hour day, and a six-day week. He also supported legislation establishing a free school system, and in 1894, he participated in Utah's convention to draft the first state constitution, which extended the vote to women.

Corinne Allen, a member of the first class of women to graduate from Smith College (1879) and an active participant in women's reform groups, instilled in Florence an appreciation of classical music, a belief in the importance of harmonious domestic life to individual and national identity, and a strong commitment to the cause of women's rights. In addition to raising her large family, Corinne Allen served as an officer of the Congress of Mothers and the Utah Federation of Women's Clubs, and helped establish the National Playground Association, the Free Public Library, and a home for working girls in Salt Lake City.

Committed to equal educational opportunities for women, the Allens encouraged their daughters to attend college. After graduating Phi Beta Kappa from the Women's College of Western Reserve University in 1904, Florence spent two years in Berlin, where she prepared for a possible career as a concert pianist and wrote music criticism for several American newspapers. She returned to Western Reserve University to earn a master's degree in political science, awarded in 1908. Her interest in courses in international law, comparative governments, and municipal law, and a professor's suggestion that she become a lawyer, "resolved [her] fast-developing psychological conflicts" about her future career.[4] Barred by her sex from attending Western Reserve University Law School, her first choice, Allen entered the University of Chicago Law School in 1909, the only woman in a class of approximately 100 students.

At Chicago, Allen studied criminal law under Roscoe Pound, whom she felt discouraged women from practicing law.[5] Allen quickly rose to the top of her class, but despite her academic success, she was unhappy in law school. At the end of her first year, she accepted an invitation from Frances Kellor, a lawyer and head of the New York League for the Protection of Immigrants, to move to New York to work for the League. Kellor introduced Allen to Florence Kelly, Lillian Wald, and other members of the Henry Street settlement community, but after participating in its work for a brief period, she abandoned her involvement in New York City's social welfare circles to commit herself fully to her legal career.

Because Columbia Law School admitted women to its summer program only, she enrolled in New York University Law School, an institution that had accorded full privileges to women since the mid-nineteenth century. No longer was Allen the only woman in her class; 82 of the 606 women enrolled in law schools in 1914 attended New York University.[6] Allen supported her legal studies by working part time for the National College Women's Equal Suffrage League. In 1911, Executive Director Maud Wood Park selected Allen to be her assistant secretary, and drew her deeply into the movement to which Allen would devote her law school summers and the first decade of her legal career.

## CAREER DEVELOPMENT

Allen graduated second in her class at New York University in June, 1913, and returned to Ohio to participate in the state suffrage campaign, study for the bar exam, and begin her legal practice. The private legal community remained inhospitable toward woman lawyers, and despite several family connections, Allen was unable to find a job in a Cleveland firm. Instead, she opened her own practice, which she devoted to legal aid and social reform work.

Like Burnita Shelton Matthews,* later to be appointed the first woman federal district court judge, Allen acquired litigation experience early in her career by representing women's organizations fighting for advances in women's status through changes in the law.[7] In 1916, Allen argued before the Ohio Supreme Court in favor of municipal suffrage for women, a legal frontier developed by the suffragists following defeats in their campaign to amend state constitutions.[8] She also worked with the Suffrage party of Cleveland on a bill granting women the right to vote for presidential electors. After the bill passed, Allen defended their hard-fought victory in court by initiating lawsuits challenging the validity of antisuffrage petitions for a referendum on the statute. Despite the success of the suits in getting many signatures invalidated, the statute was recalled by popular referendum.[9]

As World War I drew to a close, Allen represented women workers facing demotion or dismissal from wartime jobs when male soldiers returned home. In *Employees v. Cleveland Railway Company*, the National Women's Trade Union League retained Allen to challenge a National War Labor Board recommendation that the company replace 300 women workers, including 173 conductors, with men. Allen successfully argued that the War Labor Board should recommend reinstatement, but the company ignored the Board and honored an agreement to fire the women in order to settle a strike by unionized male conductors.[10]

In addition to her legal work for women's rights, Allen traveled throughout Ohio delivering speeches in support of extending the vote to women. Allen's contributions to the suffrage cause and her involvement in the Ohio Democratic party earned her an appointment as assistant prosecutor for Cuyahoga County, Ohio, in 1919. The head prosecutor reportedly considered her "the equal of virtually any male attorney in Cleveland" and predicted that she would "do a man's job in [the] office."[11] Allen was put in charge of the grand jury, which, despite its initial resistance to a female prosecutor, returned a record number of indictments during her tenure.

Shortly after ratification of the Nineteenth Amendment to the United States

Constitution, Allen announced her candidacy for judge of the Cuyahoga County Court of Common Pleas as a nonpartisan candidate. Women from both parties with whom she had worked for woman suffrage and world peace, as well as major newspapers, unions, churches, citizens' groups, and members of both political parties rallied to her cause, and in 1920, Allen became the first woman elected to sit on a court of general jurisdiction. Two years later, the same constituency mobilized "Florence Allen Clubs" throughout the state to campaign for her successful election as an independent candidate to the Supreme Court of Ohio. Allen was reelected to the court in 1928, by the largest plurality ever won for that office.

Allen's attempts to translate her popularity as a judge into a legislative victory were unsuccessful. In 1926, Allen was defeated by the Democratic incumbent in the United States Senate primary, despite efforts by major labor and other organizations to convince the electorate that Judge Allen was "the best and biggest 'man' for the job."[12] Allen campaigned for a seat in the United States Congress in 1932, but again was defeated.

Legislative losses did not tarnish Allen's image as a highly competent judge. In 1934, President Franklin D. Roosevelt appointed Allen to fill a vacancy on the United States Court of Appeals for the Sixth Circuit, making her the first woman appointed to a federal appellate court in the history of the United States and one of the highest ranking female jurists in the world at that time. Allen owed her appointment to the federal judiciary in large part to the lobbying efforts of a network of women reformers who had obtained positions in the New Deal government, led by Democratic National Committeewoman Molly Dewson, as well as such supportive male colleagues as United States Court of Appeals Judge Harold Stephens, then an assistant attorney general.[13] Despite strong support for her nomination in many quarters, the appointment of a woman to the federal appellate bench provoked controversy: Allen recalls in her memoirs that one of her Sixth Circuit brethren reportedly took to his bed for two days after her appointment.[14]

Professional women's attempts during the course of three presidential administrations to elevate Allen to the Supreme Court of the United States resulted in serious consideration but no appointment. According to political strategist India Edwards, President Harry Truman felt positively about Allen's nomination but was discouraged by the negative reaction of Chief Justice Fred Vinson and the associate justices with whom he consulted. The justices evidently believed that a woman's presence would inhibit their conference deliberations, where, with shirt collars open and shoes off, they decided the legal issues of the day.[15]

## ACHIEVEMENTS AND CONTRIBUTIONS

In her 12 years as a state supreme court justice (1922–1934) and her 25 years of service on the federal bench (1934–1959), Allen authored hundreds of opinions in cases raising many of the pressing economic, political, and social issues confronting the increasingly industrialized and urbanized United States. Her first decision on the Ohio Supreme Court held that Cleveland's City Manager Plan, which adopted a system of proportional representation, was constitutionally valid.[16] Later that term, she issued a decision construing the state Workman's Compensation Act broadly to preserve an employee's action against an employer who failed to comply with workplace safety requirements, overruling previous state Supreme Court interpretations that favored employers in the process.[17] In another decision illustrative of her general support of organized labor, she ruled that nonviolent and uncoerced picketing was lawful.[18]

As a federal judge, Allen proved to be a strong supporter of President Roosevelt's New Deal initiatives. Allen rendered her most celebrated decision in a 1938 case challenging the constitutionality of the Tennessee Valley Authority Act,[19] which authorized the construction of several dams and reservoirs in the Tennessee River watershed to control flooding, promote navigation of interstate waterways, and produce electrical power. Eighteen power companies challenged the constitutionality of the Act as violative of the commerce clause and sought to enjoin all aspects of TVA power activities. The three-judge district court panel over which Allen presided upheld the constitutionality of the statute in its entirety. The decision provided Roosevelt's New Deal government, beleaguered by several Supreme Court decisions invalidating economic recovery legislation, with a monumental victory. In *Filburn v. Helke*,[20] another important New Deal case, Judge Allen dissented from the three-judge court majority ruling that national wheat crop controls exceeded the constitutional reach of the federal commerce power. The Supreme Court reversed in *Wickard v. Filburn*[21] and generally followed Allen's reasoning that the growing practices of an individual wheat farmer affected interstate commerce and could therefore be nationally regulated.

Allen issued the first federal court ruling calling for desegregation in public housing a year after the Supreme Court declared racially segregated educational facilities unconstitutional in *Brown v. Board of Education*.[22] However, Allen was more hesitant to assert judicial power in cases involving what she perceived as discrimination in "purely social relationships." During her Sixth Circuit confirmation hearing, members of the Senate Judiciary Committee criticized her 1933 ruling for a university in a race discrimination case brought by an African-American student placed in a separate housing facility.[23]

Allen resisted attempts to limit her judicial responsibilities because of her sex with a combination of persistence, good humor, and exemplary service. As a state trial court judge, she refused an invitation extended by her fellow judges to preside over a special domestic relations court, reasoning that as an unmarried woman she lacked the personal experience with domestic relations matters possessed by her married brethren.[24] Soon after her appointment to the Sixth Circuit, Allen protested her exclusion from patent cases. Suspecting that her sex was the cause, she convinced the chief judge that her family background familiarized her with "industrial situations that many women know nothing about."[25]

Thereafter, Allen presided over numerous complex patent cases and developed a reputation as an expert in patent law.

Allen zealously advocated equality for professional working women throughout her career. She decried the double burden of paid employment and housework shouldered by most working women, yet her formula for success as a woman in a male-dominated world imposed a psychological "double standard" on women without explicit regard for its effects. In a 1926 speech, Allen admonished women to "[n]either forget nor remember that you are a woman, paradoxical as that sounds. Ask no sex favors, and don't be masculine in dress or manners; . . . unconscious femininity is an aid in public life."[26]

Allen's argument for women's participation in the professions echoed the two-pronged justification for women's enfranchisement asserted by early twentieth-century suffragists: she staked her claim on equality as well as woman's alleged moral superiority. "This is the real reason for having competent and upright women serve as judges," she noted in her memoirs. "When women of intelligence recognize their share in and their responsibility for the courts, a powerful moral backing is secured for the administration of justice."[27] In "The Outlawry of War," a speech delivered at the 1925 Conference on Causes and Cures of War organized by Carrie Chapman Catt, Allen similarly argued that woman's moral nature rendered them particularly responsible for developing an international legal system to prevent war. Having lost both of her brothers to World War I-related injuries, Allen remained throughout her life passionately committed to international law as a means of instituting world peace.

Allen's publications included *This Constitution of Ours* (1938), a survey of American constitutional history and doctrine; *The Treaty as an Instrument of Legislation* (1952), an essay on the effects of international treaties on American government; *Patris* (1908), a volume of poetry; *To Do Justly* (1959), her memoirs; and numerous articles about international law and women's rights in the *Woman Lawyers' Journal* and other periodicals. She served on the plenary board of the National Association of Women Lawyers and was an active member of the International Federation of Women Lawyers. Allen's accomplishments were widely acknowledged before and after her judicial retirement in 1959; she received the prestigious Albert Gallatin Award from New York University in 1960 and acquired numerous honorary degrees. Allen died of a stroke at the age of 82 in September, 1966.

## NOTES

1. From 1958 to 1959, her last year of active service on the bench, Allen served as chief judge of the United States Court of Appeals for the Sixth Circuit, another "first" for women.

2. Florence Allen to H. C. Herring, March 17, 1934, Florence Allen Papers, Western Reserve Historical Society Library, cited in Beverly Cook, "The First Woman Candidate for the Supreme Court—Florence Allen," *Supreme Court Historical Society Yearbook*

(1981), 19–35, a comprehensive account of the campaign to nominate Allen during the Roosevelt and Truman presidencies. For a description of the campaign to nominate Allen for a Supreme Court seat during the Eisenhower administration, see Jeanette Tuve, *First Lady of the Law: Florence Ellinwood Allen* (Lanham, Md.: University Press of America, 1984), 167–169.

3. Allen lived to see the appointment of three women to the United States district courts, but she remained the only woman to serve as a federal circuit judge until the 1968 appointment of Shirley Hufstedler to the U.S. Court of Appeals for the Ninth Circuit, two years after Allen's death. Genevieve Kline, the first woman federal judge in the United States, was appointed by President Calvin Coolidge to the Customs Courts (now the Court of International Trade) in 1928.

4. Florence Ellinwood Allen, *To Do Justly* (Cleveland: Western Reserve University Press, 1965), 23.

5. Allen's view of Pound appeared to change during her career as a judge. Ibid., 49–50.

6. Tuve, 23.

7. However, while Matthews represented the National Woman's party, Allen affiliated herself with the more moderate National American Suffrage Association. Ibid., 35.

8. Ibid., 41, and Allen, 35.

9. Tuve, 37–38.

10. Ibid., 49–50.

11. Newspaper clippings, Florence Allen Papers, Western Reserve Historical Society Library, cited by Tuve, 53.

12. "She Is the Best Man for the Job," *Labor* (July 31, 1926): 3, and Florence Allen Papers, Library of Congress Manuscript Division, Box 2, folder marked "1926 Campaign for Senate."

13. Susan Ware, *Beyond Suffrage: Women in the New Deal* (Cambridge, Mass.: Harvard University Press, 1981), 55–56, and Allen, 93–95.

14. Allen, 95.

15. India Edwards, *Pulling No Punches: Memoirs of a Woman in Politics* (New York: G. P. Putnam's Sons, 1977), 171–172.

16. *Reutner v. City of Cleveland*, 107 O.S. 117 (1923).

17. *Ohio Automatic Sprinkler v. Fender*, 108 O.S. 149 (1923).

18. *La France Electrical & Supply Co. v. Int. Brotherhood of Electrical Workers*, 108 O.S. 61 (1923).

19. *Tennessee Electric Power Company v. The Tennessee Valley Authority*, 21 F. Supp. 947 (E.D. Tenn. 1938), aff'd. 306 U.S. 118 (1939).

20. 43 F. Supp. 1017 (S.D. Ohio 1942), rev'd. by *Wickard v. Filburn*, 317 U.S. 111 (1942).

21. 317 U.S. 111 (1942).

22. 347 U.S. 483 (1954). *Detroit Housing Commission v. Walter Arthur Lewis*, 226 F. 2d 180 (6th Cir. 1955), upheld a lower court order enjoining the Detroit Housing Commission's practice of maintaining separate housing facilities for blacks and whites.

23. In her memoirs, Allen defended her decision by quoting an African-American woman friend who advised that, had she been the student in question, she would have graduated from the university rather than protest, in order to make it easier for her African-American women to follow in her footsteps. Allen, 92.

24. Ibid., 45.

25. Ibid., 102.

26. " 'Ask No Sex Favors' Judge Tells Girls," *Labor* (July 31, 1926): 3. For an interesting discussion of feminist ideology in the years following passage of the Nineteenth Amendment, see Nancy F. Cott, *The Grounding of Modern Feminism* (New Haven, Conn.:Yale University Press, 1987), 215–39, 278–83.

27. Allen, 48.

## REFERENCES

Allen, Florence Ellinwood. *To Do Justly*. Cleveland: Western Reserve University Press, 1965.

" 'Ask No Sex Favors' Judge Tells Girls." *Labor* (July 31, 1926): 3.

Cook, Beverly. "The First Woman Candidate for the Supreme Court—Florence Allen." *Supreme Court Historical Society Yearbook*. 1981: 19–35.

Cott, Nancy F. *The Grounding of Modern Feminism*. New Haven, Conn.: Yale University Press, 1987.

Edward, India. *Pulling No Punches: Memoirs of a Woman in Politics*. New York: G. P. Putnam's Sons, 1977.

Florence Allen Papers, Library of Congress Manuscript Division.

"She Is the Best Man for the Job." *Labor* (July 31, 1926): 3.

Tuve, Jeanette. *First Lady of the Law: Florence Ellinwood Allen*. Lanham, Md.: University Press of America, 1984.

Ware, Susan. *Beyond Suffrage: Women in the New Deal*. Cambridge, Mass.: Harvard University Press, 1981.

*SARAH WILSON*

# MARY ARDEN (1947– )

The Honorable Justice Mary Arden, D.B.E.[1] became a judge of the High Court of Justice in England in April 1993. Her previous experience as a barrister was as an influential consultant on company law in the financial/legal center in the City of London.[2] Indeed, as a woman, her rise to the pinnacles of City business affairs through the practice of company law, which regulates and enables domestic and international commercial transactions in the United Kingdom, was against the odds. Through her practice specializing in company law[3] as a member of Erskine Chambers (1971–1993)[4] and through her designation as a Queen's Counsel (1986),[5] Arden became, in 1993, the first woman ever to serve on the Chancery Division of the High Court.[6]

Justice Arden describes her 22 years at the bar as a busy time in which she often worked as many hours as she was awake. A benefit of her busy practice was that she met many able lawyers and worked on a variety of stimulating issues. She now finds that serving as a High Court judge requires fewer hours but demands immense concentration. That, and the personal responsibility that comes with making binding decisions, makes her judicial position a challenging one. The downside of judging, she states, is that it is more difficult to find the time for private study and writing.

## FAMILY BACKGROUND AND EDUCATION

Mary Arden was born in Liverpool on January 23, 1947. Her father was a solicitor and a diocesan registrar,[7] as his father had been. A brother who lives in Liverpool also is a solicitor and presently serves there as diocesan registrar. Arden decided at age 16 to go into the law, being drawn to the law as a natural consequence of her father's career and interests. Her original intention was to become a solicitor, but eventually she became a barrister instead. Arden found that she especially appreciated that, as a solo practitioner, a barrister is responsible for her own work. She has found it immensely satisfying to take personal responsibility for one's work and to do so with the enormous independence that barristers enjoy (subject, of course, to the fact that as a junior she sometimes assisted a Queen's Counsel and that later, as a Queen's Counsel herself, she was assisted by others).

Mary Arden attended Huyton College, an independent[8] secondary school in Liverpool, where she was variously both a day student and a boarder. She read classics—Latin and Greek—and modern history at A level.[9] Upon leaving school, she entered Girton College,[10] Cambridge, where she read law and served as the secretary of the University Law Society. She extended her study of law at Cambridge for an additional year to focus on company law, receiving a Master of Laws. Her successful study at Cambridge led to her receiving a Kennedy Scholarship for a year's study at Harvard, where she specialized in corporate law and received a second Master of Laws. Arden was especially interested in corporate law for its specification of a complex network of institutional structures and offices that define the powers and duties of individuals within a business entity.

## CAREER DEVELOPMENT

Justice Arden was called to the bar in 1971 as a member of Gray's Inn. She was admitted *ad eundem*[11] to Lincoln's Inn, where Erskine Chambers are located, in 1973. When she came to the bar, there were few female barristers in any field of law, and company law was a male reserve. Indeed, when she sought a place in chambers in which company law chiefly was practiced, she was actively discouraged from that course. Change was slow in the law, and it was particularly slow in the Chancery Bar. Company law was reputed to be a tough field for a woman, but she persevered and found her place in Erskine Chambers where she achieved a successful career at the bar.

Arden's progress was swift. By 1976, she had become a member of the Company Law Committee of the Law Society and later was a member and leader of the Insolvency Working party of that Committee. In 1978, she was a member of the Insolvency Sub-Committee of the Consumer and Commercial Law Committee of the Law Society. Both of these committees are consulted by the United Kingdom (U.K.) Department of Trade and Industry on proposed legislation. Her first publication, a paper presenting a legal overview of U.K. accounting practices, appeared in 1972, and she became a regular contributor to texts and manuals on accountancy and company law for the next 20 years.

Justice Arden's public appointments began in 1990, when she was appointed assistant recorder in the Crown Court and County Court, and a deputy High Court Judge, both part-time appointments. In 1991, she became attorney general of the Duchy of Lancaster.[12] The attorney general of the Duchy serves as counsel for the Crown should any matters affecting the Duchy's holdings come before the courts. More importantly, appointment as attorney general of the Duchy of Lancaster was a public recognition of Mary Arden Q.C. as one of the "high fliers" of the Chancery Bar. She was elected a Bencher[13] of Lincoln's Inn in 1993. Justice Arden is married to another High Court Judge, Justice Mance, who was appointed shortly after her own appointment. They have two daughters and one son.

Shortly before becoming a judge of the High Court in 1993, Justice Arden was appointed to the Financial Law Panel, a new body of growing importance to the City of London. Its charge was to recommend practical measures to resolve or otherwise deal with any uncertainty in English law that might adversely affect the financial markets in the City of London.

## ACHIEVEMENTS AND CONTRIBUTIONS

Justice Arden has been on the bench of the Chancery Division only since April of 1993, so her judicial contributions must lie mostly in the future. However, she was engaged in full-time practice as a specialist in company law for more than 20 years. While she sometimes appeared in court, most of her work was as a consultant and adviser for business clients. Her eminence as a legal consultant is exemplified by her joint authorship of *Tolley's Companies Act 1980* and by her contributions to *Tolley's Companies Act 1981*, *Tolley's Accounting Problems of the Companies Acts* (1984), Johnson and Patient's *Accounting Problems of the Companies Acts* (1985), *Tolley's Manual of Accounting* (1990), and (most recently) to Bromwich and Hopwood's *Accounting and the Law* (1992). As these contributions reveal, her written work often has involved the interactions between law and accounting. She has found such subjects to be "part of a fast moving field, which presents unique opportunities to be innovative and visionary." As she wrote in April 1993, just before her appointment to the bench, "experience and legislative history . . . have illustrated the subtlety and evolving nature of the relationship between law and accounting practice."[14]

Despite the habitual resistance of English lawyers to change, Arden has made a case for Parliament to reform the law so as to allow greater judicial review, which could enforce higher accounting standards for statutorily-mandated financial reports. In her own words, her recommendations rest on two premises: "First, it would seem desirable . . . to ensure that accounting standards are drawn in such a way that renders them as impervious as possible to circumvention. Second, it is perfectly permissible to think how to organize the law with a view to its being changed."[15] Indeed, her opinions on the "true and fair requirement"[16] have been published around the world and are thought to have had a profound influence on the development of accounting standards, setting ever higher standards for the presentation of financial statements.[17]

At least of equal importance has been Justice Arden's work as a member of the Financial Law Panel established in 1992, and now subscribed by the leading financial institutions of the city. Noting the creation of the Panel and its role in helping to preserve the role of the City of London as a great international financial center, Sir Brian Jenkins, then the lord mayor of London, said that it was created by the joint efforts of the Corporation of the City of London and the Bank of England "to provide a forum to assess questions of legal uncertainty as they affect our wholesale financial markets."[18] As the chairman of the Panel, Lord Donaldson of Lymington, has written:

> Now lawyers can live with uncertainty. Indeed, the uncharitable have been heard to remark that they live off it. But for financial markets it is quite different. So far as humanly possible, they must know where they stand. In this context it matters not whether the law is in fact uncertain. What matters is that the markets are in doubt.[19]

Thus, for example, the Legal Panel has completed work on two reports on the complex topic of "netting,"[20] and the Panel is presently at work on reducing other legal uncertainties in fund management.

Justice Arden also has written on insolvency, a field in which the new Insolvency Act 1986 demands judicial interpretations that are in accord with the needs of contemporary business practice. In that context she has described the duty of a judge in interpreting the law:

> Some people think that judges live like oysters, anchored in one place, unable to go out after anything and restricted to working on and digesting what happens to float by in the current of litigation. In insolvency law that is far from being the case; we have as our code a new Insolvency Act. . . . Thus there are many departures from previous insolvency law and the courts have seized this window of opportunity to take a fresh look at insolvency law when construing these provisions.[21]

It is fitting that Justice Arden's first opinion to be published in the *All England Law Reports* was one of statutory construction in a bankruptcy case, although the case turned on an interpretation of the Bankruptcy Act 1914 rather than on the Insolvency Act 1986.[22]

In arguing for the necessity of simplification and streamlining of Chancery Division procedures, Justice Arden has set a difficult objective—and future—for herself and her judicial colleagues, but she has concluded that: "[o]nly in this way, I believe can we meet the expectation that the public has of an efficient and effective system for the administration of justice. Such a system that I am suggesting is undoubtedly more demanding on the judge." Clearly, that is a challenge that she welcomes.

## NOTES

1. Dame of the British Empire. Upon their appointment, judges of the High Court are knighted. The Order of the British Empire is one of the orders of knighthood in the United Kingdom.

2. Unlike the expanse of metropolitan London, the City of London consists of one square mile in which are located most of the large financial institutions. Referring to "the City" in the United Kingdom is roughly equivalent to referring to "Wall Street" in the United States. The four Inns of Court—the Inner Temple, the Middle Temple, Lincoln's Inn, and Gray's Inn—which house most of the barristers in the United Kingdom, also are located within the City of London.

3. Americans would say "corporate" law.

4. Barristers in the United Kingdom are prohibited from forming professional partnerships or corporations. Instead, each barrister is a solo practitioner, although a number of barristers may share "chambers." Those sharing chambers are assisted by clerks and staff who work for the chambers as a whole. Erskine Chambers in Lincoln's Inn is an especially prestigious venue for barristers. These chambers bear the name of Lord Erskine (Thomas Erskine, 1750–1823) who was a particularly distinguished and famous barrister of his time. He was an advocate in many of the leading trials of his time and was named lord chancellor in 1806.

5. The title "Queen's Counsel" is conferred on barristers selected for their experience, knowledge, and success at the bar. A Queen's Counsel "takes silk" upon appointment, which means that a Q.C. wears a black silk gown and a slightly different wig when appearing in court.

6. The Chancery Division "deals with property, trusts, the administration of estates, bankruptcy, partnership, companies, revenue cases, probate business other than non-contentious common form business, and other matters specifically assigned." See S. H. Bailey and M. J. Gunn, *The Modern English Legal System*, 2d ed. (London: Sweet and Maxwell, 1991).

7. A diocesan registrar acts as registrar of the Consistory Court (or court of the bishop) of the diocese, and has various functions in relation to such matters as the issue of marriage licenses. The office is usually (and is in this case) combined with that of legal secretary to a bishop of the Church of England, in this instance, to the bishop of Liverpool.

8. That is, not state-supported. Americans would say a "private" school.

9. "A level" stands for advanced level and involves academic study from the age of approximately 16 to 18 years. The minimum school-leaving age in Britain is 16, so those who stay on for A levels are those who are academically-inclined, many of whom will seek admission to university.

10. Founded in 1869, Girton College was the first postsecondary institution for women at either Oxford or Cambridge. The college opened at Hitchin in Hertfordshire, 26 miles from Cambridge and moved to Cambridge in 1873. The first Girtonian passed a Cambridge Tripos (a final examination for the B.A. honors degree) in 1873. It was not until 1948 that women were admitted to full membership at Cambridge University. See M. C. Bradbrook, *That Infidel Place: A Short History of Girton College, 1869–1969* (London: Chatto and Windus, 1969).

11. In effect a membership of an Inn of Court otherwise than for the purpose of being called to the bar.

12. In 1399, Henry of Lancaster deposed Richard II and became king of England as Henry IV. On his accession to the throne, the Duchy of Lancaster was deliberately not merged in the Crown, and lands held by the Duchy are still administered separately to this day.

13. As a "Bencher," she serves as a member of the governing body of her Inn of Court.

14. Accounting Standards Board, *Foreword to Accounting Standards* (London: Accountancy Books, 1993).

15. M. H. Arden, "Accounting and the Law: A Legal Viewpoint," in M. Bromwich and A. Hopwood (eds.), *Accounting and the Law* (London: Prentice-Hall, 1992), 82.

16. The "true and fair requirement" means that the accounts drawn up pursuant to the Companies Act must give a true and fair view of the state of affairs of the company.

17. Mary Arden's opinion as counsel on "true and fair" reporting requirements were given and published through the accounting profession's Accounting Standards Committee (now the Accounting Standards Board).

18. *The Times* (October 30, 1992): 25.

19. Financial Law Panel, *First Annual Report to Subscribers* (London: Financial Law Panel, Ltd, October, 1994).

20. A broad sense of "netting" or set-off is that when companies are engaged in the transfer of funds through various accounts, especially international accounts, some of which may involve disbursements, while others may involve receipts, a financial institution may net out the balance so that only the net balance need actually be transferred.

21. From an address, "Insolvency and the Law," delivered by Justice Arden to the Insolvency Lawyer's Association at the Institute of Directors, November 10, 1993. The first sentence is based on a remark by C. Magruder in "Mr Justice Brandeis," 55 *Harvard Law Review* (1941–1942): 193.

22. *Re Dent (a bankrupt)* [1994] 2 All ER 904 (November 10, 1993).

## REFERENCES

Accounting Standards Board. *Foreword to Accounting Standards*. London: Accountancy Books, 1993.

Arden, M. H. "Insolvency and the Law." Speech to the Insolvency Lawyer's Association at the Institute of Directors, November 10, 1993.

Arden, M. H. "Accounting and the Law: A Legal Viewpoint." In *Accounting and the Law*. Eds. M. Bromwich and A. Hopwood. London: Prentice-Hall, 1992, 5–82.

Bailey, S. H., and M. J. Gunn. *The Modern English Legal System*, 2d ed. London: Sweet and Maxwell, 1991.

Bradbrook, M. C. *That Infidel Place: A Short History of Girton College, 1869–1969*. London: Chatto and Windus, 1969.

Financial Law Panel. *First Annual Report to Subscribers*. London: Financial Law Panel, Ltd., October, 1994.

Magruder, C. "Mr Justice Brandeis." *Harvard Law Review* 55 (1941–1942): 193–94.

*DONALD W. JACKSON*

# ANITA AUGSBURG (1857–1943)

Anita Augsburg left her mark on pre–World War II Germany not only as its first woman lawyer, but also as an avid suffragette and pacifist. She was a radical feminist and, as a result, in 1933, when the National Socialists came to power she was forced into exile in Switzerland. Although she is not well-known in Germany outside of feminist circles, her prominence was such that she had been placed on the Nazi party list of enemies as early as 1923. Most of the documentary evidence of her life and work was destroyed during the National Socialist regime, and what is known of her comes primarily from the memoirs of her lifetime companion, Lida Gustava Heymann, published in 1941.[1]

## FAMILY BACKGROUND AND EDUCATION

Anita Augsburg was born on September 22, 1857, in Verden an der Aller and was the youngest of five children. Her father was a lawyer, and she amused herself even as a young child by reading his law books. She was raised, however, as a typical middle-class girl of her era, and her training focused on the responsibilities of marriage, handicrafts, household management, and piano. At that time, only teaching was viewed as an appropriate career choice for a woman, and Augsburg studied at a teachers' institute.

She went to Berlin, where she taught physical education and studied acting in the evenings. Her private tutoring for the stage allowed her to become an actress and to tour in Germany, the Netherlands, and Lithuania. Her experiences in the theater also enabled her to become an accomplished public speaker and convincing advocate for her causes. In 1887, her grandmother died and bequeathed her estate to Anita, which gave Augsburg financial independence.

When she and a friend, Sophia Goudstikker, opened a photography gallery in Munich, Augsburg was launched on her life of independence.

That freedom led her to become active in women's causes, and in 1890, she joined the Global German Women's party that had been founded in 1865. The next year she participated in their meeting that formulated a petition to the *Reichstag* demanding that women be allowed to study at German universities and to achieve independence from men. As a result of that initiative, the first girl's gymnasium (high school) was opened in Karlsruhe in 1893, enabling girls to be educated like boys and prepared for entrance into universities.

That same year, Augsburg, then almost 40 years old, entered law school in Zurich, where she earned her juris doctorate in 1897. She was motivated to study law by her intense belief that the only way to win rights for women was through the law, by changing the civil code and by fighting battles in the legal arena. Her graduation preceded changes in German laws to allow women to study at German universities by ten years.

When Augsburg attended the International Women's Conference in Berlin in 1896, she met the more radical feminist, Lida Gustava Heymann, who would be her lifelong companion. Heymann was the daughter of a Hamburg politician and had been active in founding various social agencies for women, ranging from employment bureaus and food distribution centers to a business school.

## ACHIEVEMENTS AND CONTRIBUTIONS

Augsburg began contributing to the magazine, *Die Frauenbewegung* (*The Feminist Movement*), in 1895, and her articles advocated changing the civil code that limited women's possibilities to that of "the privileged German wife." In her subsequent writings, she attacked the underlying legal premises that defined female roles: marriage laws that benefited husbands in divorces and codes that regulated prostitution. She targeted the double standards embodied in the laws that, in her words, "supported the idea of the healthy woman for the dissipated man." She advocated boycotting marriage! Although none of Augsburg's work wrought reforms, she was able to highlight and bring attention to issues that had been regarded as taboo.

Augsburg's primary emphasis was extension of the franchise to women. She joined with other feminists—Minna Cauer and Lily Braun—to petition the *Reichstag* in 1901 and 1902 for the extension of the franchise to women, claiming that the female half of the population had been forgotten and that the laws were silent on the rights of women. Finally, in 1908, women were allowed to participate and to join political parties; they were granted the right to vote in 1919.

Pacifism was Augsburg's other political passion. She opposed World War I on the grounds that it and all wars were no more than expressions of men's violent aggressiveness. She advocated that women abstain from any work that would support the war effort, even in hospitals or caring for the wounded, and wrote that soldiers should be ashamed of their actions. She wrote in *Die Frauen-*

*stimmrecht* in 1913 that "only freedom and the peace movement are conducive to women's goals." Therefore, she argued that women should sit in the *Reichstag* where they could control politics and the military.[2]

The creation of the Weimar Republic at the close of the war did little to advance the cause of women in Germany. Augsburg and Heymann vigorously asserted women's rights in speeches and in print, and Augsburg argued for the creation of a matriarchal society. Rather obviously, there was no groundswell of support for their ideas. The more feasible policy changes that the two advocated were political education for women, demilitarization, prohibition of chemical weapons, protection of minorities (especially the Polish), and the end of colonial imperialism. They argued too, in both the press and their speeches, for the destruction of capitalism. As early as the 1920s, they were combatting the rising tides of anti-Semitism and National Socialism.

Hitler's assumption of power in 1933 prompted Heymann and Augsburg to leave Germany for South America. Friends advised them not to return to Europe, but they settled in Zurich and were active in the International Women's League for Peace and Freedom. Neither Heymann nor Augsburg ever returned to Germany; both died in Zurich in 1943.

Anita Augsburg did not win reforms in German laws, but she was an agitator who moved questions of women's rights onto the agenda. Her proposals were typically radical, and her methods sometimes outrageous. She was inclined to adopt strategies that would underscore the unequal treatment that women received. For example, in 1898, Augsburg dressed up as a prostitute and was attacked by police. She had engineered the incident to dramatize the lack of women's rights, the brutality of men's aggressiveness, and the prevailing double standard of morality in German law and society. She studied the law, never to practice as a lawyer but to understand how it could serve as a mechanism for the repression of women and how it could be reformed. Anita Augsburg's contributions lie in her courageous moral stands and her determination to make the plight of women a public issue.

## NOTES

1. Information used in this article is taken largely from Ute Gerhard, "Anita Augsburg (1857–1943): Juristin, Feministin, Pazifistin," in Thomas Blanke (ed.), *Streitbare Juristen* (Baden-Baden: Nomos Verlagsgesselschaft, 1990), 92–103.
2. Anita Augsburg, "Eriede auf Erden," *Die Frauenstimmrecht* (July 2, 1913): 50.

## REFERENCES

Augsburg, Anita. "Eriede auf Erden." *Die Frauenstimmrecht* (July 2, 1913): 50.
Gerhard, Ute. "Anita Augsburg (1857–1943): Juristin, Feministin, Pazifistin." In *Streitbare Juristen*. Ed. Thomas Blanke. Baden-Baden: Nomos Verlagsgesselschaft, 1990, 92–103.

*MARY L. VOLCANSEK AND LUBA DEWITT*

# SUZANNE BASTID-BASDEVANT (1906– )

Suzanne Bastid is a pioneer in the French legal academy. With the support of her husband and the influence of her father, Bastid has made her mark in the academic world through her teachings and writings on international law. The crowning result of her accomplishments in scholarship was her nomination to the prestigious *Académie des Sciences morales et politiques*, the first woman to ever receive such recognition.[1]

## FAMILY BACKGROUND AND EDUCATION

Suzanne Basdevant was born in Rennes, in Brittany, France, on August 15, 1906.[2] Her father, Jules Basdevant, had just begun his career as a professor of the law faculty there three years earlier. Not until 1918, some dozen years later, did he obtain an academic position in Paris where he was able to specialize in public international law. His own career was to provide a template for the career pursuits of his daughter.

Suzanne was the eldest of seven children: five boys and two girls. Perhaps it was the influence of her father and the masculine environment of her brothers that led her, after studying at the *lycée* Fénelon in Paris, to take a most unusual path for a young woman in the 1920s, the study of law. In 1930, Suzanne obtained the highest diploma, the *doctorat en droit*, after defending her thesis on international civil servants (*Les fonctionnaires internationaux*), a work that was awarded the Goullencourt Prize.

In 1937, she married Paul Bastid, her senior of 14 years. Paul Bastid had already carved his own scholarly reputation and was a respected political figure, as well. He was a professor on the law faculty in Paris, a deputy at the National Assembly (as his father had been) since 1924, and had served as a delegate to the Society of Nations since 1926. At the time of their marriage, Paul Bastid was the minister of Commerce. The Bastids were to have four children, three daughters, and a son who died.

## CAREER DEVELOPMENT

Suzanne Bastid was undoubtedly following in her father's footsteps when she decided to become a professor of law. She succeeded, ranking third in the *concours d'agrégation* for public law in 1932, and she was the first woman to be admitted to the faculty. She remained the only woman on the faculty until 1948. Suzanne was assigned to the law faculty in Lyon where she taught public international law and other subjects from 1933 to 1946.

During World War II, Bastid remained in Lyon where she was asked to assume responsibility for a course on international law at the *Ecole libre des Sciences politiques* that had been moved from Paris to Lyon. Her husband entered the *Résistance* and became a member of the *Conseil national de la Résistance* in 1943–1944.

In 1946, Suzanne Bastid was appointed to the faculty of law in Paris, which was, in itself, the promise of a brilliant career. She taught international law simultaneously in the law faculty of the University of Paris and at the *Institut d'études politiques* until her retirement in 1977–1978. In this position, Professor Bastid molded generations of lawyers, jurisprudential scholars, and judges, not only French but also foreign. She directed many of their theses.

Suzanne Bastid's notoriety as a scholar of international law spread and led to many invitations to lecture in various highly regarded institutions, including the Academy of International Law in the Hague (in 1951, 1957, 1962, 1966), the *Institut des hautes études internationales* at the European University Center in Nancy (France), the School of International Civil Servants in Madrid (Spain), the College of Europe in Bruges (Belgium), the *Institut universitaire des hautes études internationales* in Geneva (Switzerland), and the Sun Yat Sen University in Canton (China).

Her pedagogical activity also prompted her to assume more scientific tasks. From 1948 to 1966, she was a member of the *section des Etudes politiques et juridiques* at the *Centre national de la recherche scientifique* (CNRS), over which she presided at one time. In 1955, she founded the review, *L'Annuaire français de droit international public* (AFDI), published by the CNRS and served as its chief editor. In 1956, Bastid became a member of the *Institut de droit international* and eventually, vice president, as her father had been, in 1969. A few years later, she became a member of the *Société française pour le droit international*, founded in Strasbourg in 1967 as a replica of the American Society of International Law in the United States, of which she was honorary member as her father had been. Later, she became president and *président d'honneur* of the *Société française pour le droit international*.

All of these many duties did not distract Bastid from her writing. Her work is abundant, as is demonstrated by the hardly exhaustive bibliography at the conclusion of this piece. She wrote books, articles, prefaces and reports, all on the topic of international law and rights.

Bastid's interest in international law did not remain theoretical. She attended New York University, the Diplomatic Institute in Beijing and the University of Beida, but she was also sent on missions to Egypt, Poland, Portugal, Uruguay, Morocco, Lebanon, and Taiwan.

From 1949 to 1957, Bastid was a member of the French delegation to the General Assembly of the United Nations. In 1950, she was assigned to the administrative tribunal of the United Nations where she occupied the position of president or vice president at different times. She was designated ad hoc judge by Tunisia before the International Court of Justice on the appeal and interpretation of the judgment of February 24, 1982, *Tunisia v. Libya*, involving the disputed continental tableland in the Gulf of Gabes. She was also a member of the French commission to UNESCO in 1969, 1974, and 1982.

## ACHIEVEMENTS AND CONTRIBUTIONS

Suzanne Bastid has accomplished a great deal during her career, and she has naturally received many honors as a result. She was awarded an honorary doctorate from the University of Warsaw, named a correspondent member of the Academy of Sciences and Arts of Zagreb, and won the Manley O. Hudson Medal awarded by the American Society of International Law. She is *commandeur de la Légion d'honneur*, commander of the Cambodian Royal Order of Sahametrei, commander of the Mauritanean National Order of Merit, and officer of the Belgium Order of Leopold.

On March 22, 1971, Suzanne Bastid was elected *membre titulaire* of the *Académie des Sciences morales et politiques*, an honor that her father had previously received. That she was the first woman to be admitted at the Institute of France with the title of *membre titulaire* speaks to her contributions to the scholarly community. Her initiation to the Academy occurred on the Bastids' wedding anniversary and was particularly appropriate since her husband was also a member of the Academy and was present to witness his wife's success.

Suzanne Bastid's achievements are a long list of firsts for women in the French academic world, but her career and accomplishments extend beyond the borders of her own country. Her career established a precedent for women in French law faculties, and her honors, like her field of study, are truly international.

## NOTES

1. The *Académie des sciences morales et politiques* is one of the five academies composing the Institute of France.
2. Unfortunately, very little is included here about Suzanne Bastid-Basdevant's private

life, personal memories, or feelings since she did not respond to my request for an interview, and like most scholars, little information has been published on her life. My gratitude is extended to Monsieur Jean Foyer, president of *l'Académie des sciences morales et politiques*, who provided me with whatever information he had.

## REFERENCES

Bastid-Basdevant, Suzanne. *Les fonctionnaires internationaux*. Paris: Sirey, 1931.

Bastid-Basdevant, Suzanne. "Les conditions juridiques de la coexistence." *Politiques étrangères*. 1955.

Bastid-Basdevant, Suzanne with François Luchaire. "La condition juridique internationale des sociétés constituées par des étrangers." *La personnalité morale et ses limites*. 1960.

Bastid-Basdevant, Suzanne. "L'accession du tiers monde aux Nations Unies." *Les Nations Unies, chantier de l'avenir*. T. 1, 1961.

Bastid-Basdevant, Suzanne. "La justice dans les relations internationales." *La justice*. Institut d'études juridiques de Nice, 1961.

Bastid-Basdevant, Suzanne. "La société des Etats." *L'Encyclopédie française*. T. X.

Bastid-Basdevant, Suzanne. "Le tribunal administratif." *Etudes et Documents, Fascicule no. 22*, 1962.

Bastid-Basdevant, Suzanne. Progrès technique et déclin de la diplomatie classique. Centre Européen Universitaire de Nancy, 1962.

Bastid-Basdevant, Suzanne. Les obligations juridiques des Etats membres des Nations Unies et la coopération internationale. *Adaptation de l'O.N.U. au monde d'aujourd'hui*, 1965.

Bastid-Basdevant, Suzanne. *Diplomatie et information*. Centre Européen Universitaire de Nancy, 1965.

Bastid-Basdevant, Suzanne. *Aspects internationaux des libertés fondamentales*. Centre Européen Universitaire de Nancy, 1968.

Bastid-Basdevant, Suzanne. *La Nationalité des sociétés et la protection diplomatique*. Comité français de droit international privé, 1969.

Bastid-Basdevant, Suzanne. Les traités dans la vie internationale. Conclusion et effets. *Economica*, 1985.

*JACQUELINE LUCIENNE LAFON*

# MIRIAM BEN-PORAT (1918– )

Miriam Ben-Porat is the preeminent woman in Israeli law. While she was not the first woman District Court judge, she was the first female deputy president and president of a District Court. More importantly, Miriam Ben-Porat was the first woman Supreme Court justice in Israel. When she reached the mandatory retirement age of 70, she was the deputy president of the Supreme Court. Subsequently, she has twice been elected by the Israeli *Knesset* (Parliament) to serve as state comptroller. Once again, she was the first woman to serve in this position. In 1991, the government awarded her the Israel Prize, the country's highest award, for her special contributions to society and state. This distinguished career means that Miriam Ben-Porat is the second most important woman (after only former Prime Minister Golda Meir) in the history of Israel.

## FAMILY BACKGROUND AND EDUCATION

Miriam Shinezon was born in Whitbeck, Russia, in 1918. The youngest of three sisters and four brothers, she grew up in Lithuania where her parents owned a large textile factory. Despite the comforts and warmth provided by her large, wealthy family, she decided to make *aliya* (emigrate to the land of Israel) after finishing high school in 1936. It was a most fortunate decision; most of her family was killed during the Holocaust.[1]

Miriam Shinezon's entry into the *Yishuv* (the Jewish community in Mandate Palestine) was helped by members of her extended family who had preceded her and who were already making their mark. Since they had changed the family name to Ben-Porat, Miriam also adopted it. She was one of the first women to be accepted to study law at the Hebrew University, and in 1945, she was admitted to the bar.[2]

## CAREER DEVELOPMENT

In 1949, Ben-Porat went to work in the State Attorney's Office, the prosecutorial branch of the Israeli government. She quickly developed a reputation as a diligent, hard-nosed prosecutor. In each trial that Ben-Porat conducted, she pleaded as if it were the main trial of her life. Consequently, accused individuals frequently preferred to admit their guilt rather than to submit to her interrogation and prosecution. Her relentlessness did not spare her fellow advocates serving as defense lawyers. If, for example, a lawyer was late, Ben-Porat would not tell the judge that she had just seen him on the courthouse steps; rather, she would ask the judge to rule against him for nonappearance.[3] Ben-Porat's complete dedication to her tasks led to an impressive conviction rate and to her becoming, in 1953, deputy state attorney.

In 1959, her diligence in upholding the law earned Ben-Porat an appointment as a judge in the Jerusalem District Court. All members of the Israeli civil judiciary are selected by a nine-member, nonpartisan nominations committee dominated by its three Supreme Court justices.[4] Plainly, the appointment was based on Ben-Porat's record and not her popularity with the Chamber of Advocates (the Israeli Bar Association), for the lawyers responded in an unprecedented manner—they boycotted her swearing-in ceremony, and not one of them formally congratulated her. These acts were splashed all over the newspapers, and immediately thereafter a public apology was arranged between her and the Jerusalem Chamber of Advocates.[5]

The judicial establishment had noted a characteristic that the lawyers had missed—Ben-Porat's passionate dedication to upholding the rule of law. This became the dominant feature of her 18 years of service on the Jerusalem District Court. Among her prominent decisions was the order vacating the 1960 Jerusalem municipal elections because several hundred ballots were "blemished." The quality of her decisions and of her judicial skills led the nominations committee to appoint Ben-Porat as deputy president of the Jerusalem District and then, in 1975, to president of that court. In both instances, she was the first woman to occupy such a position. And in each instance, the appointment was greeted with approval by the Chamber of Advocates.[6]

In addition to her judicial career, Ben-Porat was an associate professor of Law at the Hebrew University from 1964 through 1978. Her specialty was contracts, commercial notes, and similar documents.[7] She authored the basic Israeli commentary on the Law of Assignment and published several articles in the *Israeli Law Review*[8] and other professional journals. She was a thorough, interesting, and demanding instructor; her exams were always extremely rigorous. Her tenure at the law school created yet another precedent: she was the only faculty member without a doctorate. That meant that Ben-Porat could not formally participate in the law school's doctoral program. Yet her contributions were so valued that the faculty permitted students to work with her and then granted the degrees under other names.[9]

## ACHIEVEMENTS AND CONTRIBUTIONS

The next precedent set by Miriam Ben-Porat came with her appointment as a Supreme Court justice in 1977. For years there had been heated public discussion about the need to make the Supreme Court more "representative" of the Israeli public. After a decade of distinguished service on the Jerusalem District Court, Ben-Porat was frequently mentioned as the woman best qualified to break the gender barrier. But the judicial elite, particularly the Supreme Court justices (who, it must be remembered, control the nominations committee), were unwilling to give the appearance that any factor other than legal merit was involved in the appointment process. So public pressure may actually have delayed her appointment. When Ben-Porat was finally appointed, the president of the Supreme Court, Yoel Sussmann, went out of his way to emphasize that "Judge Ben-Porat has been appointed to this Court because she is, in our view, an excellent jurist. Her sex does not have any connection with the appointment, and I do not know why it should. This is an appointment according to skills."[10]

Miriam Ben-Porat responded in a similar fashion. "I don't see myself as the representative of women on the Supreme Court, just as I hope that my male colleagues don't see themselves as representatives of men." Yet she also explicitly noted that "this is a change in direction in that I am the first woman justice on the Supreme Court. I see this appointment as a step beyond the many previous gains made by women in the direction of equal rights. And I am sure that many more will come after me."[11] In point of fact, appointments to the Israeli Supreme Court are not yet gender neutral, but as of 1996, there were three women justices on the 12-member court.

Israeli democracy functions without a formal, integrated written constitution, and its Supreme Court lacks the authority to exercise judicial review akin to its American counterpart. This necessarily limits the power and authority of the Israeli Supreme Court and its justices. As Miriam Ben-Porat, then the deputy president of the Supreme Court, put it in her characteristically blunt and clear style: "However negative the opinion of the judiciary may be about an arrangement, *in the absence of a constitution*, the *Knesset* possesses the authority and the power to pass a discriminatory statute, and if it has done so, there is no option but to act on it."[12] Yet because the Supreme Court retains the capacity for legislative interpretation, and because it sits as a general court of equity in its capacity as the High Court of Justice, its decisions have a considerable impact on Israeli society. How the court responds to claims for "justice" against the "system" matters. Justice Ben-Porat's service was marked by respect for the formal law embodied in the *Knesset* statutes and in court precedents, and by concern for protecting human rights. As she later said, "A judge's approach has to include upholding the law on the one hand, [and] love of one's fellow man on the other."[13]

A few examples can illustrate Justice Ben-Porat's approach. In 1984, the Supreme Court ruled that in the absence of explicit legislation, democratic principles required that the electoral process must be open to virtually all political ideologies, including the virulently anti-Arab *Kach* party. During the runup to the 1988 *Knesset* elections, the *Knesset* enacted legislation that banned explicitly racist (anti-Arab) parties. Ben-Porat joined an opinion that sustained the prohibition on *Kach's* participation in the election, but that refused to extend the ban to anti-Zionist parties. Democratic principles required a narrow interpretation of statutory limitations on the electoral process.[14]

In 1984, Justice Ben-Porat wrote the opinion establishing the legal principles governing the relations between the broadcast media and the Israeli citizenry. An investigatory team from the *Kolbotek* news program had used illegal means to obtain information by wiretaps and industrial espionage. The company sought to enjoin the Israel Broadcasting Authority from using that particular piece. In her opinion for the High Court, Justice Ben-Porat held: "It is the basic responsibility of the community to guard the freedom of expression of all forms of communication . . . The law in Israel, as in England and the United States, assumes that the weight should be on the freedom of expression and upon the right of the public to be informed; if the content is genuine and if it is of interest to the community, it can be aired, even if it has been obtained by illegal means."[15]

For Ben-Porat, this wide latitude for investigatory journalism required a concomitant responsibility for accuracy. An article in the newspaper *Ha'aretz* accused the director of the Israel Electric Authority of corruption, and it contained several inaccuracies. When the High Court panel reversed a judgment for slander against the newspaper on the basis of the communal interest in free expression, Ben-Porat wrote a powerful dissent. She insisted that it is the responsibility of the journalist to be careful in every aspect of an article. When the three-justice panel's decision was appealed, a larger panel of High Court justices sustained Ben-Porat's position. This decision governs the work of investigative journalists and serves as the basis for the study of slander in Israeli law schools.

In 1988, when she reached the mandatory retirement age for judges, the *Knesset* elected Miriam Ben-Porat to be Israel's state comptroller and public complaints commissioner (ombudsman). She quickly became the most controversial state comptroller in the annals of Israel. She has not hesitated to criticize the Government for its ineptitude, the giant *Histadrut* labor-industrial complex for waste and corruption, and politicians and political parties for irregularities and illegalities. She became the first state comptroller to name names. Ben-Porat also made history by becoming the first state comptroller to merit the public scorn of a prime minister and the first to impose fines on political parties for exceeding campaign finance limits. Yet when her first five-year term expired, Miriam Ben-Porat was unanimously reelected as state comptroller.[16]

Ben-Porat's tenure as state comptroller has been dominated by her concern that public actions conform to the established rules of law. She believes that Israel has very high standards, but that their application frequently leaves much to be desired. "There is a gap between the real world and the theoretical world.

We have many good laws, plus the norms of the Supreme Court, which compare well with those of any other democracy in the world. On the other hand, we have the grey reality that many of these norms are often not applied. This phenomenon has to be eliminated at the root.''[17]

Systemically, Comptroller Ben-Porat has waged a never-ending war against the abuse of bureaucratic power and against the politicization of public administration. The main thrust of the 1993 comptroller's report, for example, was that public officials treat taxpayers' money as if it belonged to no one.[18] Six months earlier, the state comptroller had issued an in-depth report on five local governments. It had revealed a widespread lack of concern for staying within approved budgets, a lack of thrift and efficiency, patronage support for well-connected private organizations, and improper benefits for elected officials.[19] Ben-Porat's 1993 annual report revealed the same sort of abuses at the national level. There was a cavalier attitude toward the expenditure of public funds and toward staying within budgets. Moreover, she criticized the widespread practice of appointing political cronies and party *apparatchiks* which, as she argued, leads to inefficiency and demoralization, and she noted the high salaries and extravagant perks awarded to unqualified managers and executives. She pointed out that government-owned companies were staffed by friends, supporters, and party functionaries, and she insisted on the need for greater integrity in public administration.[20]

In one of her more famous reports, state comptroller Ben-Porat criticized the most revered institution in the land, the Israel Defense Forces (IDF). During the 1991 Gulf War, the military had distributed gas masks to the Israeli public for protection against Iraqi missiles. The state comptroller found that many of the masks were defective and that the military's distribution plans and their execution were faulty. The chief of the General Staff and his predecessor both protested that their actions were faultless, and some politicians criticized the state comptroller for weakening the IDF's public image. Ben-Porat held her ground. At the end of the day, the Israeli consensus supported both her general approach and the particular action.[21]

Equally well known have been her reports criticizing the conduct of Israeli political parties. State comptroller reports have documented the cavalier attitude toward campaign finance laws that is endemic in Israel. Ben-Porat has levied large fines against the parties. She has also documented how the larger parties—Labor and *Likud*—have curried favor with smaller parties by giving them money for their campaigns in the expectation that the smaller parties will then join a *Knesset* coalition after the election. One of her reports led the attorney general to file criminal actions against *Shas*, the ultraorthodox *Sephardi* religious party. Three leaders of the party were charged with keeping two different set of records (one for public scrutiny, one for private purposes) and with illegally hiring *yeshiva* students as campaign workers. The Israeli public has developed a well-justified aversion to the machinations of the political parties, and the state comptroller's reports have fueled reform efforts.[22]

In sum, Miriam Ben-Porat believes that the democratic values of human rights and the rule of law are the hallmarks of a decent society. Even more important than her precedent-setting appointments as the first woman deputy president and president of a District Court, as the first woman Supreme Court justice, and as the first woman state comptroller in Israel have been her actions in those positions. She has dedicated her life as a lawyer, particularly as a judge and as state comptroller, to institutionalizing basic values in Israeli public life. To a considerable extent, she has succeeded in making Israel a better society.

## NOTES

1. Manfred Gerstenfeld, ''Miriam Ben-Porat: Fighting the Administration's Abuse of Power,'' in *Israel's New Future: Interviews* (Jerusalem: Jerusalem Center for Public Affairs, 1994), 135–46.

2. ''Between Shamgar and Barak,'' *Ha'Aretz* (January 1, 1986): 20–21.

3. Ibid.

4. Martin Edelman, *Courts, Politics, and Culture in Israel* (Charlottesville: University Press of Virginia, 1994), 34.

5. *Ha'Aretz* (January 1, 1986).

6. Ibid.

7. Gerstenfeld, 135–46.

8. Miriam Ben-Porat, ''The Effect of Forgery on the Rights of the Holder of a Bill,'' 1 *Israel Law Review* (1966): 141–46; and Ben-Porat, ''Extinction of Cause of Action by Release or Covenant Not to Sue,'' 4 *Israel Law Review* (1969): 201–15.

9. Ha'Aretz (January 1, 1986).

10. Edelman, 39.

11. Ha'Aretz (January 1, 1986).

12. Edelman, 24.

13. ''An Ounce of Intervention,'' *Jerusalem Post* (June 28, 1991): 10A.

14. Edelman, 43.

15. *M.E.L.Z. v. Israel Broadcasting Authority* (1984) 37 (1) P.D. 83.

16. ''A Holiday for Hypocrisy,'' *Jerusalem Post* (May 8, 1992): 8A.

17. Gerstenfeld, 136.

18. ''The Comptroller's Report,'' *Jerusalem Report* (May 11, 1993): 6.

19. ''State Comptroller Tackles Local Gov't,'' *Jerusalem Report* (December 1, 1992): 4.

20. ''The Comptroller's Report,'' *Jerusalem Report* (May 11, 1993): 6; and ''Joining the Right Political Party Helps,'' *Jerusalem Report* (May 11, 1993): 8.

21. ''Battling Ben-Porat Defends Activist Role,'' *Jerusalem Post* (June 6, 1991): 2.

22. ''Ben-Porat Blasts Election Financing. Heaviest Fines to Labor and *Shas*,'' *Jerusalem Report* (January 12, 1993): 1; and ''Ben-Porat: *Shas* Was Keeping Two Different Sets of Books,'' *Jerusalem Post* (February 24, 1993): 14.

**REFERENCES**

''Battling Ben-Porat Defends Activist Role.'' *Jerusalem Post* (June 6, 1991): 2.

''Ben-Porat Blasts Election Financing. Heaviest Fines to Labor and *Shas*.'' *Jerusalem Report* (January 12, 1993): 1.

''Ben-Porat: *Shas* Was Keeping Two Different Sets of Books.'' *Jerusalem Post* (February 24, 1993): 14A.

Ben-Porat, Miriam. ''The Effect of Forgery on the Rights of the Holder of a Bill.'' *Israel Law Review* 1 (1966): 141–46.

Ben-Porat, Miriam. ''Extinction of Cause of Action by Release or Covenant Not to Sue.'' *Israel Law Review* 4 (1969): 201–15.

''Between Shamgar and Barak.'' *Ha'Aretz* (January 1, 1986): 20–21.

''The Comptroller's Report.'' *Jerusalem Report* (May 11, 1993): 6.

Edelman, Martin. *Courts, Politics, and Culture in Israel.* Charlottesville: University Press of Virginia, 1994.

Gerstenfeld, Manfred. ''Miriam Ben-Porat: Fighting the Administration's Abuse of Power.'' In *Israel's New Future: Interviews.* Jerusalem: Jerusalem Center for Public Affairs, 1994, 135–46.

''A Holiday for Hypocrisy.'' *Jerusalem Post* (May 8, 1992): 8A.

''Joining the Right Political Party Helps.'' *Jerusalem Report* (May 11, 1993): 8.

''An Ounce of Intervention.'' *Jerusalem Post* (June 28, 1991): 10A.

''State Comptroller Tackles Local Gov't.'' *Jerusalem Report* (December 1, 1992): 4

*MARTIN EDELMAN*

# MYRA BRADWELL (1831–1882)

Myra Colby Bradwell is best known in American legal circles as the woman whose application to practice law was denied in Illinois, and that denial was upheld by the U.S. Supreme Court in its 1873 opinion, *Bradwell v. Illinois*. The 7–1 decision is often cited as an example of paternalism and sexism in nineteenth-century America. Actually, Bradwell had a distinguished career, quite apart from her petition to the nation's high court, as editor of the *Chicago Legal News*, as an advocate for women's rights, and as a champion who secured Mary Todd Lincoln's release from a mental institution in 1875.

## FAMILY BACKGROUND AND EDUCATION

Myra Colby was born on February 12, 1831, in Vermont, and was the youngest of five children. Her parents, Eben Colby and Abigail Willey Colby, claimed Boston pioneers and revolutionary soldiers for ancestors. The family moved to New York shortly after she was born and, when Myra was 12, to Cook County, Illinois. The primary features of her youth that are reported by her biographers are her Baptist upbringing and her parents' staunch abolitionism. She lived with one of her married sisters in Kenosha, Wisconsin, while attending finishing school and graduated from the Ladies Seminary in Elgin, Illinois.[1]

Myra taught school before eloping in 1852, with James Bradwell, of whom her family disapproved. James was an English immigrant who had supported himself through college and his legal studies by doing manual labor. The couple had four children, two of whom died in childhood. When James Bradwell was admitted to the Illinois bar in 1855, he joined in a partnership with Myra's brother, Frank Colby, who in less felicitous times had pursued the couple with a shotgun when they had eloped four years earlier.[2]

## CAREER DEVELOPMENT

Myra Bradwell launched the *Chicago Legal News* in 1868, as its publisher and editor. That publication was regarded as the "most important legal publication west of the Alleghenies."[3] To avoid the difficulties of the Illinois coverture law that prohibited a married woman from entering into contracts without her husband's approval, Myra obtained a special legislative charter that permitted her to own the publishing house individually and to receive the profits from it.

The next year, Myra, who had been reading law with her husband and wanted, she said, to be able to work with him in his law office, passed the Illinois bar exam. She petitioned to the state Supreme Court for her license, which was summarily rejected in a letter on the grounds that "as a married woman [she] would be bound neither by her express contracts nor by those implied contracts which it is the policy of the law to create between attorney and client." The state's high court was petitioned again and gave a formal opinion, again refusing her the license, this time because of the intentions of the legislature. The court derived the legislative intent to prevent women from entering the legal profession from their reading of the statute defining who was eligible for admission as expressly limited by the common law of England. Since during the reign of King James I, "female attorneys were unknown in England," the Illinois legislature had not intended that they be found within its jurisdiction either.[4]

Myra engaged the family friend, Senator Matthew Hale Carpenter, to seek a writ of error for the case to the U.S. Supreme Court. Hale argued that the decision of the Illinois Supreme Court denied Bradwell the "privileges and immunities of citizens in the several states," as guaranteed by the newly enacted Fourteenth Amendment to the United States Constitution. The Court announced its decision in Myra's case within days of its *Slaughter-House Cases* opinion that also asserted a violation of the privileges and immunities clause. The seven-man majority ruled rather straightforwardly that those rights that Illinois was forbidden to abridge did not include the right to practice law in state courts and simply referred to "the opinion just delivered in the *Slaughter-House Cases* [which] render elaborate argument in the present case unnecessary."[5]

Justice Bradley's concurring opinion is the one most frequently cited for its sexism, for he based his opinion, in part, on his view of the role of women:

> The civil law, as well as nature herself, has always recognized a wide difference in the respective spheres and destinies of man and woman. Man is, or should be, woman's protector and defender. The natural and proper timidity and delicacy which belongs to the female sex evidently unfit it for many of the occupations of civil life. . . . The harmony, not to say identity, of interests and views which belong, or should belong, to the family institution is repugnant to the idea of a woman adopting a distinct and independent career from that of her husband. . . . The paramount destiny and mission of woman are to fulfill the noble and benign offices of wife and mother. This is the law of the Creator.[6]

Justice Bradley's concurrence was joined by two others; only Chief Justice Salmon P. Chase, a relative of Myra, dissented but without providing a written opinion.

The decision in the *Bradwell* case is regarded as notorious in feminist circles and cited for its blatant paternalism. Paternalism is regarded as a recognition of the "importance of the relationship between people, but it often assumes and ratifies an inequality within the relationship." Frances Olsen cites *Bradwell* as a classic example of false paternalism.[7]

Notably, Illinois changed its law in 1872 to allow women to practice law, largely due to Bradwell's legislative campaign. Myra did not, however, reapply. Her only claim to being, as her primary biographer has labeled her, "America's First Woman Lawyer," lies in the decision of the Illinois Supreme Court in 1890, when Myra was dying of cancer, to acquiesce to her husband's request that she be admitted to the practice of law. The court complied and granted her admission *nunc pro tunc* (effective) as of 1869.[8]

## ACHIEVEMENTS AND CONTRIBUTIONS

By 1872, Myra Bradwell had a flourishing publication in the *Chicago Legal News*, which she continued editing until her death. It is through this vehicle that she made her other contribution to the law. The newspaper was only one part of her publishing enterprise, for the Chicago Legal News Company also printed legal forms, briefs, and law books. The 1871 Chicago fire even turned out to be a major boon for Myra and the publishing house when all of the records of the Chicago bar were destroyed. The Burnt Records Act, passed thereafter by the Illinois legislature, made the *Chicago Legal News* the only official source for publishing those lost records, including land titles.[9]

Myra's ability to obtain special concessions for her business through the legislature had not begun with the Burnt Records Act, however. Shortly after forming her company, she had reached an agreement with the legislature that at the end of each legislative session, she would be provided with copies of all newly enacted laws and that the *Chicago Legal News* publication of them would serve as evidence of their validity. Within little more than a year of its first issue, the *Legal News* was also recognized as the unofficial outlet for all judicial decisions.[10]

Myra Bradwell's legal newspaper was more than a conduit for information, laws, and judicial decisions; it also carried editorials and reported events of interest to the legal community. She was known at one point, after her husband was on the bench, to have criticized one of his opinions in her paper. She also used the paper to lampoon those with whom she disagreed, even caricaturing an enemy in its pages as he lay dying.[11] She used satire against specific judges, as well as against policies with which she disagreed.[12] She built a publishing empire that enabled the Bradwells to purchase a mansion on the shore of Lake Michigan and Myra to become one of the wealthiest women of the era.[13]

Myra used the *Chicago Legal News* as a platform for her proposals to reform the legal system and was hardly shy in attacking her own readers by pointedly writing about the faults of the practicing bar. Her primary targets were those who bribed jurors, misappropriated client's funds, drank excessively, and facilitated divorces. She did not hesitate to refer to some of her lawyer readers as "shysters" and to name the names of those who transgressed.[14] She advocated elimination of the office of justice of the peace, improved judicial salaries and working conditions, and various other legal reforms. She was a supporter of African Americans in the bar but was virulently anti-Semitic.[15] She had declared in the first issue of the *Legal News* that it was a Christian newspaper and added at a later date that she could not accommodate those of the "Hebrew faith."[16]

Myra also used the *Chicago Legal News* to advocate women's rights, in particular their access to the legal profession. She inveighed against states that prohibited women from practicing law and against law schools whose doors were not open to women. She opposed the discrimination that often targeted women once they were allowed law licenses and championed a number of individual women's causes in her paper. Her advocacy for equality of access for women was not limited to the legal profession; she lobbied on her editorial pages for women's appointments to various political positions and for their eligibility for elective offices. She also featured successes by women in both the public and private sector.[17]

Myra Bradwell's public accomplishments are not limited to those of legal journalist and editor. She also undertook at least one major cause that was personal, but with larger consequences—the plight of the widow of Abraham Lincoln. The Bradwells had known both Lincolns before he had become president, and after the assassination had helped Mary Todd Lincoln settle temporarily in Chicago. In 1875, Mrs. Lincoln had returned to Chicago to visit her son, Robert. While she was visiting, Robert engineered an insanity trial, which resulted in Mrs. Lincoln's incarceration at Bellevue Place in Batavia, Illinois, for four months. From there, she wrote to the Bradwells asking for help in securing her release. Myra responded by traveling to see Mrs. Lincoln, but she was denied admittance. She turned then to the press, where she began publishing articles in, for example, the *Bloomington Courier* and the *Chicago Times* about Mary Todd Lincoln's unfair detention.

Myra also visited Lincoln at the asylum and wrote to her almost daily, and penned letters to both Robert Lincoln and to the custodian of Bellevue Place. When the Bradwells were finally prohibited from contacting Mrs. Lincoln at all, they again turned to the press to publicize the detention. James Bradwell also gave a newspaper interview to the *Chicago Post and Mail*, attesting both to the incompetence of the doctor attending Mary Lincoln and to her sanity. Within two weeks of the publication of that article, Mary Todd Lincoln was released from Bellevue Place. She was allowed to live with her sister in Springfield and was subsequently declared sane by the Illinois courts. After some years in France, she died in her sister's home in 1882.[18]

Although Myra Colby Bradwell never practiced law, she had a decided impact on the law and on legal institutions in Illinois in the late nineteenth century. She had a distinguished career in the publishing business and proved herself to be both a very shrewd and quite capable businesswoman. If Justice Bradley truly believed in the timidity and delicacy of women, Myra Bradwell did not conform to his notions. She was a journalist with a biting sense of satire and was not above using duplicity to achieve her goals. She even faked supposedly anonymous letters to the editor of her own newspaper (herself), criticizing public officials and their actions. Her career was a testament to a woman's ability to survive and flourish in the so-called masculine professions of civil life. She was able to manipulate the legislature masterfully to achieve special concessions for herself and for her publications. She could also employ those same tactics to free a friend from an asylum, to end the use of justices of the peace, and to obtain the right of women to practice law.

Myra Bradwell has often been a sort of footnote to feminist writings because of her unsuccessful battle before the Supreme Court for the right to practice law. She deserves more for her fervor in furthering the rights of women in a variety of fields. The coverture law and limitations on women's access to both appointive and elective office were altered as a result of her tenacity and skillful legislative campaigns. She was a worthy adversary, even though not in the courtroom; she wielded her sharp pen to win her skirmishes in the press and in the legislative arena. She brought about reforms, albeit on a small scale, in the legal system and was unabashed in her willingness to criticize the failings of the system and its practitioners in print. Myra Bradwell's journalistic contributions are diminished by her anti-Semitism and the viciousness of the attacks she could mount against her enemies. Some of her tactics blatantly violated today's sense of journalistic ethics. Rarely, however, were her devious and humiliating strategies designed to further her own interests; rather, they were aimed at advancing what she saw as the interest of friends or of the larger community.

## NOTES

1. Jane M. Friedman, *America's First Woman Lawyer: The Biography of Myra Bradwell* (Buffalo, N.Y.: Prometheus Books, 1993), 35–36.
2. Ibid., 41.
3. As quoted in Carol Sanger, "Curriculum Vitae (Feminae): Biography and Early American Women Lawyers," 46 *Stanford Law Review* (May 1994): 1259.
4. *Bradwell v. Illinois*, 83 U.S. 130 (1873) at 131–32.
5. Ibid., 139.
6. Ibid., 141.
7. Frances Olsen, "From False Paternalism to False Equality: Judicial Assaults on the Feminist Community, Illinois, 1869–1895," 84 *Michigan Law Review* (June 1986): 1522–23.
8. Sanger, 1262.
9. Ibid., 1259.
10. Friedman, 79–80.

11. Sanger, 1265.
12. Friedman, 81.
13. Ibid., 91.
14. Ibid., 101.
15. Ibid., 123.
16. Ibid., 102–3.
17. Ibid., 155–65.
18. Ibid., 51–66.

## REFERENCES

Friedman, Jane M. *America's First Woman Lawyer: The Biography of Myra Bradwell.* Buffalo, N.Y.: Prometheus Books, 1993.

Olsen, Frances. ''From False Paternalism to False Equality: Judicial Assaults on the Feminist Community, Illinois, 1869–1895.'' *Michigan Law Review* 84 (June 1986): 1522–23.

Sanger, Carol. ''Curriculum Vitae (Feminae): Biography and Early American Women Lawyers.'' *Stanford Law Review* 46 (May 1994): 1259.

*MARY L. VOLCANSEK*

# BEVERLY BLAIR COOK (1927–    )

At a roundtable held in her honor, Beverly Blair Cook remarked that a "scientist who receives a prize has a conventional modest disclaimer—'I am standing on the shoulders of giants.' My response to being honored by this panel is to point to two lines of predecessors on whose scholarship I have tried to build. One is a line of male giants; the other a line of female ghosts."[1] She went on to describe the contributions of three of those "ghosts," Sophonisba Breckrinridge, Alice Paul, and Charlotte Williams.

To be sure, Cook is right: Several women contributed mightily to the study of law and courts, and their contributions have largely gone ignored or underappreciated at best. Yet, at the same time, Cook's comments are characteristically modest. For, in the general scheme of things, it was Beverly Blair Cook—not Breckrinridge, Paul, or Williams—who paved the way for women in the scientific study of courts and law. No account of the emergence of judicial process within the discipline of political science would be complete without a reckoning of her contributions.

## EDUCATION AND CAREER DEVELOPMENT

Cook's progression in the professional world of political science was, like many women of her generation, something short of linear. After receiving a Bachelor of Arts degree (with high honors) from Wellesley College in 1948 and a Master of Arts from the University of Wisconsin—Madison in 1949, she served as an instructor of political science at Iowa State University from 1949 to 1950. Following that, she entered into a domestic period, bearing and rearing four children.

In 1960, Cook resumed her graduate work at Claremont University and Graduate School, receiving her doctorate in 1962. Cook then took an assistant professorship at California State University—Fullerton, where she gained tenure in 1966. In that same year, she met Neil Cotter, another political scientist, at a National Science Foundation summer seminar; they were married five weeks later.

In 1967, Cook, Cotter, and their combined brood of eight moved to the University of Wisconsin—Milwaukee. At first, it seemed that Cook and her husband would be unable to work together in the Department of Political Science. The University, in 1969, claimed to have a nepotism rule that barred female spouses or married couples from obtaining tenure in the same department. So Cook transferred to the School of Social Welfare for a year, "while [she] helped the university discover that the rule was unwritten and in any case contradicted federal law."[2] With that matter cleared up, she moved back to the Department of Political Science, where she would produce some of her most important work and where she would remain until her retirement in 1989.

To term Cook in retirement is something of a misnomer, however. From her home in Atascadero, California, she continues to write at a breathtaking pace. Recent essays have offered a measure of significant U.S. Supreme Court decisions,[3] commented on the Court's agenda[4] and considered opinion assignment on the Burger Court.[5] Her service to the profession also continues. Over the past decade, she served on Project '87, the joint American Historical Association–American Political Science Association (APSA) Committee on the Bicentennial of the Constitution. Even more recently, she received an appointment to the Executive Committee of the Law and Courts Section of the APSA.

At the time Cook was studying for her Ph.D., an intellectual struggle of sorts was ongoing in the field of law and courts.[6] On the one side were those who supported the traditional approach to law and courts, that is, examining the legal content of judicial opinions in the style of Edward Corwin and Robert Cushman. On the other side were those scholars who advocated the scientific study of legal phenomena. Their intellectual leader was C. Herman Pritchett, who, in the 1940s, published several studies of the Roosevelt Court.[7] Rather than focusing exclusively on doctrine, Pritchett examined voting patterns in an attempt to understand systematically divisions of opinion among the justices.

This intellectual engagement was perhaps in its most heated stage by the time Cook completed her doctoral work. Important journals published acrimonious debates between proponents of the two schools;[8] articles appeared delineating the key players and their views.[9] At the end of the day, however, it was clear that Pritchett and his followers had emerged as the winners. In 1964, for the first time, judicial process articles outnumbered constitutional law pieces and, with the exception of only one year (1976), continued to dominate the field.[10]

With this debate largely settled, the victors began to see just how far scientific approaches to the study of law and courts would take them. As Thomas G. Walker notes, "theoretical innovation exploded."[11] Attitude theory, social background theory, role theory, fact pattern analysis, and others were used in attempts to explain judicial decision making. And seminal books such as Walter F. Murphy's *Elements of Judicial Strategy* and Glendon A. Schubert's *Judicial Mind*[12] were published.

Cook may not have been a part of this "heyday" period, but, during the 1970s, she became a major player. By way of illustration, consider her series of path-breaking articles on judicial socialization. Defining socialization as "individual learning of the behavioral patterns and the values of institutional roles," Cook was the first to recognize its importance for understanding what it is judges do.[13] Early pieces considered ways in which court systems attempt to socialize new judges; for example, in an article published in the *Washington University Law Quarterly*, she took up two questions relating to the introductory seminars established by the federal government to train new judges in effective case management and processing techniques: Why were they established and what impact did they have?[14] By invoking a wide range of data sources, Cook demonstrated that socialization through these seminars failed to have the desired effect of making courts more efficient.[15]

Not only were Cook's articles on judicial socialization theoretically and methodologically innovative, but they were also substantively distinct from much of the research being produced by her male counterparts. While many of Cook's peers, including Glendon Schubert, S. Sidney Ulmer, and Harold J. Spaeth, tended to focus on the U.S. Supreme Court, she set her sights on state and federal trial courts. In so doing, she rewrote the agenda for a generation of researchers to come. They heeded her warning that our understanding of the judicial process would be incomplete unless we incorporated other judicial bodies into our work.

## ACHIEVEMENTS AND CONTRIBUTIONS

Cook's earliest research shows the importance of asking interesting questions, thinking theoretically, invoking a wide range of sources, and analyzing data with rigor and sensitivity. These traits continued to characterize her later research, but her horizons grew substantially. Over the past two decades, she explored with skill questions involving criminal sentencing, judicial administration, and decision making, among many others. Still, I have little hesitation suggesting that her most important contributions came in the areas of public opinion and women on the bench.[16]

Do courts consider or mirror the views of the public in rendering judgments? This simple question has generated immense scholarly interest, not to mention debate. For, despite decades of work, analysts have resolved neither the question of why federal judges—who do not require electoral support to retain their jobs—would consider public opinion in their decisions nor the question of whether they do, in fact.[17]

What is beyond debate, however, is that Cook's work provides the starting point for virtually all important analytic discussion on public opinion and trial courts.[18] As Gregory A. Caldeira noted in his review of the field, "Some dispute the findings and interpretations, but Beverly Cook has done important research on this topic and, without doubt, has drawn scholarly interest."[19]

Cook's article in the *American Journal of Political Science* well illustrates Caldeira's point. In this work, she invokes a "representational" model to explain the sentences issued by federal district court judges in cases involving draft offenders. Her primary argument is that, for a variety of reasons, we might expect to find a relationship between public opinion and judicial decisions. First, socializing experiences teach judges that public opinion is a legitimate consideration in their sentencing. Second, the recruitment process virtually guarantees that nominees will share the attitudes and values of the local community in which they will serve. Or, to put it another way, the selection system for federal judges embeds them in the political culture of their districts. Finally, the fact that judges watch television and read newspapers means that they will have some knowledge of the prevailing public mood.

In the remaining part of the article, Cook tests her representational approach, as well as rival explanations—the legal, bureaucratic, and sociopsycholgical models—against data carefully assembled from court records. The results indicate that public opinion correlates highly with judicial sentences.

Cook's work is not without its critics. Herbert Kritzer, for example, questioned whether it was public opinion to which the judges were actually responding or to their "own doubts about the war, or their opinions concerning the degree of governmental commitment to the war."[20] Still, Cook's findings have withstood the test of time: They are always cited in influential accounts of public opinion and the courts.[21]

And, yet, what sometimes goes neglected in treatments of Cook's work on public opinion was her research strategy. At the time she was writing (the 1970s), judicial specialists avoided competitive model testing. That is to say, they would select a particular theoretical approach to decision making and test its predictions, and only these predictions, against data. Today, many researchers claim that this tack was probably unwise since we can best explain judicial decisions by invoking models that integrate many different kinds of theories.[22] But, of course, it was Cook who first had this important intuition and adopted it in her work. Seen in this way, she truly was a pioneer of the judicial process, a researcher two decades ahead of her time.[23]

Cook's contribution to legal scholarship also extended to the area of women in law. Under what circumstances are women selected to serve as jurists? Do women jurists bring a different voice to the bench? In recent years, these questions have captured the imagination of a slew of political scientists—as well they should. With two women now on the Supreme Court of the United States and with their numbers growing on the lower federal courts and state supreme courts, it seems only natural that this question move to the fore of social scientific research on the judicial process. But even before Sandra Day O'Connor* took her seat on the Court, Cook had undertaken what would become an extensive and fruitful research program on women jurists. Indeed, virtually all contemporary writings on the selection of women judges and their impact owe their origin to her studies.

Cook's research began in 1977, when she traversed the country interviewing women judges and collecting other relevant information.[24] She later created a seminal database, containing information on all state and federal women judges, which she used to explore issues concerning the ascension of women to the bench.[25] Among her more important findings is that women will become more than mere tokens in the courts only if three conditions are obtained: increases in (1) the number of judgeships, (2) the number of eligible women, and (3) the number of "gatekeepers" (those who select judicial candidates) who will give serious consideration to women.[26]

Another of her important contributions was brought to light by Sheldon Goldman, one of the nation's leading authorities on judicial selection. In his review of Cook's work, Goldman made particular note of an article she had written on Florence Allen,* the first woman federal judge and a candidate for "at least 10 of 12 vacancies on the Supreme Court that occurred during the Roosevelt and Truman administrations."[27] But, of course, Allen never received an appointment, even though, as Cook demonstrated in her article, her background (except for her sex) was comparable to others who had served on the Court.

Why did Florence Allen fail and Sandra Day O'Connor succeed? Cook takes up this question in yet another intriguing study published in *Judicature*.[28] There she derives several answers, the most significant of which is this: President Franklin D. Roosevelt did not perceive that Allen would help his political fortunes. Public opinion polls showed that, in 1938, only 37 percent of Americans favored the appointment of a woman to the Court and groups representing women's interests were not seen as central to passage of FDR's programs. As Cook demonstrates, the political environment had turned significantly by the late 1970s, enabling Ronald Reagan to do what Roosevelt found politically untenable: elevate a woman to the Court.

Still, Cook's work on Allen does more than answer an important research question. It also shows the importance of archival research. While many scholars toiling in the field rely exclusively on published reports or records, Cook draws extensively on judicial papers available in the Library of Congress, various presidential libraries, and the National Archives, to name just a few. The value of such data is evident in Cook's publications on Allen (and on several other women judges[29]): They enable scholars to capture nuances of political phenomena—nuances that may be lost in the often-sterile world of statistics and that may have some bearing on the hypotheses under investigation.

Cook's archival-based research on judicial selection continues,[30] as does her work on the equally significant question of whether women bring a distinct voice to the bench. This issue, as Sue Davis notes, is now central to the study of constitutional interpretation, feminist jurisprudence, and judicial behavior. But it was Cook who set the agenda for this entire line of inquiry.[31] She was the first to predict that women judges would be more likely than their male counterparts to advance pro-women positions in cases centering directly on the status of women.[32] She was also one of the first to suggest that they would adopt positions that would conform to those of their male colleagues in other kinds of disputes.[33] As researchers have demonstrated, both predictions tend to hold, regardless of the particular judicial body under investigation.[34]

Cook's contributions to political science do not end with her research, for over the past 30 years she has been, as Lynn Mather noted, a ''distinguished leader in the profession.''[35] Her list of professional activities is long indeed, and includes the following: stints as vice president of the American Political Science Association (1986–1987) and of the Midwest Political Science Association (1982–1984) and chair of the APSA's section on Law and Courts (1981). She has also served on the Editorial Board of the *Western Political Quarterly* and on the Program Committees of the American (1982), the Midwest (1972), and the Western Political Science Associations (1981). Finally, Cook made a major contribution to the field in her capacity as a member of the Board of Overseers of the National Science Foundation's project on the U.S. Supreme Court. Since 1984, that Board has guided the collection of a staggering amount of data on the Supreme Court, with the first release now in wide use.[36]

Among all these accomplishments, however, it is probably fair to say that Cook is proudest of her role in the founding of the National Association of Women Judges (NAWJ).[37] Her association with the NAWJ began in 1977–1978, when she was interviewing women state court judges. As she traveled around the country, she ''discovered that the women had no knowledge of women judges in other states and cities.'' Based on the work she had been conducting on early women lawyers, Cook ''recognized the similarity of the women judges' situation to that of women lawyers one hundred years earlier and thought that it was time for them to form an organization.''

Cook brought the idea to two of the judges she had interviewed. One of them, Joan Klein, ran with it planning a ''constitutional convention'' of women judges. At that meeting, Cook gave the keynote address in which she suggested that women judges ought to create their own ''sisterhood,'' just as the first women lawyers did.

As the Association began to take shape, Cook continued her involvement. In fact, it was through the NAWJ that she played a major role in bringing the organizational strength of women to the attention of the (pre-Sandra Day O'Connor) Supreme Court.[38] As she tells the story,

> [I arranged] to have women judges attending the 1980 NAWJ convention in Washington, D.C. march together into the Supreme Court building for the special tour and to impress the justices with [their] number. . . . I developed this strategy because of the report that Truman consulted with Chief Justice Vinson about the possibility of appointing Florence Allen; Vinson consulted with the brethren, and they expressed their discomfort at the idea of a woman in their private conferences.

Heeding this historical lesson, Cook thought it strategically sensible to confront Chief Justice Burger with the fact that a large number of women would soon be eligible for service on the Court. ''If they entered the building en masse,'' as Cook put it, ''then all the justices as well as the other (overwhelmingly male) personnel in the building would also understand that the day would soon come when a woman would join their conferences.''

Cook's message was delivered and, apparently, received. Chief Justice Burger was amazed ''when he walked into the huge assembly room and saw the standing room only crowd,'' composed exclusively of women. Just a one month later, the justices dropped the term ''Mr.'' from courtroom courtesy and the official reports. And exactly a year later, O'Connor ascended to the bench.

Upon reflecting on her involvement with the women judges' visit to the Court and the NAWJ more generally, Cook acknowledged that it was ''unusual'' for social scientists and lawyers to engage in this sort of cooperation. Perhaps that would be true for most of us but certainly not for Beverly Blair Cook, whom we have come to know as a leader and role model for a generation of scholars—men and women—of the judicial process.

## NOTES

1. The roundtable was held at the 1992 meeting of the American Political Science Association. Cook's remarks were published; see Beverly B. Cook, ''Ghosts and Giants in Judicial Politics,'' 27 *PS: Political Science and Politics* (1994): 78–84.

2. Ibid.

3. Beverly B. Cook, ''Measuring the Significance of U.S. Supreme Court Decisions,'' 55 *Journal of Politics* (1993): 1125–37.

4. Beverly B. Cook, ''A Critique of the Supreme Court's 1982 Agenda: Alternatives and the NYU Legal Model,'' 17 *Justice System Journal* (1994): 135–51.

5. Beverly B. Cook, ''Testing a Model of Opinion Assignment: The Burger Court,'' unpublished manuscript (1995).

6. I have adopted this discussion from Thomas G. Walker, ''The Development of the Field,'' paper presented at the Columbus Conference, Ohio State University, Columbus, Ohio (1994).

7. Herman C. Pritchett, ''Divisions of Opinion Among Justices of the U.S. Supreme Court, 1939–1941,'' 35 *American Political Science Review* (1941): 890–98; and Pritchett, *The Roosevelt Court* (New York: Macmillan, 1948).

8. See, for example, Fred Kort, ''Comment on the Untroubled World of Jurimetrics,'' 26 *Journal of Politics* (1964): 923–26; Wallace Mendelson, ''Response,'' 26 *Journal of Politics* (1964): 927; Mendelson, ''An Open Letter to Professor Spaeth and His Jurimetrical Colleagues,'' 28 *Journal of Politics* (1966): 429–32; and Harold J. Spaeth, ''Jurimetrics and Professor Mendelson: A Troubled Relationship,'' 27 *Journal of Politics* (1965): 875–80.

9. Glendon Schubert, ''Academic Ideology and the Study of Adjudication,'' 61 *American Political Science Review* (1967): 106–29.

10. Walker (1994).

11. Ibid.

12. Walter F. Murphy, *Elements of Judicial Strategy* (Chicago: University of Chicago Press, 1964) and Schubert, 106–29.

13. Beverly B. Cook, ''The Socialization of New Federal Judges: Impact on District Court Business,'' *Washington University Law Quarterly* (1971): 253.

14. Ibid.

15. As I describe soon, Cook's interest in judicial socialization remains unabated, although her later work focuses more heavily on the effect of life experiences on judicial decisions rather than those occurring on the bench. Lawrence Baum made this point when he described Cook's research on Sandra Day O'Connor, which he deemed a ''sensitive treatment of [her] life experiences and how those experiences affected her values on the bench.'' Quoted in Lynn Mather, ''Introducing a Feminist Pioneer in Judicial Politics: Beverly Blair Cook,'' 27 *PS: Political Science and Politics* (1994): 77.

16. It also bears noting that Cook was one of the first to conduct systematic research on black judges. For an early example, see Beverly B. Cook, ''Black Representation in the Third Branch,'' 1 *Black Law Journal* (1971): 260–81.

17. A recent example of the debate is Helmut Norpoth and Jeffrey A. Segal, ''Comment: Popular Influence on Supreme Court Decisions,'' 88 *American Political Science Review* (1994): 711–16; and William Mishler and Reginald S. Sheehan, ''Response,'' 88 *American Political Science Review* (1994): 716–23.

18. Beverly B. Cook, ''Sentencing Behavior of Federal Judges: Draft Cases—1972,'' 42 *University of Cincinnati Law Review* (1973): 597–633; Cook, ''Public Opinion and Federal Judicial Policy,'' 21 *American Journal of Political Science* (1977): 567–600; and Cook, ''Judicial Policy: Change over Time,'' 23 *American Journal of Political Science* (1979): 208–14.

19. Gregory A. Caldeira, ''Courts and Public Opinion,'' in John B. Gates and Charles A. Johnson, *The American Courts: A Critical Assessment* (Washington, DC: CQ Press, 1991), 317.

20. Herbert M. Kritzer, ''Federal Judges and Their Political Environments: The Influence of Public Opinion,'' 23 *American Journal of Political Science* (1979): 198.

21. Caldeira, 317; and Thomas Marshall, *Public Opinion and the Supreme Court* (Boston: Unwin Hyman, 1989).

22. Tracey E. George and Lee Epstein, ''On the Nature of Supreme Court Decision Making,'' 86 *American Political Science Review* (1992): 323–37; and Melinda Gann Hall and Paul Brace, ''Integrated Models of Judicial Dissent,'' 55 *Journal of Politics* (1993): 914–35.

23. Baum makes this point, though in a somewhat different way. As he put it, ''although multivariate models are now common in the field, Cook was among those who first showed how this kind of analysis could be done and how much we could learn from it.'' Quoted in Mather, 77.

24. A Florence E. Eagleton grant (from the Center for the American Woman and Politics, Eagleton Institute) supported this research. In addition to the Eagleton grant, Cook has received support from the National Endowment for the Humanities, the Ford Foundation, and the Social Science Research Council.

25. See Mather, 77.

26. Beverly B. Cook. ''Women Judges: A Preface to Their History,'' 14 *Golden Gate University Law Review* (1984): 573–74.

27. Beverly B. Cook, ''The First Woman Candidate for the Supreme Court,'' *Supreme Court Historical Society Yearbook* (1981): 19–35, quoted in Mather, 77.

28. Beverly B. Cook, ''Women as Supreme Court Candidates: From Florence Allen to Sandra Day O'Connor,'' 65 *Judicature* (1982): 314–26.

29. See, for example, Beverly B. Cook, ''Moral Authority and Gender Difference: Georgia Bullock and the Los Angeles Women's Court,'' 77 *Judicature* (1993): 144–55.

30. See, for example, Beverly B. Cook, ''Marion Harron,'' in *American National Biography* (New York: Oxford University Press, 1996.

31. See Mather, 78.

32. Beverly B. Cook, ''The Impact of Women Judges upon Women's Legal Rights: A Prediction from Attitudes and Simulated Behavior,'' in Margherita Rendel, (ed.), *Women, Power and Political Systems* (New York: St. Martin's Press, 1981).

33. Beverly B. Cook, ''Women Judges: The End of Tokenism,'' in *Women in the Courts* (Williamsburg, Va.: National Center for State Courts, 1978). For a review, see David W. Allen and Diane E. Wall, ''Role Orientations and Women State Supreme Court Justices,'' 77 *Judicature* (1993): 156–65.

34. For example, Allen and Wall, 156–65; and Sue Davis, Susan Haire and Donald R. Songer, ''Voting Behavior and Gender on the U.S. Courts of Appeals,'' 77 *Judicature* (1993): 129–33.

35. Mather, 77.

36. Harold Spaeth, *United States Supreme Court Judicial Database* (Ann Arbor, Mich.: Inter-University Consortium for Political and Social Research, #9422, 1995 [updated annually]).

37. Cook relayed the information that follows to Elaine Martin (letter from Cook to Martin, May 31, 1993). Cook was kind enough to supply me with a copy of the letter.

38. The information in this paragraph was relayed to me by Cook (letter from Cook to Epstein, January 23, 1994).

## REFERENCES


Allen, David W. and Diane E. Wall. ''Role Orientations and Women State Supreme Court Justices.'' *Judicature* 77 (1993): 156–65.

Caldeira, Gregory A. ''Courts and Public Opinion.'' In *The American Courts: A Critical Assessment*. Eds. John B. Gates and Charles A. Johnson. Washington, D.C.: CQ Press, 1991, 303–34.

Cook, Beverly B. ''Marion Harron.'' In *American National Biography*. New York: Oxford University Press, 1996.

Cook, Beverly B. ''Testing a Model of Opinion Assignment: The Burger Court.'' Unpublished manuscript, 1995.

Cook, Beverly B. ''A Critique of the Supreme Court's 1982 Agenda: Alternatives and the NYU Legal Model.'' *Justice System Journal* 17 (1994): 135–51.

Cook, Beverly B. ''Ghosts and Giants in Judicial Politics.'' *PS: Political Science and Politics* 27 (1994): 78–84.

Cook, Beverly B. ''Measuring the Significance of U.S. Supreme Court Decisions.'' *Journal of Politics* 55 (1993): 1125–37.

Cook, Beverly B. ''Moral Authority and Gender Difference: Georgia Bullock and the Los Angeles Women's Court.'' *Judicature* 77 (1993): 144–55.

Cook, Beverly B. ''Women Judges: A Preface to Their History.'' *Golden Gate University Law Review* 14 (1984): 573–74.

Cook, Beverly B. ''Women as Supreme Court Candidates: From Florence Allen to Sandra Day O'Connor.'' *Judicature* 65 (1982): 314–26.

Cook, Beverly B. ''The First Woman Candidate for the Supreme Court.'' *Supreme Court Historical Society Yearbook* (1981): 19–35.

Cook, Beverly B. ''The Impact of Women Judges upon Women's Legal Rights: A Prediction from Attitudes and Simulated Behavior.'' In *Women, Power and Political Systems.* Ed. Margherita Rendel. New York: St. Martin's Press, 1981, 216–39.

Cook, Beverly B. ''Judicial Policy: Change over Time.'' *American Journal of Political Science* 23 (1979): 208–14.

Cook, Beverly B. ''Women Judges: The End of Tokenism.'' In *Women in the Courts.* Eds. Winifred L. Hepperle and Laura Crites. Williamsburg, Va.: National Center for State Courts, 1978, 84–105.

Cook, Beverly B. ''Public Opinion and Federal Judicial Policy.'' *American Journal of Political Science* 21 (1977): 567–600.

Cook, Beverly B. ''Sentencing Behavior of Federal Judges: Draft Cases–1972.'' *University of Cincinnati Law Review* 42 (1973): 597–633.

Cook, Beverly B. ''Black Representation in the Third Branch.'' *Black Law Journal* 1 (1971): 260–81.

Cook, Beverly B. ''The Socialization of New Federal Judges: Impact on District Court Business.'' *Washington University Law Quarterly* (1971): 253–79.

Davis, Sue, Susan Haire, and Donald R. Songer. ''Voting Behavior and Gender on the U.S. Courts of Appeals.'' *Judicature* 77 (1993): 129–33.

George, Tracey E., and Lee Epstein. ''On the Nature of Supreme Court Decision Making.'' *American Political Science Review* 86 (1992): 323–37.

Hall, Melinda Gann, and Paul Brace. ''Integrated Models of Judicial Dissent.'' *Journal of Politics* 55 (1993): 914–35.

Kort, Fred. ''Comment on the Untroubled World of Jurimetrics.'' *Journal of Politics* 26 (1964): 923–26.

Kritzer, Herbert M. ''Federal Judges and Their Political Environments: The Influence of Public Opinion.'' *American Journal of Political Science* 23 (1979): 194–207.

Marshall, Thomas. *Public Opinion and the Supreme Court.* Boston: Unwin Hyman, 1989.

Mather, Lynn. ''Introducing a Feminist Pioneer in Judicial Politics: Beverly Blair Cook.'' *PS: Political Science and Politics* 27 (1994): 76–78.

Mendelson, Wallace. ''An Open Letter to Professor Spaeth and His Jurimetrical Colleagues.'' *Journal of Politics* 28 (1966): 429–32.

Mendelson, Wallace. ''Response.'' *Journal of Politics* 26 (1964): 927–28.

Mishler, William, and Reginald S. Sheehan. ''Response.'' *American Political Science Review* 88 (1994): 716–23.

Murphy, Walter F. *Elements of Judicial Strategy.* Chicago: University of Chicago Press, 1964.

Norpoth, Helmut, and Jeffrey A. Segal. ''Comment: Popular Influence on Supreme Court Decisions.'' *American Political Science Review* 88 (1994): 711–16.

Pritchett, Herman C. *The Roosevelt Court.* New York: Macmillan, 1948.

Pritchett, Herman C. ''Divisions of Opinion Among Justices of the U.S. Supreme Court, 1939–1941.'' *American Political Science Review* 35 (1941): 890–98.

Schubert, Glendon. ''Academic Ideology and the Study of Adjudication.'' *American Political Science Review* 61 (1967): 106–29.

Spaeth, Harold. *United States Supreme Court Judicial Database.* Ann Arbor, Mich.:

Inter-University Consortium for Political and Social Research, #9422, 1995 [updated annually].
Spaeth, Harold J. ''Jurimetrics and Professor Mendelson: A Troubled Relationship.'' *Journal of Politics* 27 (1965): 875–80.
Walker, Thomas G. ''The Development of the Field.'' Paper presented at the Columbus Conference, Ohio State University, Columbus, Ohio, 1994.

*LEE EPSTEIN*

# IRENE R. CORTES (1920– )

Irene Cortes was the third woman to be appointed to one of Asia's most important and powerful judicial bodies, the Supreme Court of the Philippines. Prior to her appointment as associate justice of that court in February, 1987, "Dean" Cortes had a long and distinguished career as a professor, scholar, and law school and university administrator. Since her mandatory retirement at age 70 in October, 1990, she has remained active in Philippine legal affairs, currently serving as vice chair of the Supreme Court's Judicial Planning, Development, and Implementation Office and professor emeritus in the College of Law of the University of the Philippines. Perhaps as important as her formal professional achievements has been Cortes's involvement in national and international committees and organizations concerned with human rights, legal reform, and, especially, the position and rights of women.

## FAMILY BACKGROUND AND EDUCATION

Irene R. Cortes was born on October 20, 1920, in Legazpi City, Albay, Philippines. Legazpi is the principal city of the Bicol region, the string of provinces that forms the long tail jutting southeastward into the Pacific Ocean from the Philippines' largest island, Luzon. Albay's best-known feature is the active and beautiful Mount Mayon, said to be the world's most perfect volcanic cone. Though connected to the capital, Manila, by highway, rail, and air routes, Bicol is an agricultural region, producing principally rice and coconuts, and is far from the capital city's influence.

Cortes was one of ten children of a comfortable Albay family. Her interest in law came naturally and early. Her father had prepared for a law career, but was shipwrecked and unable to return to complete his legal training. Though never admitted to practice, he did serve as clerk of the court in the Court of First Instance headquartered in Legazpi. As a child, Cortes was used to running to find her father at work in the court and, occasionally, to being "hushed" lest she disturb ongoing judicial business. In addition to her father, several other relatives were involved in the practice of law.

Cortes's mother trained to be a school teacher. But after a few years of teaching, she, like many other Filipino women of her class and generation, retired to rear children and supervise the farm that, given the very low salary of government employees, was the principal source of the family's income. The farm consisted of lowlands and uplands devoted principally to the cultivation of rice. Cortes recalls that her mother managed as many as 100 workers during the farm's best years.

Though she considered other options, principally medicine and journalism, by the time she had completed secondary school, Cortes had decided on a legal career. She enrolled in the Philippines' leading institution of higher education, the University of the Philippines (UP). She completed her prelaw Associate of Arts degree with honors in 1940 and began studying for her Bachelor of Laws (L.L.B.) in the UP College of Law. However, she was unable to complete her degree immediately due to the outbreak of war between the United States and Japan, and the Japanese invasion of Manila.

Fleeing the invasion, Cortes reports that she caught the last train out of Manila to Bicol, arriving in Legazpi a day before the Japanese established control over the city. Walking to the city at 4:00 A.M. to collect some of her things, she discovered its government buildings already occupied. She then walked some 20 kilometers into the countryside to a village where the mayor, who knew her father, helped her get home to the family farm in the village of Libon. She had hardly arrived at the lowland farm when her family packed up and joined the exodus to the hills, to the family's upland property. Because their property was a flourishing rice farm, Cortes's family was fortunate during the war years: they always had enough food and managed to wait out the Japanese occupation in relative safety. However, both Cortes's parents died of natural causes during this period, and when the war ended, she was delayed for a year, serving as an English teacher in Libon, before resuming her studies.

Once she did resume her studies, Cortes completed her L.L.B. (cum laude) in 1948. She took the bar exams that same year. While waiting for the top ten score that was the result of her exam, she returned to Albay.

## CAREER DEVELOPMENT

At the University of the Philippines, Cortes recalls that the only woman professor she encountered in law school insisted that women could not succeed in the law unless they "thought like men." However, she also recalls being impressed by several UP professors who were achievers and sources of inspiration. Principal among these was Vicente G. Sinco, professor, law dean, university president, organizer of the postwar Department of Foreign Affairs under President Sergio Osmena, and prolific author whose *Political Law* Cortes edited for its eleventh edition. Serving to some degree as mentor for the young Cortes, it was Sinco who invited her to join the UP Law Faculty in 1954. Prior to going to UP, she had worked briefly with the Duran law office, taught in the law school of Foundation College, and concurrently served as a legal assistant with Community Publishers, Inc., all in Manila.

After a year of teaching, Cortes decided to improve her academic credentials by seeking an advanced degree, so she enrolled in the Master of Laws (L.L.M.) program at the University of Michigan. She spent ten months in Ann Arbor tackling the work necessary to succeed with her studies while struggling to find appropriate housing and learning to cope with the domestic chores—room cleaning and washing—that are unfamiliar to Filipinos of middle-class background whose families employ servants for these purposes. Nevertheless, she found the law school work enjoyable and was impressed by a number of her professors, some of whom became lifelong friends.

Completing her L.L.M. in 1956, Cortes returned to her teaching duties at UP. But in the 1960s, she accepted the challenge of UP President Carlos Romulo to seek her doctorate and returned to Michigan to study for the Doctorate of Juridical Science (S.J.D.). She completed the work for the degree in 1966, and her dissertation, "The Philippine Presidency: A Study of Executive Power," was published by the UP Law Center in the same year. Before returning to the Philippines, Cortes took the opportunity to travel, visiting the great cities of Europe, and the pyramids of Egypt, traveling on the proverbial $10 per day budget and doing things that, after the fact, she was told no woman traveling alone should do.

Before leaving to study for her S.J.D., Cortes had already been given administrative responsibilities, serving briefly as acting secretary of the UP College of Law. Upon her return, she was once again appointed to this position, as well as to the post of faculty adviser for the *Philippine Law Journal*. Her administrative career began in earnest in 1970, when she became the first woman dean of the college and the chair of the UP Law Research Council. In 1970, she was also appointed to the Albino Z. Sycip Professor of Law Chair. Her responsibilities were further augmented in 1973, when she became concurrently supervisor of the UP Law Center, the research and training organization affiliated with the College of Law. She continued to serve in all these capacities until 1978.

## ACHIEVEMENTS AND CONTRIBUTIONS

Cortes was dean of the UP College of Law during one of the University's most turbulent periods. The early 1970s were years of student activism in the Philippines, a period that reached its zenith with the declaration by radical groups that the University was a commune, resulting in the suspension of classes and acts of vandalism and violence. Like other academic units, the Law School had to suspend classes during the commune. But it largely escaped the serious damage that resulted from the bombings and destruction of property that other units suffered. Once classes resumed, however, all was not peace and quiet, for the Law School experienced a series of "rumbles," essentially gang warfare, among student fraternities. Events like these served as part of the rationalization for President Ferdinand Marcos's declaration of martial law and suspension of democratic government in September, 1972.

Despite their turbulent beginnings, the 1970s were also years of accomplishment for Cortes and the UP College of Law. As dean, she took the lead in curriculum reforms that introduced practical clinical education into Philippine legal training. Such clinical education has now become accepted in most Philippine law schools, and the courts presently allow student attorneys to participate in virtually all phases of legal practice, including appearing in court under the supervision of a licensed attorney. Cortes also succeeded in organizing for the first time an effective alumni association and foundation that has subsequently been an important source of support for the College and its programs. She still serves on the board of the law school's foundation.

As supervisor of the UP Law Center, Cortes encouraged the expansion of the Center's traditional research mission to include sociolegal research of several kinds. In collaboration with social scientists, the Center undertook an expansive study of the legal profession—the characteristics and attitudes of lawyers, legal aid, studies of tribal law, and collaborative research on law and population with Harvard and Tufts universities.

In 1978, Cortes gave up her administrative duties in the College of Law and returned to teaching. In that year she also began service as vice chair of the National Commission on the Role of Filipino Women, a position she held until 1985. The chair of the Commission was First Lady Imelda Marcos. But since Mrs. Marcos never did anything in connection with the Commission, Cortes, as vice chair, was responsible for administering the Commission and its activities. Her role on this national commission was a precursor to her later service on the United Nations Committee on the Elimination of Discrimination Against Women (CEDAW). She became a member of CEDAW in 1982 and served as its vice chair from 1984 to 1986. In these capacities, she had the opportunity to be involved in the major world conferences on the status of women, serving as adviser to the Philippine delegation to the U.N. International Women's Conference at Mexico City in 1975, and as a delegate to the conferences in Copenhagen (1980) and Nairobi (1985). Cortes also participated in a number of other international conferences on the political and social status of women.

The University of the Philippines administration apparently could not do without Cortes's talents for very long. In 1982, she was appointed vice president for Academic Affairs for the University, a position she held until her appointment to the Supreme Court in 1987. During her tenure she also served concurrently as acting vice chancellor for Academic Affairs of the UP flagship campus at

Diliman in 1983–1984, and in 1986–1987, as executive vice president of the University of the Philippines.

Cortes appears to have weathered the incessant meetings, formalities, and crushing workloads associated with her vice presidential offices with reasonable good humor. She reports that she especially enjoyed the opportunities the positions gave her to get to know a wide variety of people within the UP system.

Cortes reports that she had no idea that her name was being put forward seriously for appointment to the Supreme Court when it was being reformed by President Corazon Aquino after the 1985 People Power Revolution and the downfall of the authoritarian Marcos regime. Apparently, she was being strongly supported by three former Supreme Court justices and Marcos opponents who were influential advisers to Aquino on legal matters: former Chief Justice Roberto Concepcion; his close friend former Associate Justice Jose B. L. Reyes; and the Supreme Court's first woman member, former Associate Justice Cecilia Muñoz Palma*. Though told by her colleagues that she was a "shoo-in" for an appointment, she was not among the initial group of Aquino appointees. However, she was named to the Court some nine months later, on February 1, 1987. She served until the Philippines' mandatory retirement age of 70, retiring as of October 20, 1990.

The period of Cortes's service was an important and exciting time for the Philippine Supreme Court. It had the duty of beginning to explicate a constitution newly adopted in 1987, a constitution that substantially expanded the powers of the Supreme Court in an effort to forestall the reemergence of a Ferdinand Marcos-like dictator. Unfortunately, in Cortes's opinion, the 1987 constitution is both too verbose and less clear than the 1935 constitution that served the Philippines until Marcos declared martial law. As a result, the Supreme Court was called upon early and often to determine the operational meaning of the constitution.

The need to address disputes over the meaning of the new constitution was one significant feature of Supreme Court performance during Cortes's tenure. Another was the need to reduce the decisions backlog that had built up during the last years of the Marcos regime. Cortes describes attacking piles of cases that were literally "so dusty we hated to touch them," and of facing four-day-a-week decision-making sessions with agendas containing over 100 items. The fight against the backlog meant that Saturdays and Sundays became workdays like any other for the justices. But the fight against the backlog bore considerable fruit. In the years of Cortes's service, the Court regularly disposed of substantially more cases than were filed each year, peaking at over 5,800 disposed-of cases in 1990.

Personally, Cortes rates her decisions involving freedom of information (especially *Legaspi v. Civil Service Commission*) and freedom of speech and press as among her most significant. But the opinions for which she will probably be most remembered are those she penned in the "Marcos return cases" of 1989, cases in which the Court, through Cortes, upheld the government's refusal to allow the return of the exiled dictator or, later, his body, to the Philippines.

Cortes has not been idle in her retirement. She currently serves the Supreme Court as vice chair of the Judicial Planning, Development, and Implementation Office (JPDIO), reporting to the chief justice, its chairman. The JPDIO is charged with monitoring the performance of the judiciary and exploring a wide variety of projects to promote judicial reform.

As an academic, Cortes has produced a substantial body of work. In addition to her published dissertation, *The Philippine Presidency* (1966), she is author/editor of *Philippine Administrative Law, Cases and Materials* (second edition, 1984), *Emerging Trends in Law* (1983), and *The Constitutional Foundations of Privacy* (1970), as well as other legal research manuals and monographs. Her articles and chapters, appearing in a wide variety of Philippine and international sources, have concentrated most heavily on constitutional law and rights, especially the rights of women, and on law and population issues. In addition, she has written extensively on the reform and restructuring of Philippine legal education.

**REFERENCES**

Cortes, Irene R. *Essays on Legal Education*. Quezon City: University of Philippines Law Center, 1994.

Cortes, Irene R. *Philippine Administrative Law: Cases and Materials*. Rev. 2d ed. Manila: Community Publishers, 1984.

Cortes, Irene R. *Emerging Trends in Law*. Quezon City: University of Philippines Press, 1983.

Cortes, Irene R. *Philippine Manual of Legal Citations*. Quezon City: University of Philippines, College of Law, Legal Resources Center, 1983.

Cortes, Irene R. *Discrimination against Women and Employment Practices*. Manila: National Commission on the Role of Filipino Women, 1982.

Cortes, Irene R. *Women's Rights under the 1973 Constitution*. Quezon City: University of Philippines Press, 1976.

Cortes, Irene R. *The Constitutional Foundations of Privacy*. Quezon City: University of Philippines Law Center, 1970.

Cortes, Irene R. *The Philippine Presidency: A Study of Executive Power*. Quezon City: University of Philippines Law Center, 1966.

Curriculum vitae of Irene R. Cortes, July 22, 1991.

Personal interview with Irene R. Cortes, August 5, 1994, at the Supreme Court, Manila.

*C. NEAL TATE*

# TAKAKO DOI (1928–    )

Takako Doi is one of the most important figures in Japanese postwar politics. Having experienced the tragedy of war, the taste of hunger, and the male-dominated Japanese society, she rose to become the first woman in Japan to accomplish many things. In college, she was the first woman to lead her rugby team as its manager. In politics, she was the first woman ever to hold the position as chairperson of any political party, and to become the first woman speaker of the powerful Lower House of the Japanese *Diet*.

As a friend of the oppressed, Doi has worked to improve human rights for all. To Doi, all injustice and discrimination is a question of basic rights, rights that must forever be guarded and protected with never-ending diligence. She is a people person and enjoys the simple things of life. Her desire to sing at *karaoke* lounges and play *pachinko*, a Japanese-style pinball gambling machine, has won her the confidence and support of the average citizen.

Doi helped to bring about change in Japanese politics by working with the other minority parties to bring an end to the Liberal Democrats' control of the *Diet*. From an historical standpoint, her election as speaker of the House of Representatives was as significant as the election of the Hosogawa coalition government.

In addition, Doi is well known for her work as a guardian of the constitution and has gathered grassroots support for her pacifist policy and environmental concerns. While she has worked hard for the rights of women and children, she has also won the support of labor unions, farmers, fishermen, the ordinary worker, and the owners of small businesses. Doi has also played the role of consumer advocate and was strongly against the 3 percent consumer tax enacted in 1989.

## FAMILY BACKGROUND AND EDUCATION

Takako Doi was born on November 30, 1928, in Kobe, Japan. Her father was a prominent doctor who practiced both pediatrics and internal medicine. Her mother was a well-educated, free-spirited feminist whose name was Kiyo, but bore the nickname *Oden Chan*, which referred to her large buttocks. Takako loved it when her maternal grandmother, who used to sleep with a small Samurai sword known as a *Kaiken* by her side, would tell her tales of Japanese folklore. Her favorite was a gruesome story of the battle of Tobafushimi, wherein her grandmother would dramatize the story with realistic speech and action. Takako, with her older sister, younger sister, and two younger brothers would be frightened by the story, which delighted the old woman.

Her father's family were farmers from Hiroshima. He attended Kyoto Medical School (*Kyoto Isen*) and developed a very conservative personality. Before crossing a bridge, he would always check to make sure it was safe, and if there was any doubt, he would refuse to cross. He was a refined, quiet man who liked the better things in life and was determined to live a well-organized life. He used to count calories and eat each meal at precisely the same time every day. Doi's father worked until he was 86 and died at the age of 90. At the age of 80, he suffered a heart attack but returned to his practice in order to care for his loyal patients who depended on him for both medical and personal matters.

In those days, Japanese girls were treated differently from boys, and parents would often use the expression "because you are a girl . . . (*onna dakara*)," whenever they wanted to put their daughter in her "proper place." However, this was never done in the Doi household. The three daughters and two sons were treated alike by their parents.

In the spring of 1935, Takako Doi entered first grade, and there began her lifelong crusade to help the weak and the underdog. On the first day of school, after the entrance ceremony was over and the children were lined up in the school yard, she came to the rescue of a little girl with polio who was being bullied by a boy student. He was tormenting the child by pushing her shoulder and pulling her hair. When he picked up a rock to throw at his victim, Takako decided it was time to step in and take action. She fought with the boy and physically dissuaded him from any further aggression toward the girl. Both Takako and the boy were severely scolded by the teacher, but she never agreed to apologize to the brute. After school, the boy threatened Takako and said that he would not forget what she had done. Intimidated somewhat, she was reluctant to return to school the following day. Nevertheless, when she arrived at school a little tardy, she was relieved to discover that the boy had not arrived yet. She realized that he was equally afraid of her when eventually he had to be dragged into the classroom by his mother.

During the Second World War, it was considered unpatriotic to listen to American music. Nevertheless, Doi often listened to Mickey Mouse records in the privacy of her own home without objection from either of her parents. In 1938, her father was drafted in the army medical corp and was stationed first in Osaka, but on July 5 of the same year, he was sent to China to care for the wounded on the front lines. Fortunately, he returned safely the following year and resumed his medical practice in Kobe.

In April of 1941, Doi entered the No. 3 Hyogo Prefectural School for Girls. She studied English there until the attack on Pearl Harbor, when the subject was banned from the classroom. She also participated in track and field wherein she used a heavy wooden stick in place of shot put due to the need to preserve iron for the war effort. Her studies were soon suspended, and Doi was required to work in a bearing factory making iron balls. Since this factory was directly related to making armaments, it was often a target of U.S. air strikes. Doi lived in constant fear of attack and dashed to the shelters at the sound of the air raid sirens.

By 1945, the war had escalated to a point where the United States was now systematically conducting air raids and had launched a major offensive on the port town of Kobe and its surrounding areas. Everyone in the family slept with an emergency kit next to their pillow, for air raids could come at any time. At 11:00 P.M. on March 17, the biggest attack on Kobe occurred; this traumatic event would have a profound, lasting effect on Doi's life. When the sirens sounded that evening, her mother instructed her to take her younger brother to the school grounds. There was total chaos; people were screaming and crying, and Doi saw people killed or injured before her eyes. Her father, as a doctor, was naturally called upon to aid the injured, and she was required to help him. One of the injured was a man whose arm had been seriously damaged to the extent that it had to be removed, and at that time there was no anesthesia. Doi was ordered by her father to hold the arm while he conducted the amputation. Takako's first-hand experience of the pain and suffering of war would lead to her lifetime work as a champion of peace and opponent of violence in any form.

In addition to the damage done to human life (2,598 dead and 8,559 injured) in Kobe, many structures were also destroyed. More than 4,600 homes were firebombed, and her house was one of them. Doi and her family were left with only the clothes they were wearing. Fortunately, however, Dr. Doi was able to set up a temporary practice at a nearby clinic soon after the attack.

Doi's parents sent her to Kyoto to attend Kyoto Women's College. Although there was only a little food to eat and people subsisted mainly on sweet potatoes and pumpkins, she realized her good fortune in being able to study. The rules were very conservative at this prestigious institution, but Doi had no trouble complying with them.

On August 7, 1945, while Doi was preparing to come home for summer vacation, she heard that a big bomb had been dropped on Hiroshima. At the time, she did not realize that it had been an atomic bomb. After returning home to be with her family, they listened together to Emperor Hirohito's voice for the first time on the radio declaring that the war was over. She had to pinch her own hand; she just couldn't believe it. For the first time in many years, Doi had a reason to look forward to tomorrow. Until then, she had not known if she would live or die.

On August 30, General Douglas MacArthur arrived in Atsugi with the occupation forces. Her father, having experienced the brutality of Japanese military life first hand, believed that it was dangerous for a young woman to live away from home and wanted her to leave Kyoto Women's College and return home. However, her mother disagreed and told him that the college would take responsibility for looking after their daughter. Doi was allowed to stay.

In her formative years, Doi was profoundly influenced by Abraham Lincoln, as portrayed by Henry Fonda in her favorite movie, *A Young Mr. Lincoln.* After seeing how Lincoln tried to help liberate the blacks, she was determined to become a lawyer and work for the rights of the oppressed and weak. She was moved to tears at seeing the dramatization of Lincoln's assassination and the compassion he displayed for the less fortunate of society.

To achieve her goal, Doi transferred from Kyoto's Women's College to the faculty of law at Doshisha University at the end of her sophomore year in 1949. She was now 20. Out of a class of 150 students, she was one of only two females. Without even expressing an interest in the position, Doi was elected to the student council as the sole female member. As a student, Doi was an activist and an outspoken critic of the Korean War, and even in these early years, she recognized the importance of democracy and majority rule. To protest a tuition hike, the council adopted a measure calling for a boycott of classes and final exams. Doi, who had voted against the idea but went along with the majority resolution and did not attend class or take finals, felt betrayed by some of her fellow classmates when some of those who favored the action ignored the boycott and sat for examinations. Doi also made it clear to everyone in these early days that she was a staunch pacifist opposed to violence in any form. She consistently voted against any measure where force was suggested.

Doi would always sit in the front row of the class so she could absorb everything her professors were saying. She joined a study group to prepare for the bar exam, and in the process, took a special interest in Article 14 of the Japanese constitution which, on the surface, guarantees equality of the sexes. Doi questioned laws that violated this ideal, laws such as the one that required women (but not men) to wait six months before they could remarry.

Professor Shinobu Tabata of Doshisha University probably had more influence on Doi's professional career than any other person. He taught constitutional law and was a strong supporter of human rights, of the Japanese pacifist position as required by Article 9 of the constitution, and of democracy at the grassroots level. Upon graduation, Doi gave up the notion of becoming a lawyer owing to her lack of confidence in her ability to pass the bar exam, and even more so to her desire to go on to graduate school and continue her studies under Professor Tabata. Her interest now shifted to legislation and judicial interpretation. In 1951, Doi entered the master course at Doshisha in the area of politics. Her thesis research addressed the authority of the *Diet* to conduct investigations pursuant to Article 62 of the constitution.

## CAREER DEVELOPMENT

In 1956, Doi completed her graduate studies, and two years later she took a teaching position as an instructor of constitutional law at Doshisha University. She continued to work closely with Professor Tabata and also taught at Kwansei Gakuin University and Seiwa Women's College. Her courses were well attended, and she was initially very nervous in front of a class in a large auditorium with more than a thousand seats. Within a couple of years, the butterflies in her stomach disappeared, and Doi taught with vigor and enthusiasm. Her 168 cm stature may have helped her command respect, as she was noticeably tall for a Japanese woman.

In 1962, Professor Tabata established a constitutional research center dedicated to the study of issues related to preserving the constitution. The center was founded with private funds, and Doi and others sold paper to raise money for its operation. Doi was also responsible for establishing groups around the country to work for the preservation of the constitution. She encouraged the average citizen to take an interest in the affairs of government in order to maintain true democracy. During this period, Doi also became a well-known radio personality at Kyoto Broadcasting Station and Mainichi Broadcasting Station. Her main program was a Saturday afternoon show dealing with women's issues entitled ''Women's Forum and Living for Tomorrow'' (''Josei no Hiroba-Asu e no Kurashi'').

In 1965, Doi became the first woman to be appointed to a civil service commission in Japan. In December of that year, she began her service on the Kobe Civil Service Commission for a term of four years. In 1969, she also became director of the Committee to Protect the Constitution (*Kempo o Mamoru Kai*).

In early December 1968, Tomomi Narita, chairman of the Socialist party, suddenly telephoned Doi and asked her to run for the Lower House as a representative from Hyogo District No. 2. Her mentor, Professor Tabata, also urged her to enter politics. Despite these encouragements, Doi was very reluctant to give up her teaching career and her study of the constitution. She tried desperately to find some way to reject their proposal. But in January 1969, on her way home from teaching at Kwansei Gakuin University, Doi noticed something disturbing in the newspaper's headlines. The newspaper had erroneously reported that she had decided to run for political office. Upon arriving at her residence, Doi immediately lodged a complaint at the newspaper's office. The paper was surprised by her call and failed to take her complaint seriously.

Since such a public announcement would have the appearance of a conflict of interest and would jeopardize her image of neutrality and fairness, Doi resigned from the Civil Service Commission. When she went to city hall to tender her resignation, the vice mayor refused to accept it. He reasoned that since she had not herself decided to run for public office, there was no need for her resignation. More importantly, however, he also insulted Doi by suggesting that politics would be no place for a woman, and she could save herself a lot of disappointment by abandoning any notion of a political career.

In a moment of frustration and anger, and to express her resentment regarding discrimination against women, Doi decided to run for political office after all in order both to spite the vice mayor and to satisfy her personal need for challenge. She knew that half of the sovereignty of any democracy belonged to women. But on the bus ride home, Doi realized that she would be leaving the academic world of constitutional law and entering the hectic world of politics. She wondered why she had spent so many years studying the constitution. With no prior experience in politics, Doi felt totally unprepared for what lay ahead.

In February, 1969, the Socialist party officially declared Doi a candidate at its general meeting. Her father, though he had been opposed to the idea, secretly asked his patients to support her. Doi began traveling around her district and worked very hard to meet the people who lived and worked there. Her teaching at Doshisha University continued until March, and she concluded her work at Kwansei University in September, whereupon she became a full-time politician.

On December 7, 1969, campaigning for the general election officially began. Although Doi lacked sufficient funds and preparation, she began to campaign wholeheartedly, standing outside train stations and the gates to major companies to greet the arriving workers in the morning. Doi would talk so much that her voice would become hoarse. People would cheer her and offer words of encouragement, though most of the press declared that she had little chance at winning. After 20 days of campaigning, Doi won her first political contest with 69,395 votes, a margin of 1,400 votes over her opponent. In order to fully appreciate her level of support, Doi went to a vacant baseball stadium that had a seating capacity of 43,000. As she stood in the middle of the field, she realized the tremendous support she had achieved and the significant responsibilities that would follow.

As the media began to pay more attention to Doi, a question often asked related to her unmarried status. Surprised at the inquiry, she simply replied that she never had the opportunity to marry. In a country where all women are expected to marry, Doi was considered to be unique in this regard. In fact, high-ranking politicians occasionally insulted her on this issue. For example, in February 1989 former Vice Prime Minister Shin Kanemaru said that Doi could not be compared to British Prime Minister Margaret Thatcher inasmuch as she was single and did not know men, whereas Thatcher had a husband.

Doi, however, was no stranger to mixing it up politically with her male colleagues, and many suffered the wrath of her harsh questioning. On March 19, 1970, she had her first opportunity to question the Cabinet before a national audience, an event that would earn her the title of the "evil questioner." In support of her party's no-confidence resolution stemming from the Liberal Democrats' railroading of the conditions for the return of Okinawa without adequate discussion at the *Diet*, Doi made a speech in which she criticized the speaker of the Lower House. She declared that he should be ashamed of himself, as a public official, as a member of the *Diet*, as speaker, and most importantly, as a man, for being afraid to include the minority parties in the negotiating process.

On one occasion in the Lower House, the ‘‘evil questioner’’ once quoted from a fifth grade textbook dealing with the subject of industrial pollution. Doi asked the Minister of Education why the textbook explained that in order to prevent pollution factories had to install filters in their smokestacks, but that the cost of the equipment could drive the companies into bankruptcy, which suggested the Government ought not be too harsh on companies. The minister, forced to admit that he was not familiar with the book, was left in a state of panic at the question. Doi declared that the health of citizens should always be at the forefront of concern.

In February, 1987, Doi even took on former Prime Minister Yasuhiro Nakasone and publicly stated that he was a dangerous man. She declared that his policies were an assault on democratic principles and that he was trying to destroy the peace that Japan had enjoyed since the war. Doi felt Japan's role in the world was destined to be that of a ‘‘conscientious objector’’ and that the Nakasone Cabinet had developed a hawkish policy.

## ACHIEVEMENTS AND CONTRIBUTIONS

In July of 1971, Doi became a member of a special committee dealing with environmental protection and pollution control. She worked hard with Takeo Miki, former chairman of the Office for Environmental Protection, to draft legislation that provided for strong measures against industrial pollution. Through her efforts, Japan was able to clean up much of the pollution created during the 1970s, a period of rapid development. She also took a great interest in the Osaka Airport Noise Pollution case and went to the area around the airport to experience first hand what the surrounding residents heard every time a jumbo jet took off or landed. She could not believe what she saw and heard; the noise and vibration were so immense that the area was virtually uninhabitable. The government took the position that since the airport had complied with international standards for airport design, it had no responsibility for alleviating the problem. A civil suit on the matter went to the Supreme Court, but the case was eventually settled by the parties in March of 1984.

Takako Doi has always considered equality between the sexes an issue of basic human rights. In the early 1970s, she began to take an active interest in encouraging Japanese women to play a more aggressive role in improving the status of their gender. In 1975, the Ten Years of the Woman began under a United Nations resolution, and Doi helped to implement its principles. In 1979, the Convention on the Elimination of All Forms of Discrimination Against Women was ratified by several countries in Copenhagen, and Doi attended the signing ceremony. While Japan was a signatory to the convention, it took a wait-and-see attitude in terms of revising domestic laws that conflicted with the convention. Many areas of Japanese law needed to be revised, including the Nationality Law, which basically granted Japanese nationality only to children with Japanese fathers. Doi also wanted to end employment and educational discrimination, and to abolish the requirement that only high school girls had to take home economics courses.

In 1985, after ten years of battle with the Ministry of Justice and two previously unsuccessful attempts, Doi was finally able to introduce legislation that would grant Japanese nationality to the children of Japanese women who married non-Japanese husbands. In a committee meeting she sarcastically commented that the old law had always been a violation of Article 14 of the Japanese constitution, but that it took an international convention to push the Japanese government into action. Doi argued that international conventions must take priority over the constitution.

Since her election to the *Diet*, Doi has consistently taken an interest in foreign policy, especially with other Asian nations. The political right has criticized her for arguing publicly that Japan should apologize for its sins of the Second World War and for stating that the late Emperor Showa (Hirohito) was responsible for the Pacific war. At a press club meeting in Tokyo in January, 1989, just after the death of the emperor, she told a German journalist, ''I think the late Emperor was responsible for the war, because it was fought in his name in accordance with the old Constitution.'' At that time, Hirohito was considered the sovereign of Japan and supreme commander of the Imperial Armed Forces. Nevertheless, Doi had been one of the first to visit the Imperial Palace to sign a register to wish for the late Emperor's recovery.

In January, 1972, Doi visited China and met with former premier Zhou Enlai. At the meeting she suggested that Japan and China exchange animals as a sign of friendship. She told him that the children of Japan would love to receive a panda for Tokyo's Ueno Zoo. Zhou replied that such an exchange would have to wait until the two nations formally restored diplomatic relations and might serve as a memorial of the event. After the exchange finally occurred, Doi was given credit for the formation of ''panda diplomacy.''

Doi also took considerable interest in improving the situation with the Korean residents of Japan. During World War II, the Korean soldiers who fought in the Japanese army were considered Japanese citizens, but they were stripped of that status after the war and had to fend for themselves when accused of participating in war crimes. In addition, whereas the bodies of Japanese soldiers were returned to their hometown and given a proper burial, the remains of Korean soldiers have yet to be sent to their final resting place. Doi believes that the Japanese government should pay compensation to those who suffered because of the Japanese military effort.

Another example of her compassion involves her attention to a 28-year-old Korean who was denied reentry into Japan after studying music in the United States for two years. Son Ae was a Korean born in Japan who refused to be fingerprinted every time her alien registration was renewed. The Justice Ministry had categorically denied reentry permits to such individuals. However, through Doi's efforts, the Ministry changed its position for the first time and granted the student permission to re-enter Japan.

Surprisingly, Takako Doi is not a socialist, although she is a member of the Socialist party (referred to in English as the Social Democratic party of Japan, or SDPJ). Doi, being raised in an upper middle-class family, always supported the principles of capitalism. As a constitutional scholar, she had decided early in her career to dedicate her life to guarding the constitution, and it was this ambition that prompted her to join the Socialist party. When the Liberal Democrats suggested that the constitution be amended to allow for the establishment of a military force, Doi joined the opposition because of its position on preserving the constitution, especially Article 9, which prohibits Japan from maintaining a military force.

When, in 1985, the Socialist party abandoned its Marxism/Leninism approach and adopted Western-style social democracy, Doi became engaged in party work. When the party celebrated its fortieth anniversary that year, Doi organized women's forums to oppose nuclear development and military expansion, and to create a nuclear-free zone.

In July 1986, the SDPJ suffered a tremendous defeat in the general election and was left with only 85 seats in the Lower House. The party leadership turned to Doi to revitalize the organization, and they elected her as the first woman chairperson of the Social Democratic party of Japan. At first, Doi was reluctant to run for the post, not wanting to give up her committee work. But after consulting with her longstanding mentor, Professor Tabata, and receiving his words of encouragement, she changed her mind. Doi felt that her work for the party was analogous to a hen helping her chick out of its shell; she would chip away from the outside, and the party would peck from the inside. In the summer of 1991, after serving as chairperson of the SDPJ for almost five years, Doi resigned from the party leadership and returned to committee work.

In August of 1993, Doi again set a new record by becoming the first woman speaker of the powerful Lower House. She was elected over the liberal party candidate, Seisuke Okuno, by a margin of 264 to 222 votes. In her capacity as speaker, Doi has continued to strive for political reform and political justice. She has helped Japan to transform its political system from one influenced by money and big business to one responsive to the needs of the people.

Doi dismisses the notion of becoming Japan's first woman prime minister and continues to be a driving force in Japanese politics. Her life has been a model for young women, and she has challenged many of them to take responsibility for their own destiny. Takako Doi has brought about tremendous improvement in the status of women and has made many efforts to preserve peace and to ensure economic and political justice for all.

## REFERENCES

The Committee to Support Takako Doi (ed.). *Takako Doi*. Tokyo: Yumiko Haneda, 1987.

Doi, Takako. ''Watashi no Ririku Sho'' (''My Personal History''). In *Nippon Keizai Shimbun*, September 1–30, 1993.

Doi, Takako. *My Way*. Tokyo: Shuppan Shinsha, 1986.

Itagaki, Hidenori. *Kibo no Kakumei—Doi Takako no Chousen* (*A Revolution of Hope—The Challenge of Takako Doi*). Tokyo: DHC Co. Ltd., 1993.

Tabata, Shinobu. *Hisen Heiwa no Ronri* (*The Theory of Peace and Nonaggression*). Tokyo: Houritsu Bunka Sha, 1992.

*WILLIAM B. CLEARY*

# RUTH BADER GINSBURG (1933– )

On August 10, 1993, in the East Room of the White House, Ruth Bader Ginsburg stood before Chief Justice William Rehnquist. With her husband, Martin Ginsburg, holding the Bible and President Bill Clinton looking on, she recited the oath of office as the 107th justice of the United States Supreme Court. Although Ginsburg is only the second woman to rise to the bench of the nation's highest court, her contribution to the history of American law was made well before this momentous occasion. As an educator and an advocate, Ruth Bader Ginsburg worked diligently throughout the 1970s to advance the rights of women in the United States. And it was largely her own experiences with discrimination that motivated her to pursue legal and social change.

Justice Ginsburg's life presents a portrait of the often romanticized American success story. Born in the Flatbush neighborhood of Brooklyn, New York, to first-generation Americans, Ginsburg overcame innumerable personal, social, and professional obstacles to reach the nation's highest court. What is most fascinating about the second woman in history to serve on the United States Supreme Court is her lifelong streak of independence, and it is this trait that makes journalists and scholars squirm when assessing her career as a judge and, most recently, as a justice of the United States Supreme Court. An understanding of that independence is possible, however, when seen in light of her common-sense approach to law, combined with the experiences that she brought with her to the Court.

## FAMILY BACKGROUND AND EDUCATION

Joan Ruth Bader was born on March 13, 1933, in Brooklyn, New York, to Celia Amster and Nathan Bader.[1] In the throes of the Great Depression, the neighborhood was home to a mix of recent immigrants, and first- and second-generation Americans of Jewish, Irish, and Italian descent. Ruth was the second Bader child but was raised virtually as an only child. Her older sister, Marilyn, died of meningitis at the age of six when Ruth was just one year old. But Marilyn left her younger sibling with the nickname, ''Kiki,'' a name that followed young Ruth during her childhood and adolescent years.

Ruth's father was a furrier and a haberdasher. Her mother, Celia, had graduated from high school and worked for a short time in the garment industry to support her brother's college education. But once a wife and mother, home was where she was expected to be, regardless of her talents or intellect. Celia had the most profound influence on young Ruth; she ensured that her daughter received a proper education and taught her the love of books and diligent work habits. Tragically, Celia Bader fell ill with cancer while Ruth was in high school and passed away the day before her daughter's graduation ceremony where Ruth was to be honored for her academic achievements. Not surprisingly, it was to her mother that Ruth Bader Ginsburg dedicated her nomination to the Supreme Court on the day of President Clinton's announcement in the Rose Garden.

> I have a last thank-you. It is to my mother . . . the bravest and strongest person I have known, who was taken from me much too soon. I pray that I may be all that she would have been had she lived in an age when women could aspire and achieve and daughters are cherished as much as sons.[2]

Ruth Bader's early education in the New York City public school system was a mix of social activities and serious studies. She was a member of the twirling squad, the academic honor society, and the booster club for the high school sports teams. Even in these early years, she was able to juggle the competing demands on her life, a skill that would serve her well throughout her college education and her early years of married life.

Graduating sixth in her class from James Madison High School, Bader enrolled at Cornell University in 1950. In her freshman year, she met her future ''life partner,'' Martin Ginsburg, who was a sophomore. As their relationship developed, Ruth and Martin discussed career options that they both could share and settled on plans to attend law school more out of compromise than a passion for law. While Martin began his first year at Harvard Law, Ruth finished her senior year at Cornell, graduating first in her class in 1954, with a degree in government. Shortly after graduation, they were married.

The Ginsburgs' plan to pursue law school was interrupted by Martin's Selective Service notice. Assigned to a station in Oklahoma, the new Mrs. Ginsburg moved with her husband to the Midwest and sought out a civil service job. It was here that Ruth Ginsburg witnessed, at first hand, employment discrimination against women. Though qualified for a GS-5 position, Ginsburg's revelation of her pregnancy resulted in her disqualification from an available job at that level in the local Social Security office and her relegation to clerk typist, which was three steps below her qualification.

When Martin's tour of duty was completed in 1956, the family returned to the East Coast with their young daughter, Jane, and Ruth enrolled and Martin reenrolled at Harvard Law School. Out of 400 students, Ruth was one of but nine women admitted to the law school that year. Mrs. Ginsburg made the Law Review and maintained excellent grades. But juggling the competing demands of motherhood and academics became even more complicated when her husband was diagnosed with cancer. Ruth worked tirelessly to keep Martin up to date on his classes by taking notes and typing his papers during his medical treatment all the while maintaining her own studies. When Martin graduated and received an offer from a New York law firm in 1958, Ruth transferred to Columbia Law School to complete her final year of law school, where she graduated tied for first in her class.

Ruth and Martin have two children, Jane and James, and are the proud grandparents of Jane's two children, Clara and Paul. The Ginsburg household has never been "traditional." Much ado has been made about the fact that Martin is the cook in the family and that throughout their marriage, he assumed many of the household chores. Martin is a renowned tax attorney in his own right and is also a professor of law. Jane has followed in her parents' footsteps and is a professor of law at Columbia University. Son, James, who attributes his love of music to his parents, is the owner of a growing classical music production studio in Chicago.

## CAREER DEVELOPMENT

Having completed her education in 1959, Ruth Ginsburg once again confronted gender discrimination in seeking employment. Despite her stellar academic record, she was not hired by any of the prestigious New York firms and was not even granted an interview for a Supreme Court clerkship, an opportunity that would have been offered to a male counterpart with her qualifications. "A woman, a Jew and a mother to boot" were not characteristics likely to endear her to the very male, black-robed justices of the Supreme Court.[3] Ginsburg eventually secured a clerking position with U.S. District Judge Edmund L. Palmieri and worked with him until 1961.

Following her clerkship, Ginsburg was invited to participate as a research associate on a comparative legal studies project funded by the Carnegie Foundation through Columbia University. She seized the opportunity to travel to Sweden to study its legal and judicial system and there, by coincidence, she witnessed the beginnings of a feminist movement. But the young Mrs. Ginsburg was not yet attuned to the legal concerns of women. The comparative studies project resulted in two co-authored books on Swedish law, and to this day, Ginsburg maintains her academic interest in that country's laws and judicial system.

In 1963, Ginsburg sought to enter the academic world. Columbia, New York University, and Fordham University law schools expressed no interest in hiring her, but she was offered a position at Rutgers University. Ginsburg was only the second woman hired by Rutgers and was one of the first 20 women to hold a tenure-earning position in the nation's law schools. Recalling her previous experience with pregnancy and employment ten years earlier, she hid her second pregnancy by wearing oversized clothes in fear of not being granted tenure. Son, James, was born, and in 1966, Assistant Professor Ginsburg was promoted to associate professor. Three years later, she attained the rank of professor, teaching civil procedure, conflict of laws, and constitutional law, and publishing on a variety of legal topics that included her continued interest in Scandinavian and international law.[4] Ginsburg remained at Rutgers until 1972.

It was during her later years at Rutgers that Ginsburg developed an interest in women's issues and law. Her first article on the topic was published in 1971 in the *Journal of Family Law*, and the title, "Sex and Unequal Protection: Men and Women as Victims," might have provided some indication of what was to come. That same year she wrote her first Supreme Court brief in the landmark case, *Reed v. Reed*.[5] Ginsburg took her professorship to Columbia University in 1972, after having been tentatively courted by Harvard Law School. Soon after, she signed on with the American Civil Liberties Union as the director of their new Women's Rights Project.

For the next eight years, Ginsburg devoted her time to teaching, writing, and litigation. She developed one of the earliest courses on sexual equality and law, and finding that there were no contemporary textbooks on the topic, with Herma Hill Kay and Kenneth Davidson, she published *Text, Cases, and Materials on Sex-Based Discrimination* in 1974. Between 1971 and 1980, Ginsburg published over 20 articles and lectures, two monographs, and the case book on gender discrimination, wrote nine Supreme Court briefs, and presented oral argument in six cases before the justices. She also filed and litigated numerous cases in the lower courts on behalf of women and men claiming gender discrimination.

In 1976, with the election of the first Democratic president in eight years, Professor Ginsburg had hoped to be appointed as the first woman solicitor general of the United States.[6] She would have been following in the footsteps of some very prominent jurists (Archibald Cox, Thurgood Marshall, Erwin Griswold, and Robert Bork, for example) who had previously served as the nation's legal representative before the Supreme Court. But the offer from President Jimmy Carter never came.

Quite late in the Carter administration Ruth Bader Ginsburg received a nomination to the United States Court of Appeals for the District of Columbia Circuit. She first donned her black robes in 1980 and remained on the bench until her nomination to the U.S. Supreme Court on June 14, 1993, by President Bill Clinton. As a member of the D.C. Circuit, Judge Ginsburg authored over 70 opinions on a broad range of constitutional, statutory, and administrative matters.

The confirmation hearings of Ruth Bader Ginsburg for the Supreme Court before the United States Senate Judiciary Committee in July of 1993 were relatively docile. With the exception of several anti-abortion activists and a few conservative speakers, there was overwhelming support for Judge Ginsburg's confirmation as the 107th justice of the nation's highest court. This support was reflected by the entire Senate on August 3, 1993, with their 96–3 vote in favor of confirmation.[7] Justice Ruth Bader Ginsburg was sworn in on August 10, 1993, and took her seat on the Supreme Court.

As a justice, Ginburg's tenure is still quite new. In her first term on the Court (1993–1994), she authored 27 opinions (nine majority, ten concurring, and eight dissenting).[8] The legacy she will leave as an associate justice of the United States Supreme Court will best be judged by time.

## ACHIEVEMENTS AND CONTRIBUTIONS

Ruth Bader Ginsburg became an active participant in the women's movement rather late in the day relative to many of her contemporaries; nonetheless, her imprint on the law of sexual discrimination in the United States will last for generations. As a result of her litigation through the Women's Rights Project of the American Civil Liberties Union (ACLU), the legal status of men and women in the United States has changed dramatically. What must be remembered in assessing her contributions to the development of law as an educator, a scholar, lawyer, judge, and now, justice is Ginsburg's longstanding devotion to equality and civil rights. As Eleanor Holmes Norton,* the delegate to Congress from the District of Columbia, noted: ''Ruth Ginsburg's roots are deep in the Bill of Rights.''[9]

Described by one colleague as a ''steel butterfly,''[10] Professor Ginsburg was never the outgoing instructor that students seek out in selecting their classes. She was reserved and measured in her public speaking (even to this day), and her strongest suit as an early academic was found in her scholarly writings. Through her work on Sweden and international law, which merited her the attention of the Swedish government, Ginsburg's early academic career might have appeared traditional. She, like others, was carving out a typically narrow scholarly niche for herself in the academic ivory tower through publications. That would all change, however, with her foray into gender discrimination law and her subsequent involvement with the ACLU.

While still at Rutgers, Professor Ginsburg successfully litigated a challenge to a New Jersey regulation that demanded the resignation of school teachers who became pregnant. With her move to Columbia University as the first woman to be granted tenure at the law school, her involvement in fighting for equality blossomed. Understanding full well the impact of gender discrimination in society, Ruth Bader Ginsburg volunteered and served as the founding director of the Women's Rights Project. In that capacity, she crafted a strategy of legal change that rested on incremental challenges to the law on narrowly proscribed grounds. Most interesting is that in many of the cases that Ginsburg argued, her client was not a woman but a man. By challenging laws that discriminated against men, Ginsburg and her colleagues were able to guide the nation's highest court to an acknowledgment that any discrimination, be it against men or women, violated the principle of equality.

Many briefs with Ruth Bader Ginsburg's name as counsel, or *amicus curiae* (friend of the court), are scattered throughout the volumes of the *Federal Reporter* and *Supreme Court Reports*. A wholesale treatment of her legal arguments would demand a book-length work. The cases discussed herein are those that Justice Ginsburg considers her most important litigation matters, as noted in her response to the Senate Judiciary Committee.[11]

Lawyer Ginsburg's name first came before the nine justices in 1971, with her submission of the appellant's briefs in *Reed v. Reed*.[12] Although she did not orally argue this case, it was her approach that persuaded the Court to rule that a gender-based classification was inconsistent with the equal protection clause of the Fourteenth Amendment to the United States Constitution. Previously, equal protection arguments had been used successfully to challenge racial discrimination. In *Reed*, the Court ruled that an Idaho statute that gave preference to males over females as executors of estates was unconstitutional.

In *Moritz v. Commissioner of Internal Revenue*, Ginsburg teamed up with her husband, Martin, to argue against a tax deduction permitted for daughters and married men who provided care to their elderly parents, but not to her client, a single man.[13] As Ginsburg notes, this case was the "fraternal twin to *Reed* . . . and the only occasion, at least before 1980, in which a provision of the Internal Revenue Code has been declared unconstitutional."[14] The case was decided by the Court of Appeals for the Tenth Circuit in 1972, and the Supreme Court subsequently denied review.

The mere filing of Ginsburg's brief and the Supreme Court's grant of certiorari in the case of *Struck v. Secretary of Defense* seemingly prompted the United States Air Force to reverse its policy mandating the discharge of pregnant officers in 1972.[15] As a result of the change in policy, the lower court decision upholding the discriminatory policy was vacated by the United States Supreme Court.

In 1973, Professor Ginsburg argued her first case before the Supreme Court. In *Frontiero v. Richardson*, Ginsburg and the ACLU challenged the federal laws that allowed male military members certain spousal and family benefits, but denied similar benefits to the spouses of female soldiers.[16] While the Court agreed that the statutes were unconstitutional, it did not fully adopt the line of reasoning that Ginsburg had urged. Ginsburg argued that the Court should recognize that gender, like race, is a "suspect" classification under equal protection analysis and thus, any law or governmental action that distinguished between men and women could be subjected to the "strict scrutiny" standards the Court had previously outlined for racial distinctions. Four of the justices agreed with Ginsburg, but she could not win over a majority to the notion. To date, the Court has yet to recognize gender classifications as "suspect."

Ginsburg went on to argue five more cases before the Supreme Court on gender issues. In *Edwards v. Healy*[17] and *Duren v. Missouri*,[18] the Court overturned state laws that distinguished between men and women regarding jury service. Two cases challenged the distribution and entitlement of Social Security benefits where the rules discriminated against the disbursement of a deceased woman's Social Security benefits to her surviving widower.[19] Ginsburg's single loss before the high court came in *Kahn v. Shevin*, when the justices upheld a Florida law that permitted property tax exemptions for widows, but not widowers, on the basis that these laws benefited women who had traditionally been economically disadvantaged.[20]

This last case offers scholars a crisp view of Ruth Ginsburg's philosophy of gender equality and, at the same time, the intellectual rift that has divided feminists since the 1970s. The division centers around the question of whether or not the law should accommodate or make allowances for women on the basis of legitimate distinctions between the genders or, alternatively, as Ginsburg seemingly advocates, that any and all legal distinctions between the genders should be eliminated. Because of Ginsburg's consistent reliance on equal protection analysis and an "egalitarian feminist" approach, she has drawn the ire of a number of women's rights organizations who fear the loss of benefits related to motherhood and child care. And because Ginsburg believes that equality should serve as the guiding legal principle in gender cases, she has been vocally critical of the Supreme Court's 1973 decision, *Roe v. Wade*,[21] legalizing abortion for being too broad and couched in unnecessary legal reasoning regarding privacy rights.[22]

Despite her career as a liberal, path-breaking lawyer and scholar, some argue that Judge Ginsburg is a different person as a jurist. She has been categorized as a moderate and a centrist, and during her stint on the D.C. Court of Appeals, she sided slightly more often with her conservative colleagues than with the liberal wing of the bench. But sitting on an intermediate appellate court that is bound by precedent and subject to Supreme Court review does not permit the independence of thought that some of her critics seem to expect. Even as an attorney, however, Ruth Ginsburg fashioned for the Court a strategy of incremental change rather than revolution. Her approach to legal reasoning relied on a strong belief in the value of precedent and a modicum of judicial restraint. But throughout her life, Ginsburg has always exhibited that streak of independence, a trait that has not disappeared with her elevation to the Supreme Court.

During her first term on the Supreme Court, Justice Ginsburg did not exhibit the restraint at oral arguments typical of newcomers to the bench. In fact, the media made some fuss over her ambitious queries and interjections.[23] The traditional "first-term" studies of her performance also indicate that Ginsburg did not suffer from "the freshman effect" in receiving assignments of majority opinions, nor did she hesitate to submit concurring or dissenting opinions.[24] Clearly, her intellect and experience on the Court of Appeals quickly earned Ginsburg the respect of her eight colleagues.

Substantively, Justice Ginsburg has continued to take the independent path and defies classification as a conservative or liberal. One assessment in advance of her appointment defined her approach as "political liberalism and judicial conservatism. Her conservatism . . . reflects not mindless deference but a willingness to be restrained by the constitutional text, history and structure."[25] That philosophy has seemingly held true. She has most frequently sided with the "middle" justices (David Souter and Anthony Kennedy), but "she had moderate agreement rates with all of her colleagues whether they were conservative, liberal, or something in between."[26]

Ruth Bader Ginsburg has received numerous honorary degrees and has been invited to deliver many endowed lectures over her years as a scholar, practitioner, and judge. In 1993, she received the Margaret Brent Women Lawyers of Achievement Award from the American Bar Association Commission on the Status of Women in the Profession. But perhaps the most significant accolade Ginsburg received in recent years came from a man whom she first encountered in 1956. The occasion of their introduction was an invitation to a social hosted by the dean of Harvard Law. At the social, Ginsburg and the other eight women who had been admitted that year were questioned by the dean regarding their academic and career intentions. He pointed out to them that they were, in essence, displacing men who had also applied for admission, and implicit in his discussion was evidence that he wanted somehow to ensure that the women were not simply seeking husbands through their enrollment. Ginsburg's recollection of that evening was one of shock.

At a Supreme Court anniversary celebration over 40 years after this incident, it was that former dean of Harvard Law that named Ruth Bader Ginsburg and Thurgood Marshall as the two lawyers who had most significantly changed the course of legal history in modern times.[27] It was a high compliment coming from Dean Erwin Griswold, one of the nation's most renowned and respected constitutional scholars. But it was more than that. The accolade was an implicit commentary on how significantly life had changed for women in America and in the legal profession. And Justice Ruth Bader Ginsburg was a major force in effecting that change.

## NOTES

1. The biographical information included in this and the following section was obtained from a number of newspaper and magazine articles published following Ginsburg's nomination to the Supreme Court. "Women Call Ginsburg Mentor, Role Model," *St. Louis Post Dispatch* (June 16, 1993): 1C; David Margolick, "Trial by Adversity Shapes Jurist's Outlook," *New York Times* (June 25, 1993): A1; Linda P. Campbell and Linda M. Harrington, "Judge Ruth Bader Ginsburg: Portrait of a 'Steel Butterfly,' " *Chicago Tribune* (June 27, 1993): C7; David Von Drehle, "Conventional Roles Hid a Revolutionary Intellect; Discrimination Helped Spawn a Crusade," *Washington Post* (July 18, 1993): A1; Timothy M. Phelps and Jack Sirica, "Master of Law, Careful Jurist," *News-*

*day* (July 19, 1993): 4; and Sara Fritz, ''Without Great Expectations, Ginsburg Found Her Way to the Top,'' *Los Angeles Times* (July 21, 1993): A5.

2. ''White House Briefing (Announcement by President Bill Clinton of his nomination of Ruth Bader Ginsburg for Supreme Court Justice),'' *Federal News Service* (June 14, 1993).

3. Quoted in Fritz.

4. See, for example, Ruth Bader Ginsburg, ''The Competent Court in Private International Law,'' 20 *Rutgers Law Review* (1965): 89; Ginsburg, ''Civil Procedure, Basic Features of the Swedish System,'' 14 *American Journal of Comparative Law* (1965): 336; Ginsburg, ''Proof of Foreign Law in Sweden,'' 14 *International and Comparative Law Quarterly* (1965): 277; and Ginsburg, ''Recognition and Enforcement of Foreign Civil Judgments: A Summary View of the Situation in the United States,'' 4 *International Lawyer* (1970): 237.

5. 404 U.S. 71 (1971).

6. As of this writing, the nation still has not seen a woman appointed to the position of solicitor general.

7. Senators Strom Thurmond (Republican of South Carolina), Jesse Helms (Republican of North Carolina), and Don Nickles (Republican of Oklahoma) cast the dissenting votes, and one senator was not present for voting.

8. Christopher E. Smith, Joyce Ann Baugh, Thomas R. Hensley, and Scott Patrick Johnson, ''The First-Term Performance of Justice Ruth Bader Ginsburg,'' 78 *Judicature* (September–October, 1994): 76.

9. Quoted in Fritz.

10. Campbell and Harrington, ''Judge Ruth Bader Ginsburg: Portrait of a 'Steel Butterfly,' '' (June 27, 1993), quoting Columbia Law School Vice Dean Vivian Berger.

11. ''Senate Judiciary Committee, Initial Questionnaire (Supreme Court),'' published in United States Senate, Committee on the Judiciary, ''Hearings Before the Committee on the Judiciary, United States Senate, 103d Congress, 1st Session on the Nomination of Ruth Bader Ginsburg, to be Associate Justice of the Supreme Court of the United States'' (Hearings held on July 20, 21, 22 and 23, 1993) (Washington, DC: U.S. Government Printing Office, 1994), 83–91.

12. 404 U.S. 71 (1971).

13. 469 F.2d 466 (10th Cir. 1972), *cert. denied*, 412 U.S. 906 (1973).

14. Ibid., 85.

15. *cert. granted*, 409 U.S. 947, *judgment vacated*, 409 U.S. 1071 (1972).

16. 411 U.S. 677 (1973).

17. 421 U.S. 772 (1975), argued with *Taylor v. Louisiana*, 419 U.S. 522 (1975).

18. 439 U.S. 357 (1979).

19. *Weinberger v. Wiesenfeld*, 420 U.S. 636 (1975) and *Califano v. Goldfarb*, 430 U.S. 199 (1977).

20. 416 U.S. 351 (1974).

21. 410 U.S. 113 (1973).

22. Speech at New York University in March 1993, cited in Fritz; and David A. Kaplan and Bob Cohn, ''A Frankfurter, Not a Hot Dog,'' *Newsweek* (June 28, 1993): 29.

23. Tony Mauro, ''Our Nattering, Chattering High Court,'' *New Jersey Law Journal* (April 11, 1994): 18.

24. Smith, Baugh, Hensley, and Johnson, 76.

25. ''Wise Choice: Judge Ruth Bader Ginsburg,'' *The New Republic* (July 5, 1993): 7.

26. Smith, Baugh, Hensley, and Johnson, 76.

27. Bill Hewitt, Nina Burleigh, Rochelle Jones, Margie Sellinger, and Luchina Fisher, ''Feeling Supreme,'' *People* (June 28, 1993): 49.

## REFERENCES

Campbell, Linda P., and Linda M. Harrington. ''Judge Ruth Bader Ginsburg: Portrait of a 'Steel Butterfly.' '' *Chicago Tribune* (June 27, 1993): C7.

Fritz, Sara. ''Without Great Expectations, Ginsburg Found Her Way to the Top.'' *Los Angeles Times* (July 21, 1993): A5.

Ginsburg, Ruth Bader. ''Civil Procedure, Basic Features of the Swedish System.'' *American Journal of Comparative Law* 14 (1965): 336.

Ginsburg, Ruth Bader. ''The Competent Court in Private International Law.'' *Rutgers Law Review* 20 (1965): 89.

Ginsburg, Ruth Bader. ''Proof of Foreign Law in Sweden.'' *International and Comparative Law Quarterly* 14 (1965): 277.

Ginsburg, Ruth Bader. ''Recognition and Enforcement of Foreign Civil Judgments: A Summary View of the Situation in the United States.'' *International Lawyer* 4 (1970): 237.

Hewitt, Bill, Nina Burleigh, Rochelle Jones, Margie Sellinger, and Luchina Fisher. ''Feeling Supreme.'' *People* (June 28, 1993): 49.

Kaplan, David A., and Bob Cohn. ''A Frankfurter, Not a Hot Dog.'' *Newsweek* (June 28, 1993): 29.

Margolick, David. ''Trial by Adversity Shapes Jurist's Outlook.'' *New York Times* (June 25, 1993): A1.

Mauro, Tony. ''Our Nattering, Chattering High Court.'' *New Jersey Law Journal* (April 11, 1994): 18.

Phelps, Timothy M., and Jack Sirica. ''Master of Law, Careful Jurist.'' *Newsday* (July 19, 1993): 4.

Smith, Christopher E., Joyce Ann Baugh, Thomas R. Hensley, and Scott Patrick Johnson. ''The First-Term Performance of Justice Ruth Bader Ginsburg.'' *Judicature* 78 (September–October, 1994): 76.

United States Senate, Committee on the Judiciary. ''Hearings Before the Committee on the Judiciary, United States Senate, 103d Congress, 1st Session on the Nomination of Ruth Bader Ginsburg, to Be Associate Justice of the Supreme Court of the United States.'' Hearings held on July 20, 21, 22, and 23, 1993. Washington, DC: U.S. Government Printing Office, 1994, 83–91.

Von Drehle, David. ''Conventional Roles Hid a Revolutionary Intellect; Discrimination Helped Spawn a Crusade.'' *Washington Post* (July 18, 1993): A1.

''White House Briefing (Announcement by President Bill Clinton of his nomination of Ruth Bader Ginsburg for Supreme Court Justice).'' *Federal News Service* (June 14, 1993).

''Wise Choice: Judge Ruth Bader Ginsburg.'' *The New Republic* (July 5, 1993): 7.

''Women Call Ginsburg Mentor, Role Model.'' *St. Louis Post-Dispatch* (June 16, 1993): 1C.

*REBECCA MAE SALOKAR*

# BRENDA MARJORIE HALE (1945– )

Justice Brenda Marjorie Hale's career in British law is a combination of multiple experiences as an academic lawyer, a practicing member of the Manchester bar, a law commissioner, and since January of 1994, as a judge of the Family Division of Britain's High Court of Justice.[1] In the course of her career, she has achieved a number of significant "firsts" as a woman through the positions she has attained.

While teaching law over 18 years at Manchester University, Hale has taught a variety of legal subjects, but she came to be widely recognized for her expertise in family law. It was that expertise that led to her appointment to the Law Commission in 1984, where Hale believes she has made her most important contribution to the development of British law. As a law commissioner, she contributed heavily to the eventual enactment of the Children Act 1989, and by her own testimony, it is her proudest achievement in a legal career that, judging from her record to date, promises much more to come.

## FAMILY BACKGROUND AND EDUCATION

Brenda Hale was born to school teacher parents on January 31, 1945, and spent her formative years in Richmond, a lovely, though quiet, market town in the Yorkshire dales. Her father was headmaster of a small grammar school.[2] The countryside surrounding Richmond is best known to James Herriot fans as the setting of the television series, "All Creatures Great and Small." Hales's father died when she was 13, and her mother, who had previously assisted her husband at the grammar school, was named the headmistress of a local primary school.

Brenda Hale was educated at Richmond High School for Girls where eventually she was named "head girl."[3] That school's headmistress recognized young Brenda's intellectual potential for university and suggested that she might read economics. Brenda, who had become interested in the British constitution and government, asked about studying law. To her credit, the headmistress's response was, "What a good idea!"

Hale attended Girton College, Cambridge,[4] first as an Exhibitioner and later as a Scholar of the College to read law.[5] Reading law at Cambridge or Oxford, even today, is quite different from studying for a graduate professional degree at many law schools in the United States. Law is studied there as an academic subject rather than as professional training. The differences were even greater when Hale read law. For example, Roman law was a compulsory subject in her first and second years. Of course, that requirement demanded Latin proficiency of entering students, a qualification that only those expressly preparing for a university education like that offered by Oxford or Cambridge usually would have had. But Roman law and legal history were subjects that Hale especially enjoyed. Indeed, she received the George Long Prize for Roman Law. Her affinity for such subjects no doubt was a suggestion of her inclination for a career as an academic lawyer, as were her academic distinctions at school and at Cambridge. She received first class honors for her law qualifying exam and for her Law Tripos Part I[6] and a "starred"[7] first class for her Law Tripos Part II. She also received the Teresa Montefiori Prize given by Girton College for all-around excellence.

## CAREER DEVELOPMENT

After receiving her degree from Cambridge in 1966, Hale began her career as a law lecturer at Manchester University. While teaching law, she studied privately for the bar, passing her bar examination in 1967, and completing her obligatory meals[8] at Gray's Inn. She received the Council of Legal Education Prize as the best bar candidate for Michaelmas term in 1967 and was called to the bar in 1969. Hale completed her pupillage[9] in Manchester and practiced as a member of the Manchester bar.

While teaching law at Manchester, she was regularly promoted: to lecturer in 1968, to senior lecturer in 1976, to reader in 1981, and to a professor's chair from 1986 to 1989. She took leave in 1984, however, to serve as a member of the Law Commission. Hale was appointed professor of English Law at King's College (London) in 1989, and she continues to serve King's as a visiting professor.

When Hale was appointed to the Law Commission in 1984, she became the first woman to serve as a commissioner. The Law Commission is a statutory body created in 1965 to promote reform of the law. The Commission has five members and is headed by a judge of the High Court. By tradition, the remaining four members consist of one barrister, one solicitor, and two academic lawyers. While serving on the Law Commission (1984–1993), Hale did leading work on

Commission Reports on *Illegitimacy* (2nd Report, 1987), *Facing the Future: A Discussion Paper on the Ground for Divorce* (1988), *Review of Child Law: Guardianship and Custody* (1988), *Matrimonial Property Law* (1988), *Distribution on Intestacy* (1989), *The Grounds for Divorce* (1990), *Rape Within Marriage* (1992) and *Domestic Violence and Occupation of the Family Home* (1992).

Hale also led the work on the Commission's various consultations or working papers on family law and on laws affecting mentally incapacitated adults. She was a key participant in the preparation of interdepartmental government working party reports on the *Review of Child Care Law* (1985), which contributed to the adoption of the Children Act 1989, and on the *Review of Adoption Law* (1992).

While serving as a law commissioner, Hale was appointed an assistant recorder, recorder, and deputy High Court judge in 1989.[10] She was also named a Queen's Counsel[11] in 1989. Hale was appointed to the High Court of Justice and assigned to the family division in January of 1994.

## ACHIEVEMENTS AND CONTRIBUTIONS

Several of Justice Hale's early articles were reports of recent cases and developments in family law (broadly described), which appeared in *The Solicitors' Journal*, the earliest one in 1973 and the last in 1978. Two interesting examples are a 1976 article, "The Unborn Child and the Law of Tort," and a 1977 article on the law of rape under the Sexual Offences (Amendment) Act 1976. The article on the possibility of an unborn child being the victim of a tortious act focused on the Congenital Disabilities (Civil Liability) Act 1976, which grew out of a Law Commission Report responsive to the tort cases involving congenital defects resulting from the use of the drug "thalidomide" by pregnant women. In her 1977 article on rape and the revisions resulting from the Sexual Offences Act, Hale highlights the two most important changes the law implemented. First, it would no longer be possible to offer evidence or to cross-examine witnesses at trial regarding the sexual experience of a complainant except those experiences with the defendant himself. Second, the revision allowed for the protection of the anonymity of the complainant in media accounts of a criminal charge or trial for rape.

Some of Hale's longer pieces have appeared as chapters in books. Notable among these is her chapter on "Families and the Law" in a 1982 book, *Families in Britain*.[12] In that piece, she recounts the transition in family law from its old role of defining—unimodally—the creation, composition, and dissolution of the family unit and its relationship with the outside world, to a new role in which the law may accommodate a variety of family arrangements while continuing to protect those who may suffer some serious disadvantage in a relationship.

Her 1976 book, *Mental Health Law*, was a pioneering text that went into its third edition in 1990. The first edition of another pioneering book, *Parents and*

*Children: The Law of Parental Responsibility*, was published in 1977 and went into its fourth edition in 1993. The book that Hale regards as her greatest academic achievement is her collection (with David Pearl) of cases and materials on family law. *The Family, Law and Society: Cases and Materials* was first published in 1983, and its third edition was released in 1991.

In 1984, Hale was the co-author with Susan Atkins of the book, *Women and the Law*.[13] The authors' characterization of their book in the introduction is quite pertinent to the appreciation of their contribution:

> We seek to understand how the law has perceived women and responded to their lives. Our object is not to give a biased account of the law but to uncover the extent to which the law itself is biased towards a particular view of life. Even today that view can readily be recognized as one reflected in male rather than female eyes.

Among Hale's more recent articles is one that attempts to assess recent reforms in British family law from her perspective as the first woman law commissioner for England and Wales. She recounts the smug complacency of the early 1950s, which prompted some prominent lawyers and judges to assert that women had achieved equality with men. In this article, Hale notes, "They seem to have been unaware of the extent of the remaining legal, social and especially economic disadvantages suffered by women and assumed that formal equality of opportunity to own property was the same as substantive equality."[14] According to Hale, this began to change in the 1950s and 1960s, and while the changing perceptions of reality involved some men, she gave credit to Betty Friedan for providing the catalyst for modern feminism in 1963, and the resultant possibility of a greatly expanded cast of potential roles for women. Hale noted that the law followed these changing perceptions in the instance of the United Kingdom, for example, in the Equal Pay Act in 1970 and the Sex Discrimination Act in 1975.

The thorny issue she reaches at the end of her article is a suggestion for the proper resolution of spousal support and fair distribution of marital property on the dissolution of a marriage. Apart from the interests of children of a marriage, a proper resolution might be one that takes into account not simply the abstract legal status of husband and wife, but the actual advantages and disadvantages that have resulted from the roles they have filled during the marriage (including the economic and social contribution of each), and the prospects of each for the future. As of the writing of this article in 1994, Hale was not persuaded that a legal resolution of this nature was on the horizon.

The Children Act 1989 was a product of combined efforts of government of the day and the Law Commission; it was also stimulated by a report on child abuse in the County of Cleveland in 1987. Hale cites the Children Act as her most important contribution to date, and it has been described as "The most comprehensive and far reaching reform of child law which has come before Parliament in living memory."[15] As Hale herself has written, "It is impossible to exaggerate the effect which the Act will have upon the practice of all who are concerned with court decisions and social services for children.''[16]

These results were due in no small part to Hale's contribution, for when she joined the Law Commission in 1984, it began a ''wide-ranging review of private law as part of its family law program.'' Thus, it was possible both to reform the law and to coordinate the revision of public and private law relating to children. The Law Commission's recommendations were published in 1988.[17]

It is evident that Justice Brenda Marjorie Hale's career as a woman in law has not just recorded a number of firsts for a woman. The perspective she has brought to her work as a woman and as a legal scholar, and her unending concern for women and families have allowed Justice Hale to make a unique contribution to the development of English family law.

## NOTES

1. The Family Division ''exercises the matrimonial and domestic jurisdiction of the High Court, which includes defended divorce cases and matters relating to the wardship, guardianship, custody, maintenance of adoption of children, and deals with non-contentious or common form probate business. It also hears appeals from magistrates' courts in domestic (family) proceedings.'' S. H. Bailey and M. J. Gunn, *The Modern English Legal System*, 2nd ed. (London: Sweet and Maxwell, 1991).

2. In the United Kingdom, a grammar school traditionally has been a secondary school with rigorous admission standards for academically inclined students, many of whom will go on to university. In the recent past, several professional careers, including law, were open to students who had completed grammar school but chose not to attend university.

3. The title of ''head student'' in a school is bestowed upon a senior student based on character and leadership qualities as well as academic achievement. The head student serves as a role model for juniors and is charged with helping to maintain a school's traditions and standards of behavior.

4. Founded in 1869, Girton College was the first postsecondary institution for women at either Oxford or Cambridge. It was not until 1948 that women were admitted to full membership at Cambridge University. See M. C. Bradbrook, *That Infidel Place: A Short History of Girton College, 1869–1969* (London: Chatto and Windus, 1969).

5. An ''exhibitioner'' is the recipient of a fixed-sum award from a college at Cambridge. Unlike the common usage in the United States, a ''scholar'' in British academia is a recipient of a scholarship from a college.

6. Tripos, Parts I and II, refers to the two honors examinations for the B.A. degree at the conclusion of the third year of study. It is a term unique to Cambridge University and, like many English traditions, has a curious origin. According to the Oxford English Dictionary, formerly a holder of a Cambridge Bachelor of Arts degree was designated each year to dispute in a ''humorous or satirical style,'' the candidates for the B.A. degree. The person assigned this task sat on a three-legged stool while conducting his disputation, hence the origin of the term *Tripos*.

7. First-class honors are the highest class conferred, but a starred first class is reserved for special distinction for a few.

8. By tradition, eating a certain number of obligatory meals in the dining room of an inn was equivalent to being in residence at an inn for a required number of terms.

9. Pupillage is a required period of experiential practical training in which a pupil works with an established barrister who serves as a tutor and mentor.

10. An assistant recorder and recorder sit on the Crown Court. Only solicitors and barristers of ten years' standing can be appointed.

11. The title "Queen's Counsel" is conferred on barristers selected for their experience, knowledge, and success at the bar. A Queen's Counsel "takes silk" upon appointment, which means that a Q.C. wears a black silk gown and a slightly different wig when appearing in court.

12. R. N. Rapoport, M. P. Fogarty, and R. Rapoport, eds., *Families in Britain* (London: Routledge, 1982).

13. Susan Atkins and Brenda Hoggett [B. Hale], *Women and the Law* (London: Basil Blackwell, 1984).

14. Brenda Hoggett [B. Hale], "Recent Reforms in Family Law: Progress or backlash?" 11 *Dalhousie Law Journal* (1987–1988): 6–20.

15. Lord Mackay, speaking before the House of Lords. *Hansard*, H.L. Vol. 502, col. 488.

16. Brenda Hale, "Introduction," in R. White, ed., *Clarke, Hall and Morrison, Law Relating to Children and Young Persons (Special Bulletin: A Guide to the Children Act 1989)* (London: Butterworths, 1990), viii.

17. See J. Masson and M. Morris, *The Children Act Manual* (London: Sweet and Maxwell, 1992), 9. The Law Commission's Report was No. 172.

## REFERENCES

Atkins, Susan, and Brenda Hoggett [B. Hale]. *Women and the Law*. London: Basil Blackwell, 1984.

Bailey, S. H., and M. J. Gunn. *The Modern English Legal System*, 2d ed. London: Sweet and Maxwell, 1991.

Bradbrook, M. C. *That Infidel Place: A Short History of Girton College, 1869–1969*. London: Chatto and Windus, 1969.

Hale, Brenda. "Introduction." In *Clarke, Hall and Morrison, Law Relating to Children and Young Persons (Special Bulletin: A Guide to the Children Act 1989)*. Ed. R. White. London: Butterworths, 1990, vii–viii.

Hoggett, Brenda [B. Hale]. "Recent Reforms in Family Law: Progress or Backlash?" *Dalhousie Law Journal* 11 (1987–1988): 6–20.

Masson, J., and M. Morris. *The Children Act Manual*. London: Sweet and Maxwell, 1992.

Rapoport, R. N., M. P. Fogarty, and R. Rapoport, eds. *Families in Britain*. London: Routledge, 1982.

*DONALD W. JACKSON*

# ROSALYN HIGGINS (1937– )

Rosalyn Higgins is one of the world's most respected and honored public international law scholars, having served as Professor of International Law at the London School of Economics of the University of London since 1981. She is perhaps best known for her four volumes on United Nations global peacekeeping operations, published between 1969 and 1981, but her entire scholarly contribution is immense, and it has been continuous over the past 30 years. Indeed, the publications listed in her curriculum vitae are so many that they are subdivided into subject headings, which include international legal theory, United Nations law, the use of force, state and diplomatic immunities, human rights, and international petroleum law. Her most recent book, originally given as a course of lectures on public international law at the Hague in 1991, is *International Law and the Avoidance, Containment and Resolution of Disputes.*[1]

## FAMILY BACKGROUND AND EDUCATION

Rosalyn Higgins was educated at Burlington Grammar[2] School in London. She entered Girton College,[3] Cambridge in 1955, and was named a Major Scholar[4] of the College in 1958. Higgins was awarded the Teresa Montefiore Prize by Girton College for overall distinction in 1958. Also in 1958, she served as the United Kingdom Interne in the Office of Legal Affairs of the United Nations. She received her B.A. in law with First Class Honors[5] from Cambridge University in 1958, and her L.L.B. in international law, also with First Class Honors, from Cambridge in 1959. Rosalyn Higgins was one of a small group of students who gathered at Cambridge University in the late 1950s to study international law in an academically rigorous way, but with a practical commitment to put their knowledge to work, coupled with their idealistic personal commitments to the international rule of law.[6]

In 1959, Higgins received a Commonwealth Fund (Harkness) Fellowship[7] and a Graduate Fellowship for study at Yale Law School, from which she received her Doctorate of Juridical Science in 1962. During her doctoral studies at Yale, Higgins was also named a visiting fellow at the Brookings Institution in Washington, D.C. In addition, the Rockefeller Foundation awarded her a fellowship to continue her research after her return to the United Kingdom.

Professor Higgins has been married to the Rt. Hon. Sir Terence Higgins since 1961. He has been the Conservative Member of Parliament for the Worthing (West Sussex) constituency since 1964. They have one daughter and one son.

## CAREER DEVELOPMENT

Higgins' first academic appointment in the United Kingdom was as a junior fellow in International Studies at the London School of Economics from 1961 to 1963, during which time she completed her doctoral dissertation and produced her first book, *The Development of International Law Through the Political Organs of the United Nations* (1963), an elaboration of her Yale dissertation. From 1963 to 1974, she was a staff specialist in International Law at the Royal Institute of International Affairs (Chatham House), but she returned to the London School of Economics as a visiting fellow from 1974 to 1978. During those years, she also served as a visiting professor of International Law at Stanford University (1975) and at Yale (1977). From 1978 to 1980, Higgins was professor of International Law at the University of Kent at Canterbury. She was appointed to her present position, Professor of International Law at the University of London, in 1981.

As a member of the bar who has chambers in Lincoln's Inn Fields, Rosalyn Higgins was made a Queen's Counsel[8] in 1986, and she became a Bencher[9] of the Inner Temple in 1989.

Professor Higgins received an Honorary Doctorate from the *Université de Paris XI* in 1980, the Wolfgang Friedman Medal for services to international law from Columbia University in 1985, the *Ordre de Palme Academique* in 1988, the Honorary Life Membership Award of the American Society of International Law, and an Honorary Doctorate from the University of Dundee in 1992. She has served as chair of the Public International Law Advisory Board of the British Institute of International and Comparative Law since 1992.

## ACHIEVEMENTS AND CONTRIBUTIONS

Higgins' extensively footnoted first book (1963) documented the practices of United Nations political organs[10] with reference to different aspects of international law, and by recording them, contributed to the development and understanding of customary rules of public international law. Perhaps even more interesting was the analytic perspective from which she explored the relationships between law and politics—so as better to understand both—at a time when legal scholars and political scientists, at best, viewed one another with suspicion, and, at worst, entirely ignored one another. In her own words, here is a summary of her perspective:

> The belief that law and politics are not necessarily inimical leads to certain consequences of importance so far as this particular study is concerned. In the first place, it means that it has not been considered beyond the ambit of the lawyer to comment on the political and diplomatic pressures causing certain legal decisions to be taken; on the contrary, the necessity of interdisciplinary co-operation between lawyers and political scientists is predicated. Secondly, it is argued here that political considerations must be taken into account when interpreting ambiguous or imprecise legal rules. To insist that every international problem admits of an 'impartial' legal answer is essentially a dishonest position.[11]

A decade later, when evaluating the desirability of adjudication of international disputes by a third party, rather than simply reciting conventional dogmas about the desirability of third party adjudication, Higgins continued her broad perspective by calling for scholars to recognize the variety of sources and contents of international conflicts so as to produce a typology of conflicts, and to seek to relate varying conflict situations to suitable alternative forms of dispute resolution.[12]

Professor Higgins' monumental work is her four-volume compendium of United Nations' peacekeeping operations. Volume I on the Middle East was published in 1969, Volume II on Asia in 1970, Volume III on Africa in 1980, and Volume IV on Europe in 1981. Volumes I and II received the 1971 Certificate of Merit of the American Society of International Law.

When delivering a 1971 memorial lecture, "United National Peacekeeping: Past Lessons and Future Prospects,"[13] Professor Higgins summarized for her audience some lessons from her first two volumes. At that time, the only enforcement action that the United Nations (U.N.) had taken was in Korea, and that had been possible only because of the Soviet Union's 1952 boycott of the Security Council. While recognizing the deep divisions that then separated the communist bloc from the West and acknowledging that political consensus among U.N. members would have made still greater efforts possible, she nonetheless concluded that the United Nations' "record in containing hostilities has been a good one." She cited the U.N. presence in Cyprus as a leading example and argued that U.N. efforts were often undervalued. Nonetheless, she conceded that U.N. intervention had been more efficacious in stopping fighting than in securing peaceful settlements. In 1971, her concerns for the future of the U.N. were about the role that the People's Republic of China would play, given its veto in the Security Council, and whether a "man of vision" could be found to serve as secretary general, "to point the way forward."[14]

Professor Higgins has also voiced concern about the conduct of the United States in international affairs. Writing in 1987, she began by outlining the then-contending "systems of world public order" and the relationship of each to the rule of international law. She identified the liberal democracies of the Western alliance—led by the United States—as a system which, since World War II, had expressed a view of international law as a "system of law that regulates international relations and is applicable to all, regardless of economic or political system or the stage of development." Higgins identified the socialist or Soviet system as one that emphasized the "primacy of treaties as a source of law." Those were the abstractions, but she pointed out that neither system had been consistent in their appreciation of international law. Higgins then noted, for example, that the disenchantment of the United States with the United Nations sometimes stemmed from its inability to command a majority in the U.N. or to secure support there for its own objectives.

Higgins also commented on the United States' reluctance to ratify international human rights covenants and the absence of any international scrutiny of its otherwise enviable human rights record. After noting the willingness of the Soviet bloc to use force, both to sustain its hegemony in Eastern Europe and to support "national liberation" in the Third World, she also listed U.S. intervention in Grenada, its bombing in Libya, and its support of the Contras in Nicaragua. Higgins found that the United States' conduct in international affairs increasingly seemed to reflect the view that the ends it sought justified the means it had chosen, including its unilateral use of force.

Finally, looking at third-party adjudication of international disputes, Higgins noted that neither the United States nor the Soviet Union warmly welcomed the jurisdiction of the International Court of Justice. In the instance of the case brought by Nicaragua before that Court, the United States had withdrawn from the hearing on the merits of the case and had chosen to ignore the Court's judgment. Her point in this recitation of the actual conduct of the "world order system," especially that led by the United States was that "a commitment to the rule of law is an essential element of a democratic public-order system. But the linkage between that nature of a public-order system and its record in relation to international law is not always easy to show."[15] Panama and Haiti could be added as even more recent examples.

The importance of Higgins' contribution was recognized by Robert Turner, then president of the United States Institute of Peace:

> True to her reputation for scholarly excellence and intellectual courage, she presents an honest appraisal of the serious challenges to the international legal regime and directs no small measure of responsibility for at least some of the problems to the United States. She is certainly aware that many Americans would be far more critical of their own nation's policies than she has been in this overview essay, and those of us who would quarrel with some the critical European public opinion she documents must recognize the accuracy of her observation and resist the temptation to "shoot the messenger." She has by any standard, done us a great service.[16]

In 1989, 20 years after publishing her first volume on U.N. peacekeeping operations, Higgins again evaluated the U.N.'s efforts, but this time focused on its role in international human rights enforcement. She has been a member of the United Nations Committee on Human Rights since 1985 (as one of 18 jurists charged with the duty to monitor and encourage compliance with the International Covenant on Civil and Political Rights). The effectiveness of the Covenant on Civil and Political Rights rests on the obligation of a state that has ratified it to report to the U.N. Committee on Human Rights each five years after its initial report. States must report in accordance with formal guidelines set by the U.N. Committee with reference to each obligation they have taken under the Covenant. Professor Higgins noted the incongruity between the widespread but diffuse support of the work of the Committee, the frequent failure of states to meet their reporting obligations, and the reluctance of member states to fund adequate international human rights enforcement. In the end, Higgins made a stringent plea for preserving integrity. ''Questions of integrity are inevitably raised when states praise certain structures for human rights, but starve them of funds; when they urge the importance of impartial scrutiny, but fail to submit their own reports; when they laud knowledgeable examination, but urge short reports and brief questions.''[17] She worried that the viability of the U.N. Committee was threatened by such failures. ''It would be bitterly ironic,'' she wrote, ''if, having won the battle to place human rights at the legitimate center of international concern, the liberal democracies throw away the fruits of that victory by a failure to recognize that, in large part, the integrity of the Covenant now lies in their own hands.''[18]

A final example of Higgins' contributions came in 1993 when she wrote of the present United Nations in the context of the former Yugoslavia. Suffice it to say that Higgins is profoundly disturbed and disappointed by the international response to the disintegration of Yugoslavia. At a time when the end of the cold war offered the prospect of the U.N. fulfilling its peace enforcement role as originally prescribed in the Charter to include the use of collective military sanctions under Articles 42 and 43, she found the U.N.'s peacekeeping posture in Bosnia and Herzogovina to be inappropriate, insufficient, and futile. She herself was willing to entertain such a measure as the prosecution of war crimes and crimes against humanity through a standing international criminal court, but in fact, did not expect that the Serbian and Bosnian Serb leaders would ever be brought to trial. She concluded:

> Just as the excesses of nationalism can kill the hopes of real democracy in Eastern Europe, so ill-conceived and short-sighted action by states can kill the hopes of real efficacy in the United Nations. The events in the former Yugoslavia in the early 1990s will be seen as a time in history when there was a real opportunity to implement important international changes for the promotion of peace. Wittingly or unwittingly, we have failed to seize the moment, and the harm is likely to prove irreparable.[19]

Higgins' idealism and her commitment to the rule of law, christened at Cambridge more than 30 years ago, clearly have not waned, though at present they are sorely tried.

## NOTES

1. R. Higgins, *International Law and the Avoidance, Containment and Resolution of Disputes* (Oxford: Oxford University Press, 1994).

2. In the United Kingdom, a grammar school traditionally has been a secondary school with rigorous admission standards for academically inclined students, many of whom will go on to university.

3. Founded in 1869, Girton College was the first postsecondary institution for women at either Oxford or Cambridge. The college opened at Hitchin in Hertfordshire, 26 miles from Cambridge, and moved to Cambridge in 1873. The first Girtonian passed a Cambridge Tripos in 1873. It was not until 1948 that women were admitted to full membership at Cambridge University. See M. C. Bradbrook, *''That Infidel Place'': A Short History of Girton College, 1869–1969* (London: Chatto and Windus, 1969).

4. Unlike the common usage in the United States, a scholar in British academia is a recipient of a scholarship from a college.

5. The Tripos are the Honors examinations for the B.A. degree at Cambridge. First-class honors are selectively conferred on the outstanding students at each examination.

6. P. J. Allott, ''John McMahon: An Appreciation,'' in J.E.S. Fawcett and R. Higgins (eds.), *International Organization: Law in Movement (Essays in Honour of John McMahon)* (London: Oxford University Press, 1974), ix–x.

7. At the time, Harkness Fellowships were roughly the reverse of Rhodes Scholarships for study in England; they provided support for study in the United States.

8. The title ''Queen's Counsel'' is conferred on barristers selected for their experience, knowledge, and success at the bar. A Queen's Counsel ''takes silk'' upon appointment, which means that a Q.C. wears a black silk gown and a slightly different wig when appearing in court.

9. As a ''Bencher,'' she serves as a member of the governing body of the Inner Temple, one of the four Inns of Court of which barristers are members.

10. As of the writing of her book, the political organs were the General Assembly, the Security Council, the Secretariat, the Trusteeship Council, and the Economic and Social Council.

11. R. Higgins, *The Development of International Law through the Political Organs of the United Nations* (London: Oxford University Press, 1963), 9.

12. R. Higgins, ''The Desirability of Third-Party Adjudication: Conventional Wisdom or Continuing Truth?'' in Fawcett and Higgins, 37–52.

13. Dr. Rosalyn Higgins and Brigadier Michael Harbottle, *United Nations Peacekeeping: Past Lessons and Future Prospects* (Annual Memorial Lecture) (London: The David Davies Memorial Institute of International Studies, November 25, 1971).

14. Higgins and Harbottle, 11–14.

15. R. Higgins, ''Contending Systems of World Public Order and International Law: An Overview,'' 25 *Atlantic Community Quarterly* (Summer, 1987): 145–59.

16. R. F. Turner, ''International Law, the Use of Force and Reciprocity: A Comment on Professor Higgins' Overview,'' 25 *Atlantic Community Quarterly* (Summer, 1987): 160–74 at 160.

17. R. Higgins, "The United Nations: Still a Force for Peace," 52 *Modern Law Review* (January, 1989): 1–21 at 20.

18. Ibid., 20–21.

19. R. Higgins, "The New United Nations and the Former Yugoslavia," 69 *International Affairs* (July, 1993): 465–83 at 482–83.

## REFERENCES


Allott, P. J. "John McMahon: An Appreciation." In *International Organization: Law in Movement (Essays in Honour of John McMahon).* Eds. J.E.S. Fawcett and R. Higgins. London: Oxford University Press, 1974, ix–x.

Bradbrook, M. C. *"That Infidel Place": A Short History of Girton College, 1869–1969.* London: Chatto and Windus, 1969.

Higgins, Rosalyn. *International Law and the Avoidance, Containment and Resolution of Disputes.* Oxford: Oxford University Press, 1994.

Higgins, Rosalyn. "The New United Nations and the Former Yugoslavia." *International Affairs* 69 (July 1993): 465–83.

Higgins, Rosalyn. "The United Nations: Still a Force for Peace." *Modern Law Review* 52 (January, 1989): 1–21.

Higgins, Rosalyn. "Contending Systems of World Public Order and International Law: An Overview." *Atlantic Community Quarterly* 25 (Summer 1987): 145–59.

Higgins, Rosalyn. "The Desirability of Third-Party Adjudication: Conventional Wisdom or Continuing Truth?" In *International Organization: Law in Movement (Essays in Honour of John McMahon).* Eds. J.E.S. Fawcett and R. Higgins. London: Oxford University Press, 1974, 37–52.

Higgins, Rosalyn. *The Development of International Law Through the Political Organs of the United Nations.* London: Oxford University Press, 1963.

Higgins, Rosalyn, and Brigadier Michael Harbottle. *United Nations Peacekeeping: Past Lessons and Future Prospects* (Annual Memorial Lecture). London: The David Davies Memorial Institute of International Studies, November 25, 1971.

Turner, R. F. "International Law, the Use of Force and Reciprocity: A Comment on Professor Higgins' Overview." *Atlantic Community Quarterly* 25 (Summer, 1987): 160–74.


*DONALD W. JACKSON*

# LEONILDE IOTTI (1920– )

Leonilde Iotti was born to a rather humble home that combined a strong commitment to socialism with an equal attachment to Roman Catholicism. That mixture would prove eventually to define Iotti's political contributions. She joined the Italian Communist party and rose through its ranks, though her place was usually decided solely on her attachment to the party leader, Palmiro Togliatti, who was also her lover. After Togliatti's death in 1964, Iotti was finally recognized in her own right. Her highest position was as president of the Italian Chamber of Deputies, the third highest post in the nation. From that platform, she was able to mold the law and sought to champion the legal rights of women, children, and the family.

## FAMILY BACKGROUND AND EDUCATION

Nilde Iotti was born in Reggio Emilia, capital city of the region Emilia Romagna, on April 10, 1920. In the early days of the reconstruction after the First World War and industrial development, her family could be said to belong to the upper working class. Her mother, Alberta Vezzani, was self-educated and helped the family financially by doing laundry for others, while her father, Egidio, was among the few who found employment in the railroad company, at least until 1923, when he was fired because of his involvement in the unions.

Nilde Iotti's birthplace is particularly relevant to her development. Prior to the unification of Italy in 1860, the territory had belonged to the Vatican State and subsequently became a stronghold of the Socialist party. The ideological and practical conflict that derived from the "cohabitation" of secular and clerical forces ameliorated the quality of both, producing a very lofty and sophisticated political debate while smoothing the edges of animosity in everyday life.[1]

Iotti's family reflected the regional characteristics: her mother was Catholic, and her father was among the early socialists of Italy.[2] Thus, Iotti was raised to appreciate the richness of both traditions. When the time came to mount an opposition to the fascist regime, both Catholics and socialists shared organizations and manpower; and when it became necessary to increase the resistance to an overt opposition, they looked for the best organized and most motivated group, and joined forces under its flag. It was then that the Communist party rose above the Socialist party in Emilia, a lead that it was able to hold for decades to come.

Iotti completed her education in Reggio in 1938 and intended to pursue a graduate degree. She wanted to be a physician, but the *excursus studiorum* would have been too long and expensive for her family, and the mandatory attendance rule would have forced Iotti to be a boarder. The family financial situation worsened in 1935, when her father died. Iotti then decided, instead, to earn a graduate degree in literature and philosophy, a four-year program (while medicine was six) that encouraged attendance to class while not making it an iron-clad rule. She also chose this degree because it would most certainly qualify her for teaching and thus, allow her to support both herself and her family. Unexpectedly, Iotti was given a scholarship by the railroad union because she was an orphan. That made the best educational institutions of Italy available to her.

Iotti's choice was the *Università Cattolica di Milano*, which was an easy commute and, at the same time, an intellectual gymnasium from which she was certain to benefit. The ideology of the institution was strongly opposed to socialism and communism, but it was also evolving into antifascism. Thus, in a comparative spirit, logic was presented in its widest and truest application, and dialectic was encouraged. Iotti had chosen *La Cattolica* because she believed herself to be a strong Catholic, but during her studies she realized she was a sentimental Catholic, not a believing one. By the time she graduated *summa cum laude* in the 1942–1943 academic year, she had experienced an ideological crisis of identity not uncommon at the time in Italy and not restricted to those in their twenties.

## CAREER DEVELOPMENT

Nilde Iotti did not, in the fullest sense, take part in the partisan war raging in Italy but, rather, taught philosophy in a high school. She became increasingly aware of the Communist party's (PCI) ideas, involvement, and commitment to antifascism. As an independent, she chose to fight some battles alongside them, but she was not yet fully committed to the cause. Everything in her background and experience led her toward social issues, and very soon she began collaborating with the Union of Italian Women (UDI). In the long winter of 1945, Iotti was part of a team of women of various political beliefs whose task was to survey the social, economic, and sanitary conditions of needy families in the areas hardest hit by the war. The membership of UDI was more than 20,000 women, and they formed an intense network that did not stop at the survey stage, but also provided for distribution of aid. Iotti was becoming known, and her postwar popularity derived from her involvement with UDI. Iotti became national secretary of the organization in the fall of 1945.

The year 1946 was politically important for Italy, because the political parties had finally agreed to hold local administrative (town and provinces) elections in March. These would be followed by a general election on June 2, in which the institutional choice between monarchy and republic, and the election of a Constituent Assembly were to take place. Beyond the institutional relevance of these elections, there was also the new and unmeasurable element of women's votes. In fact, it was during these elections that universal suffrage, including women, was granted in Italy. Not only could women vote, but they could be elected to public office.

The national leadership of the Communist party disagreed with the northern regional groups on strategies to achieve control of the government. To smooth the revolutionary tones of Reggio Emilia's comrades, the party supported the notion that the selection of candidates to the Constituent Assembly not be limited to those who had bravely fought for the liberation of Italy, the ''heroes,'' but also include moderates, sympathizers, and intellectuals.[3] Nilde Iotti was asked to be a candidate for all of these reasons. That March, she ran successfully for a position on Reggio's council. In June, she was elected to the national Constituent Assembly with 15,936 votes and as a result had to relinquish her position on the town council. Years later, Iotti would recall her short tenure as a local politician with fondness. ''Were I to form a list by importance of the positions I covered in my career, there is no doubt in my mind that I would place first my election as town councilwoman.''[4] It was the first stage of a long career in which Iotti would distinguish herself for her concern and attention to women, families, and the needy.

Early in her political career, Iotti became personally acquainted with the leader of the Communist party, Palmiro Togliatti, establishing a platonic friendship at first and later becoming his lover. Her personal life affected her political career and influenced her legislative initiatives. Iotti was ostracized by the party apparatus for her role of ''home wrecker,'' and was tolerated as Togliatti's lover. But it was only after Togliatti's death that the party would consider her one of its own.

As one of the 20 women out of 556 constituent assemblymen, Iotti was among the five women selected to be part of the Committee of Seventy-five, the inner group responsible for the actual drafting of the constitution. Composed of the best jurists and the most dedicated and enlightened members of each political party, Iotti was chosen over the ''heroes'' of the PCI because of her graduate degree in philosophy. In addition, the ''heroes'' were too busy helping the party strengthen its constituency to be involved in the drafting of the constitution. Three subcommittees were formed to focus on specific constitutional areas: the rights and duties of the citizenry, the structure of the state, and economic and social liberties and duties.

Iotti joined the first subcommittee that developed constitutional language and policies on education, family issues, welfare, and church-state relations. All were subjects for which the sensitivity of a woman would be fundamental. Iotti's upbringing and her understanding of the nuances of both the Catholic and socialist traditions were essential in drafting the new fundamental law of the land. The result was a marvelous blend of the three greatest mass movements and ideologies of the Italian political tradition: liberalism, Catholicism, and socialism.

The members of each subcommittee were teamed so as to allow opposites to find solutions that the majority of Italians could accept. Iotti was teamed with Camillo Corsanego, who had been leader of the Popular party and who was a lawyer and a university professor teaching ecclesiastical law. Together, they were to draft the articles related to the family.[5] The inexperienced Iotti was ultimately the loser in this match. While it is true that no article of the constitution as she had originally drafted was approved, it is also true that every article that touches on women's issues reflects her battles and contributions: equality of treatment by the law, equal opportunities for employment (including the judiciary), the curtailment of *patria potestá* resulting in equal rights for wives and husbands, the rights of illegitimate offspring, maternal protection, and safeguards for minor children. All of them, in their final draft, were touched and molded by Iotti.

The conflicts among the drafters over the rights of women and principles of family life revolved around a fundamental issue: whether to legalize or ban divorce. The final wording of the constitution that prohibited divorce did not betray weakness on behalf of the Communist party or of Nilde Iotti; rather, it reflected the attitude of a very strong faction in the Constituent Assembly that was determined to reach a compromise not to be mistaken for *consocialization.* The drafters sought to find formulas in which both the clerical and anticlerical spirit of the nation could be represented.[6] This was the spirit encouraged by Togliatti and the policy pursued by Iotti and leaders of the three major parties.[7] Thus, Iotti did not fail in her role as Founding Mother.

Three months after the drafting of the constitution by the Constituent Assembly began, the Communist party condoned extramarital relationships, but the party membership, then more moralistic than some Catholics, disapproved and ostracized those living together outside wedlock. Albeit a Founding Mother of the new constitution, Nilde Iotti was not spared this harsh and cruel treatment for her relationship with Togliatti. She was forced to live an almost clandestine existence and was accused of being a Catholic sent to spy on the leader of the PCI. Condemnation was so strong that, in 1948, many in the party opposed Iotti's candidacy to the first legislature of the new republic whose creation she had contributed to and whose fundamental law she had written.

The 1948 election, held at the beginning of the cold war, marked the most heated political competition in Italian history. Ultimately, the Christian Democratic party made a clean sweep. Palmiro Togliatti's leadership, characterized by the avoidance of open conflict with Catholics and the persistence of Nilde Iotti in the party, was deemed by Moscow and by the grass roots of the PCI as being among the reasons for the electoral defeat. This climate of suspicion against Iotti, who was not an orthodox communist, became extremely uncomfortable for her. She endured it successfully even after an attempted assassination of Togliatti.[8]

Although the PCI hierarchy continued to distrust Iotti, her role as Togliatti's companion began to gain acceptance after his convalescence from the attempted assassin's bullets. Since the morality of the party prevented them from having children of their own, the couple took in a young girl, Marisa Malagoli, to live with them in 1950.[9] Despite repeated attempts to adopt Marisa, the law provided Togliatti's wife with the right to block any legal recognition of the relationship between Marisa, Iotti, and Togliatti. It was not until 1961 that the relationship was legalized. A car accident in 1950, involving Togliatti, Iotti, and Marisa, provided the opportunity for the PCI to allow, for the first time, the circulation of pictures of Togliatti with Iotti and the child. The relationship was then official, albeit not entirely accepted or free from suspicions.

At 30 years of age, Iotti began to fashion a place of her own in the history of the party and of the nation. The previous four years had molded her into a more prudent, reserved, "fighting" person, and she resembled those communist women who had fought in the resistance. In 1951, Iotti was prepared for the political fight over family issues and civil rights, and that year she supported a law limiting the freedom of the press when the press targeted children and teenagers. She fought against violence and political ideologies (especially capitalism) that were transmitted through cartoons, which she thought should be vehicles of moral and ethical tenets. She opposed the North Atlantic Treaty Organization (NATO) by arguing that a military alliance could never build peace. She fought "imperialistic America" for building bacteriological weapons. When at all possible, Iotti avoided taking a stand on rhetorical propaganda issues and concentrated instead on those social issues that had always been her main interest. Thus, she took a very strong stand alongside employees of the *Officine Reggiane*, who were fighting to avoid closure of their factory. She became a strong speaker for improving the working conditions of women in the rice fields. Iotti also opposed an electoral reform law that would have altered the representation of smaller parties in the national assemblies.

In the general elections of 1953, Iotti was again successful, despite continued opposition from party representatives in her home district of Reggio. Her reelection guaranteed her acceptance into the party hierarchy. Although she cannot be considered one of the most prolific bill writers in the Chamber of Deputies, Iotti never missed an opportunity to take the rostrum on issues in which politics and pedagogy merged. Such was the case in 1954, when she supported new standards for the teaching of history in primary and secondary schools. Notwithstanding her dedication and energy on behalf of these issues and her membership in the PCI hierarchy, strong opposition in her district prevailed. To avoid an embarrassing loss in the 1958 election, Iotti did not represent Reggio but Bologna.

Because of her political achievements—a member of the Central Committee since 1956, a participant of the executive council of the UDI, a representative for three legislatures, and her recognition as ''Mother of the Constitution''—Iotti was finally given the opportunity to deliver a keynote address at the IX PCI Congress in 1960. Significantly, she chose two of her favorite topics, the emancipation of women and the PCI relationship with the Catholic world. Iotti's hypothesis was that women's issues could only reach the forefront if women could unite notwithstanding their ideological differences. As a woman who knew how to read public opinion, Iotti advocated neither divorce nor abortion, although both issues were emerging on the political scene. But the following year, with Togliatti, Iotti proposed a bill aimed at ''Suppressing articles 559, 560, 561, 562 and 563 of the criminal code, relating to adultery and *concubinato*.''

In 1962, Iotti was elected to the Executive Council of the PCI after she gave one of the keynote addresses at the X Congress, an address that focused on uniting the left-wing parties through the brotherhood of the working class in both urban and rural areas. Although not one of her best speeches, this address signified an ideological maturity for the party. From the immediate reactions to the address and Iotti's behavior during this Congress, it became obvious that censorship by the party was lifted. As a result, Iotti became more outspoken.

Definitive proof of Iotti's political maturity and of her role in the party came in 1964, when Togliatti suffered a cerebral hemorrhage and died. Telegrams of condolence from communist leaders around the world reached Nilde Iotti, and not Rita Montagnana, Togliatti's legal wife. For the first time, the Italian Communist party daily newspaper openly talked about Iotti and her grief, and mentioned the sorrow of Togliatti's daughter. At the funeral, Iotti and Marisa were considered the official family of the great leader. Nilde Iotti lost her friend, companion, and tutor, but she gained an independence and strength that could only come from within herself.

## ACHIEVEMENTS AND CONTRIBUTIONS

In 1966, at the XI Congress, Iotti was given the task of explaining and defending the policy of the party—inspired by her—on the issue of divorce. In analyzing her very lengthy address and comparing it to the PCI's position in the Constituent Assembly, it must be noted that there was no progress.[10] The PCI's aim was to drastically change laws governing both the family and marriage while not breaking definitively with the Catholic groups. The length of the address denotes, on the other hand, that Iotti had become even more active and certainly more listened to than in the past. Within Italian society, she became above and behind party lines, an opinion-leader.

In 1967, however, the socialists rather than the Communist party proposed modifications in Italian family and marriage laws. Once it became clear that the PCI either had to side with the Socialists or present its own bill, Iotti was charged with designing a strategy. After a moderate conciliatory approach, Iotti introduced a bill, "Modifications of the laws of the civil code dealing with family and succession issues." The proposal summarized all the battles Iotti had fought since the days of the Committee of Seventy-five, moving the debate beyond party ideologies by crafting the bill as a women's issue.[11] Because of her perseverance, a new bill legalizing divorce was approved in 1970. Iotti was also actively involved in the citizen referendum that resulted in the definitive adoption of the new law.

The early 1970s saw great successes for the PCI and for Iotti. In 1972, she was appointed vice president of the Chamber of Deputies, and her opinions were more and more appreciated. She became a strong supporter of the strategy that led to an historic compromise between the Catholic party (Christian Democrats) and the communists. It came naturally to Iotti because it, too, summarized all of her battles since 1945. At the XIV Congress of the PCI held in March, 1975, it was Nilde Iotti who formally introduced the compromise. Her reputation as someone who could blend more than one tradition placed her in the national limelight. After the success of the PCI party in the elections of 1976, Iotti was appointed to the most prestigious committee chairmanship given to the opposition, the Committee on Constitutional Affairs.

Since the death of Togliatti, Nilde Iotti had slowly gained a place of her own in the party. Her increasingly visible role as councillor, adviser, and expert to the new leadership of the party demonstrated her status as "Mother of the PCI." This was a moral victory for Iotti who had been suspected of being a Catholic spy within the party just 20 years earlier. It only seemed natural that at the XV PCI Congress in the spring of 1979, the opening speech was given by her rather than by the secretary general. It was a recognition of her newly acquired status within the party, but it was also a difficult task since the party had to come to terms with the issue of left-wing terrorists and explain to the membership the successes and failures of the "historic compromise" years. In a very brief opening address, not only did Iotti deal with these issues, but she also laid out future directions for the PCI. The historic compromise had reached its final stage; the future would mean a more co-responsible role of the PCI in the government of the nation.

But 1979 was an important year for Iotti not only because of her *super partes* role within the party, but also because of Italy's early general elections of June 3, 1979. The party suffered a loss in popular support, and so did Iotti. Her reelection to the Chamber and her status within the party made Iotti the most qualified candidate for the presidency of that assembly. On June 20, 1979, with 433 votes out of 630, Nilde Iotti was elected president of the Chamber of Deputies, assuming the third most powerful political position in Italy. For the first time, an Italian governmental institution was to be led by a woman, 33 years after universal suffrage was granted.

A continuing governmental crisis literally halted legislative production of both chambers, and Iotti found herself in the position of having to defend and, at the same time, bring reforms to Parliament. Three issues seemed to dominate the agenda: institutional reform, the political parties' overwhelming penetration of society, and morality. The most urgent issue for Iotti was institutional reform, specifically with respect as to whether Parliament could become more efficient in its legislative mandate. The other two issues were ignored while perfecting the equality of both Chambers was tackled. From her observations, Iotti became so convinced of the urgency of reform that she invested the Central Committee of the party with the issue by placing it on the party's political platform. She concluded that three pillars of the 1948 constitution were to be somehow modified, if not totally amended—a sad conclusion for a Founding Mother but an honest one.

Iotti's reform agenda centered on the bicameral structure of Parliament, the high number of representatives (630 deputies and 315 senators), and the electoral law, with the thought that these modifications would result in a truly proportional system rather than the Italian hybrid. The first two issues were so blatantly fundamental to the functioning of Parliament that they were easy to advocate. Iotti suggested diversification of the fields of competence between the two branches of the legislature and proposed that a bill, initiated in one chamber, would have an expedited process in the other. As for the size of the legislative body, Iotti recommended reducing the number of deputies to about 400 and the number of senators to about 200. The issue of amending the electoral law was more difficult since it was viewed as the guarantee of democracy. Not easily resolved, the reform issues were to remain on the political agenda for several years.

Iotti was reelected president of the Chamber of Deputies in 1983, an election that also proved successful for the Socialist party. Increasingly, Iotti found herself having to defend the independence and autonomy of the legislative branch vis-à-vis the executive, which, notwithstanding its ample coalition, preferred to govern through decree-laws, thus bypassing the Parliament's function and role. The death of Secretary General Enrico Berlinguer in June of 1984 set into motion a debate within the PCI in which Iotti took a very active role by bringing back to the forefront the issues of institutional reform and the proposed amendments to the constitution. Increasingly, the debate within the party concentrated on the electoral law, and Iotti opposed the faction that advocated majority rule over proportional law.

March, 1987, marked another important moment in the legislative life of Iotti as well as that of the nation. Following yet another governmental crisis, the president of Italy, a Christian Democrat, appointed Iotti to "explore" the possibilities of forming a new governmental coalition or to suggest the call for early elections. It was the first time a woman was asked to lead the Cabinet and the first time a member of the Communist party was offered the possibility of abandoning the opposition benches. Iotti knew that her task of forming a government was close to impossible, but she willingly played her role as ''notary-public'' in confirming that early elections would have to be called. The electoral failure of the PCI led to a change of leadership and platform. For the first time, the new generation that had lived through and fought the battles of 1968 was to guide the fortunes of the Communist party. The new secretary general, Achille Occhetto, began the move of the PCI toward the center as the PDS (the Party of Democratic Left).

A new political setting confronted Nilde Iotti. Within the party, which was divided between proponents of the status quo and reformers, Iotti assumed a centrist position. She accepted the change toward a more European, less Gramscian Communist party, yet she defended Togliatti's earlier views and policies. She followed the new secretary general in 1989, remaining in the PDS and supporting him on his decision for new policies, but Iotti also criticized him for having taken too much time to achieve change and for permitting a split within the party. During the Gulf War, she openly sided with the pacifist movements and the most active Catholic groups in stark contrast with the official policies of the PCI. Nilde Iotti had come full circle. All of her critics, both within and outside of the party, once again accused her of being a Catholic.

The birth of the new Communist party signaled the slow death of the old *partitocrazia* (government by parties) and the beginning of what has been called by the media, ''the peaceful revolution of Italy.'' After the 1991 referendum in which Italians overwhelmingly voted in favor of changing the electoral law, a new political fever spread throughout the nation. The ''old'' parties and the ''old'' political personalities were to be removed from office for a true new beginning.

Iotti was still the president of the Chamber on her seventieth birthday, and on the occasion of a party given in the chamber, she began a retrospective of her years in politics. ''When I look back at my legislator's life, I feel a sense of dread for all I could have done and have not.''[12] After the general elections of April 5, 1992, she was not elected to a fourth term as presiding officer of the Chamber of Deputies, nor did her party succeed in electing her president of the Republic. As a deputy, the Founding Mother of Republican Italy was appointed to the special bicameral Committee for Institutional Reform charged with writing amendments to the fundamental law of the land, the same constitution that she had played a key role in drafting years earlier.

No longer in the limelight, Iotti has continued to fight her battles for women's rights and remains a model for many within her party and the nation. ''Never do I forget that I am a woman, nor do I ever forget, based on my personal experience, how hard it is for women to participate in politics.''[13]

## NOTES

1. See Giovanni Guareschi, *The Little World of Don Camillo*, translated by Una Vincenzo (New York: Tronbridge, Pellegrini and Cudahy, 1950); and Guareschi, *Don Camillo and His Flock*, translated by Frances Fenaye (New York: Pellegrini and Cudahy, 1952).

2. He was a follower of Camillo Prampolini, who is considered the father of Emilia Romagna's reformists.

3. The majority of the party membership was made up of blue-collar workers, farmers, and union people who would encounter major obstacles in the writing of a constitution.

4. Gianni Corbi, *Nilde* (Milano: Rizzoli, 1993), 42.

5. Articles 29, 30, and 31 of the Italian constitution were their special assignment, but they were free to contribute, as both did, on the drafting of all other articles at the Committee stage and on the floor.

6. For example, while the indissolubility of marriage was sanctioned in Article 29, the duty to provide for the well-being of illegitimate offspring can be found in Article 30. If the liberals conceded that the state can interfere in the private and economic spheres of the family, then the communists ceded to a temporary ban on divorce, and the Catholics accepted regulations in favor of the illegitimate.

7. This is best seen in the debates over Article 7. For details on this debate, see Maria Elisabetta de Franciscis, *Italy and the Vatican: The 1984 Concordat Between Church and State* (New York, Bern: Peter Lang Publishing, 1989); and Corbi, 68.

8. In an interview in 1981, Iotti recalled that at the time she had told Togliatti she would never, for any reason, not even their relationship, interrupt her political battles, and that Togliatti appreciated her for her commitment. Corbi, 98–99.

9. Marisa, age seven, was one of nine children of a farmer. Her older brother, the family wage-earner, had been killed by the State Police during a Union demonstration. Togliatti and Iotti intended to educate Marisa, relieving the family from some of its financial burdens.

10. For the details of these debates, see La Costituzione della Repubblica nei lavori preparatori dell'Assemblea Costituente, Volume VI, *Resoconto Sommario*: hearings of October 30, 1946, at 630–36; November 5, 1946, at 637–41; November 6, 1946, at 643–54; November 8, 1946, at 655–62; November 12, 1946, at 663–68; and November 13, 1946, at 669–76; and in Volume VII, January 15, 1947, at 101–9; and January 16, 1947, at 111–16.

11. The concluding paragraph of the bill read as an invitation to all representatives to bring about justice by returning equality to people (women) whom the collective conscience of Italy considered noncitizens and, therefore, titulars of fewer rights. Corbi, 192–93.

12. Corbi, 238.

13. Ibid., 42.

## REFERENCES

Corbi, Gianni. *Nilde*. Milano: Rizzoli, 1993.
"La Costituzione della Repubblica nei lavori preparatori dell'Assemblea Costituente."

Volumes VI and VII. *Resoconto Sommario*. Hearings of October 30, November 5, 6, 8, 12, 13, 1946; and January 15, 16, 1947.
de Franciscis, Maria Elisabetta. *Italy and the Vatican: The 1984 Concordat Between Church and State*. New York: Peter Lang Publishing, 1989.
Guareschi, Giovanni. *The Little World of Don Camillo*. Trans. by Una Vincenzo. New York: Tronbridge, Pellegrini and Cudahy, 1950.
Guareschi, Giovanni. *Don Camillo and His Flock*. Trans. by Frances Fenaye. New York: Pellegrini and Cudahy, 1952.

*MARIA ELISABETTA DE FRANCISCIS*

# BARBARA CHARLINE JORDAN (1936–1996)

Barbara Jordan distinguished herself in the male-dominated fields of law and politics, and achieved national recognition with dignity, courage, and perseverance. She had many obstacles to overcome, including gender discrimination and racial prejudice, before she was elected the first African-American woman to the Texas State Senate since Reconstruction.[1] The hurdles cleared and the long road traveled by Jordan to become the chair of the U.S. Commission on Immigration Reform began in her hometown of Houston, Texas.

## FAMILY BACKGROUND AND EDUCATION

Barbara Jordan grew up the youngest of three daughters of Benjamin and Arlyne Jordan. The Jordans were a working-class family who stressed the importance of education. Jordan attended Houston's public schools where she became very active and involved in her high school's debate team. Her renowned oratorical skills were nurtured and developed while attending Phyllis Wheatley High School. This is where she decided on a career in law after hearing a speech by an African-American woman lawyer.[2]

Jordan remained in Houston after graduation to attend Texas Southern University where she majored in political science and history. She continued to develop her oratorical skills and won many awards and championships. After graduating *magna cum laude* from Texas Southern in 1956, she attended Boston University's Law School. This was Jordan's first extended stay outside the South, where she found the racial climate of the day stifling and oppressive. Although Boston's race relations were not ideal, Jordan also had to confront another kind of discrimination—gender. In 1956, America's law schools did not enroll large numbers of women, let alone African-American women. Jordan graduated with a Bachelor of Law degree in 1959.

## CAREER DEVELOPMENT

Jordan initially contemplated remaining in Boston after she passed the Massachusetts bar examination. She interviewed at a couple of insurance companies but decided her future was in Houston, practicing law in the same neighborhood where she was raised. She opened her own law practice, which she ran out of her parents' home. To earn extra money to obtain an office for her practice, Jordan taught government during the summers at Tuskegee Institute. In 1961, she was able to open a law office in downtown Houston. Her client base was not large enough to support herself solely on her earnings from the practice, so she worked as an administrative assistant for a local judge to supplement her income.

Houston, like so many other cities during the 1960s, was engulfed by a climate of racial uneasiness. The goals and aspirations of the civil rights movement were being articulated loudly, and political, economic, educational, and social demands were placed on politicians and lawmakers by an African-American community that was frustrated by the slow pace of change in the city. Jordan became particularly interested in school segregation issues, which served as her catalyst for entering politics.

As late as 1961, Houston's public schools were still segregated despite a number of court cases that had been brought against the school district. Jordan decided that her best position to effect change was as an elected official. Her political aspirations were the result of observing Houston's political milieu; she simply did not like what she saw.

Jordan first became interested in the intricacies of political campaigning during the Kennedy-Johnson presidential race in 1960. Instrumental in mobilizing African-American voters in Harris County, Jordan traveled to churches, schools, and other venues to speak about the importance of voting. After the campaign, Jordan was thoroughly convinced that she wanted to run for public office and began to make a name for herself by capitalizing on her ability to deliver a speech. Chris Dixie, a labor organizer and fellow Democrat, encouraged her to run for a seat in the Texas House of Representatives in 1962.[3] She ran as a liberal Democrat on the theme, "Reform and Retrenchment," but lost both her 1962 and 1964 bids for a seat in the Texas state legislature.

Undeterred, Jordan ran for office again in 1966. Fortunately, a redistricting of the state had just been completed, and as a result, the Eleventh District in Houston was created.[4] The young 30-year-old Jordan ran in this new district and defeated her opponent, thereby becoming the first African American elected to the Texas state legislature since 1883.[5]

Jordan firmly believed that the best way she could contribute to women and to African Americans was through the law. She served as chair of the Labor and Management Relations Committee and as vice chair of the Legislative, Congressional, and Judicial committees. Her other committee assignments in the state legislature included Education, Environmental Matters, Finance, Interstate Cooperation, State Affairs, and Elections.

Jordan was instrumental in passing a bill that established the Fair Employment Practices Commission. The Commission's responsibility was to ensure that the citizens of Texas were not discriminated against on the basis of race, gender, religion, color, age, or national origin in the workforce.[6] She also used the law to assist underrepresented segments of American society—for example, women and men who worked in low-paying jobs. Jordan also worked tirelessly for passage of Texas' first minimum wage law.

Barbara Jordan's hard work and dedication did not go unnoticed. She was named outstanding freshman senator during her first term in the Texas Senate. She was very successful in getting bills passed that she introduced, which led to her election as *pro tempore* of the Texas legislature in 1972. She became the first African-American woman to earn this distinction. But Barbara Jordan had ambitions that went beyond the boundaries of Texas. In 1972, she threw her hat into the ring for a seat in the United States House of Representatives.

Again, a fortuitious redistricting had recently taken place. Following the Supreme Court decision of *Wesberry v. Sanders* (1966) in which the Court ruled that state legislatures must apply the principle of ''one man, one vote'' in their decennial reapportionments to ensure equal representation, a new congressional district was established in Texas. That district was in Houston, and Jordan ran for Congress from the newly created Eighteenth Congressional District. The population of the newly formed district was dominated by racial and ethnic minorities, primarily African Americans (50 percent) and Mexican Americans (15 percent). Jordan won the Democratic primary and went on to capture the congressional seat in the general election.

Jordan joined three other Democratic African-American women in the United States House of Representatives—Shirley Chisholm of New York, Yvonne Burke of California, and Cardiss Collins of Illinois.[7] In 1972, along with Andrew Young of Georgia, Barbara Jordan simultaneously became the first African American to be elected to Congress from the South in the twentieth century.[8]

## ACHIEVEMENTS AND CONTRIBUTIONS

Barbara Jordan served three consecutive terms (six years) in the House of Representatives, and her contributions and achievements made her a national political figure. She landed a spot on the Judiciary Committee during her first term with the help and advice of former President Lyndon B. Johnson. Her presence and participation on the Judiciary Committee during the impeachment hearings of President Richard Nixon truly propelled her to the national spotlight in 1974. During her tenure, however, Jordan remained committed to the belief that the law could be used to bring about equal representation in voting.

One of Jordan's most important contributions while serving in Congress was her fight to extend the Voting Rights Act of 1965. The original legislation prohibited states from using discriminatory tactics to prevent mainly African Americans from voting in the Deep South, but Texas was not targeted by that prohibition. However, Jordan received numerous complaints from African Americans and Mexican Americans about unfair, discriminatory acts by voting officials that prevented minorites from exercising their right to the franchise.

When the Voting Rights Act was up for renewal in 1975, Jordan worked to put Texas under its purview. She proposed an amendment to the bill that would allow ballots to be printed in Spanish since English-only ballots prevented some Texas citizens from voting, thus perpetuating discriminatory testing devices. As a result of her efforts, Texas came under the jurisdiction of the Voting Rights Act of 1975, allowing the United States attorney general to file suits on behalf of individuals. While the original bill had permitted individuals to bring suit, many of those who suffered under the discriminatory practices could not afford the expense of litigation on their own. Thus, without the involvement of the national government and the Department of Justice, many people would have remained victims of local election officials who simply chose to ignore or not enforce the law. Jordan's political skills and knowledge of the law not only allowed African Americans full participation in the voting process, but also permitted people who did not speak English as a first language to exercise their constitutional right to vote.

Jordan's contributions to passage of civil rights legislation designed to eradicate racial discrimination goes without question; however, her work on legislation to fight gender discrimination is equally noteworthy. Jordan voted in favor of the ratification of the Equal Rights Amendment (ERA) while she was in the Texas state senate and in the U.S. House of Representatives. She also supported federally funded abortions by voting against the Hyde Amendment, which prohibited the use of federal funds for abortions. Although she never married or had children, Jordan saw the importance of these issues to women who led very different lives from her own. Although she espoused the "bootstrap" philosophy, which stated that women must work to improve their own individual situation, much as she herself had done, Jordan's commitment to improving the social conditions of all meant that government had to be involved. And new laws and legislation were the best possible tools available to Jordan to effect social change.

Jordan's national reputation was solidified after she served as one of the keynote speakers for the Democratic National Convention in 1976. Using her customary oratorical prowess, she delivered a powerful and moving speech on the need for national unity. For many Americans who were hearing and seeing her for the first time, Jordan could have been the presidential or vice-presidential candidate. She avidly campaigned for presidential candidate Jimmy Carter. Many of her colleagues, constituents, and fans encouraged her to accept a Cabinet post in Carter's administration, and indeed Carter met with her to discuss positions in various governmental agencies. But Jordan had her sights set on only one office—attorney general. Carter was not in a position to offer her this post, and Jordan declined to accept any other. Perhaps she was simply ahead of her time. Nearly 20 years later, Janet Reno* became the first woman to be appointed attorney general under President Bill Clinton.

Barbara Jordan retained her congressional seat during the early years of the Carter administration, but in 1977, she announced that she would not seek a fourth term. After her departure from Congress, Jordan held the Lyndon B. Johnson Chair in Public Policy at the University of Texas at Austin and finally the chair of the U.S. Commission on Immigration Reform. She also served as an adviser to Governor Ann Richards of Texas on ethical issues in the 1980s.

In her last years, Jordan continued to use her great oratorical skills on behalf of her beloved Democratic Party and to urge Americans to participate in their government. Her keynote address at the Democratic National Convention in 1988 was memorable, but perhaps more memorable was seeing Jordan on the first night of the 1992 convention in New York City. After being diagnosed with multiple sclerosis in the late 1980s, she had all but disappeared from the public speaking circuit. When she returned to the public eye that night in 1992, she needed the assistance of a wheelchair. At first sight, Jordan seemed tired and physically broken. And while she had lost some of the fire of her oratory, her message was still the same. She spoke to all Americans, but especially to those who had suffered the burdens of poverty and discrimination. She noted that although the American dream had not entirely been lost, it needed reviving. Her message to women was one of future hope and promise. "That horizon of gender equity is limitless for us, and what we see today is simply a dress rehearsal for the day and time we meet in convention to nominate Madame President."[9] And once again, Jordan articulated her faith in the law, the Constitution, and her country.

Barbara Jordan passed away on January 17, 1996, at the age of 59, from complications of leukemia. It was one of the few battles in her life that Jordan could not win. She had overcome the constraints of classism and poverty, and she had prevailed over racism and sexism at a time when the number of African Americans and women in law school and in political office was not very large. Jordan even managed to win over a national media that had, early on, been critical of her commanding physical presence and unmarried status even though these traits were unrelated to her effectiveness in politics. In her distinctive style, Jordan built bridges between liberals and conservatives during her three decades of public service. And she won over those students lucky enough to be selected for her ethics seminar at the University of Texas.

While Jordan will be remembered for her symbolic "firsts" in Texas and national politics, it will be her interminable sense of fairness and justice combined with her oratorical skills that will serve as her legacy. "She was not a great speaker who could make nonsense sound convincing, like William Jennings Bryan or Ronald Reagan. She was a great speaker who was usually right.''[10]

## NOTES

1. Gerald David Jaynes and Robin M. Williams, Jr. (eds.) *A Common Destiny—Blacks and American Society* (Washington, D.C.: National Academy Press, 1989), 69.
2. Judith Graham, *Current Biography Yearbook 1993* (New York: H. W. Wilson, 1993), 290.
3. Barbara Jordan and Shelby Hearon, *Barbara Jordan—A Self-Portrait* (Garden City, N.Y.: Doubleday, 1979), 112.
4. Graham, 291.
5. Lucius J. Barker and Jesse J. McCorry, Jr., *Blacks and the Political System* (Cambridge, Mass.: Winthrope, 1980), 236.
6. Jordan and Hearon, 149.
7. John Hope Franklin, *From Slavery to Freedom* (New York: Alfred A. Knopf, 1988), 463.
8. Jaynes and Williams, 69.
9. Patricia Corrigan, ''Barbara Jordan's Powerful Message,'' *St. Louis Post-Dispatch* (July 18, 1992): 3D.
10. Michael Lind, ''Jordan's Rules,'' *The New Republic* (February 12, 1996): 6.

## REFERENCES

Barker, Lucius J., and Jesse J. McCorry, Jr. *Blacks and the Political System*. Cambridge, Mass.: Winthrope, 1980.

Corrigan, Patricia. ''Barbara Jordan's Powerful Message.'' *St. Louis Post-Dispatch* (July 18, 1992): 3D.

Franklin, John Hope. *From Slavery to Freedom*. New York: Alfred A. Knopf, 1988.

Graham, Judith. ''Barbara Jordan.'' In *Current Biography Yearbook 1993*. New York: H. W. Wilson, 1993, 289–93.

Jaynes, Gerald David, and Robin M. Williams, Jr. (eds.). *A Common Destiny—Blacks and American Society*. Washington, D.C.: National Academy Press, 1989.

Jordan, Barbara, and Shelby Hearon. *Barbara Jordan—A Self-Portrait*. Garden City, N.Y.: Doubleday, 1979.

Lind, Michael. ''Jordan's Rules.'' *The New Republic* (February 12, 1996): 6.

*CASSANDRA R. VENEY*

# SYLVIE KANIGI (1953–   )

Sylvie Kanigi became the first woman prime minister of Burundi, a small central African nation, in mid-1993. Her appointment, followed less than a month later by that of Agathe Uwilingiyimana* as prime minister in neighboring Rwanda, marks a political watershed in modern African history. Like Uwilingiyimana, Kanigi became her country's head of government at a crucial time in the political transition away from dictatorship and minority ethnic rule to attempts at liberal democracy. While she was in office for only about one year, her tenure in that post certainly has left a lasting impact on Burundi, one of Africa's most troubled nations. Like neighboring Rwanda, Burundi has suffered through periods of ethnic genocide in the past 30 years.

## CAREER DEVELOPMENT

Unfortunately, very little is known in the West about Kanigi's early life. She is a member of the Tutsi ethnic minority, which for centuries ruled in both Rwanda and Burundi over the majority Hutus. However, she overcame the hostility between the two groups, marrying a Hutu man, who died in 1993, and raising five children with him.[1] A graduate in economic management from Burundi University, Kanigi held economic civil service jobs until 1991, when she was made senior consultant in the prime minister's office. There she was in charge of economic reform and reported directly to the president and prime minister.

Kanigi had the difficult job of trimming the budget deficit by slashing funding for a Tutsi-dominated army long accustomed to preferential treatment. A key part of her job in 1992 and 1993 was to deal with Western donors demanding economic changes in Burundi, a former Belgian colony whose economy is heavily dependent on coffee and tea exports. Kanigi has said that this post was very important to her, for the way she managed these economic reforms would impact the lives of millions of poor Burundians.[2]

## ACHIEVEMENTS AND CONTRIBUTIONS

Sylvie Kanigi's career took on an explicitly political spin following the election of Melchior Ndadaye in June 1993 as Burundi's first Hutu president. Honoring an election campaign promise to appoint a minority Tutsi to the post of prime minister, President Ndadaye turned to Kanigi, offering her the premiership in July, 1993.[3] This arrangement of splitting key government posts between traditionally dominant minority Tutsis and the majority Hutu ethnic group was an admirable political concession, but of course made the tasks of both the president and prime minister all the more difficult. It is with this scenario that Kanigi, who had never held high political office, found herself thrust into the limelight of the premiership of a nation with a history of genocide and authoritarian government.

Matters were further complicated by the fact that Kanigi was a member of the Tutsi-dominated political party of former President Pierre Buyoya, a former military officer whom Mr. Ndadaye had defeated in the June, 1993 elections.[4] Many observers have speculated that outgoing President Buyoya explicitly requested that the new president appoint Kanigi to the prime minister's post.

In an interview shortly after her appointment as prime minister, Kanigi said:

> I was extremely surprised to be appointed. As you know there are not many women prime ministers in Africa; I must be the only one now. There were probably some in the past—one in the Central African Republic, one in Uganda—these were precedents but I was extremely surprised and I believe that this is a good surprise for Burundian women primarily, but for African women too.[5]

The new prime minister also emphasized that her highest political priority would be to help bring about ethnic reconciliation between the Tutsis and Hutus, which she said was essential for her economic development plans.[6] Unfortunately, as in neighboring Rwanda, the new prime minister did not have a chance to implement her desired economic policies, as ethnic violence and the killing of not only President Ndadaye, but also his successor, would plunge Burundi into another round of ethnic massacres.

On October 21, 1993, Tutsi paratroopers stormed the national palace in a predawn attack and captured and killed President Ndadaye and six Cabinet ministers. Furthermore, the coup leaders imposed a curfew, cut telephone service, seized control of the state radio, and closed Bujumbura's international airport. In addition, at least 600,000 Hutu civilians fled to neighboring Rwanda as some Tutsis, apparently encouraged by the coup leaders, began widespread massacres of Hutus in the countryside.[7] Shortly after the coup, in the face of widespread public opposition, the takeover appeared to falter as alleged coup leaders in the army sought to distance themselves from this ethnic violence that had erupted after the murder of President Ndadaye. One of the purported coup leaders even offered that the army officers who had orchestrated the takeover attempt would step down in exchange for amnesty.[8]

As the violence continued, the generals requested that Prime Minister Kanigi and Cabinet ministers who were taking refuge at the French embassy in the capital city form a new government to restore order in the aftermath of the bloody ethnic battles. However, the ministers remained within the embassy, reportedly suspicious of the army's true intentions. Two days later, Kanigi addressed the country via state radio and urged the part of the army responsible for the coup attempt to return to their barracks. Kanigi also vowed "severe punishment" for those responsible for initiating the coup.[9] Thus, the prime minister, who had not been in office for even four full months, now found herself in charge of her nation after a failed military uprising.

On November 1, 11 days after the coup attempt and the killing of President Ndadaye, Prime Minister Kanigi left the refuge of the French embassy to talk with surviving provincial leaders and representatives of both loyal and rebellious factions of the Tutsi-dominated army.[10] She emphatically rejected the coup leaders' requests for a general amnesty, maintaining that the coup plotters must be prosecuted. Furthermore, the prime minister vowed to set up a special commission to prepare for a new presidential election. She also said she was arranging an inquiry into the October 21 coup, which later collapsed. Under the Burundian constitution, the speaker of the Parliament was to assume control upon the death of the president. However, he was killed in the coup attempt, leaving Kanigi in de facto control of the government of Burundi.[11]

Sylvie Kanigi's government salvation efforts were also given a huge boost when two former Tutsi presidents, Pierre Buyoya and Jean Baptiste Bagaza, both former military strongmen, rallied behind Kanigi's government.[12] A semblance of order was restored, and plans were made for a new presidential election. Unfortunately, ethnic violence continued in the countryside, with Kanigi's de facto government able to do little to stop the killing, which has been estimated at nearly 100,000 dead. This is a significant number for a nation of less than 6 million people.[13]

In early January, 1994, the Burundian Parliament finally agreed on a successor for the slain Melchior Ndadaye when they elected Agriculture and Livestock Minister Cyprien Ntaryamira, a 38 year-old Hutu, to fill Ndadaye's unexpired five-year term. This caused considerable hostility from some Tutsi groups and parties who saw this as a civilian coup, since the Parliament had only hours before amended the national constitution to make this election possible. Still, Prime Minister Kanigi, a Tutsi, retained her post and expressed loyalty for the new president.[14] Ethnic violence continued in the capital and the countryside, however, and Burundi remained racked with ethnic tension. Finally, in February of 1994, Sylvie Kanigi was replaced in the role of prime minister by another Tutsi member of her party, Anatole Kanyenkiko.[15] Newly elected President Ntaryamira was later killed when his plane was shot down in Rwanda in April, 1994, an assassination that brought further ethnic carnage to both Rwanda and Burundi.

After being replaced as prime minister, Sylvie Kanigi took a job in the banking industry of Burundi, a post seemingly appropriate to her economics training and the crisis management skills she obviously developed as de facto head of state following the killing of President Ndadaye. In her position as a civilian, Kanigi offered some of her personal opinions on the problems of Burundi.[16] Specifically, she has stated that democracy came too fast to Burundi, and that ethnic tensions were not conducive to multiparty democratic government. Unfortunately, the pained history of her nation may bear out these pessimistic opinions.

## NOTES

1. A. Hartley, ''Burundi Premier Lists Curfew, Army Chiefs Disown Coup,'' *Reuters News Service* (October 26, 1993) (newswire).
2. Ibid.
3. ''Prime Minister Kanigi Takes Office,'' *Agence France Press* (July 19, 1993) (newswire).
4. ''Prime Minister Kanigi: Situation Still Confused; Warns of Country's Destruction,'' *BBC Summary of Foreign Broadcasts* (October 30, 1993) (radio broadcast).
5. ''Ministers to Hold First Cabinet Meeting Since Coup,'' *BBC Summary of Foreign Broadcasts* (November 9, 1993)(radio broadcast).
6. Ibid.
7. ''President Killed in Military Coup,'' *Facts on File* (October 28, 1993): 813, E3.
8. Ibid.
9. D. Lorch, ''Specter of Hate Stalks Burundi, Too,'' *New York Times* (April 26, 1994): A9.
10. ''Burundi Prime Minister Leaves Embassy,'' *United Press International* (November 2, 1993) (newswire).
11. C. Watson, ''Burundi Coup Survivors Try to Impose Order,'' *Reuters News Service* (November 4, 1993) (newswire).
12. ''Former Burundi Strongmen Rally Behind Kanigi,'' *Reuters News Service* (November 5, 1993) (newswire).
13. R. Press, ''Burundi Army Learns Democracy Has Roots,'' *Christian Science Monitor* (October 19, 1993): 1.
14. D. Muvira, ''Burundi's Parliament Elects Hutu as New President,'' *Reuters News Service* (January 13, 1994) (newswire).
15. ''New Premier for Burundi,'' *Agence France Press* (February 7, 1994) (newswire).
16. T. Griffiths, ''Political Vacuum Boosts Violence in Burundi,'' *Reuters News Service* (September 11, 1994) (newswire).

## REFERENCES

''Burundi Prime Minister Leaves Embassy.'' *United Press International*. Newswire (November 2, 1993).

''Former Burundi Strongmen Rally Behind Kanigi.'' *Reuters News Service*. Newswire (November 5, 1993).

Griffiths, T. ''Political Vacuum Boosts Violence in Burundi.'' *Reuters News Service*. Newswire (September 11, 1994).

Hartley, A. ''Burundi Premier Lists Curfew, Army Chiefs Disown Coup.'' *Reuters News Service*. Newswire (October 26, 1993).

Lorch, D. ''Specter of Hate Stalks Burundi, Too.'' *New York Times* (April 26, 1994): A9.

''Ministers to Hold First Cabinet Meeting Since Coup.'' *BBC Summary of Foreign Broadcasts*. Radio Broadcast (November 9, 1993).

Muvira, D. ''Burundi's Parliament Elects Hutu as New President.'' *Reuters News Service*. Newswire (January 13, 1994).

''New Premier for Burundi.'' *Agence France Press*. Newswire (February 7, 1994).

''President Killed in Military Coup.'' *Facts on File* (October 28, 1993): 813, E3.

Press, R. ''Burundi Army Learns Democracy Has Roots.'' *Christian Science Monitor* (October 19, 1993): 1, 32.

''Prime Minister Kanigi: Situation Still Confused; Warns of Country's Destruction.'' *BBC Summary of Foreign Broadcasts*. Radio Broadcast (October 30, 1993).

''Prime Minister Kanigi Takes Office.'' *Agence France Press*. Newswire (July 19, 1993).

Watson, C. ''Burundi Coup Survivors Try to Impose Order.'' *Reuters News Service*. Newswire (November 4, 1993).

*KEVIN HILL*

# CARRIE BURNHAM KILGORE (1838–1909)

Carrie Burnham Kilgore was the first woman graduate of the University of Pennsylvania Law School and the first woman lawyer in Pennsylvania. After many rebuffs from lower courts in that state, she was eventually admitted to practice before the Supreme Court of Pennsylvania in 1885, and before the United States Supreme Court in 1890. Her life is marked by nearly insuperable obstacles that she overcame with patience, imagination, and determination.

## FAMILY BACKGROUND AND EDUCATION

Caroline Burnham was born in 1838 in Craftsbury, in extreme northern Vermont. Her family was somewhat advantaged in that her father, James, was a woolen manufacturer of means. Her mother, Eliza Arnold Burnham, formerly a teacher, died when Carrie was three. Her father died when she was 12 years of age, and an appointed guardian decided that Carrie had completed enough education for a young woman and made her work in the family woolen factory or in the kitchen.

Carrie began teaching school when she was 15 years old and used her earnings from her teaching position and domestic work on the side to continue her own education at Craftsbury Academy and Newbury Seminary in Vermont. She enrolled in a classical course of studies, one rarely chosen by women students of that time. Carrie also overworked herself and became undernourished. In her weakened state, she caught typhoid fever. Following her recovery, Carrie left Vermont and moved west to Sun Prairie, Wisconsin, where an older sister lived.

## CAREER DEVELOPMENT

Carrie Burnham was not one to stay with a single job or profession for very long. It seems that her persistent interest in education and knowledge prompted her to travel and seek additional training in a variety of subjects. In Wisconsin, Carrie Burnham taught in the lower grades and eventually moved to Madison, where she taught Latin, Greek, and mathematics at a high school. There she met the man whom she would marry much later, Mr. Damon Kilgore, a former Methodist minister and lawyer who was superintendent of schools. Later, Carrie taught classics, physiology, and drawing in a private academy, Evansville (Wisconsin) Seminary.

Increasingly interested in physiology, Burnham left Wisconsin and went to New York City to attend the Hygeio-Therapeutic College; she was in the first class of women admitted to the Bellevue Hospital Clinics. She also took classes in the Normal Institute for Physical Education in Boston. Within two years, Burnham had her medical degree. She worked for a summer as a doctor at the Normal Institute and then moved to Philadelphia.

In Philadelphia, Carrie returned to teaching and succeeded in introducing a course of gymnastics in the public schools. She also became administrator of a "French School" for Young Ladies. But by the time she got to Philadelphia, her interests had shifted once again, this time to the study of law. Damon Kilgore had also left Wisconsin and moved to Philadelphia, where he opened his own law practice. In 1865, she began to read law informally with her future husband. Five years later, Carrie formally registered as Kilgore's student with her own intentions to practice law.

Interestingly, it was Damon Kilgore who initially became active in the women's rights movement, and not surprisingly, Carrie's activism soon followed. She registered as a voter in the state of Pennsylvania and paid the poll tax in 1871, but her ballot was rejected on election day nonetheless. So she sued, arguing her own case before the Pennsylvania Supreme Court in 1873; the court denied her right to vote on the grounds that neither the state constitution nor tradition gave women the franchise. Carrie continued to campaign for women's suffrage, twice representing the state of Pennsylvania in national suffrage conventions.

Kilgore made several efforts to enroll in law school. In 1871, the University of Pennsylvania Law School rejected her application. Then, based on having read the law with Damon, Kilgore tried to obtain permission to take the bar examination in 1873 and 1874. The Board of Bar Examiners demurred, and her efforts to appeal its negative decision to the courts and the state legislature were unavailing. Finally, in 1881, she was admitted to Pennsylvania Law School where she achieved her dream and graduated in 1883. The 45-year-old Kilgore was the first woman graduate from the law school.

Carrie Burnham and Damon Kilgore were finally married in 1876. Since both were keenly aware of the low estate of married women's rights, they signed a prenuptial contract that, in effect, nullified the legal barriers against married women in Pennsylvania, or any other state or territory of the United States. Damon and Carrie had two children: Carrie, born in 1877, and Fanny, born in 1880. Carrie spent her time taking care of her children and husband and continued to pursue her goal of practicing law.

## ACHIEVEMENTS AND CONTRIBUTIONS

With a law degree in hand, Kilgore now struggled to be admitted to practice before the courts. Clearly, if she could not practice in the courts as an accepted attorney, she would be unable to litigate and her law career would be greatly circumscribed. During this era, admission to one court in a state usually enabled one to practice in all other courts in the state through the rule of reciprocity. But the rule did not hold for a woman counselor. In Pennsylvania, as in many other states, the court system was highly fragmented. Kilgore therefore sought admission to the courts one at a time. Not surprisingly, she won immediate admittance to the Orphans' Court of Philadelphia, a specialized trial court of inferior jurisdiction. But she needed admission to the Court of Common Pleas, the key trial court of general jurisdiction in Pennsylvania.

The *New York Times* took an interest in chronicling Kilgore's battle for justice, writing stories during the period 1883–1885 about her adventures in various courts and eventually editorializing on her behalf. Much of the coverage focused on what she wore in her various appearances, but even in this, the *Times* was supportive. The *Times* found her garb ("toilet") attractive and feminine, yet with a propriety befitting an attorney and in no way masculine. She wore black silk or black velvet several times, and dispensed with trimmings on her garments, sporting a simple hair style without "bangs, frizzes, [or] puffs."

Philadelphia had four separate Common Pleas courts, each with three judges and each completely independent of the others. In December, 1883, Carrie Kilgore went into Common Pleas Court No. 2, accompanied by her husband and another male political ally, former state senator Horatio Gates Jones. The judges of this bench were deemed more opposed than other judges; Kilgore was taking the battle to the heart of resistance. Presiding Judge Hare listened to Senator Jones, who based much of his argument for Kilgore's admission to the court on the precedent of her admission to the Orphans' Court. But Judge Hare discounted the Orphans' Court admission, saying that each court was the judge of its own rules. He concluded that he must refuse her application owing to the uniform rule and practice of courts in Pennsylvania against admission of women lawyers. As a judge, he could not introduce such an innovation and suggested that a legislative route be pursued. Judge Hare went even further by demonstrating how existing state law, which excused married women from liabilities for certain frauds and debts, could allow a married female lawyer to escape liability for financial defalcations with her clients' money.

But perseverance was the bedrock of Kilgore's strategy. The next working day she appeared in Common Pleas Court No. 1 before Judge Thayer. Again, Senator Jones spoke for her, now escalating the level of argumentation. He quoted from the Bible and Plato to demonstrate that a woman's intellectual capacity was equal to that of a man's. Jones compared Mrs. Damon Kilgore to the Prophetess Deborah, who saved the Jewish people; Mrs. Kilgore would "save many of her fellow-creatures from injustice and oppression if she were given a chance and a reasonable fee." He found a state law requiring courts to admit to legal practice "all persons learned in law," and he also discovered a judicial decision that interpreted "person" to mean "citizen." Jones cited yet another decision that declared women to be "citizens" even if they were not entitled to vote. He even had an answer for Judge Hare's earlier argument that Kilgore, as a married woman, could not be a financially responsible lawyer owing to the laws of the state that suspended a married woman's fiscal encumbrances. In her pre-nuptial agreement, Kilgore had waived all the privileges legislation gave married women, which meant that she retained all the liabilities of a single woman or a man under the law.

After his presentation, Jones submitted a written motion that preserved the right to appeal to the state Supreme Court, should the lower court rule against Kilgore. But Court No. 1 did not act. Six weeks later, Damon Kilgore presented a petition on behalf of his wife to Court No. 2, which had at least rendered a decision. That petition recounted her efforts to gain acceptance from the Court of Common Pleas and her appearance before a committee of the state legislature to request a change in the law. Carrie Kilgore asked the Court to set a time for argument so that she could prove that denying her application constituted a denial of her civil right to earn her living in her profession and to demonstrate further that such a denial violated the United States Constitution and the principle of equal rights. The presiding judge indicated that the court would not go back into a case it had already decided, but that if Mr. Kilgore filed the petition, the court would consider it.

The *Times* correspondent noted that Court No. 1 seemingly intended to avoid any decision whatsoever. But a month later, that court also rebuffed Kilgore's petition. However, the panel of three judges split: Judge Pierce wrote a long dissenting opinion in which he embraced many of the arguments the Kilgores had been asserting and added yet another powerful argument to the case. He submitted that in many legal matters, a woman "would rather suffer injustice and wrong than confer with a man," a problem that would be remedied by allowing women to practice law. In a rousing statement, Pierce wrote:

> [Are women] to be denied these rights and privileges because men a thousand years ago, assuming and asserting their claims to superiority when they were in a state of ignorance far below the ordinary intelligence of the women of today, and largely actuated by selfish motives, struck down their rights and bound them in the swaddling clothes of what they are pleased to term feminine propriety, and by the manly protection of depriving them

of their property as tenants by the courtesy, and of reducing to their own possession their personal estate when they become their wives? How long are these relics of semi-barbarism to be perpetuated?

Court No. 2 eventually rejected Carrie Kilgore's request as well and was similarly divided with a dissent from Judge Finletter. The Kilgores next appealed to the Common Pleas Court No. 3, but were again turned down. This rejection prompted the *Times* to publish an editorial criticism of Judge Ludlow who had issued the ruling, picking apart his arguments and logic. Ludlow had employed a natural law justification to point out the distinctions between the stronger and weaker sexes, and thus, the need for special protections for women. The *Times* rebuked him, ''We fear that ridicule may be the reward of Judge Ludlow when he leaves the beaten track of the law and wanders amid the flowery glades of social and physiological disquisition.''

Finally, the Kilgores submitted their arguments to what was expected to be the most receptive of the tribunals, Court No. 4, the last of the Common Pleas courts in Philadelphia. In May, 1884, Court No. 4 admitted Carrie Kilgore to the practice of law. Presiding Judge Russell Thayer, who was considered a great and unparalleled jurist of the Pennsylvania Bench, according to the *Times*, announced his court's 2–1 vote and justified the majority decision squarely on the state statute that permitted judges of courts of record to admit persons to practice as attorneys. Denying that he was engaging in judicial activism, Judge Thayer found no barriers as to age, color, citizenship, or sex in the law governing admissions; the only requirement was that the applicant be honest and learned in the law. The Kilgores were present in the courtroom as the decision was announced, and Carrie immediately approached the bench to take the oath of office.

The following year, 1885, the Pennsylvania legislature passed an act explicitly permitting the admission of women to practice before the state Supreme Court, and Carrie Kilgore gained admission to practice before that tribunal in 1886. This admission admitted her to all of the state courts. A year later, Kilgore was appointed the first woman master in chancery in the state.

Damon Kilgore died in 1888, leaving Carrie with their two young daughters and only a small legacy. But Carrie was able to take over his practice, losing only one client. She continued to practice law for many years. Having overcome so many gender barriers to her legal career throughout her life, Carrie Kilgore found a new interest and a new challenge in her golden years: gravity. She joined the Philadelphia Aeronautical Recreation Society, a Philadelphia group interested in balloon flight, and at the age of 70, Kilgore was the first woman in southeastern Pennsylvania to make a balloon ascension, remaining aloft for several hours. Carrie Kilgore died of cancer a year later and was buried in her hometown of Craftsbury, Vermont.

## REFERENCES

Irwin, Inez Haynes. *Amazons and Angels: A Hundred Years of American Women.* Garden City, NY: Doubleday, Doran, and Co., 1933.

*New York Times* (December 16 and 18, 1883; February 10, March 9 and 20, May 4, 1884; and June 30, 1909).

Thomas, Dorothy. ''Carrie Kilgore.'' In *Mothers of Achievement in American History: 1776–1976.* Eds. American Mothers Committee, Bicentennial Project 1974–1975. Rutland, VT: Tuttle, 1976.

*GREG CASEY*

# HELEN KINNEAR (1894–1970)

On International Women's Day, March 8, 1993, the Canadian postal service issued a commemorative stamp bearing the portrait of Helen Alice Kinnear and the words, ''Helen Alice Kinnear 1894–1970—Legal Pioneer.'' Two ceremonial celebrations were held: the first at the Helen Kinnear Children's Centre in Port Colborne, hometown and resting place of Judge Kinnear; the other in Cayuga, her birthplace and the judicial seat where Kinnear presided as county judge from 1943 to 1962. This was the first national recognition and celebration of this Canadian woman who achieved a remarkable number of ''firsts'' over the course of her life.[1] Despite a generation of feminist scholarship, little is known about Helen Kinnear, a modern woman of our time. Even an official 1992 poster bearing the names of 100 significant Canadian women distributed by the Canadian government to public institutions did not include the name Helen Kinnear.

## FAMILY BACKGROUND AND EDUCATION

Helen Kinnear was born on May 6, 1894, in Cayuga, a small community in southern Ontario. She was raised in rural peace, prosperity, and Presbyterianism. Kinnear was the youngest of four children, and like her two brothers and one sister, she was a gifted and serious student. The Kinnear family, from the first generation on the Niagara Peninsula, were ardent Liberals. ''Liberal by birth and Liberal by conviction,'' Helen would later respond to anyone who asked. James Kinnear, Helen's grandfather, nominated William Lyon MacKenzie as Liberal candidate for the Parliament of Upper Canada in 1851. Louis, Helen's father, a classics teacher and lawyer, won the Liberal nomination in Welland County in 1911. Although he lost the election, Louis remained actively associated with Liberal party politics, setting the stage for Helen, who would become his law partner in 1920.

In the spring of 1917, Helen Kinnear graduated from the University of Toronto with Honors in History and English. In September of the same year, she enrolled in Osgoode Hall Law School and graduated with Honors in 1920. Called to the bar on the morning of October 21, Kinnear joined her father's law office in Port Colborne that afternoon; the sign ''Kinnear & Kinnear'' was already in place. Helen Kinnear, at age 26, became the first woman to practice law on the Niagara Peninsula. At the same time, she began a journey toward political power.

To understand Kinnear, one must understand the locale where she spent nearly the first half of her life. For centuries, the Niagara Peninsula was home to a significant population of Native peoples. The permanent arrival of Europeans began in the 1790s, and the Niagara Peninsula attracted settlers like the Kinnears: farmers, teachers, and lawyers who established roots and prospered around the Peninsula. Port Colborne, located about 20 miles from Niagara Falls on the southeastern tip of the Peninsula, was also a summer resort for wealthy and distinguished families from the southern United States. From 1889 to 1933, the refreshing shores of Lake Erie in Port Colborne were a convenient alternative to the lands of the scorned Yankees. The Southerners came with their entourage of ''colored'' servants, accents, foods, and culture, all a source of wonder and curiosity in the local community. Called ''Southern Comfort'' by the locals, this resort of 28 cottages was among the historical forces that shaped the village home of Helen Kinnear.

Kinnear grew up just outside the wrought iron gates of Southern Comfort. Inequality and discrimination of race and class were lived out every summer in Kinnear's neighborhood with the arrival of the vacationing Americans. Whether or not these influences led to her later commitment to social reform is not clear. What is clear is that Kinnear, white and privileged, was to be a role model in the reform of social and political injustices for women who, like servants of color, were excluded from the social, political, and economic processes dominated by white men in Canada and elsewhere.

## CAREER DEVELOPMENT

Throughout the 1920s, Helen Kinnear traveled around the Niagara Peninsula organizing campaigns, chairing committees, and holding offices in local and regional branches of the Liberal party. In interviews, speeches, and sermons, she forged debate on the inequities of Canadian democracy and how they must be remedied. Kinnear argued that women must have a ''definite place'' in the political system of Canada because women represented 52 percent of the voting public and yet their representation in Parliament was less than 1 percent. She charged her beloved party with the responsibility for change and demanded that the party, from the hierarchy to the grass roots, encourage and support women in politics. Democracy, according to Kinnear, was a form of government "worth fighting for," yet the glaring inequality of women in Canadian society was elemental and conspicuous.

In 1924, Louis Kinnear died suddenly, and Helen was left to carry on the work of a general law practice alone. She kept up her political pace, attempting without success, to gain her party's nomination in both provincial and national elections when the opportunity arose. In the fall of 1932, in the midst of the Great Depression, Kinnear closed her law office and decided to take a six-month journey. With sister Jennie, her mother, and a friend, the four women set off by automobile for California. Kinnear's journal notes on the trip provide interesting and amusing observations and anecdotes of the drive west, with comments on California and the new Hollywood scene.

Besides enjoying the sights of California, Kinnear made contacts through women lawyer friends and set up an informal course of study for herself. She focused on two areas, the juvenile defender and the insanity defense. She would use this knowledge nearly 22 years later, in 1954, when she was appointed to two Royal Commissions: the Royal Commission for the Criminal Law Relating to Sexual Psychopaths and the Royal Commission Relating to the Defense of Insanity.

When Kinnear returned to Port Colborne in 1933, she opened a new law office. Her devoted sister, Jennie, became the office manager, and a young capable secretarial assistant, Dorothy Neff, was hired. Neff, a staunch Tory who worked for Kinnear for over a decade, remembers her warmly: "We never talked politics." Kinnear continued her activities on behalf of the Liberal party.

Helen Kinnear was the first woman to appear as counsel before the Supreme Court of Canada. In December 1934, she was named King's Counsel (K.C.), a prestigious honor awarded by the provincial government to practicing lawyers who excelled as counsel. She was the first woman in the British Commonwealth so honored. When Kinnear heard the news, she expressed her hope that the award was based on her legal merits rather than political influence. As a result, her popularity on the speakers' circuit increased and Kinnear continued to challenge the male hierarchy of the Liberal party, hoping to gain the party nomination to the federal Parliament for the Welland riding.

In 1941, after two serious campaigns for political office, Kinnear succeeded in gaining the Liberal nomination for Welland riding for the upcoming election for federal members of Parliament. After 21 years of hard work, Helen Kinnear, K.C., respected lawyer, political activist, and distinguished citizen, had a real chance to go to Ottawa. To the great surprise and even greater disappointment of her supporters, Kinnear relinquished her opportunity to sit in Parliament by giving up her nomination to a man. This seemed completely out of character for the woman the Welland riding had come to know over the past two decades. It was a tough decision for Kinnear and one that ended her career in politics.

Two years later, however, Helen Kinnear was sworn in as a county judge, the first woman appointed a judge by the government of Canada. For Kinnear, the appointment was "more than a personal achievement"; she considered it a milestone, a "victory" for women, and an acknowledgment that women, indeed, had a "definite place" in Canadian legal administration. In an article Kinnear wrote in 1954, she reflected on the relationship of politics and the Bench. She observed that the county judge's independence was so carefully protected that the judge was required to

> Step completely out of politics on his appointment and to refrain from expressing any political opinion afterwards. Indeed on his appointment he loses the right to vote and sit in the councils of the nation. Those are precious rights he gives up, but the wisdom of the rule has been proved through the years, not only as a means of removing from his mind any reason for bias and ensuring a judicial approach, but also make it perfectly clear to the world that he is not open to influence. The same reasons lie behind his security of tenure.[2]

Kinnear recognized and acknowledged the role of politics, however, in a system that relied on the appointment of judges.

> The system of appointment so far adopted has produced results which are generally good. The most careful consideration should be given before that system is changed, lest the change result only in a shifting of responsibility without any guarantee of improvement. Though there is a different method of appointment in England, political influence has its place there too, with much the same result as here. So it would appear from Dr. Jackson's resume of the subject in 1940 and his statement that "the pressing political claims to appointment in England does at least end when the appointment is made; the debt is paid and the political account is closed."[3]

Helen Kinnear believed in public service, and she felt that it should not be a bar to judicial appointment. "So long as fitness for judicial work is the basis of appointment, a record of public service should be an asset. We may be thankful that never in the history of Canada have we departed from the system of appointing judges in favour of the elective system with its inevitable risks."[4]

The County Court in Canada to which Kinnear was appointed was a court of inferior jurisdiction for a fixed area, created by provincial statute as provided under the British North America Act (1867), which gave the legislature of each province exclusive power to pass laws on the administration of justice in the province.[5] This included the constitution, and maintenance and organization of provincial courts of both civil and criminal jurisdiction.

County judges were required to be barristers of at least ten years standing and were federally appointed by the governor general. Salaries and pension rights were fixed by the Parliament of Canada. The remuneration set in 1951 was $8,000 per annum. Helen Kinnear observed that the compensation had not kept pace either with the increase in the jurisdiction of county judges or the cost of living. The chief duty of the county judge was to act in the county to which the judge was appointed. The county judge was also a surrogate court judge with wide jurisdiction over the estates of deceased persons, and over the guardianship and custody of children. A county judge was also appointed local judge of the High Court of Justice for the Province. Kinnear described the scope of a county or district judge's jurisdiction as "the Jack of all trades in the administration of justice in Ontario."

Under the British North America Act, criminal law fell under federal jurisdiction, but under the Criminal Code the county judge had jurisdiction to try persons accused of any criminal offenses, except murder or treason, with or without a jury. At the time, the county courts in Canada tried four times as many criminal cases as the Supreme Court. Theft and related crimes formed a large proportion of the criminal work.

Many other duties were assigned under particular statutes. Duties under specific statutes included chair of the Board of Criminal Audit, which audited accounts and debts incurred by the county in the administration of criminal justice. The county had concurrent jurisdiction over magistrates and juvenile court judges under the Children's Protection Act and the Children of Unmarried Parents Act, which determined paternity and liability for maintenance of any illegitimate child. Summary trials under the Landlord and Tenant Act were conducted by a county court judge, and Judge Kinnear found that the housing shortage caused a great increase in applications by landlords of rented premises. With the increase in construction since World War II, there was a great increase in mechanics' lien actions. The county judge presided over recounts in federal, provincial, and municipal elections and had a wide appellate jurisdiction in municipal matters. The county judge also heard appeals from summary convictions by the criminal court magistrate, most commonly offenses under the Highway Traffic Act and the Liquor Control Act.

Helen Kinnear was appointed judge for Haldimand County. The judicial seat was in Cayuga, her birthplace. Although required to sit in the county to which they were appointed, judges in smaller counties were often called upon to help in the busier counties. Kinnear traveled from her own county to Welland County, nearly 40 miles away, once a week for nearly two years. In 1948 and 1949, she assumed the complete administration of justice at the county court level in the County of Lincoln; this was in addition to her own duties.

## ACHIEVEMENTS AND CONTRIBUTIONS

Helen Kinnear was one of 63 county judges in Ontario. Nine, including Kinnear, were also juvenile court judges. An early advocate of probation for juvenile offenders, Kinnear studied the causes of juvenile delinquency to ascertain why so many young men "find their way to the prisoner's dock." Because of her interest and experience in this area of the law, Kinnear was the founding president of the Juvenile and Family Court Judges Association (1952–1954).

As a member of the Royal Commission on "Insanity as a Defense in Criminal Cases and Criminal Law Relating to Sexual Psychopaths," Kinnear served with

Ontario Chief Justice J. McRuer and Dr. Desrochers of Quebec City. The final report, issued in 1958, pioneered the argument for the segregation and treatment of sexual offenders, notwithstanding the fact that the availability of medical resources in the prison system was bleak. In 1958, according to the Commission, one psychiatrist rendered services to a population of 800 inmates, and those services were directed principally at the acutely mentally disturbed. The Commission's recommendations respecting "dangerous sexual offenders" in the criminal justice system were enacted and continue to form the basis of the existing law in Canada.

Many of Judge Kinnear's decisions are bound in seven volumes and maintained in the law library in the Court House in Cayuga. The range of cases she determined was in keeping with the wide jurisdiction of the county court and her additional juvenile court duties. Her decisions are models of clarity in the description of facts and analysis of applicable law. Her keen mind coupled with a straightforward and fair approach, Judge Kinnear was held in high regard by her peers and her community. Among her many recognitions is an award from the John Howard Society of Canada, the social welfare agency in the field of criminal justice. Kinnear was the first woman so honored in the history of this society.

In 1961, illness forced her retirement from an ever-increasing workload. That same year, Helen and Jennie Kinnear moved back to their hometown of Port Colborne. They bought a new home, entertained friends, and traveled back and forth to Toronto where Kinnear was frequently a guest speaker at conferences and gatherings. In 1967, Jennie died, and for the first time in her life, Helen Kinnear was alone. Helen herself died just three years later, on April 25, 1970, and was laid to rest in the family plot in Oakwood Cemetery, Port Colborne.

Helen Kinnear, like many women of her generation, shared the social and political goals fought for by many nineteenth-century women. The exclusion of women from social, political, and economic realms, solely on the basis of sex, was an affront to the cherished ideals of democracy. During the course of a life that spanned 75 years, Kinnear never wavered in her commitment to reform social injustice. She understood the nature of power and carved a path for women in law and politics. In her own "demure" way, she distinguished herself in both areas.

## NOTES

1. *Editors' Note*: This chapter is part of a larger biographical project on Kinnear being conducted by Doris Corbett. The project was sparked by the curiosity of Justice Marie Corbett who, upon her appointment as the forty-ninth woman judge in Canada, wondered who was the first woman to be appointed judge in Canada. With the support of Justice Corbett, the Osgoode Society, and the Law Foundation of Ontario, research seed money was found to commission the biography. The issuance of the postal stamp commemorating Kinnear was at the urging of Justice Corbett who engaged the support of the Honorable Kim Campbell, then minister of Justice.

2. Helen Kinnear, ''The County Judge in Ontario,'' 32 *Canadian Bar Review* (1954): 145.

3. Ibid., 145–46.

4. Ibid.

5. County Courts merged with the Supreme Court of Ontario in 1990, creating a single superior trial court.

## REFERENCE

Kinnear, Helen. ''The County Judge in Ontario.'' *Canadian Bar Review* 32 (1954): 21–43, 127–60.

*MARIE CORBETT AND DORIS CORBETT*

# CLAIRE L'HEUREUX-DUBÉ (1927– )

Claire L'Heureux-Dubé has had a long and distinguished career in the legal profession. She began her career as a lawyer and has sat as a judge of the *Cour Supérieur du Québec*, the *Cour d'Appel du Québec*, and the Supreme Court of Canada. Throughout the stages of her career as a law student, practitioner, and judge, she was consistently one of the first women to hold those positions. While her contribution to the development and reform of family law in Québec and Canada is particularly noteworthy, in her career as a judge Justice L'Heureux-Dubé has been a generalist, writing important decisions in all fields of law.

In addition to her work as a judge, her intellectual contribution to law in Canada has included work on family law reform in Quebec, a major report on the Department of Manpower and Immigration filed under Canada's Public Inquiries Act, and numerous scholarly articles, predominantly in the field of family law. Justice L'Heureux-Dubé has been an active member of a number of legal and educational institutes and has received honorary doctoral degrees from seven Canadian law schools.

L'Heureux-Dubé's career has been shaped by her commitment to justice in a practical form. A self-described "pragmatic idealist," Justice L'Heureux-Dubé espouses a vision of law that places a commitment to equality and justice over the technical formalities of law.

## FAMILY BACKGROUND AND EDUCATION

Claire L'Heureux was born on September 7, 1927, in Quebec City, the capital of the province of Quebec. She was the first of four daughters born to Paul L'Heureux and Marguerite Dion. Her father served as a colonel in the army and in civil life was a collector of customs and excise successively in Rimouski,

Quebec, and Montreal. Her mother, who suffered from multiple sclerosis throughout her adult life, devoted her time to raising her four daughters.

When Claire L'Heureux was seven years old, her family moved to Rimouski after her father was transferred there from Quebec City. She received her elementary and secondary schooling in Rimouski at the private convent school, *Collège des Ursulines*. After graduating from the *Collège* with first prize and the Medal of the Lieutenant Governor, Claire L'Heureux went on to complete a Bachelor of Arts degree at the College Notre-Dame de Bellevue. She graduated *magna cum laude* from this liberal arts program and was again the recipient of the Medal of the Lieutenant Governor.

Following the receipt of her bachelor's degree, Claire L'Heureux enrolled in the Faculty of Law of Laval University. One of only two women among a class of 40 students, she graduated *cum laude* in 1951, receiving special awards in civil law and in labor law. She was admitted to the bar of the province of Quebec in 1952.

Claire L'Heureux married Dr. Arthur Dubé (deceased 1978), a professor of engineering at Laval University. The couple had two children, Louise, a lawyer, and Pierre (deceased 1994).

## CAREER DEVELOPMENT

At the time of her graduation from law school, it was virtually unheard of for women to practice law. Claire L'Heureux-Dubé's prospects for employment as a lawyer would have been slim to none had she not worked part-time as a legal secretary for the law firm of Samuel S. Bard in Quebec City during her years of legal studies. Thus, upon completion of her legal studies, the firm offered her a position as a salaried lawyer. Upon accepting the position, L'Heureux-Dubé became one of only a handful of women lawyers practicing in Quebec. While clients of the firm, which had been renamed Bard, L'Heureux and Philippon, were initially resistant to the idea of dealing with a woman lawyer, one of the partners of the firm actively encouraged clients to make use of her services.

During her early years of practice, L'Heureux-Dubé worked primarily in the area of commercial law, dealing with the firm's predominantly business-oriented clientele. She was not confined to office work and became one of only a very few women at the time who appeared in court on behalf of clients.[1] In 1968, the passage of the federal Divorce Act generated an avalanche of family law cases, and L'Heureux-Dubé became actively involved in the burgeoning family law side of the practice. After becoming familiar with the shortcomings of the law and the courts in this area, she developed a strong interest in family law reform in Quebec.

L'Heureux-Dubé was quickly perceived as an expert in the area and was named president of the Family Law Committee and of the Family Court Committee of the Quebec Civil Code Revision Office (1972–1976). In their law reform initiatives, which were subsequently incorporated into the Civil Code of Quebec, these committees addressed problems that included biases in the treatment of women by the law and in the courts and the inequality of treatment between so-called legitimate and illegitimate children. Between 1970 and 1973, she lectured in family law in the professional training program of the *Barreau du Québec*. She also gave courses at the Faculty of Law of Laval University. L'Heureux-Dubé was active in the *Barreau du Québec*, serving as a counsellor of the *Barreau* and delegate at the General Council forum in 1968–1970, and sitting on a number of committees of the *Barreau* until the time of her appointment to the bench.

In 1969, L'Heureux-Dubé received the honor of Queen's Counsel and became a senior partner of her law firm, which was renamed L'Heureux, Philippon, Garneau, Tourigny, St-Arnaud and Associates. It was at this time that the firm began to acquire a reputation as a specialist firm in the area of family law. The firm's approach favored mediation in the area of family law; the courts were seen as a last resort for the resolution of problems arising from marriage breakdown.

On February 9, 1973, L'Heureux-Dubé was appointed a judge of the Superior Court of Quebec. While she was appointed to sit primarily in Quebec City, she was also required to serve as a circuit judge. This meant frequent trips to more remote communities in Quebec that were not served by permanent judicial institutions. L'Heureux-Dubé was the first woman to sit as a judge in Quebec City and only the second in the province of Quebec. Initially, her appointment was not well received by the other judges sitting in Quebec City, partly because she was a woman, and partly because of her work in the area of family law, which at the time was not considered a serious area of practice.[2] The initial resistance was soon transformed into more cordial working relations.

As a sitting judge, L'Heureux-Dubé was keenly aware that she might easily be assigned to sit primarily on family law matters, thus subjecting her to a form of "ghettoization." She resisted this possibility by insisting that she be allowed to sit on cases dealing with all areas of law. Thus, in spite of her deep and abiding interest in family law, she became a generalist judge, writing opinions in a wide range of legal areas.

On August 13, 1973, just a few months after her appointment as a judge of the Superior Court, the chief justice of the Superior Court assigned L'Heureux-Dubé to sit as a commissioner under Part II of the Inquiries Act to investigate and report on allegations of misconduct within the Department of Manpower and Immigration in Montreal. She reluctantly accepted the task, which would take her away from her work as a judge and require her to conduct hearings in Montreal away from her home and her young children. The Commission of Inquiry proved a difficult and challenging task. Her report was filed and published some two and a half years following her appointment and after a review by the Commission of Inquiry of over 500 files related to the allegations of wrongdoing on the part of immigration officials. During the course of the proceedings, L'Heureux-Dubé developed rules for the conduct of public inquiries that would serve as a model for future inquiries.[3]

On October 16, 1979, L'Heureux-Dubé was appointed to the Quebec Court of Appeal. At the time of her appointment, she was the only woman ever to be appointed to that court, and she remained the only woman on the court for another eight years. In 1979, only one other woman in Canada was sitting as a judge on a Court of Appeal. This was Bertha Wilson* of the Ontario Court of Appeal, who was later to be her colleague at the Supreme Court of Canada.

While at the Court of Appeal, L'Heureux-Dubé continued to insist on being a generalist. During her tenure on this court, she wrote opinions in all areas of law, including, for the first time, criminal law. Her achievements in law were amply recognized at this point in time: she was awarded honorary doctoral degrees by the law faculties of two Quebec universities, Laval University and the University of Montreal, as well as by one law school outside of Quebec, Dalhousie University.

On April 15, 1987, L'Heureux-Dubé was appointed to the Supreme Court of Canada. She joined Justice Bertha Wilson on the panel of nine justices, becoming the first woman from Quebec and the second woman in Canadian history to sit as a justice of the Supreme Court of Canada. The appointment meant a move from her home in Quebec City to the seat of the Supreme Court in Ottawa, Ontario. While she remained free to work and write her opinions in her mother tongue, the realities of life in Ottawa and work at the court would involve a significant shift in her language of work and her cultural environment. L'Heureux-Dubé arrived at the Supreme Court at a time when it faced a heavy backlog of cases, and an atmosphere of overwork and burnout. Despite the initial difficulties, she has become a prolific and significant contributor to the work of the Court. Since her appointment to the Supreme Court, Justice L'Heureux-Dubé has been recognized with additional honorary doctoral degrees from the University of Ottawa, the University of Toronto, Queen's University (Kingston), and the *Université du Québec à Rimouski.*

## ACHIEVEMENTS AND CONTRIBUTIONS

L'Heureux-Dubé's contributions to the jurisprudence of the Supreme Court of Canada reflect both her continuing desire to bring her judgment to bear on a broad range of legal issues, and her depth of understanding and commitment to family law reform. She has written important opinions in all areas of public and private law, including family law, administrative law, criminal law, and constitutional law. She brings a pragmatic and flexible approach to most issues, combined with a clear awareness of the social, political, and economic contexts in which the cases arise. Justice L'Heureux-Dubé remains a generalist; some of her most significant contributions to law in Canada lie in the approach she brings to the range of cases she decides. Elements of her approach focus on placing cases in a social, economic, and political context; judicial notice and the use of academic authority; and human rights and equality.

In her opinions, Justice L'Heureux-Dubé is careful to place cases in their social, political and economic context. This approach is designed to ensure that decisions affecting the rights of individuals are not taken in a sterile legal vacuum. In a dissenting opinion concerning sex discrimination in the structure of income tax deductions for business expenses and child care, Justice L'Heureux-Dubé wrote:

> We must keep foremost in our minds the unequal cost of child care that women have traditionally borne, the effect of such cost on the ability of women to participate in businesses or otherwise be gainfully employed and, finally, the impact of child care on women's financial ability and independence. In my view, such a "contextual" approach is an attempt to attack the problem of privilege and to understand the diversity of people's experiences.[4]

One of the most significant examples of this contextual approach in the area of family law is Justice L'Heureux-Dubé's majority opinion in *Moge v. Moge*.[5] This case signaled a shift in direction for the Supreme Court of Canada in the area of spousal support. Previously, Canadian judicial opinion favored an approach to spousal maintenance premised on the idea that women who received support payments were to become self-sufficient after a period of time. In her decision, L'Heureux-Dubé openly acknowledged that the economic consequences of marriage breakdown could, for many women, last a lifetime. She also directly addressed the feminization of poverty as an "entrenched social phenomenon" in Canada.[6] The approach taken in this decision moved toward a model of substantive equality for women following marriage breakdown, as opposed to more traditional formal equality approaches.[7] In a subsequent decision, L'Heureux-Dubé urged that: "Interpretation and application of family law, especially the law of support, in a manner consistent with Parliamentary intention therefore implicitly requires sensitivity to the social realities experienced by those most affected."[8]

In her significant dissenting opinions in *R. v. Seaboyer*[9] and *R. v. Osolin*,[10] both of which dealt with evidentiary issues in sexual assault cases, Justice L'Heureux-Dubé explored the social context of violence against women in Canadian society. Her dissent in *Seaboyer* provides a thorough analysis and critique of the rules relating to the admissibility of evidence of a woman's past sexual history in sexual assault trials.[11] In *Osolin*, L'Heureux-Dubé also notes the impact of the "further victimization [of women] at the hands of the criminal justice system" on the level of reporting of sexual assaults.[12]

In yet another case, Justice L'Heureux-Dubé expanded on the growing problem of child abduction in Canada before reaching an interpretation of the Criminal Code that would cover the case of a man who had taken a boy from a park for the purposes of photographing him by a river.[13] She has explored the problem of child sexual abuse in Canada, citing extensively from statistical and scholarly sources before ruling that a child's videotaped evidence was admissible in cases of child sexual abuse.[14]

Placing law within a social context requires, in some cases, an elaboration of the ways in which judges can use different sources of information. L'Heureux-Dubé is an advocate of the expansion of the doctrine of judicial notice, and a number of her recent opinions have articulated the need for judicial notice of social and economic factors affecting the context in which cases arise.[15] In *Willick*, she states:

> Where social data and research are relevant to the creation of a rule of law, they take on a general character that goes far beyond the specific context in which they have been raised. They are part and parcel of the rule of law which they help to substantiate. . . . As such, the concept of jurisprudential social authority is intrinsic to the notion of jurisprudence itself. Intrinsic to jurisprudence, in turn, is the power and, to some extent, responsibility, of the court to actively inform itself of authority that will aid it in evaluating the merits of the legal arguments before it and in ultimately reaching its legal conclusions. The judiciary's long-recognized function as a policy finder sometimes compels it to consider social authority even when the parties do not, themselves, present relevant evidence on relevant questions of public policy.[16]

Her opinions, particularly in the area of family law, make significant use of social science data and literature to examine the impact of law on issues such as the structure of the family and the feminization of poverty.[17]

Justice L'Heureux-Dubé sees judicial opinions as performing a dual role. On the one hand, they resolve the issues in dispute before the court; on the other hand, the text of the opinions serves an educative function.[18] Many of her opinions cite current scholarship extensively and engage openly with the academic debates.

As a justice of the Supreme Court of Canada, Claire L'Heureux-Dubé has written numerous opinions that emphasize her commitment to equality and recognize the diversity of the Canadian population. In one dissenting opinion, for example, Justice L'Heureux-Dubé accepted an expansive definition of the family that would include same-sex couples.[19] Her analysis in this case also urged a broad and liberal approach to the interpretation of human rights instruments. In another dissenting opinion, Claire L'Heureux-Dubé explained how the grounds of sex discrimination and age discrimination may well overlap in the way in which some mandatory retirement policies may have a differential impact on women.[20] Concerns with women's equality are also reflected in the setting of a social context in her application of the rules and doctrines of all areas of law, including family and criminal law.[21]

In her long and distinguished career, Claire L'Heureux-Dubé has made significant contributions to the development of Canadian law. As a judge, her approach to legal issues reflects a commitment to resolve disputes within a broader understanding of the social conditions that give rise to them. Her scholarship, law reform efforts and judicial opinions have contributed to significant developments in family law in Quebec and in Canada. Her commitment to social equality and justice is reflected in a range of legal opinions, covering a wide spectrum of issues.

**ACKNOWLEDGMENT**

I would like to thank Madam Justice Claire L'Heureux-Dubé for her time in providing me with some of the background information for this article.

**NOTES**

1. In the commencement address that she delivered at the Northern Illinois University College of Law, Claire L'Heureux-Dubé stated: "when I graduated from law school there were very, very few women who even practiced law and of course no female judges. There were just as few, if any, members of visible minorities who practiced and no minority women. Everything around us said tacitly or explicitly that law was, *de facto*, the exclusive domain of white, middle and upper-class, able-bodied men." Cited in Claire L'Heureux-Dubé, "The Legal Profession in Transition," 13 *Northern Illinois University L. Rev.* (1992–1993): 93 at 95.

2. Writing about her early family law practice, L'Heureux-Dubé stated: "at the time, this area was practically ignored by the legal community. The profession, judges as well as lawyers, perceived family law as the exclusive domain of those who 'knew nothing else.' Family law practitioners were perceived as lacking the skills to take on the major corporate law case or the sensational cases in criminal law." Claire L'Heureux-Dubé, "Recent Developments in Family Law," 6 *Canadian Journal of Women and the Law* (1993): 269.

3. "Report of the Commission of Inquiry Relating to the Department of Manpower and Immigration in Montreal" (Ottawa: Information Canada, 1976).

4. *Symes v. Canada*, 4 S.C.R. 695 (1993) at 826.

5. 3 S.C.R. 813 (1992).

6. Ibid., 853.

7. *Willick v. Willick*, 6 F.L.R. (4th) 161 (1994) at 193.

8. Ibid., 188.

9. 2 S.C.R. 577 (1991).

10. 4 S.C.R. 595 (1993).

11. *R. v. Seaboyer*, 2 S.C.R. 577 (1991) at 651–55.

12. *R. v. Osolin*, 4 S.C.R. 595 (1993) at 628.

13. *R. v. Chartrand*, 2 S.C.R. 864 (1994).

14. *R. v. L. (D.O.)*, 4 S.C.R. 419 (1993).

15. *Moge v. Moge*, 3 S.C.R. 813 (1992) at 874.

16. *Willick v. Willick*, (1994) at 189.

17. *Moge v. Moge*, (1992); *Willick v. Willick*, (1994). In a recent address, L'Heureux-Dubé stressed the need for judges to make themselves aware of statistical information regarding marriage breakdown and related issues. She stated: "The impact of marriage

breakdown on women is precisely the sort of factual issue that calls for the application of the judicial notice doctrine. . . . The preferred solution is to make sure that judges are familiar with the general factual data so that they can be applied by them to the circumstances of the particular cases with which they must deal.'' Cited in L'Heureux-Dubé, ''Recent Developments,'' 277.

18. Claire L'Heureux-Dubé, ''The Length and Plurality of Supreme Court of Canada Decisions,'' 28 *Alberta Law Review* (1990): 581 at 595.

19. *Mossop v. Canada*, 1 S.C.R. 554 (1993).

20. *Dickason v. University of Alberta*, 2 S.C.R. 1103 (1992).

21. See, for example, *R. v. Osolin* (1993) and *R. v. Seaboyer*, (1991).

## REFERENCES


Abella, Rosalie S., and Claire L'Heureux-Dubé, eds. *Family Law—Dimensions of Justice*. Toronto: Butterworths, 1983.

L'Heureux-Dubé, Claire. ''Au-delà des mythes: justice.'' *Canadian Journal of Women and Law* 7 (1994): 1–14.

L'Heureux-Dubé, Claire. ''Economic Consequences of Divorce: A View from Canada.'' *Houston Law Review* 31 (1994): 451–98.

L'Heureux-Dubé, Claire. ''By Reason of Authority or by Authority of Reason.'' *University of British Columbia Law Review* 27 (1993): 1–18.

L'Heureux-Dubé, Claire. ''Recent Developments in Family Law.'' *Canadian Journal of Women and the Law* 6 (1993): 269–77.

L'Heureux-Dubé, Claire. ''The Legal Profession in Transition.'' *Northern Illinois University Law Review* 13 (1992–1993): 93–103.

L'Heureux-Dubé, Claire. ''Nomination of Supreme Court Judges: Some Issues for Canada.'' *Manitoba Law Journal* 20 (1991): 600–24.

L'Heureux-Dubé, Claire. ''The Length and Plurality of Supreme Court of Canada Decisions.'' *Alberta Law Review* 28 (1990): 581–88.

L'Heureux-Dubé, Claire. ''The Quebec Experience: Codification of Family Law and a Proposal for the Creation of a Family Court System.'' *Louisiana Law Review* 44 (1984): 1575–640.

L'Heureux-Dubé, Claire. ''Deciding Child Custody: New Developments in Quebec.'' In *The Child and the Courts*. Eds. Ian F.G. Baxter and Mary A. Eberts. Toronto: Carswell, 1978.

L'Heureux-Dubé, Claire. ''Le droit de ne pas divorcer.'' *Cahiers de Droit* 10 (1969): 121–66.

''Report of the Commission of Inquiry Relating to the Department of Manpower and Immigration in Montreal.'' Ottawa: Information Canada, 1976.


*TERESA SCASSA*

# JUTTA LIMBACH (1934– )

Jutta Limbach is the first woman to be elected president ("Chief Justice") of Germany's Federal Constitutional Court and the seventh president to preside over the 45-year-old tribunal entrusted with the guardianship and authoritative interpretation of the Basic Law (Germany's constitution). Elected on September 7, 1994, and barring unforeseen circumstances, she will lead Germany's highest court, and arguably the world's most powerful constitutional tribunal, into the first two years of the twenty-first century. As president, she also represents the court in all of its relations with outside groups and organizations. Limbach is also the fifth-ranking official in the German Federal Republic, behind the federal president, the federal chancellor, the president of the council of state governments (*Bundesrat*), and the president of the national parliament (*Bundestag*).[1]

## FAMILY BACKGROUND AND EDUCATION

Jutta Limbach, whose maiden name was Ryneck, was born in Berlin on March 27, 1934. She was raised in a family devoted to social causes and active in the Social Democratic party (SPD). Her great grandmother, Pauline Staegermann, founded the Berlin Women's Labor Association in 1885 and is reported to have been jailed for an "offense against the sovereign" (*Majestätsbeleidigung*). Elfriede Ryneck, her grandmother, was an SPD member of the Weimar constitutional convention, the *Reichstag*, and the Prussian state Parliament. Her father, an engineer, was barred from the practice of his profession during the Nazi period; immediately after the war, as a member of the SPD, he became the district mayor of Pankow in East Berlin. As an active Social Democrat, however, he found life in the Soviet Zone of Occupation increasingly intolerable, so he fled with his family to West Berlin in 1948. There the family found a new life just as the young daughter, Jutta, was about to discover her own vocation.

Motivated early on by a passion for social justice, a trait undoubtedly inherited from her socially active forbearers, Jutta embarked on the study of journalism but then turned to law in the hope that a legal background would bolster her journalistic career. After passing her first state law examination, she advanced to the practical phase of her legal training, spending the next two and one half years apprenticing in the courts of Kiel and Speyer. During this time she decided to remain in the law and become a judge. She passed her second state examination in 1962, qualifying shortly thereafter for a junior judgeship. Instead of taking a judicial post, however, she set her sights on a doctoral degree, now resolved to enter the male-dominated world of legal scholarship.

Jutta earned her doctorate in 1966, upon the completion of a dissertation in legal sociology under the direction of Ernst E. Hirsch, a professor of civil law at the Free University of Berlin. While serving as an assistant to Professor Hirsch, she began working on her *Habilitationsschrift*, a major publication required of candidates wishing to qualify for a professorship at Berlin University. She met this requirement in 1971, whereupon she received a call to occupy a chair in law at the Free University of Berlin. Meanwhile, during all these years of training and preparation for a major professorship, she joined the SPD, married Peter Limbach, a legal counselor in the Federal Ministry of Interior in Bonn, and gave birth to three children. She would later refer to her marriage as an "itinerant" one, commuting as she did between Berlin, her native city and place of work, and Bonn, where her family resided.

## CAREER DEVELOPMENT

Jutta Limbach would spend the next 18 years of her life holding a distinguished professorship in civil law and legal sociology at the Free University. During these years she produced an impressive list of monographs and articles dealing with various issues of public and private law. Her interest in legal sociology manifested itself in numerous publications on various aspects of family law. Empirical and critical, much of her work was directed toward achieving equality for women in marriage, improving the protection and security of nonmarital children, and placing a cautious stamp of the law's approval on long-lasting unions between men and women outside of marriage. After leaving the legal academy for politics in 1989, she turned her attention increasingly to the problems of law and justice in the former (East) German Democratic Republic (GDR). Careful research, clear exposition, and sound judgment were the terms often used in characterizing her published work.

As noted earlier, Jutta Limbach joined the SPD in 1962, at the age of 28. Later in her career she would become much more active in party affairs, but mainly as an academic legal adviser. She served on an advisory committee of the Federal Ministry of Youth, Women, and Health and later, as a consultant on legal affairs to the SPD's national executive committee. In March of 1989, just months before the collapse of the Berlin Wall, she became the senator of justice in West Berlin's senate (i.e., "Cabinet"), a position in the eye of many a political storm during most of the city-state's postwar history. Her tenure of five years as senator, however, would be longer than that of all her predecessors.

Serving originally in the senate of a left-leaning SPD–Green party coalition government, she proceeded to institute a number of legal reforms, including the reorganization of the attorney general's office in West Berlin. On another front, she drew the fire of conservative critics when, in response to a letter from the "Red Army Faction" (RAF), a terrorist group, she displayed her readiness to end the forced isolation of RAF prisoners and allow them some degree of contact with each other and other prisoners.

Her performance as senator of justice received enough applause and support to propel her into that position once again after the first all-city election on December 2, 1990, subsequent to Germany's unexpected reunification. But Limbach would now hold her portfolio in a grand Christian Democratic Union (CDU)–Social Democratic party coalition government under the leadership of Eberhard Diepgen (CDU), Berlin's new lord mayor. Her presence in a CDU-led senate was another sign of Jutta Limbach's general political acceptability. Her reappointment as senator was also fortuitous because she would now command the spotlight of public attention in proceeding forthwith to reorganize East Berlin's court system and call for the dismissal of former GDR officials who had abused their trust and authority while serving the communist regime.

Under her leadership, shortly after reunification, all East Berlin courts were shut down, their judges and prosecutors dismissed, and all their records transferred to judicial districts in the Western part of the city. At the same time, Limbach was largely responsible for establishing the Working Group on (GDR) Governmental Criminality, an organization responsible for investigating the records of thousands of GDR officials, including border guards accused of shooting would-be escapees, and for opening prosecutions against large numbers of them. She insisted publicly that GDR officials found to have committed crimes under the old regime be brought to trial. The more important of these trials, including that of Erich Honecker, the former general-secretary of the Communist party and GDR head of state, took place on her doorstep in Berlin.

For some of these decisions and policies, Limbach was severely taken to task in the reunited Berlin's house of representatives. Members of her own party faulted her for the speed and harshness with which the eastern bench and bar were dismantled. She freely admitted before the house that some mistakes were made in the course of rebuilding Berlin's system of justice. She expressed disappointment at Honecker's release in mid-trial, but defended the decision to let him go as fully consonant with the principle of legality.

## ACHIEVEMENTS AND CONTRIBUTIONS

Candor, toughness, confidence, and a willingness to admit error marked Limbach's stewardship in the rough and tumble period following reunification. The weekly magazine *Der Spiegel* dubbed her "Jutta Courage" for the independence, decisiveness, and rectitude she displayed in the conduct of her office. Independent-minded and still very much the legal scholar, she eschewed partisanship and cared little about the response her actions would provoke among her friends and colleagues in the SPD. In her view, the needs of the state prevailed over those of party. As it turned out, she was in the right place at the right time and doing the right things when nominated as a judge of the Federal Constitutional Court.

The choice of Jutta Limbach for president of the Federal Constitutional Court resulted from a combination of chance and circumstance. When the term of Vice-president Ernst-Gottfried Mahrenholz was about to expire in 1993, a major parliamentary battle erupted over the selection of his successor. The Social Democratic party (SPD), holding the right to nominate the person to fill this particular seat, chose Herta Däubler-Gmelin, a prominent member of the national Parliament and deputy chairman of the SPD. But Christian Democratic members of the *Bundestag's* Judicial Selection Committee (JSC), the 12–member parliamentary committee empowered by law to elect one-half the members of the Constitutional Court that the Basic Law requires the *Bundestag* to choose, refused to accept the nomination. For months, the SPD stood fast before the opposition of the CDU, threatening to hold up other nominations, including those of the CDU, until Däubler-Gmelin was accepted.[2]

Däubler-Gmelin herself broke the logjam when she withdrew her nomination. Jutta Limbach, who was high on the list of potential SPD nominees, surfaced as the compromise candidate acceptable to the CDU. The SPD had insisted on placing a woman at the head of the Second Senate, and Limbach had made no secret of the fact that a seat on the court would be a "dream come true" (*Traumziel*). The SPD could applaud her progressive views on social and cultural issues; the CDU could applaud her for standing up for law, order, and corrective justice in the eastern half of Berlin. In reality, however, she was more pragmatic than ideological, and for this reason, she was also likely to be well received by her new colleagues in Karlsruhe.

On March 4, 1994, Jutta Limbach was unanimously chosen vice president of the Constitutional Court, the plan being that she would eventually succeed to the presidency itself. In any event, with her election, she became the first female vice president to occupy the Second Senate's center chair. Several weeks later, as chance would have it, the president and presiding justice of the First Senate, Roman Herzog, was elected President of the Federal Republic. On September 7, 1994, the *Bundestag*'s JSC unanimously chose Limbach as his successor, ensuring that she would remain at the Court's helm until 2002, the year of her scheduled retirement. As president, she would continue to preside over the Second Senate, while the new vice president would take his seat at the center of the First Senate.

Vice President Limbach arrived in Karlsruhe in the midst of a major constitutional conflict. Barely had she taken her seat when she presided over two days of oral argument on the question of the validity of German participation in military operations outside the territory of the North Atlantic Treaty Organization (NATO). A few weeks later, in a momentous decision, she joined the majority in sustaining the constitutionality of Germany's participation in United Nations peacekeeping operations. Her continued presence on the Second Senate would of course take on considerable importance, given its exclusive jurisdiction over high profile "political" cases such as the *Military Deployment Case*. Months later, as president, she would cast the critical fifth vote in the famous *Markus Wolf Case,* which nullified the prosecution of East Germans who had spied against West Germany. Had the vote been four to four, the spy trials would have continued, risking more tension between the two halves of the country.

Apart from these cases, it is too early to assess Justice Limbach's record on the Constitutional Court or her contribution to Germany's developing constitutional jurisprudence. In public speeches and interviews, however, she has expressed her opinions on several constitutional issues, including her disappointment over the recent failure of the postunification Joint Commission on Constitutional Revision to revise the Basic Law in certain respects. In an interview in the magazine *Der Spiegel*, she described the Basic Law as "the best of all German constitutions" but added that it would be better if had been amended to include selected plebiscitary elements and state social objectives such as adequate housing and employment for all.[3] She would also amend, as indeed she had proposed, the Basic Law's provisions on marriage and family to redefine the family in the light of changing social reality and to guarantee the right of all children to be free of violence and abuse.

In the same *Der Spiegel* interview, Justice Limbach praised the Federal Constitutional Court for doing its part in modernizing the Basic Law through interpretation, mentioning particularly its vindication of the right to informational self-determination and decisions requiring the equal treatment of the sexes. Asked whether she would have voted with the majority in striking down aspects of a liberalized abortion statute passed in 1992, Limbach responded by saying that she would have been more respectful of the "compromise worked out so thoughtfully and ably in the *Bundestag*." These opinions and responses are poor guides as to how President Limbach will actually vote in particular cases coming before her senate. Her principal role will be to guide the process of collective decision making on the court. It is safe to predict that the ultimate assessment of her achievements may rest on how effectively she guides that process rather than her particular opinions on constitutional matters.

## NOTES

1. For readers of this biographical sketch, it is important to note a few details about the Federal Constitutional Court and its members. The court, which is located in Karlsruhe, is divided into two senates (First Senate and Second Senate) of eight members each and mutually exclusive jurisdiction. Thus, each Senate speaks in the name of the court as a whole. The court's president normally presides over the First Senate and the vice president over the Second, although, as with Wolfgang Zeidler and Jutta Limbach, the presiding justice of the Second Senate may also be elected to the presidency. All members of the court are elected for a single, nonrenewable term of 12 years unless they first reach the compulsory retirement age of 68. Jutta Limbach was 60 years of age at the time of her election. Accordingly, her term will end in 2002, after eight years in office.

2. Since a two-thirds vote in the JSC is necessary to elect a justice, each party's nominees must be acceptable to the other.

3. (July 11, 1994): 160–63.

## REFERENCES

''Interview with Jutta Limbach'' (in German). *Der Spiegel* (July 11, 1994):160–63.

Limbach, Jutta. *Frauenrechte im Grundgesetz des geeinten Deutschland: Diskussion in der Gemeinsamen Verfassungskommission.* Baden-Baden: Nomos, 1993.

Limbach, Jutta. *Gemeinsame Sorge geschiedener Eltern.* Heidelberg: C.F. Müller, 1988.

Limbach, Jutta. *Der Verständige Rechtsgenosse.* Berlin: Schweitzer, 1977.

*DONALD P. KOMMERS*

# BURNITA SHELTON MATTHEWS (1894–1988)

In 1949, Burnita Shelton Matthews became the first woman federal district court judge in the United States, appointed by President Harry Truman to the U.S. District Court for the District of Columbia. Only the second woman Article III judge,[1] Matthews earned her appointment by her committed professional service at the bar and her feminist activism. Her work on behalf of the National Woman's party, which she began while still in law school, brought her to the attention of women colleagues and other feminists. By virtue of her highly visible role as the party's primary speaker on behalf of the Equal Rights Amendment in congressional hearings, she came to know many members of Congress, an association she considered significant in securing her appointment as a federal judge.

Matthews's tenure as a district judge drew praise from her brethren on the bench. When she took senior status in 1968, a long-time colleague on the federal court, Judge Edward Tamm, told her: "[D]uring the tenure of your service you have established a national reputation, not only for judicial temperament and bearing but for great courage, profound judicial learning, and an absolute and complete fairness."[2] During her 18 years on the bench, only two other women received appointments to the federal district court, but Matthews vindicated, if vindication were required, those who believed that sex was not a suitable criterion for choosing judicial officials. It would be another ten years after her retirement before pressure from an active women's movement caused an upsurge in the number of women named to the federal bench.

**FAMILY BACKGROUND AND EDUCATION**

Burnita Shelton was born on December 28, 1894, in Burnell, a tiny town in Copiah County, Mississippi, south of Jackson. Her father, Burnell Shelton, was a planter, later elected clerk of Chancery Court for Copiah County, and then county tax collector and sheriff. Her mother, Lora Barlow Shelton, graduated from Whitworth Bible College in Brookhaven, Mississippi. Shelton, the only daughter in a family of five living children, attended public schools in Barlow and Hazlehurst, to which the family had relocated. Her mother died when Shelton was young, and her responsibilities expanded to include caring for her siblings.

Shelton's interest in law emerged early, sparked by visits to the courthouse in Hazlehurst, Mississippi, where her father was court clerk. Even as a child she won prizes for her oratorical skills, prompting a local attorney to comment to her father that he "ought to make a lawyer out of that little girl."[3] Instead, her family sent two of her brothers to law school, and, after a single year at Whitworth Bible College, she was dispatched at age 18 to the Cincinnati Conservatory of Music to study piano and voice in preparation for a career in teaching or concert work.

At night while at the Conservatory, she read legal tomes, including Blackstone's *Commentaries*, a practice she continued during the four years she taught music in public schools in Texas, Mississippi, and Georgia. Her reading deepened her interest in the law, but she was appalled at the position women occupied in it and affronted by Blackstone's notion that women benefited from laws that gave husbands control over their wives.

In order to study law formally, Matthews needed to move to a city with a law school that admitted women. World War I created openings in government for women and while living in Atlanta, Matthews applied for a position in Washington., D.C. She married in 1917, but her husband, Percy A. Matthews, almost immediately went off to war.[4] In 1918, she received an assignment to the Veterans Administration. The job permitted her to support herself while she attended evening classes at the National University Law School. This demonstration of resolve prompted her father, despite his ongoing misgivings about her decision, to offer to pay for her legal education, but Matthews declined his help. The only woman in her graduating class, she received her Bachelor of Laws in 1919, and a Master of Laws and Master of Patent Law in 1920. She was admitted to the bar of the District of Columbia that same year, and to the Mississippi state bar and the U.S. Supreme Court bar in 1924.

Matthews did not feel mistreated in law school on account of her sex. She was elected vice president of her class and counted many friends among the male students. Still, she later recalled sexist jokes from professors and mocking criticism of Belva Lockwood, the first woman admitted to the Supreme Court bar.

While in law school, Matthews was recruited by a classmate to join the woman suffrage picket line organized by the militant National Woman's party (NWP) in front of the White House. Fearful that an arrest would impair her legal career, Matthews was careful to stay within the law. She also concealed her extracurricular activity from her male classmates, some of whom denounced the pickets as traitors. Once suffrage was won in 1920, Matthews continued to work with the National Woman's party at the request of Alice Paul, the party's charismatic leader, advising on legal matters and conducting research on laws affecting women in each of the states.

## CAREER DEVELOPMENT

After Matthews graduated from law school, she experienced sex discrimination at first hand. Her application for a position as a lawyer in the Veterans Administration was rejected solely because she was a woman. Her efforts to find a place in an established law firm proved futile. Having little choice, she hung out her own shingle in an office opposite the District of Columbia courthouse, volunteering to defend indigent criminals and to serve as guardian *ad litem* in civil matters involving minors and incompetent persons. The hostility of her male associates was not subtle. When she applied for membership to the Washington, D.C. Bar Association, her check was returned with a claim that her sponsors had withdrawn; two women colleagues met the same fate.

With her private law practice growing slowly, Matthews had time to devote to NWP activities. Matthews represented the party in congressional hearings on the Equal Rights Amendment (ERA) at least seven times between 1925 and 1948.[5] Her testimony inventoried the numerous instances of discrimination against women that she and her staff had uncovered in state legal codes concerning the property rights of married women, child custody, inheritance, jury service, civil service pay rates, and occupational exclusion.[6] She was vehement that statutes that presumed to "protect" women served rather to privilege men. Matthews's advocacy of equal treatment extended even to military service for women, which ERA opponents frequently pointed to as the most odious outcome of constitutional equality. Matthews viewed the Equal Rights Amendment simply as the "most dignified . . . easiest . . . most permanent" way to establish equality and eliminate discrimination against women in national as well as state law.[7]

In addition to her advocacy of the Equal Rights Amendment, Matthews assisted the party in its efforts to modify discriminatory state and federal laws. Matthews drafted several state statutes, which were then conveyed to NWP workers in specific states. Her bills included the D.C. law allowing women to serve on juries, and statutes adopted by several states eliminating preferences for males in inheritance and equalizing pay for women teachers. Matthews also authored amendments to the nationality laws of the United States, equalizing citizenship rights: a 1931 amendment repealed a provision that revoked the U.S. citizenship of a woman who married an alien ineligible for citizenship; in 1934, a second change permitted an American woman married to a national of another country to transmit her U.S. citizenship to their children born abroad as would an American man.

Matthews's professional duties for the NWP extended beyond women's rights. In the 1920s, she represented the party in a condemnation action, incidentally bolstering her private practice. In 1925, Chief Justice William Howard Taft, eager for a separate building for the Supreme Court, chose a site behind the Capitol owned by the National Woman's party and occupied by the "Old Brick Capitol," a Washington landmark. When the chief justice refused to reconsider, Matthews asked Congress for $1 million in compensation, citing the building's historical significance and the obvious desirability of the location. After a court battle, the jury awarded the NWP almost $300,000, the largest condemnation award ever made by the government to a property holder in such an action. Word of mouth brought her several clients whose property had been similarly condemned, and Matthews continued to specialize in real estate transactions throughout her career.

Matthews described herself as a general lawyer, concerned with the full range of lawyerly responsibilities rather than an exclusive focus on women's legal status. Still, during the 1930s, her firm, known as Matthews, Berrien, and Greathouse, consisted of herself, and two other NWP attorney activists, Rebekah Greathouse and Laura Berrien. In addition to her private practice and political work, from 1942 to 1948 Matthews taught evidence at the Washington College of Law, a coeducational school founded in 1895 by two women lawyers.

Matthews won substantial acclaim for her legal acumen, both on behalf of women and in private practice. She served as a member of the committee of experts on women's work of the International Labor Organization, president of the National Association of Women Lawyers and the Women's Bar Association of D.C., and as a member of the legal research committee of the Inter-American Commission of Women. She was thus a reasonable choice for the federal bench, and by July 1949, the General Federation of Women's Clubs and the National Federation of Business and Professional Women's Clubs were campaigning on her behalf. According to a *Washington Post* account, she had by then "long since been recognized as one of the nation's leading women attorneys."[8]

Although it came officially from the president, the nomination of Burnita Shelton Matthews to the federal bench resulted in no small measure from the application of many feminist activists and, in particular, the efforts of India Edwards, chair of the Women's Division of the Democratic National Committee. Burnita Matthews was one of four women attorneys India Edwards recommended to President Truman as he selected 27 new federal judges in October 1949. Thanks to women's organizations, Truman and the attorney general had already received numerous expressions of support for her appointment. When Edwards found out, late on October 14, that the president's choices were all men, she mounted a full court press on behalf of Matthews (whom she considered the strongest of the four), sending special delivery letters to party and administration officials, including the president, to warn of dire consequences were the judicial appointments all men. The next day, Edwards received a call asking her to bring Matthews to the White House, and that afternoon, Matthews's name appeared on the list of judicial nominations that went to the Senate Judiciary Committee.[9] Because the list of appointments came to the Senate so late in the term, the Senate held many over for confirmation until the next session. On October 21, 1949, Matthews received a recess appointment from Truman; her permanent appointment followed on April 7, 1950, after Senate confirmation.

Although the National Woman's party and the National Association of Women Lawyers were jubilant, other reactions were more ambivalent. A leading attorney later told Edwards that it was not likely the D.C. bar would ever endorse another woman; they had endorsed Matthews, he said, only so they would not appear "antifemale."[10] One of her colleagues, Judge T. Alan Goldsborough, said publicly that Matthews's sex was a defect. According to some accounts, her fellow judges received her coldly and agreed among themselves to assign her the least appealing judicial responsibilities. But Matthews recalled later a kind gesture from Judge Edward Tamm, who vacated his chambers to make room for her, and she always maintained that her colleagues treated her equitably.

The press treatment of her appointment was favorable almost to the point of effusion; her sex was a prominent theme. The *Chicago Daily Tribune* titled a story it ran in April, 1950: "Her Black Robe Does Not Hide Her Femininity."[11] The Memphis *Press-Scimitar* wrote a story published in October, 1952, enthusing: "Nation's Only Woman U.S. District Judge Is Lovely Feminist from Deep South."[12] In news stories regarding specific cases in which she was the judge, however, no mention was made of her sex.

## ACHIEVEMENTS AND CONTRIBUTIONS

Matthews became known as one of the hardest working judges on the District Court, often doing more than her share, always aware of the scrutiny she was under. Because of its jurisdiction over local cases, the U.S. District Court in the District of Columbia had an unusually diverse docket, including criminal matters such as murder and rape and civil matters such as divorce, estate, and custody awards not customarily adjudicated in federal courts. Still, the court's location guaranteed a certain amount of visibility. In 1955, Matthews made news when she allowed to stand the action of the Passport Service in denying a passport to African-American personality Paul Robeson because he refused to answer questions concerning alleged communist affiliations. She also presided over the 1957 trial in which Jimmy Hoffa, then vice president of the teamsters' union, was acquitted of bribery, another highly publicized case. Matthews was rarely overruled and did not hesitate to issue decisions counter to those of judges on district courts elsewhere. In a 1962 case, she interpreted the requirements of the Sherman Anti-Trust Act differently from the holdings in five other district court cases. The Supreme Court ultimately upheld her reading of the statute.[13]

As a district judge in the years before the passage of federal laws prohibiting sex discrimination by private employers (the first was the Equal Pay Act of 1963), Matthews had little opportunity to rule on legal equity for women. When necessary, as in *Schneider v. Rusk*,[14] Matthews cited cases to demonstrate that the government could, if it wished, treat groups such as women as a special class.

Sitting by temporary designation as a circuit judge, however, she wrote one opinion she clearly found gratifying. In a 1974 case, *Evans v. Sheraton Park Hotel*,[15] she upheld the decision of U.S. District Judge Gerhard Gesell that sex-segregated local unions per se violated Title VII of the 1964 Civil Rights Act. In her opinion, Matthews quoted Justice William Brennan's opinion in *Frontiero v. Richardson*,[16] where he took note of Congress's increasing sensitivity to sex-based classifications, including both the enactment of Title VII and the submission to the states of the Equal Rights Amendment, which he quoted in full. In sum, Brennan said, "Congress itself has concluded that classifications based upon sex are inherently invidious." Matthews echoed him: "Such recognition by the Supreme Court should quell any doubts that Congress in enacting Title VII found classifications based on sex inherently invidious." Matthews went on to observe that Evans, in filing her lawsuit, brought about the merger of the two sex-segregated locals and thus "performed a valuable public service in bringing this action, entirely consistent with the intent of Congress."

If her judicial responsibilities constrained her activism, she nevertheless stayed true to her feminist principles. Shortly after her appointment, she wrote to Alice Paul, asking her to sign a picture of herself so that Matthews could hang it in her chambers. In substantive ways, she sought opportunities for women wherever she could. Throughout her career, Matthews hired only women law clerks, an act both conspicuous and important at a time when few male judges would consider employing them in this role. In the 1960s and 1970s, she wrote letters to sitting presidents supporting appointments for a former law clerk, Sylvia Bacon. In 1975, she recommended Bacon to President Gerald Ford for a seat on the Supreme Court, chiding him: "Mr. President, it is time that a qualified woman of the United States be given such an opportunity."[17]

Though raised in the Jim Crow South, Matthews also evinced a sympathy for black advancement that earned her the affection and gratitude of key figures in the African-American community. In 1958, she championed the efforts of the Washington Bar Association, an African-American organization, to place a black attorney on the Committee on Admissions and Grievances of the U.S. District Court. The lawyer, William B. Bryant, himself later became a district court judge. De Long Harris of the Bar Association credited her with a major role: "Certainly, this objective could not have been attained at this time without your efforts in our behalf."[18] Ten years later, at her retirement, he wrote again: "No individual, group or Association has ever had a more faithful or effective friend.''[19]

Matthews also earned the friendship of educator and civil rights activist Mary McLeod Bethune, serving on the Advisory Committee of the Mary McLeod Bethune Foundation. In 1955, when Bethune died, the National Council of Negro Women asked Matthews to speak at the memorial service. Matthews also supported voting rights for residents of the District of Columbia, a show of support for the African-American community.

Matthews took senior status on March 1, 1968, but continued to serve as a judge by designation and assignment until 1983, variously on the district court and on two federal appellate courts. At this juncture in her career, she reaped bountiful sentiments of regard from colleagues. Judge William Jones wrote: ''Your life is living proof that a woman need not take second place to any man.''[20] *The Daily Washington Law Reporter* called her 18 years on the bench ''distinguished,''[21] the Women's Bar Association recognized her as Woman Lawyer of the Year, and the D.C. Bar Association presented her the Distinguished Service Award, ''in recognition of her many years of dedicated service and outstanding contribution to the administration of justice.''[22] By then, even Judge Goldsborough had acknowledged that his assessment of her had been incorrect.

Of women and the law, Matthews had said in 1950: ''To rise to eminence they usually must be a little better, work a little harder and show a little more in results than their male colleagues.''[23] She more than met her own standard and to the end of her life remained committed to equal treatment for women, still affronted by the male bias prevalent in the legal profession. When, in 1974, the American Bar Association (ABA) presented her with a standard certificate in recognition of 50 years of ABA membership, the form letter came addressed to ''Mr. Matthews.'' Judge Matthews noted on the letter in pen, ''After 50 years a member, I find this inexcusable! BSM.''[24] Judge Matthews died in Washington, D.C. on April 25, 1988, at the age of 93.

## NOTES

1. Article III is a reference to the section of the U.S. Constitution that provides for the judicial branch of the United States. Article III courts are distinguished from other courts authorized by Congress under its legislative powers in Article I or by statute principally in that appointments carry life–time tenure. The first woman appointed to an Article III court was Florence Allen.*

2. Edward Tamm to Burnita Shelton Matthews, February 7, 1968, microfilm M-73, papers of Burnita Shelton Matthews, Schlesinger Library, Radcliffe College, Cambridge, Massachusetts (hereinafter, BSM papers).

3. *Washington Post* (November 7, 1949).

4. After the war, Percy Matthews returned to work as an attorney and field investigator for the Veterans Administration. In May, 1934, he received a commission as captain in the Judge Advocate General's Department of the Army Reserve and was recalled to

active duty during World War II, serving chiefly as staff judge advocate at military bases in the United States. Promoted to lieutenant colonel in 1947, he also served on the legal staff of the occupation army in Europe and Africa. He retired as a lieutenant colonel on March 31, 1955, and died in 1969. The Matthews had no children.

5. Kate Greene, ''Torts over Tempo: The Life and Career of Judge Burnita Shelton Matthews,'' 56 *The Journal of Mississippi History* (August, 1994): 191–92.

6. See, for example, ''The Denial of Justice to Women—A Summary of Discriminations,'' in U.S. Senate, Committee on the Judiciary, 77th Congress, 1st session, Committee Print, ''Equal Rights'' (August 15, 1941).

7. U. S. Senate, Subcommittee of the Committee on the Judiciary, 75th Congress, 3rd session, ''Hearings on S.J. Res. 65'' (February 7, 8, 9, and 10, 1938).

8. *Washington Post* (November 11, 1949).

9. India Edwards, *Pulling No Punches: Memoirs of a Woman in Politics* (New York: G. P. Putnam's Sons, 1977), 185–86.

10. Ibid.

11. April 21, 1950, microfilm M–73, BSM papers.

12. October 10, 1952, microfilm M–73, BSM papers.

13. *U.S. v. Wise*, 370 U.S. 405 (1962).

14. 218 F. Supp. 302 (1963).

15. 502 F.2d 177 (1974).

16. 411 U.S. 677 (1973) at 687.

17. Burnita Shelton Matthews to Gerald Ford, November 19, 1975, folder 27, box 1, BSM papers.

18. De Long Harris to Burnita Shelton Matthews, November 14, 1958, folder 34, box 2, BSM papers.

19. De Long Harris to Burnita Shelton Matthews, February 7, 1968, microfilm M-73, BSM papers.

20. William B. Jones to Burnita Shelton Matthews, February 8, 1968, microfilm M-73, BSM papers.

21. 96 *The Daily Washington Law Reporter* (March 1, 1968): 379.

22. Biographical sketch of Burnita Shelton Matthews, Senior U.S. District Judge, U.S. District Court for the District of Columbia, folder 12, box 1, BSM papers.

23. *Harvard Law School Record* (October 11, 1950).

24. Chesterfield Smith to BSM, January 2, 1974, folder 24, box 1, BSM papers.

## REFERENCES

Edwards, India. *Pulling No Punches: Memoirs of a Woman in Politics*. New York: G.P. Putnam's Sons, 1977.

Greene, Kate. ''Torts Over Tempo: The Life and Career of Judge Burnita Shelton Matthews.'' *The Journal of Mississippi History* 56 (August, 1994): 181–210.

Greenhouse, Linda. ''Burnita Shelton Matthews Dies at 93.'' *New York Times* (April 28, 1988): D27.

''Matthews, Burnita Shelton.'' *Current Biography*. New York: H.W. Wilson, 1950, 385–87.

Matthews, Burnita Shelton. Interview with Alice O'Donnell. Federal Judicial Center, Washington, D. C. (January 10, 1985).

Matthews, Burnita Shelton. Papers of Burnita Shelton Matthews. Maintained at Schlesinger Library, Radcliffe College, Cambridge, Mass.

Smith, J. Y. "Burnita S. Matthews Dies." *Washington Post* (April 27, 1988): B6.

United States Senate, Committee on the Judiciary. "The Denial of Justice to Women—A Summary of Discriminations." Committee Print, "Equal Rights." 77th Congress, 1st session (August 15, 1941).

United States Senate, Subcommittee of the Committee on the Judiciary. "Hearings on S.J. Res. 65." 75th Congress, 3rd session (February 7, 8, 9, and 10, 1938).

*CYNTHIA HARRISON*

# BEVERLEY McLACHLIN (1943– )

The Honorable Madam Justice Beverley McLachlin, a former lawyer and academic and now Justice of the Supreme Court of Canada, has written some of the most significant judgments in Canadian law in areas such as equality rights, evidence, trusts, and damages for personal injuries. She has also had considerable impact through speaking and presenting papers across the country and internationally. Her influence stems from the strength of her judicial approach, which combines rigorous analysis and logic with open-mindedness and an understanding of the social context in which legal problems are embedded, and from her enormous productivity.

## FAMILY BACKGROUND AND EDUCATION

Beverley McLachlin was born in Pincher Creek, Alberta, in 1943 to Ernest and Eleanora Gietz. The family owned a ranch and lumbering operation. Beverley McLachlin and her siblings, Leonard, Conrad, Judi, and Ronald, grew up in a family in which self-reliance and hard work were expected. She lived close to a small town with a public library created by the efforts of volunteers in the community. An excellent student, and not particularly attracted to the conventional career options for women at the time (nursing, teaching, or secretarial work), Beverley McLachlin went to the University of Alberta where she earned a Bachelor of Arts (1965) and Master of Arts (1968) in philosophy, and her Bachelor of Laws in 1968. (In recent years, she has also received honorary doctorate of laws degrees from the University of British Columbia, the University of Alberta, and the University of Toronto.)

In 1964, Beverley McLachlin was selected for the World University Service Summer Seminar, which that year meant a study tour of Algeria. The experience brought her together with other students from across the country, some of whom have had comparable careers to her own (for example, Raymond Chrétien, Canada's ambassador to the United States). It exposed her to Third World poverty and to a very different religious, political, and cultural environment.

After obtaining her baccalaureate in philosophy, McLachlin wrote to the then-dean of the University of Alberta Law Faculty, Wilbur F. Bowker, and asked for some information about the Law Faculty and its process for admission. Despite the preliminary nature of her inquiry, she received back a letter informing her that she had been admitted. She decided to go to law school, and the study of the law proved to be well suited to her abilities and interests. She combined it with work toward her master's degree in philosophy, writing her thesis on "The Role of Rules in the Concept of Law." Between her second and third years at law school, she married Roderick (Rory) McLachlin, a biologist. After winning the Horace Harvey Gold Medal in Law, she took an articling position in Edmonton with the firm of Wood, Moir, Hyde and Ross, and was called to the bar of Alberta in 1969. She moved, in 1971, to the small and remote community of Fort St. John, British Columbia, with the firm of Thomas, Herdy, Mitchell & Co., to join her husband who was employed in that area.

## CAREER DEVELOPMENT

In 1972, Beverley and Rory McLachlin moved to Vancouver, where she took a position as a litigation associate with the firm of Bull, Housser and Tupper, working on some major litigation. In 1975, she was first appointed associate professor at the University of British Columbia Faculty of Law. Her major areas of teaching and research were evidence, civil litigation, and creditors remedies. In 1976, she gave birth to her son, Angus. A tenured professor by 1981, she was appointed to the County Court of Vancouver, and five months later, to the Supreme Court of British Columbia. In 1985, McLachlin was appointed to the Court of Appeal for the Province of British Columbia, and in September, 1988, she was named chief justice of the Supreme Court of British Columbia. Tragically, her husband Rory, who had been ill for some time, died just after that appointment.

Beverley McLachlin had little time to make an impact as chief justice of the Supreme Court of British Columbia (though she did lay some of the groundwork for the successful merger of the County and Supreme courts that was to come) because her elevation to the Supreme Court of Canada and move to Ottawa took place less than one year later, on March 30, 1989. (An often-quoted observation made by one of the speakers at her swearing-in in the Supreme Court of Canada was that she had "moved through the courts more rapidly than many lawsuits.") She became the third woman to sit on that court, following Justices Bertha Wilson* and Claire L'Heureux-Dubé.* When she was appointed, a photographer asked for a shot of the three women together, and they readily agreed. The photograph shows three female Supreme Court justices in the red robes with ermine trim, seemingly conscious of being, and delighted to be, in a place where no woman had gone before.

Madam Justice McLachlin serves on the Supreme Court to the present day. She has become one of the Court's most prolific and influential writers. In 1992, she married Frank McArdle, a lawyer and executive director of the Canadian Institute for Advanced Legal Studies (which organizes lecture programs in Cambridge, England and other international locations for a Canadian audience of judges and lawyers).

## ACHIEVEMENTS AND CONTRIBUTIONS

As both a lawyer and an academic, Beverley McLachlin was sometimes a "first woman" (the first woman to be chief justice of the Supreme Court of British Columbia, and the first woman full professor at the Law Faculty), and invariably an "early woman." She joined the law firms where she practiced, the faculty where she taught, and the courts where she sat at a time when there were few female predecessors. Her reputation as a lawyer was solid, and her mentor at the firm of Bull, Housser and Tupper, W. J. Wallace, Q.C. (later to serve on the Court of Appeal), was one of the senior and most distinguished litigators in the province. At the Law Faculty, McLachlin was a popular teacher, known for a sense of humor and for clarity of presentation, and she was a well-regarded scholar in the fields where she wrote (civil procedure, evidence, and damages for personal injuries).

Although the legal and academic phases of her career were more than merely preparatory for the judicial career that was to come, it is as a judge that Beverley McLachlin has made her most important contributions. In an article entitled "The Role of Judges in Modern Commonwealth Society," McLachlin sets out her understanding of the role of a judge:

> To perform their modern role well, judges must be sensitive to a broad range of social concerns. They must possess a keen appreciation of the importance of individual and group interests and rights. And they must be in touch with the society in which they work, understanding its values and tensions. The ivory tower no longer suffices as the residence of choice for judges. . . . It is impossible to eliminate the judge's personal views. But by a conscious act of considering the other side of the matter the judge can attain a level of detachment which enables him or her to make decisions which are in the broader interest of society. In the end, the judge can know no other master than the law, in its most objective sense.[1]

At the same time, McLachlin had written previously about the new expectations placed on judges as a result of the advent in 1981 of constitutional protection for rights and freedoms under the Canadian Charter of Rights and Freedoms:

> [J]udicial decision making under the Charter must be flexible and responsive. Our courts must be capable of addressing a plethora of social and moral problems which only a short decade ago were non-litigable. . . . In addressing the problems presented by the Charter, the courts must strive for objectivity; their decisions should reflect not their personal views so much as the collective views of society.[2]

Responsiveness to society and obedience to the law are not necessarily consistent objectives, and reconciling them in her decision making has been a conscious and not always easily achieved task for Madam Justice McLachlin. Her most salient intellectual characteristics are her rigorously logical and analytical mind, and her openness to new ideas and to the questioning of previous assumptions. She places a high value on maximizing the internal consistency and coherence of the law, but she seems to recognize the limits of logic. She knows it can dictate legal results inconsistent with ordinary judgment or common sense, and she has remained attentive to the ways that legal conclusions impact peoples' lives. Her experiences as a woman, in particular as a woman who lost a husband through a difficult illness and raised her son on her own for some time, have likely helped her to do this.

McLachlin is sometimes described as one of the "liberals" on the Court in the sense that she puts considerable emphasis on individual rights, on the importance of freedom of expression, and on holding the state to a high standard when it comes to the interests of accused persons in the criminal justice system. Clearly, she does proceed from a set of philosophical principles deriving from classic liberalism, particularly with respect to the "fundamental freedoms" (religion, expression, association, and assembly). Moving beyond classic liberalism, however, some of her judgments seem to carry on with the direction set by Madam Justice Bertha Wilson in *R. v. Morgentaler*,[3] working out the implications of affording full human rights to women as women (that is, avoiding the fallacy of taking the male biology and life experience as generically human). Furthermore, while she recognizes the importance of safeguarding the rights of accused persons, McLachlin has also written or concurred in judgments emphasizing the interests of the community and society as a whole.

As applied in the context of Charter litigation, McLachlin's judicial philosophy assumes a collaboration with Parliament in which the judiciary seeks truly to understand the policy objectives of legislation. Where the judge concludes there is violation of Charter rights, it is the obligation of the justice to indicate to Parliament, in the light of those policy objectives, ways in which the legislation could be made consistent with the Charter. In the context of common law principles, her judicial approach is to innovate where current societal norms require and fundamental legal principles permit. These approaches are exemplified in the two areas that are examined in detail here: equality jurisprudence and the law of damages for personal injuries.

"Equality" has taken on a significantly different meaning in Canada than it has in the United States, reflected in (and to some extent due to) the Supreme

Court of Canada's interpretation of the equality provisions (section 15) of the Canadian Charter of Rights and Freedoms.[4] Section 15 specifically contemplates taking positive steps to remedy inequality and emphasizes that the inequalities between people based on characteristics such as (but not limited to) race, sex, age, and disability are the kind requiring remedy. The Canadian approach to constitutional equality jurisprudence has room for substantive, outcome-based considerations as much as for formal, treatment-based ones. Not only in constitutional cases, but also in her extrajudicial writing and in some judgments in private law cases, Justice McLachlin has provided leadership in developing that approach. At the same time, she has on occasion resolved a conflict between the promotion of equality and the promotion of other Charter-protected values in favor of the other values.

In some extrajudicial writing, Justice McLachlin has shown a concern for inequality on a systemwide basis. A 1991 paper, ''Crime and Women—Feminine Equality and the Criminal Law,'' examined three areas where the criminal law could be seen to impact particularly on women, and she concluded that

> [I]n the past, and to some extent the present, our criminal law has failed to accord equality to women. It has often placed the burden of social problems on the backs of women through the so-called ''feminine'' crimes related to reproduction and sexuality. It has, at least until recently, failed to recognize the situation in which many women, such as battered women, find themselves, and the way that situation impacts on the traditional criminal law defences. And it has, through the misapplication of invalid stereotypes, often treated female offenders as less than fully responsible, and female victims with cruel insensitivity.[5]

With respect to the composition of the judiciary, she commented that

> [I]t is widely accepted that the court should be representative of a cross-section of Canadian society. This means that it should include women and people from varied social and ethnic backgrounds. It is no longer acceptable to have a bench composed entirely of aging white males.[6]

Justice McLachlin begins a 1991 paper with an anecdote that may shed some light on the personal perspective that underlies some of these concerns:

> One of my most poignant memories dates to a summer evening when, as a young university student, I found myself seated on a bus coming from some event or other beside a young woman of about my age from the Blood Indian Reserve, near Cardston, Alberta. Although we had been born within miles of each other in a sparsely populated part of the world, we had never met, and quite naturally fell to comparing cultural notes. At a certain point, as I touched on some aspect of my normal, happy childhood, my companion's face closed in an expression I can only recall as embittered hatred. ''I was taken away to residential school,'' she said.
>
> It was thus that I first became acquainted with the pain that can be inflicted by well-

meaning persons acting under the aegis of the state, interfering in the family and the relations between a child, her parents and her culture. At the time I did not perceive the incident as involving religion, but now I know that it did. The people who enforced the residential school policy used words like "education," "advancement," and "enlightenment" to justify their conduct. But the underlying goal was in large part the simple one of attempting to replace a native culture and religion with the established Christian religion of the majority.[7]

The equality jurisprudence itself provides a clear illustration not only of Justice McLachlin's understanding of equality issues, but also her general judicial philosophy and, indeed, her intellectual honesty. While on the British Columbia Court of Appeal, she wrote the decision that was appealed to the Supreme Court of Canada in the first test of the meaning of Section 15 of the Charter. In *Andrews v. Law Society of British Columbia,*[8] the issue was the constitutional validity of the requirement that members of the bar in British Columbia be Canadian citizens. Major unresolved issues were the extent to which Section 15 would be read as open to all kinds of equality claims, and the extent to which Section 1 of the Charter[9] would have a role in assessing the reasonableness of particular limitations on equality. The Supreme Court differed strongly from Justice McLachlin's Court of Appeal decision on those issues, although it did agree in the outcome—that the citizenship requirement was unconstitutional.

In the ensuing years, the question has been the extent to which the *Andrews* approach will be maintained. In three important Section 15 decisions handed down in May, 1995 (*Miron v. Trudel,*[10] *Egan v. Canada,*[11] and *Thibaudeau v. Canada*[12]), Justice McLachlin appears as the strongest defender of the Supreme Court of Canada's approach in *Andrews.* Writing for the narrow majority in *Miron v. Trudel,* where the issue was whether exclusion of unmarried partners from accident benefits available to married partners under the standard insurance policy prescribed by the provincial "Insurance Act" violated the equality provisions of the Charter, Justice McLachlin discussed what she saw as problematic in the approach of the minority in the case (and, implicitly, in her own earlier approach). "My colleague Gonthier asserts that discrimination under s. 15(1) is conclusively rebutted by a finding that the ground on which the equal treatment is denied is relevant to the legislative goal or the functional values underlying the impugned law. With respect, I cannot agree."[13]

She also referred in *Miron* to the concurrently released *Egan* case, which involved the denial of benefits under a statute to same-sex couples, where she dissented from the majority's conclusion that the denial was constitutional:

The danger of using relevance as a complete answer to the question of whether discrimination is made out, and thus losing sight of the values underlying s. 15(1), is acute when one is dealing with so-called "biological differences." . . . This is the lesson of *Bliss v. Attorney General of Canada* . . . and *Brooks v. Canada Safeway Ltd.* . . . Much as this court did in *Bliss*, La Forest J. [for the majority in *Egan*] relies on the biological differences between heterosexual and homosexual couples to find that the "Old Age

Security Act'' does not discriminate on the basis of sexual orientation. Following the lesson of *Brooks*, I would respectfully suggest that more is required; if we are not to undermine the promise of equality in s. 15(1) of the Charter, we must go beyond the biological differences and examine the impact of the impugned distinction in its social and economic context to determine whether it, in fact, perpetuates the undesirable stereotyping which s.15(1) aims to eradicate.[14]

The third case, *Thibaudeau*,[15] was about the tax regime governing child maintenance payments—they are taxable in the hands of the recipient parent and deductible from the income of the paying parent. Justices McLachlin and Claire L'Heureux-Dubé, the two women members of the Court, dissented as they had in an earlier case, which also involved the impact of neutrally drafted provisions of the Income Tax Act on taxpayers (mainly women) with responsibility for children.[16] Justice McLachlin concluded that the benefits of this scheme to custodial parents were somewhat illusory and that, ''The actual situation of thousands of custodial parents in Canada belies the contention that the family law regime corrects the inequality created by the deduction/inclusion scheme within the couple.''[17]

In cases not involving Charter equality claims, McLachlin has written reasons clearly flowing from a concern for equality. In both *Norberg v. Wynrib*[18] and *Peter v. Beblow*,[19] an expansion of traditional equitable principles permitted her to rectify inequalities. *Norberg* concerned a young woman who sought assistance from a physician for her addiction to prescription painkillers; rather than treating the addiction, he exploited it by providing her with more drugs in return for sex. Although all levels of court below failed to grant her a remedy, either for sexual assault, negligence, breach of contract, or breach of fiduciary duty, she succeeded in the Supreme Court of Canada. Two of the judges (McLachlin and L'Heureux-Dubé) found for her on the basis of a breach of fiduciary duty on the part of the physician. In *Peter v. Beblow*, a woman who was in a spousal relationship with a man, but not married to him, claimed a share in the property he had acquired during the 12 years they had cohabited and she had performed the domestic work involved in raising their blended families. Writing for the majority of the Court, McLachlin said:

I share the view . . . that ''there is no logical reason to distinguish domestic services from other contributions.'' The notion that household and childcare services are not worthy of recognition by the court fails to recognize the fact that these services are of great value, not only to the family, but to the other spouse. . . . The notion, moreover, is a pernicious one that systematically devalues the contributions which women tend to make to the family economy. It has contributed to the phenomenon of the feminization of poverty which this Court identified in *Moge v. Moge*.[20]

In *R. v. Khan*,[21] McLachlin's concern for the vulnerability of children to sexual abuse, along with a desire to establish a unifying underlying principle for the rule against hearsay, led to a dramatic shift in some of the traditional rules of evidence. Chief Justice Lamer later described *Khan* as "a triumph of principled analysis over a set of ossified, judicially created categories."[22] The "principled approach" of Madam Justice McLachlin in *Khan* has also been the basis for a change by the Supreme Court to the common law rule about prior inconsistent statements.[23]

As for the instances involving competing principles in which McLachlin does not give primacy to equality, the freedom of expression cases (*R. v. Keegstra*,[24] *R. v. Butler*,[25] and *R. v. Zundel*[26]) are significant. The majority in the first two cases upheld legislation restricting freedom of expression (where the expression amounted to hate propaganda or obscenity, respectively) in part because of the legislation's impact in promoting equality for religious and racial minorities and women. Justice McLachlin, dissenting with others, would have struck down the legislation. For the majority in the third case, *Zundel*, she wrote the decision striking down legislation that restricted freedom of expression by prohibiting "spreading false news," used to charge the publisher of Holocaust denial literature. Another clear example is *R. v. Seaboyer*,[27] in which McLachlin wrote for the majority, striking down the "Criminal Code" sections protecting complainants in sexual assault cases from cross-examination on previous sexual conduct, on the basis that it violated the constitutional rights to a fair trial of accused persons. Illustrating her attempt at a collaborative approach, she wrote detailed guidelines into the judgment that provided the basis for subsequent legislation replacing that which was struck down.

In 1981, then-Professor Beverley McLachlin commented in an article in the *Canadian Bar Review* that"[f]ew deficiencies in the law have been more remarked upon in recent years than the absence of coherent principle in the law on damages for personal injuries."[28] In that piece, and in her subsequent judicial writings, she has been a strong advocate for what is called the "functional compensation" approach, which seeks to assess damages on the basis of how the award can actually restore, as well as possible, the injured plaintiff to his or her pretrial position. This approach takes into account the plaintiff's actual condition and the use to which the money can be put. It requires the plaintiff to demonstrate "a reasonable or fair function which the money claimed will serve."[29] In a pure form, it leads to the conclusion that an insentient plaintiff, as long as his or her needs and those of dependents are being met, is not entitled to further damages, for example, for lost future income. In the 1981 Supreme Court of Canada case of *Lindal v. Lindal*,[30] Justice Dickson quoted from the McLachlin article and affirmed the functional approach to damages for nonpecuniary loss, which had previously been applied in the 1978 trilogy of *Andrews*,[31] *Teno*,[32] and *Thornton*.[33] The most controversial aspect of the "trilogy" was its imposition of a "rough upper limit" or ceiling on awards for nonpecuniary damages of $100,000 in 1978 dollars.[34] Although McLachlin's article suggested that the functional approach to damages would be "arguably capable of providing a comprehensive rationale for damages for personal injuries generally"[35]—that is, not only with respect to nonpecuniary loss but in all aspects of assessment of damages—the courts have not uniformly taken up that suggestion.

This is illustrated by one of Justice McLachlin's own early decisions on the Supreme Court of Canada. *Watkins v. Olafson*[36] (a unanimous decision) considered an issue that was directly addressed in her 1981 article: whether periodic payments could be substituted for a lump-sum judgment. McLachlin had advocated in her 1981 article that periodic payments would be "more in accord with the fundamental principles underlying the law on damages than is the lump-sum system presently in force."[37] However, sitting on the Court in 1989, she concluded that "the well established limits on judicial law making powers as well as the complexities associated with the introduction of the concept of periodic payments into our law, preclude the court from ordering periodic . . . payments."[38] In *Ratych v. Bloomer*,[39] issues of double compensation and collateral benefits came up for decision. A police officer was injured while on duty due to the negligence of the defendant. He was unable to work for some months, but continued to be paid pursuant to the terms of his collective agreement, without losing any "sick credits." In this case, Justice McLachlin took the same view of the functional approach as she had in her article, writing that "The trend away from a moralistic view of tort suggests that the process of assessing damages should focus not on how the tortfeasor may be appropriately punished, but rather on what the injured person requires to restore him to his pre-accident state."[40] Thus, writing for a 5–4 majority, she concluded that the plaintiff should only be compensated for real losses and that he had suffered none with respect to his inability to work. However, the principle established has been significantly eroded by subsequent cases, such as *Cunningham v. Wheeler*[41] (where Madam Justice McLachlin dissented), which held that payments received for loss of wages pursuant to a private insurance policy should not be deducted from the lost wage claim of a plaintiff.

Despite these negative examples, in many areas Justice McLachlin has been able to persuade the majority of her view. In *Watkins*, it was the necessity of giving allowance for the effect of taxation in calculating the cost of future care.[42] In *Toneguzzo-Norvell v. Burnaby Hospital*,[43] it was the deduction for living expenses during the "lost years."[44]

These cases illustrate not only a particular perspective on the law of damages, but also an approach to judging: an attempt to achieve logical consistency by finding an underlying principle, a respect for the limits of the judicial role, a quest for fairness for both sides of the dispute, and an ability to take the long view (in other words, persistence) while acknowledging a change of mind where appropriate.

Having assisted in laying some of the foundations for Charter interpretation, in rethinking the rule against hearsay, in rationalizing some of the principles for awarding damages for personal injury, and in recognizing in law the inequalities affecting women and children in society, Madam Justice McLachlin has already established a strong place in Canadian juridical history. Still relatively young to be sitting on the senior Canadian court, she seems likely to become a predominant figure in this judicial era.

**ACKNOWLEDGMENT**

The contribution of Jennifer Fell, in third-year law at the University of British Columbia, to the researching and drafting of this profile is gratefully acknowledged.

**NOTES**

1. Beverley McLachlin, "The Role of Judges in Modern Commonwealth Society," 110 *Law Quarterly Review* (1994): 260 at 266.

2. Beverley McLachlin, "The Charter: A New Role for the Judiciary?" 29 *Alberta Law Review* (1991): 540 at 548.

3. [1988] 1 S.C.R. 30. In the *Morgentaler* case, the Supreme Court struck down the "Criminal Code" provisions on abortion. Justice Wilson approached the case as one involving liberty for women, expanding on the traditional meaning of that concept.

4. Section 15 reads:

**Equality before and under the law and equal protection and benefit of law**
15.(1) Every individual is equal before and under the law and has the right to the equal protection and equal benefit of the law without discrimination and, in particular, without discrimination based on race, national or ethnic origin, colour, religion, sex, age or mental or physical disability.
**Affirmative action programs**
(2) Subsection (1) does not preclude any law, program or activity that has as its object the amelioration of conditions of disadvantaged individuals or groups including those that are disadvantaged because of race, national or ethnic origin, colour, religion, sex, age or mental or physical disability.

5. Beverley McLachlin, "Crime and Women—Feminine Equality and the Criminal Law," 25 *University of British Columbia Law Review* (1991): 1 at 22. Although the statements made were well-supported, a group called "R.E.A.L. Women" complained about them to the Canadian Judicial Council as promoting "radical feminism," a complaint that was dismissed without a hearing.

6. McLachlin, "The Role of Judges," 267.

7. Beverley McLachlin, "Who Owns Our Kids? Education, Health and Religion in a Multicultural Society," *Cambridge Lectures 1991* (Montreal: Editions Y Blais, 1991), 147.

8. [1989] 1 S.C.R. 143.

9. Section 1 reads:

**Rights and freedoms in Canada**
1. The *Canadian Charter of Rights and Freedoms* guarantees the rights and freedoms set out in it subject only to such reasonable limits prescribed by law as can be demonstrably justified in a free and democratic society.

As may be seen, it explicitly permits limits on rights and freedoms in the interests of the community as a whole, beyond those that may be implicit in the definitions of the rights.

10. [1995] 124 DLR (4th) 693.
11. [1995] 124 DLR (4th) 609.
12. [1995] 124 DLR (4th) 449.
13. [1995] 124 DLR (4th) 693 at 741.
14. Ibid. at 743.
15. (25 May 1995) No. 24154 (S.C.C.) [unreported].
16. *Symes v. Canada*, [1993] 4 S.C.R. 695.
17. [1995] 124 DLR (4th) 449 at 515.
18. [1992] 2 S.C.R. 226.
19. [1993] 1 S.C.R. 980.
20. Ibid., 993.
21. [1990] 2 S.C.R. 532.
22. *R. v. Smith*, [1992] 2 S.C.R. 915 at 930.
23. *R. v. B(K.G.)*, [1993] 1 S.C.R. 740.
24. [1990] 2 S.C.R. 697.
25. [1992] 1 S.C.R. 452.
26. [1992] 2 S.C.R. 731.
27. [1991] 2 S.C.R. 577.
28. Beverley McLachlin, ''What Price Disability? A Perspective on the Law of Damages for Personal Injury,'' 59 *Canadian Bar Review* (1981): 1.
29. Ibid., 11.
30. [1981] 2 S.C.R. 629.
31. *Andrews v. Grand & Toy Alberta*, [1978] 2 S.C.R. 229.
32. *Arnold v. Teno*, [1978] 2 S.C.R. 287.
33. *Thornton v. School District 57 (Prince George)*, [1978] 2 S.C.R. 267.
34. An approach that may or not itself be consistent with the functional analysis, as pointed out by Justice Esson in his dissent in *Knutson v. Farr* [1984] 5 W.W.R. 315 at 336.
35. McLachlin, ''What Price Disability,'' 9.
36. [1989] 2 S.C.R. 750.
37. McLachlin, ''What Price Disability,'' 17.
38. [1989] 2 S.C.R. 750 at 764.
39. [1990] 1 S.C.R. 940.
40. Ibid., 963.
41. [1994] 1 S.C.R. 359.
42. With lump-sum awards, which under Canadian law are considered taxable income, the taxes reduce the size of the award available to meet the plaintiff's needs. The Supreme Court of Canada in the trilogy of cases declined to ''gross up'' awards in order to take into account the impact of future taxation, but in the 1981 article, when discussing this issue, McLachlin stated that this was ''inconsistent . . . with the basic principles of functional and full compensation which it claims to support'' (McLachlin, ''What Price Disability,'' 29). Writing for the unanimous court in *Watkins*, Justice McLachlin concluded that the trilogy cases did not preclude the taking into account of taxation, and that it should be done where supported by the evidence.
43. [1994] 1 S.C.R. 114.
44. In this case, a child was severely injured at birth, resulting in a substantially lowered life expectancy. Given that there would be an award for loss of earning capacity for the years the plaintiff would actually live, as well as the years she would have lived

but for the injury, the question arose as to whether a deduction should be made for personal living expenses during those "lost years." For a unanimous Court, Justice McLachlin reasoned that the deduction should be made; otherwise there would be an element of duplication and overcompensation of the plaintiff.

## REFERENCES

McLachlin, Beverley. "The Role of Judges in Modern Commonwealth Society." *Law Quarterly Review* 110 (1994): 260–69.

McLachlin, Beverley. "The Charter: A New Role for the Judiciary?" *Alberta Law Review* 29 (1991): 540–59.

McLachlin, Beverley. "Crime and Women—Feminine Equality and the Criminal Law." *University of British Columbia Law Review* 25 (1991): 1–22.

McLachlin, Beverley. "Who Owns Our Kids? Education, Health and Religion in a Multicultural Society." *Cambridge Lectures 1991*. Montreal: Editions Y Blais, 1991.

McLachlin, Beverley. "What Price Disability? A Perspective on the Law of Damages for Personal Injury." *Canadian Bar Review* 59 (1981): 1–51.

*C. LYNN SMITH*

# SOIA MENTSCHIKOFF (1915–1984)

Soia Mentschikoff's career marked the beginning of the breakdown of the formidable barriers that had excluded women from the legal profession in the twentieth century. She was a lawyer, a law professor, a law school dean, and a principal drafter of the most important legal code in American law, the Uniform Commercial Code. Her genius as an advocate, her political acumen, and her powerful and charming personality took her where no woman had been before.

Mentschikoff was the first woman partner in a Wall Street law firm, Spence, Hotchkiss, Parker and Duryee; she was the first woman professor at the University of Chicago and Harvard Law schools and the first woman dean of an accredited law school, the University of Miami; she was the first woman president of the American Association of Law Schools; and finally, Attorney General Nicholas Katzenbach recommended her to President Lyndon B. Johnson for appointment to the United States Supreme Court. Mentschikoff combined this remarkable life in the law with a devotion to her parents and brother, to her husband, Karl Nickerson Llewellyn, a leading Legal Realist, and to her nieces, whom she raised from the ages of nine and seven.

## FAMILY BACKGROUND AND EDUCATION

Soia Mentschikoff was born in Moscow in 1915. Her father, Roman Mentschikoff, who reputedly was the son of Prince Sergei Mentschikoff, had lived in the United States and was an American citizen. Her mother, Eugenia Ossipov Mentschikoff, came from an important White Russian aristocratic family. Eugenia was a devout Russian Orthodox, and Soia was a practicing believer all her life. In 1917, the Mentschikoffs fled the Russian Revolution and returned to New York City's Upper West Side. Her father found work as a typewriter salesman for Eagle Pencil Company, and her mother did fine sewing at home.

Mentschikoff attended New York public schools and Hunter College, an academically demanding, free public college for women. Hunter had an ethnically diverse student body, most of whom lived in New York City and commuted from home. Mentschikoff was president of her sophomore and junior classes, and in her senior year, she was head of the entire student body. She won the Constitutional Law Prize at graduation in 1934.

Mentschikoff went on directly to Columbia Law School, which had admitted its first women law students seven years earlier. She was one of 18 women in the entering class of 254 students. Throughout law school Mentschikoff worked as a research assistant to her contracts professor and future husband, Karl Nickerson Llewellyn, the well-known teacher and scholar of sales law and the leading Legal Realist of the time. In his great commercial law articles of this period, Llewellyn acknowledged his debt to Mentschikoff and her fellow research assistant, Henry Harfield, often footnoting their disagreements with him on specific points. In one footnote, Llewellyn thanked Mentschikoff for her ''sustained and shrewd critique which has improved the paper more than I altogether enjoy recognizing,'' a most unusual acknowledgment of a research assistant by a law professor.[1]

## CAREER DEVELOPMENT

After graduation from Columbia in 1937, Mentschikoff sought work as a litigator, although for a woman to be a trial lawyer at that time was a rarity. Nevertheless, she found a small law firm, Scandrett, Tuttle and Chalaire, in New York City that was willing to let her do litigation, where Mentschikoff specialized in labor law. She was the only woman attorney during her four years at the firm.

In 1941, Mentschikoff became general counsel to a woman in the business of manufacturing mannequins. Mentschikoff successfully defended the business against charges of violating wartime labor regulations on the grounds that the entrepreneur was going through menopause at the time. This was almost surely the first time in American law that a lawyer argued that a woman's biology had psychological consequences relevant to a legal judgment of her actions. The woman's business was dissolved not long after Mentschikoff joined it, owing to a shortage of necessary materials needed for the war.

Mentschikoff then joined the Wall Street firm of Spence, Hotchkiss, Parker, and Duryee, as an associate. At the time, this corporate law firm was considered ''huge'' with 17 male partners and 10 to 15 associates, including one other woman. During the war years, some women were hired by New York law firms to replace the young men who went off to war. But in 1945 most of these women were sent home to make room for the men who had now returned. Mentschikoff, however, was promoted to partner and was the first woman partner at any Wall Street firm. Although she practiced law for only the first decade of her career, throughout her life Mentschikoff described herself as a lawyer.

Mentschikoff subsequently joined the faculty of Harvard Law School as a visiting professor and began her career as an academic. Later, she moved to Chicago and was appointed professorial lecturer at the University of Chicago Law School, where she remained for two decades. But, in 1967, five years after the death of her husband, Mentschikoff began a series of visiting assignments at the University of Miami in Florida. In 1974, she was named dean of that law school, and she remained there until 1982.

## ACHIEVEMENTS AND CONTRIBUTIONS

In 1943, Mentschikoff signed on to the successful 25-year campaign to create a code of laws governing commercial transactions. She became deeply involved in the drafting process, and in the subsequent efforts to secure the approval of the legal and business communities and to gain acceptance of the new Uniform Commercial Code by all the state legislatures. By 1967, the Code was adopted by every state except Louisiana, making the laws on sales and financing of personal property, commercial paper, bank deposits and collections, letters of credit, documents of title, and investment securities virtually uniform throughout the country.

This project was launched in 1940 by Karl Llewellyn and William Schnader, the President of the National Conference on Uniform State Laws. Six years out of law school, when she was 27 years old, Mentschikoff became Llewellyn's chief lieutenant in this campaign. This monumental enterprise would probably not have been possible without their complementary talents and their extraordinary partnership. The traditional announcement by Mentschikoff's parents of the marriage of their daughter to Mr. Karl N. Llewellyn on October 31, 1946, was accompanied by a small formal card:

*S.M.*
*and*
*K.N.L.*
*want you to know*
*that they have become partners in life*
*as in law.*

Mentschikoff's partnership with Llewellyn ended with his sudden death in 1962. Her association with the Uniform Commercial Code enterprise continued throughout her lifetime.

Mentschikoff's first sustained work on the Code project was during a four-month leave from Spence, Hotchkiss in 1943. She negotiated the leave at Llewellyn's request in order to work on the Uniform Revised Sales Act as the assistant reporter.[2] This version of the Act was based on Llewellyn's drafts written in 1940 and was revised the following year.[3] At this point, responsibility for drafting broadened considerably. Llewellyn and Mentschikoff met with the advisory committee for four or five days each month, reviewing the drafts they had prepared and then revising the Code to deal with the comments of committee members.

Mentschikoff described her contribution to the drafting process as that of an innocent, a nonexpert. If she could understand it, she said, anyone could; if she could set it up in a pattern, it would be intelligible to nonexperts. Knowledge of the law can be a great hindrance when one's approach is what can one do that is sensible rather than how does one change the existing law. Llewellyn wrote that "the cure [for confusion] came when [his] ideas got to be worked over by a non-expert [Mentschikoff] . . . ; reorganized and worked through along lines inherently required but blocked off by conventional training from ever being seen."[4] His characterizations point to Mentschikoff's skill in cutting through abstractions and focusing on the underlying transaction. Her questions emphasized reality and what the parties wanted to get out of it. Her focus was on the craft of the law and how to make things happen that needed to get done.

In 1944, the drafting of the proposed Uniform Commercial Code became a well-funded and official joint project of the National Conference of Commissioners on Uniform State Laws and the American Law Institute. Llewellyn was appointed the chief reporter.[5] He hired Mentschikoff as the associate chief reporter and appointed associate and assistant reporters for each article of the Code. These reporters drafted their assigned Code Articles and then met with Mentschikoff and Llewellyn every few weeks. While Mentschikoff and Llewellyn retained overall editorial responsibility and control, the drafting team was greatly enlarged. Because Mentschikoff was not the reporter for any particular article, it is hard to identify her hand specifically in particular Code provisions.

Forty years later, Mentschikoff spoke of the time when she worked on the Code and her admiration of the eminent old men who were sitting around working "like dogs"[6] on these drafts to prepare them for presentation to the annual meeting of the National Conference. Did Mentschikoff bring to the Code ideas that were distinctly her own? While she was committed to the notion of writing consumer protection into the Code, she did not succeed in doing so. For example, Mentschikoff favored including provisions obligating lenders and sellers to make full disclosure in consumer transactions. Her colleagues countered that the Code would get bogged down in a fight between finance companies and consumers, and would not be enacted. That position ultimately won the day.

The institutions involved in the codification process were quite conservative, and there was considerable concern among the members of the American Law Institute about the radical ideas of the chief reporter whom they viewed as wild-eyed, at best. In fact, Llewellyn was not always easy to deal with, nor was he receptive of criticism. A letter between the two participants, now in the Llewellyn archive, suggested that if there was any difficulty with Mr. Llewellyn, it was advisable to see Miss Mentschikoff about the matter as she was always reasonable.[7] Mentschikoff played this traditional woman's role of facilitator in relation to Llewellyn in many other situations as well.

Mentschikoff also played a key role in the campaign for passage of the Code state by state. The biggest battle was in the New York Law Revision Commission, which held lengthy hearings and heard extensive testimony from many whose interests would be affected by the proposed legislation. Mentschikoff, along with other key drafters, testified before the Commission on the meaning and import of the new laws. She used her enormous skills as an advocate to try to persuade the commissioners that the Code's proposed changes to New York law were significant improvements. The Commission hearings and a study of the Code's proposed changes to New York law resulted in the redrafting of many of the Code's provisions.

While Mentschikoff would continue to work on the Uniform Commercial Code throughout her life, a career change was imminent. Before the fall term of 1947, Dean Erwin Griswold of Harvard Law School called on Soia Mentschikoff at her office in New York and offered her a visiting professorship at Harvard Law School. At that time, women students were still not admitted to Harvard Law School, and there were no women professors. While other elite law schools had some women students, there were only a handful of women law professors in the country. Mentschikoff accepted the offer and spent two years in Cambridge, Massachusetts. Llewellyn joined her as a visiting professor the following year.

Mentschikoff was an enormously successful teacher of commercial law at Harvard. In addition to a seminar on Commercial Arbitration, she taught large classes that included many World War II veterans. As the sole woman professor at Harvard Law, however, life was not always easy. For example, on the first day of class in the fall of 1948, Professor Mentschikoff found poems left on the podium in the style of various poets, including an Ogden Nash-like rhyme, "A woman Professor—I'd rather caress 'er," and also one that ended, "But why—why learn sales from a dame—Ain't we enough in the dark?" She read them to herself and after a long silence began class without comment. In response to a question later as to why she had not read them aloud, Mentschikoff explained that she had thought, "Would Austin Scott have read such verses? Would Roscoe Pound? And so I didn't read them."

A love affair between Mentschikoff and the class of 1949 developed quickly. They formed a new moot court club. Instead of naming it after preeminent attorneys like Holmes, Williston, or Griswold, as was the custom, they called it the "Soia Mentschikoff" club and won their way to the final round. Forty years later, many students recalled her confidence in them, and her continued advice and support in their professional and personal lives. Many credit her with teaching them how one apt phrase or word could clarify an issue or protect a client or a nation from catastrophe, and how a sense of timing and balance could be crucial to a successful negotiation.

At the end of her two-year visit, Griswold invited Mentschikoff to join the permanent faculty. He made no similar offer to Llewellyn whose problems with alcohol had plagued his year in Cambridge. Griswold, who described himself as a committed teetotaler, characterized Llewellyn's teaching as an unmitigated disaster. Mentschikoff refused the offer and Griswold believed that she was angry at him for this slight to her husband for the rest of her life.

After the Harvard visit and their return to New York, Llewellyn tried unsuccessfully to get Mentschikoff an appointment to the Columbia University faculty. But in 1951, Dean Edward Levi of the University of Chicago received authorization to make a few new appointments of outstanding law professors to that institution's law faculty. The overwhelming first choice of the faculty was Karl Llewellyn. When inquiring about Llewellyn, Levi learned of the existence of Mrs. Llewellyn for the first time. His informants were extremely enthusiastic about Mentschikoff and assured him that she would be a great asset to the faculty. Dean Levi invited Llewellyn and Mentschikoff to come to the University of Chicago Law School, but he was unable to offer Mentschikoff a professorship because of Chicago's anti-nepotism rule. Instead, Mentschikoff was given the title of professorial lecturer with all of the privileges and status of a professor except tenure. Mentschikoff recalled that she left the decision entirely up to Llewellyn, although at the time she thought Chicago was little more than stockyards. They accepted.

While not a regular member of the faculty at the University of Chicago, Mentschikoff was still treated as a full, tenured faculty member. She expressed no resentment publicly about this arrangement. Professor Mentschikoff was a firm believer in the individualistic meritocratic principle—if you're first rate, you'll make it—despite contrary evidence that Mentschikoff clearly witnessed with respect to talented women. However, tenure, in her view, was irrelevant. In her first decade at Chicago, Mentschikoff was a member of a small committee that issued a strongly critical report on the status of women at the university but interestingly, that report made no mention of the anti-nepotism rule.

Mentschikoff was an active participant in the institutional life of the law school. She was a key adviser to Dean Levi in law school matters, as well as a neighbor and close friend of both the dean and his wife, Kate. Mentschikoff taught Commercial Law and Elements of Law, a famous first-year jurisprudence course created by Levi. She also taught courses on law in the undergraduate school. Her students at Chicago spoke less of her magic in the classroom and more of her being a great teacher in discussions outside the classroom and by example. She gave both the men and women students counsel and support in their personal lives as well as in their search for careers. Many of these relationships continued long after graduation.

Interestingly, Mentschikoff gave an annual talk to the Law Wives Association, counseling them that their job as wives of law students, as it would be as wives of lawyers, was to support their husbands in every way. Their husbands needed to devote all of their time to succeeding in their legal studies, and a wife's job was to make that possible. Many of her women students saw a clear contradiction between this advice and Mentschikoff's own life, but she never seemed to recognize the contradiction.

Mentschikoff began a study of commercial arbitration, one of the empirical studies funded by the Ford Foundation at the Law School. In true Legal Realist tradition, she brought in Ernest Haggard, a social psychologist, to examine and report on the social and psychological context of this alternative method for resolving commercial disputes. Mentschikoff published two articles based on this study, but no final volume ever appeared.

Mentschikoff and Llewellyn bought a big house near the law school and established a warm, busy, and lively household. Mentschikoff's parents lived in their own apartment on the third floor. In the mid-1950s, Mentschikoff's two young nieces, Alexandra (Sandy) and Jeanne, joined the family. Young faculty often stayed with them, either when they first arrived in Chicago or when they were between moves. Colleagues from the Uniform Commercial Code project who had now become distinguished judges and leading lawyers would also visit. It was not uncommon to see one of these gentlemen in the neighborhood walking Mentschikoff's dog or cleaning the snow off her car in the early morning after a storm. At least one night a week, students, friends, and colleagues were invited to drop in for conversation. These were essentially Llewellyn's evenings where he was center stage in discussions that were often directly or indirectly about the nature of law. While Mentschikoff joined in, she was primarily a warm and welcoming hostess.

In 1962, Karl Llewellyn died very suddenly. They had been married for 16 years and Mentschikoff was devastated by his death. She sold their house, but stayed at the law school in Chicago for another 12 years. During those years she became active in a number of public organizations, serving as a member of the United States delegation to the Hague Conference, the Commission on the Rights, Liberties, and Responsibilities of American Indians, the panel of arbitrators of the International Center for the Settlement of Investment Disputes, and the executive committee of the Council for the Study of Mankind.

In 1967, Mentschikoff accepted a one-semester appointment as distinguished visiting professor at the University of Miami Law School during the winter quarter. She would return to Miami for the following seven winters in the same capacity. Mentschikoff loved Miami's informality and was well known for wearing sneakers and sweatsuits to school both before and after she became dean. Long solitary walks on the beach were one of her greatest joys.

In 1974, Mentschikoff accepted the deanship of the University of Miami Law School after a round of hard bargaining in which she won unique independence for the law school with respect to the control of its budget, fund raising, and other matters. In her eight-year tenure as dean, she made an indelible mark on that institution. Mentschikoff brought a group of outstanding, dedicated young faculty with her, she instituted a tutorial program and made important additions to the curriculum, she oversaw the construction of a new law school, and she attracted outstanding students. As a result, she gained national recognition for the University of Miami as a first-rate law school. The faculty characterized her alternately as ''Czarina'' and ''Earth Mother,'' reflecting two important aspects of her personality that made this accomplishment possible.

Mentschikoff retired in 1982. In the good periods of her very last days, she finished dictating an expert affidavit on the significance of ''good faith'' in the Uniform Commercial Code. She died of cancer on June 18, 1984.

## NOTES

1. Karl N. Llewellyn, ''Through Title to Contract and a Bit Beyond,'' 15 *New York University Law Quarterly Review* (1938): 159, n.1.
2. Soia Mentschikoff, ''Reflections of a Drafter,'' in Symposium entitled ''Origins and Evolution: Drafters Reflect upon the Uniform Commercial Code,'' 43 *Ohio State Law Journal* (1982): 535, 537.
3. Zipporah Batshaw Wiseman, ''The Limits of Vision: Karl Llewellyn and the Merchant Rules,'' 100 *Harvard Law Review* (1987): 465, 486.
4. ''Staff Production Report on the Uniform Commercial Code'' 2 (1952).
5. Wiseman, 490.
6. Mentschikoff, 540.
7. Karl Llewellyn Papers, J. xxv7. University of Chicago.

## REFERENCES

Llewellyn, Karl N. ''Through Title to Contract and a Bit Beyond.'' *New York University Law Quarterly Review* 15 (1938): 159–217.

Mentschikoff, Soia. ''Llewellyn the Civilian.'' *Tulane Law Review* 56 (1982): 1125–70.

Mentschikoff, Soia. ''Reflections of a Drafter.'' In Symposium entitled ''Origins and Evolution: Drafters Reflect upon the Uniform Commercial Code.'' *Ohio State Law Journal* 43 (1982): 535–44.

Mentschikoff, Soia. ''Peaceful Repossession Under the Uniform Commercial Code: A Constitutional and Economic Analysis.'' *William and Mary Law Review* 14 (1973): 767.

Mentschikoff, Soia. *Commercial Transactions: Cases and Materials*. Boston: Little, Brown, 1970.

Mentschikoff, Soia. ''Highlights of the Uniform Commercial Code.'' *Modern Law Review* 27 (1964): 167–89.

Mentschikoff, Soia. ''Commercial Arbitration.'' *Columbia Law Review* 61 (1961): 761, 846–69.

Mentschikoff, Soia. ''Letters of Credit: The Need for Uniform Legislation.'' *University of Chicago Law Review* 23 (1956): 571–619.

Mentschikoff, Soia. ''The Significance of Arbitration—A Preliminary Inquiry.'' *Law and Contemporary Problems* 17 (1952): 698–710.

Mentschikoff, Soia, Ernst von Cammerer, and Konrad Zweigert, eds. *Ius Privatum Gentium* (*Festschrift fur Max Rheinstein*). Siebeck: Tubingen, Mohr, 1969.

Mentschikoff, Soia, and Nicholas DeB. Katzenbach. *Unification of International Private*

*Law*. Report of the American Bar Association Special Committee. Chicago: American Bar Foundation, 1961.
Mentschikoff, Soia, and Irwin P. Stotzky. ''Law—the Last of the Universal Disciplines.'' *University of Cincinnati Law Review* 54 (1986): 695–744.
Mentschikoff, Soia, and Irwin P. Stotzky. *The Theory and Craft of American Law—Elements*. New York: M. Bender, 1981.
''Staff Production Report on the Uniform Commercial Code'' 2 (1952).
Wiseman, Zipporah Batshaw. ''The Limits of Vision: Karl Llewellyn and the Merchant Rules.'' *Harvard Law Review* 100 (1987): 465, 486–545.

*ZIPPORAH BATSHAW WISEMAN*

# CONSTANCE BAKER MOTLEY (1921– )

While on a mission in Mississippi during the 1960s, Constance Baker Motley received a warning: "Put those papers inside the *Times*," her client told her, "We are being followed [by the state police]. We don't want them to know who you are." "There we were, frightened to death, driving to Meridian," Motley said about that trip with James Meredith. "This occurred going through a wooded area. The state police just followed us all the way. They knew it was [Medgar Evers'] car, because they had been following him for years."[1]

It was in Mississippi that Medgar Evers was hated, hounded, and within a year, killed.[2] But it was not only in Mississippi that Motley, then with the National Association for the Advancement of Colored People (NAACP), Legal Defense and Educational Fund, Inc. (the Inc. Fund), was endangered. During a trial in Alabama, she stayed in Arthur Shores's home in Birmingham and remembered that the lawyer's home had been bombed about 15 times. "At night we were guarded by African-American men with machine guns, and during the day others carrying handguns escorted us to and from court."[3]

Standing in harm's way, Motley stood somewhere else as well. In her view, blacks stand on the shoulders of each paladin who has stood up for them.[4] Where they stand, there, too, stand nonblacks, regardless of gender or other identification. To all of this, Motley's life and work attest.

## FAMILY BACKGROUND AND EDUCATION

Constance Baker was born in New Haven, Connecticut, on September 14, 1921, one of twelve children born to Willoughby Alva Baker and Rachel Huggins Baker, only six of whom survived infancy.[5] Her father was a cook working in hotels, restaurants, and for a Yale University fraternity. Her parents, who had emigrated from Nevis, British West Indies, expected Constance to become a hairdresser. While in the eighth grade, she had thought of becoming an interior decorator but changed her mind before graduating from high school in 1939. Not that it mattered; she had not yet met Clarence Blakeslee.[6]

Blakeslee, a white businessman, entered Baker's life in the fall of 1940, when he called a public meeting to determine why blacks in New Haven were making little use of the community center he had built for them. What black community leaders would not tell him, Constance Baker did: blacks would take greater interest in the center if they were members of its board of directors. Perhaps the leaders were not surprised by her audacity in raising the issue. A civil rights activist at age 15, she had been secretary of the New Haven Adult Council as well as president of the New Haven Youth Council. In any event, these guiding lights, preferring to let sleeping dogs lie, were annoyed by her candor. But she impressed Blakeslee, who asked the center's director to have her call at his office.[7]

When they met, Blakeslee, who had checked Baker's high school record, asked why the honors graduate had not gone to college. She gave the same reason that blacks and others had given to him before—she could not pay for college. Blakeslee made the same offer he had made before: he would pay. When she told him that she wanted to be a lawyer,[8] Blakeslee replied, "I don't know much about women and law but if that's what you want to do, I'm ready to pay for it."[9]

Motley's interest in law stemmed from her awareness of a critical race relations case decided by the Supreme Court during her high school years. The state of Missouri, in order to avoid establishing a law school for black students, had made it a practice of paying the tuition of its prospective black students at out-of-state law schools. In *Missouri ex. rel. Gaines v. Canada*, the Supreme Court rejected Missouri's discriminatory tactics and required the state to provide a legal educational facility for blacks within its state boundaries.[10] To Motley, the case highlighted the roles that law, lawyers, and courts could play in effecting significant social reforms—reforms that could personally impact her life and future as a black American.

With Blakeslee paying part of the costs, Baker enrolled at Fisk University in February, 1941, and transferred to New York University in June, 1942, majoring in economics. She graduated from its Washington Square College in October, 1943. Several months later, in February, 1944, she began her studies at Columbia Law School. Its dean had earlier opposed the admission of women, but Baker, who had long dreamed of helping her people, was not deterred. She graduated in 1946, certain that no one would believe that she would succeed in law.[11]

But she did succeed and not just on the battlefront of law; Baker also managed the homefront, balancing needs at home with demands at the office and dangers in the field.[12] In doing so, she was encouraged by Joel Motley, the insurance broker and law school graduate whom she married on August 18, 1946, and by their son, Joel, Jr., who was born in May, 1952.[13] Asked the secret to her simultaneous success in meeting familial and professional demands, Motley answered, "Juggling."[14] It helped that, as her son said, "There was no question in our house that history was being made."[15] In large measure, that history was being made by his mother, "a dogged opponent of Southern segregationists."[16]

Encouragement for Baker was in short supply. Few took her career seriously: "Most people thought it laughable; there were not that many black men lawyers," she recalled.[17] This was more true in Baker's early years in the legal profession than years later when a white woman lawyer charged that racist politics inside and outside the American Bar Association[18] kept the legal profession "too pale and too male."[19] Fortunately, said Motley, her work at the Inc. Fund exposed her to two of those few black men, Charles Hamilton Houston and William Henry Hastie, who were models for young attorneys.[20]

## CAREER DEVELOPMENT

Baker approached graduation from law school with some trepidation. "Frankly, I cannot say that I was thrilled and happy to be going forth into a world hostile to women in the professions and still segregated as to blacks."[21] Like the other women in her class, she had endured a third year marked by "high hopes but few offers." In her case, Motley did not even enjoy a receptionist's offer to take a seat when she visited a white Manhattan firm in search of a job, let alone a partner's offer to hire her. In retrospect, her failure to find employment at a traditional firm was not a purely negative omen, for it meant that she would stay on at Inc. Fund. Motley had joined director-counsel Thurgood Marshall's staff as a law clerk in 1945, while still in law school, and became a research assistant after graduation in 1946. She only became an associate special counsel in 1949, after notifying Marshall that if she were to bear the responsibilities of that position, she should be classified and paid accordingly. Motley became the staff expert on housing, taking on a caseload large enough to occupy a small firm.[22]

Beginning in 1946, Motley accompanied Marshall to court in almost all the cases he argued. These included cases that nullified restrictive covenants in 1947, won Ada Lois Sipuel's right to study law at the University of Oklahoma in 1948, opposed school segregation in Hempstead, New York, in 1949, gained Herman Sweatt's admission to the law school at the University of Texas in 1949, sought a citation of contempt against the University of Alabama Board of Trustees in 1949, and banned public school segregation in 1954.[23]

But Motley did more than accompany Marshall to court. She also took charge of many cases, including the well-known cases resulting in the admission of James Meredith to the University of Mississippi, Charlene Hunter (Gault) and Hamilton Holmes to the University of Georgia, and Harvey Gantt to Clemson College in South Carolina. From 1949 until 1964, she fought school and other desegregation in courts in 11 states and the District of Columbia.[24] "She was a plodder," a former colleague said, "but she knew her stuff."[25]

In 1961, Jack Greenberg succeeded Thurgood Marshall as head of the Inc. Fund (with the new title of general counsel), and Motley was promoted to associate counsel.[26] According to Greenberg, segregationists "found her tougher than Grant at Vicksburg. She dug into a position and wouldn't let go in the face of all kinds of threats, evasion, obfuscation, and delay."[27]

Charlene Hunter-Gault would think this military analogy fitting. "It seemed as if this was the most important mission in her life. In fact, she often talked about the South in those days as if it were a war zone and she was fighting a revolution." In court, however, the client received scant attention from her attorney. "No one—be it defendant or plaintiff—was going to distract her from carrying out her task to a successful conclusion."[28]

## ACHIEVEMENTS AND CONTRIBUTIONS

Motley's career is adorned with "firsts" and "virtually firsts" among blacks and women. In February, 1964, she was elected to the New York State Senate—the first black woman, the second woman, and the third black in its history. Motley remained a senator until February, 1965, when she was elected president of the Borough of Manhattan, the first woman to become president of any borough in New York City. As president, she was the only woman on the New York City Board of Estimate.[29]

In the mid-1960s, on the very day that her argument of a case before the U.S. Supreme Court impressed him, Attorney General Ramsay Clark recommended that President Lyndon B. Johnson appoint Motley to a federal judgeship. Johnson chose instead to nominate her to the United States Court of Appeals for the Second Circuit, but he encountered stunning opposition from southern senators and from federal judges. As a result, Johnson shifted her nomination to the United States District Court for the Southern District of New York.

Formally nominated in January of 1966, Motley was finally confirmed by the Senate in August of that year, the first black woman so honored. The only other women on the federal bench were two on District courts, one on a Court of Appeals, and one Customs Court judge.[30] Motley was the only woman on the nation's largest (27 members) federal district court until President Jimmy Carter appointed Mary Johnson Lowe, another African American, in the late 1970s. Motley was also the second woman to be chief judge of a federal district court, a position she relinquished to take senior status on October 1, 1986.[31]

Having hurdled barriers erected against women, especially black women, in the law,[32] Motley wanted to advance further. "But that same power that could make [her] a judge," wrote Bruce Wright, "could keep her where she was, despite her superior qualifications, which could match those of any candidate, no matter the color or sex."[33] She never reached the appellate level, because "the opposition to me as a woman and a 'liberal' has remained."[34]

Motley's experience bears the tell-tale marks of this opposition where the scrutiny and assumptions are reserved for blacks and women by white racists and sexists. ''As the first black and the first woman,'' she explained, ''I am proving in everything that I do that blacks and women are as capable as anyone—of course there is more scrutiny—and I am aware of that.'' Nor is that all. ''Here in New York you get the best and you get the worst. With the worst, they come in here and [given her race and gender] they assume I don't know my job.''[35]

Lawyers, her fellow judges, and other courtroom participants projected onto her their anxieties about their own inadequacies, thus masking their fear of justice and of competition. Motley encountered this fear, as she explained, both as a black and as a woman. That is why, in reviewing her career, this National Women's Hall of Famer[36] said, ''I have spent most of my time trying to decide who is in the good guy camp and who is in the bad guy camp.''[37]

Bad guys were as boorish as they were racist in devising a means of marginalizing Motley. One technique was their blatant refusal to use her title when addressing her. One instance occurred in the 1950s when Motley, as the first black woman attorney to try a case in Mississippi, sought to equalize black and white teachers' salaries. The local newspaper played up the trial, and local people flocked to it. The trial commanded attention for many reasons: it was the first such assault on Jim Crow in this century, and it involved two black New York lawyers, one of whom was a woman. Although the judge addressed her as ''Mrs. Motley,'' opposing counsel did not, perhaps preferring the appellation trumpeted by the local press: ''that Motley woman.''[38]

Years later, Motley attended a school established for the instruction of new federal judges. Making introductions, the group's chairman hailed other participants' legal accomplishments but mentioned only Motley's membership on the Boards of the United Church Women and the Young Women's Christian Association. An offended Supreme Court Justice Tom Clark grabbed the microphone and announced, ''Just a minute, Mr. Chairman, I would like to say something about Mrs. Motley . . .'' He had forgotten the exact number of cases she had argued (he said 20—the count was 10), but he remembered the exactitude that enabled her to win nine. He also reminded them of her humanity by paying her a simple courtesy: as he had when she appeared before the U.S. Supreme Court, he addressed her as ''Mrs.''[39]

Motley fought for equality on gender and racial fronts alike. Asked, in 1988, to review her career as a black woman in the law, she criticized federal judges who, ''always ruling on somebody else's affirmative program,'' refused, steadfastly, ''to adopt one of their own for women.'' She had seen only one other woman argue a case in the Fifth Circuit Court between 1949 and 1964, when she herself litigated civil rights cases in Washington, D.C., and in 11 southern states. Moreover, she remembered that in 1966 women staffers in the United States Attorney's office in New York were not allowed to try criminal cases. In

1988, that was no longer so. Furthermore, some 60 women, most of them President Carter's appointees, sat on federal benches.[40]

Heartened by the progress, Motley has gone so far as to predict that twenty-first century law will be largely a woman's calling. However, she tempers this optimism with reality; "The reality is that although women have made tremendous progress in the legal profession, there is not going to be much change without an affirmative action program in the federal courts." To ensure such change, Motley argues that presidents and senators would have to be pressured into supporting affirmative action.[41]

While the courts neither can nor should handle all societal problems, wrote Motley in 1978, they must not avoid the problem of ensuring that power, including their own, is shared with blacks, women, and other minorities.[42] But Motley knew of no guarantee that they would. "Some people just can't imagine a Federal judge being anything else but a white male."[43]

Fundamentally, the problem is not one of race or gender either singly or taken together; it is one broader in scope and deeper in complexity. As Suzanne Harper contends, the problem is institutionalized white supremacy whose "central nexus" she identifies as "the intricate connections of race, class, gender and sexuality."[44] In exquisite elaboration, Patricia Hill Collins asserts "the significance of seeing race, class, and gender as interlocking systems of oppression," namely, that this encourages our "thinking inclusively about other oppressions, such as age, sexual orientation, religion, and ethnicity." It is, of course, imperative that these not be seen as the singular oppressions of black women, Collins adds.

> But these systems and the economic, political, and ideological conditions that support them may not be the most fundamental oppressions, and they certainly affect many more groups than Black women. Other people of color, Jews, the poor, white women, and gays and lesbians have all had similar ideological justifications offered for their subordination.[45]

To understand what Collins wrote is to understand what Motley fought—not just one oppression (racism), but a multiplicity of oppressions. It is in this light that Motley's career, especially while a lawyer, is properly appraised. Given its incredibly enervating and expansive nature, the struggle against racism required a concentration of resources—psychopolitical and socioeconomic—that made impractical the direct assault that other oppressions merited. And yet, so multifaceted and hydra-headed was this horror that to chip away at it was to undermine the others.

Take, for example, *Brown v. Board of Education of Topeka*, the public school desegregation decision of 1954. Its history justifies consideration of Derrick Bell's contention that the decision "should be seen as furthering the nation's foreign and domestic interests far more than it helped black people gain the critically important citizenship right to equal educational opportunity."[46] There are, of course, those who refuse to carry criticism of *Brown* this far, but even many of them would agree with Bell that other minorities—and whites as well—have benefited from black protest against racism.[47] That is they would concur in Motley's opinion that *Brown* opened a closed society, sparking drives for equal rights not only by public interest law firms representing nonblack minorities, but also by women, poor people, prisoners, consumers, and environmentalists.[48]

In fighting her way through and beyond *Brown*, Motley has secured a place in history. The emphasis here on her career at the bar is not intended to deflect attention from her performance on the bench where, as Michelle Washington wrote, she has demonstrated that "a passionate commitment to justice and equality before the law are principles guiding judges as well as advocates. Earlier she challenged the openly racist laws oppressive of her people, now she goads the judiciary to make real the promise of democracy."[49]

Motley has been a federal judge for almost 20 years, an achievement impressive when made by a white man, notable when made by any woman or black, and singular when made by a woman who is black. Still, she considers "lasting and significant" the years she spent as a lawyer with the Inc. Fund.[50] Like the years themselves, she has proven herself pivotal in American life and law. For while standing on the shoulders of all human rights paladins, Constance Baker Motley stood shoulder to shoulder with many.

## NOTES

1. Marie Brenner, "Judge Motley's Verdict," *New Yorker* (May 16, 1994): 70–71.

2. Ibid., 70; and Taylor Branch, *Parting the Waters: America in the King Years, 1954–63* (New York: Simon and Schuster, 1988), 824–25.

3. Constance Baker Motley, "Standing on His Shoulders: Thurgood Marshall's Early Career," *The Black Letter Journal* (Spring 1989): 9.

4. Ibid.

5. Floris Barnett Cash, "Constance Baker Motley (1921– )," in Jessie Carney Smith (ed.), *Notable Black Women* (Detroit: Gale Research, 1992), 779; and Jack Greenberg, *Crusaders in the Courts: How a Dedicated Band of Lawyers Fought for the Civil Rights Revolution* (New York: Basic Books, 1994), 34.

6. Constance Baker Motley, "Some Recollections of My Career," 6 *Law and Inequality* (1988): 35–36; and Kathleen Thompson, "Motley, Constance Baker (1921– )," in Darlene Clarke Hine (ed.), *Black Women in America: An Historical Encyclopedia*, Vol. 2 (Brooklyn: Carlson Publishing, 1993), 822.

7. Cash, 779; Motley, "Some Recollections," 35–36.

8. Motley, "Some Recollections," 35–36; Cash, 779; Beverly Jensen, "Alexander, Harris, Kennedy, Motley & Murray: Attorneys-at-Law," *Black Enterprise* (August, 1977): 23; and Jack Greenberg, *Race Relations and American Law* (New York: Columbia University Press, 1959), 40.

9. Motley, "Some Recollections," 35.

10. Jensen, 23; Greenberg, *Race Relations*, 40; and *Missouri ex. rel. Gaines v. Canada*, 305 U.S. 337 (1938).

11. Motley, ''Some Recollections,'' 36.
12. Brenner, 70–71.
13. Cash, 779–80.
14. Jensen, 23.
15. Brenner, 70.
16. Greenberg, *Crusaders*, 34.
17. Jensen, 23.
18. Jerold S. Auerbach, *Unequal Justice: Lawyers and Social Change in Modern America* (New York: Oxford University Press, 1976), 65–66 and 210–17.
19. Bruce Wright, *Black Robes, White Justice* (New York: Carol Publishing Group, 1990), 86.
20. Personal interview with Constance Baker Motley, September 12, 1978, New York.
21. Constance Baker Motley, ''Civil Rights: Our Legacy and Our Responsibility,'' 64 *North Dakota Law Review* (1988): 121.
22. Constance Baker Motley, ''My Personal Debt to Thurgood Marshall,'' in Robert Goldman and David Gallen (eds.), *Thurgood Marshall: Justice of All* (New York: Carroll and Graf Publishers, 1992), 160–61, 163–65; Thompson, 824; Cash, 780; Greenberg, *Crusaders*, 207; Mark V. Tushnet, *Making Civil Rights Law: Thurgood Marshall and the Supreme Court, 1936–1961* (New York: Oxford University Press, 1994), 36; and Richard Kluger, *Simple Justice: The History of Brown v. Board of Education and Black America's Struggle for Equality* (New York: Alfred A. Knopf, 1976), 273.
23. Motley, ''My Personal Debt,'' 163–65.
24. Motley, ''Some Recollections,'' 37–38; and Thompson, 824.
25. Kluger, 273.
26. Greenberg, *Crusaders*, 295.
27. Ibid., 34.
28. Brenner, 66–67.
29. Motley, ''Some Recollections,'' 38.
30. Motley, ''My Personal Debt,'' 164–65; Motley, ''Some Recollections,'' 39; Geraldine R. Segal, *Blacks and the Law: Philadelphia and the Nation* (Philadelphia: University of Pennsylvania Press, 1983), 228; Cash, 781; and Thompson, 824.
31. Motley, ''Some Recollections,'' 166.
32. ''Constance Baker Motley,'' *Almanac of the Federal Judiciary*, Vol. 1 (Englewood Cliffs, N.J.: Prentice-Hall Law and Business, 1994), 50.
33. Wright, 86.
34. Motley, ''Some Recollections,'' 166.
35. Howard W. French, ''Guiding Wedtech Trial, a Sure Hand,'' *New York Times* (August 7, 1988): 32.
36. Brenner, 67.
37. Motley, ''Some Recollections,'' 35.
38. Ibid., 37–38; Greenberg, *Crusaders*, 38–39.
39. Motley, ''Some Recollections, 38–39; Cash, 780.
40. Motley, ''Some Recollections,'' 37–39.
41. Ibid., 40.
42. Constance Baker Motley, ''The Role of Law in Effecting Social Change,'' *The Crisis* (January, 1978): 26–27.
43. French, 32.

44. Suzanne Harper, "Subordinating Masculinities/Racializing Masculinities: Writing White Supremacists Discourse on Men's Bodies," 2 *Masculinities* (Winter 1994): 2.

45. Patricia Hill Collins, *Black Feminist Thought: Knowledge, Consciousness, and the Politics of Empowerment* (London: HarperCollins Academic, 1991), 225.

46. Derrick Bell, *And We Are Not Saved: The Elusive Quest for Justice* (New York: Basic Books, 1987), 107–8.

47. Derrick Bell, *Race, Racism and American Law* (Boston: Little, Brown and Co., 1974), xxxix.

48. Motley, "Civil Rights: Our Legacy and Our Responsibility," 132.

49. Michelle Washington, "Constance Baker Motley: Black Woman, Black Judge," 1 *Black Law Journal* (Summer 1971): 179.

50. Brenner, 71.

## REFERENCES

Auerbach, Jerold S. *Unequal Justice: Lawyers and Social Change in Modern America.* New York: Oxford University Press, 1976.

Bell, Derrick. *And We Are Not Saved: The Elusive Quest for Justice.* New York: Basic Books, 1987.

Bell, Derrick. *Race, Racism and American Law.* Boston: Little, Brown and Co., 1974.

Branch, Taylor. *Parting the Waters: America in the King Years, 1954–63.* New York: Simon and Schuster, 1988.

Brenner, Marie. "Judge Motley's Verdict." *New Yorker* (May 16, 1994): 70–71.

Cash, Floris Barnett. "Constance Baker Motley (1921– )." In *Notable Black Women.* Ed. Jessie Carney Smith. Detroit: Gale Research, 1992.

Collins, Patricia Hill. *Black Feminist Thought: Knowledge, Consciousness, and the Politics of Empowerment.* London: HarperCollins Academic, 1991.

"Constance Baker Motley." *Almanac of the Federal Judiciary.* Volume 1. Englewood Cliffs, N.J.: Prentice-Hall Law and Business, 1994.

French, Howard W. "Guiding Wedtech Trial, a Sure Hand." *New York Times* (August 7, 1988): 32.

Greenberg, Jack. *Crusaders in the Courts: How a Dedicated Band of Lawyers Fought for the Civil Rights Revolution.* New York: Basic Books, 1994.

Greenberg, Jack. *Race Relations and American Law.* New York: Columbia University Press, 1959.

Harper, Suzanne. "Subordinating Masculinities/Racializing Masculinities: Writing White Supremacists Discourse on Men's Bodies." *Masculinities* 2 (Winter 1994): 2.

Jensen, Beverly. "Alexander, Harris, Kennedy, Motley & Murray: Attorneys-at-Law." *Black Enterprise* (August 1977): 23.

Kluger, Richard. *Simple Justice: The History of Brown v. Board of Education and Black America's Struggle for Equality.* New York: Alfred A. Knopf, 1976.

Motley, Constance Baker. "My Personal Debt to Thurgood Marshall." In *Thurgood Marshall: Justice of All.* Eds. Robert Goldman and David Gallen. New York: Carroll and Graf Publishers, 1992.

Motley, Constance Baker. "Standing on His Shoulders: Thurgood Marshall's Early Career." *The Black Letter Journal* (Spring 1989): 9.

Motley, Constance Baker. "Civil Rights: Our Legacy and Our Responsibility." *North Dakota Law Review* 64 (1988): 121.

Motley, Constance Baker. "Some Recollections of My Career." *Law and Inequality* 6 (1988): 35.

Motley, Constance Baker. "The Role of Law in Effecting Social Change." *The Crisis* (January, 1978): 26.

Segal, Geraldine R. *Blacks and the Law: Philadelphia and the Nation*. Philadelphia: University of Pennsylvania Press, 1983.

Thompson, Kathleen. "Motley, Constance Baker (1921– )." In *Black Women in America: An Historical Encyclopedia*. Volume 2. Ed. Darlene Clarke Hine. Brooklyn: Carlson Publishing, 1993.

Tushnet, Mark V. *Making Civil Rights Law: Thurgood Marshall and the Supreme Court, 1936–1961*. New York: Oxford University Press, 1994.

Washington, Michelle. "Constance Baker Motley: Black Woman, Black Judge." *Black Law Journal* 1 (Summer 1971): 179.

Wright, Bruce. *Black Robes, White Justice*. New York: Carol Publishing Group, 1990.

*GILBERT WARE*

# EMILY FERGUSON MURPHY (1868–1933)

Emily Murphy was the first woman magistrate in Canada and in the British Empire. Although she was neither a university graduate nor a trained lawyer, she made a singular contribution to the evolution of the justice system in Canada, along with several other women magistrates from the same era.[1] The significant mark left by these women was a working conception of familial justice that endeavored to depart from the ''conveyor belt'' intuitive practices of the past, and rather to substitute a person-oriented system designed to address the problems of particular individuals and fashion responses that seemed to meet their needs. In Canada, the female magistrates were among the earliest advocates and practitioners of socialized justice.[2]

Emily Murphy demonstrated from childhood an independence of mind and later developed a vision of her role as a woman that belied the traditional stereotype of the quiet, compliant female. She was very much her own person and highly self-motivated, combining zest for life, a keen interest in people, a passion for social justice, an abiding curiosity, and boundless energy. It was these strong personal qualities that she brought to her career and were the primary influences on her work as a magistrate. They also propelled her into active involvement in some of the leading feminist and social reform causes of the period from 1900 to 1930.

In her work and attitudes, Emily Murphy stood at the confluence of maternal and rights-based feminism and was heavily influenced by the social purity and social gospel movements. Like many of the social and moral reformers of that age, she reposed great faith in the answers of science, especially medical science, to major social problems.

## FAMILY BACKGROUND AND EDUCATION

Emily Murphy was born in Cookstown, Ontario, on March 14, 1868. Her parents, Isaac and Emily Ferguson, were Irish Protestants and members of the Church of England.[3] As their third child and first daughter, Emily benefited from her father's belief that all children, female as well as male, needed a sound education. After private tutoring and special instruction in writing and Latin, she was sent to the Bishop Strachan School for Girls in Toronto, at the age of 15.[4] While still at school, she met her future husband, Arthur Murphy, a theological student at Wycliffe College. They were married on August 24, 1887.[5]

Emily Murphy was a devoted wife and mother and ready to follow her husband on his pastoral rounds and missionary work as an Anglican priest, first in Ontario and later in Manitoba.[6] She also accompanied him on an extended visit to Britain and the Continent between 1898 and 1900, and it was there that she was, for the first time, introduced to the grinding poverty with which she would become so well acquainted as a magistrate.[7] However, not to be outdone by her husband, Emily Murphy developed her own career as a writer and journalist, publishing widely in a chatty, humorous style under the pen name ''Janey Canuck.''[8] Moreover, she increasingly dedicated herself to community service and the cause of the legal protection of women and children.[9]

## CAREER DEVELOPMENT

It was in Edmonton, to which the Murphy family moved in 1907, that Emily Murphy's most notable contributions to the cause of social welfare and reform were made. Soon after her arrival, she became involved in the campaign for the enactment of the Dower Act to afford an interest to wives in the matrimonial property.[10] She remained a leader in the cause of women's rights within marriage until the latter years of her life. Her interest in the welfare of juveniles, especially young girls, was no less determined. She assisted the Superintendent of Neglected Children with revisions to the Alberta Children's Protection Act.[11] Although not a lawyer herself, she had been a frequent visitor to court and an observer of court procedures. Moreover, she came from a family of lawyers. All three of her brothers were members of the profession and were supportive and generous with their advice, especially during her early years as a magistrate.[12]

On June 12, 1916, the Honorable Charles W. Cross, the attorney general of Alberta in the Liberal government of Arthur Sifton, wrote to Emily Murphy that the lieutenant governor had been pleased to appoint her ''as Police Magistrate in and for the Province of Alberta, and a Commissioner under the Children's Protection Act.''[13] After consulting widely with family and friends, Murphy agreed to take on the challenge. As the *Morning Bulletin* reported on June 14, ''Edmonton will have its first woman police magistrate and Alberta will have taken another step in the path of social reform, leading every other province in the Dominion.''[14]

Emily Murphy's appointment, applauded by her family and friends, was not received with the same enthusiasm throughout the justice system. She had to deal with a number of irritants and in particular, lack of cooperation from the police. Her honor was not daunted by this sort of churlishness. She knew that she had the support of successive attorneys general and she had no compunction about reporting the problems to the attorney general and requesting action. The tone of the letters, though always respectful, suggest that she expected an immediate response.[15]

The antipathy toward Murphy was not limited to law enforcers and civil servants. Occasionally she ran into hostility and rudeness from lawyers. In *R. v. Nora Holt* in 1917,[16] Eardley Jackson, representing the accused who had been sentenced by Magistrate Murphy to a $50 fine and two months in jail for being unlawfully in possession of a loaded pistol, was heard to remark, ''To hell with Women Magistrates, this country is going to the dogs because of them. I would commit suicide before I would pass a sentence like that.''[17] In this instance, the judge dealt directly and decisively with the problem, writing to Jackson and advising him that''[u]nless I receive from you an apology in writing, I shall regretfully be obliged to henceforth refuse you admittance to this Court in the capacity of Counsel.''[18] At a more general level, it was defense lawyers whose clients were found guilty by Emily Murphy who would threaten to appeal on the ground that as a woman she lacked the jurisdiction of a magistrate.[19] The threats were never followed through.

Judge Murphy, unlike most of the male magistrates of the era, believed that the roots of much crime and deviance, especially among women, lay in social and economic deprivation. Magistrates in particular, she believed, were key agents in improving the lot of those unfortunates who came before them, as well as in spreading the more general message for social and moral reform. In an article on magistrates' courts in *Maclean's* magazine in October, 1920, she wrote:

> A police magistrate is closer to the human side of his city than anyone in it—or ought to be—and sees all phases of its life. Added to this, he is in a position where his findings and opinions are recorded constantly in the local newspapers, so giving him a continuous access to the public conscience. . . .
>
> And pray how many of us come out publicly in favour of temperance enactments; in a campaign against venereal disease, or against the exploitation of girl-children for immoral purposes? For some reason all of us are strangely silent about these things, concerning which we have intimate knowledge, when it is our plainest duty to warn the public—the uninformed, unsuspecting public—from off the rocks and hidden shoals.[20]

Murphy referred to the role of magistrate as that of ''magistrate-physician,'' a person who would not only diagnose the patient and prescribe a course of treatment, but also follow up to ensure that the prescription was working and the cure achieved.

In her daily life as a magistrate, Emily Murphy was true to the vision she had of that position in the community. One of her biographers reveals that "[e]very woman who came to her court was interviewed by Emily Murphy, or one of her helpers, in the dingy little office where so much of her work was done."[21] As her Magistrate's Notebook reveals, she demonstrated particular empathy with juvenile offenders and adults who were first offenders or were the victims of economic deprivation, serious sexual abuse, their own naivete, or rank exploitation.[22]

In other cases, Judge Murphy went out of her way to secure family support for those who had fallen afoul of the law or had become destitute in circumstances that she found understandable. A number of the cases she heard involved girls or women who had forsaken their families or husbands in small towns or remote communities, or had refused to follow their husbands to those communities, and as a result, had fallen on hard times or into bad company in the city. In cases involving complaints of lack of support or charges that an estranged parent, often the wife, had neglected the children, Judge Murphy would try, where she thought it appropriate, to effect a reconciliation between the husband and wife so that the family would be brought together again. In this effort, she seems to have been careful to appear even handed, reminding both adults of their obligations to each other and to the children.

In those cases where Murphy felt she had no choice but to sentence an offender to a jail term and if the result was likely to be hardship to the family, she would take special steps to make arrangements for the care of the children and to report to the partner whom she felt had been wronged. She was especially solicitous of the children and the personal sensibilities of men serving overseas during the Great War.

Judge Murphy evinced a strong desire to divine the causes of the problems of those who came before her and to craft responses that seemed to her conducive to reformation or some other appropriate solution. In the case of juvenile offenders, a range of responses existed under the Children's Protection Act, including imprisonment, committal to an industrial school, refuge, or charitable society, followed by placement in a foster home or probation.[23] Neglected children were treated in the same way as juvenile offenders, except that the option of imprisonment was not open to the judge.

Adult sentencing, although it was open to a judge, was generally confined to two outcomes: fine or imprisonment. Murphy, however, sometimes seized the opportunity to use her discretion by suspending the sentence on an undertaking of good behavior. Where Judge Murphy could, she would try to find shelter, placements, or jobs for those whom she conditionally discharged, which she felt would provide the context for a new start in life.[24] She was clearly frustrated by the limited range of options available for adult offenders and argued vigorously for the introduction of adult probation. For example, she felt that the fining of prostitutes was tantamount to licensing the trade and was, in any event, typically paid for by a pimp. The standard jail term was useless, in her opinion, because the environment made rehabilitation unavailable or impossible to achieve.[25]

At the level of the criminal process, she found the representation of the poor by private practitioners troublesome, and in 1931, she lent her support to a campaign by the women barristers of Edmonton to introduce a public defender system.[26]

There were limits, however, to Emily Murphy's understanding and patience. The judge's notebook suggests that she could be particularly tough on seasoned prostitutes—the "harpies" as she referred to them. Little mercy was shown to women who she believed were incorrigible, exploited other women or girls, or neglected their own children. Although young delinquents and offenders were generally treated more leniently, those whom Judge Murphy saw as recidivists could expect tough treatment. She was no less well disposed to delinquent children who were brought before her under the Children's Protection Act and who she was satisfied had willfully refused to take responsibility for their actions.

References to the ethnic origin of some of those whom she sentenced suggest an association in her mind between delinquency or insanity and certain minority, immigrant groups. Blacks and Swedes seem to have excited the most frequent comment from her.

The few entries in Judge Murphy's notebooks in which she dealt with male offenders suggests that, as with the women, she had no time for recidivists and exploiters. At preliminary hearings, she committed various pimps and procurers for trial by the Supreme Court without regret. Moreover, she despised those men who were responsible for supplying drugs to women and controlling women's lives, typically by running them as prostitutes.[27] She was willing, however, to use leniency in the case of those who she felt had uncharacteristically gone astray. Emily Murphy was less understanding of some of the lawyers who represented prostitutes before her at fees which she claimed ranged from $25 to $400. She referred to these lawyers simply and bluntly as "living on the avails."[28]

Interestingly, in regards to criminality, Magistrate Murphy did not believe that women necessarily dominated virtue. While conceding that men statistically offended far more than women, she was inclined to believe that a portion of female criminality never came to light because it was hidden from view and that men committed crime more openly. In tune with the opinion of many psychiatrists of her era, she classified so-called criminals into two groups: the malevolent and the feeble-minded. The feeble-minded, who she thought the more dangerous because they were basically irresponsible and incurable, were overrepresented, she believed, among female offenders.[29] Murphy felt that the feeble-minded of either sex should be permanently incarcerated. She argued that certain allowances had to be made in punishing women, because they were, in some instances, victims of nervousness and hysteria. Generally, however, she deprecated the comment attributed to her fellow magistrates, ''your sex has saved you.'' On one occasion, she argued that a woman implicated with her lover in the murder of a policeman should go to the gallows along with him.[30]

Judge Murphy took seriously her own injunction to magistrates to follow up on the fate of those who came before them. Whatever she thought of individual offenders and whether they provoked her sympathy or ire, she demonstrated interest in what happened to them, often visiting Fort Saskatchewan Jail and the Alberta Mental Hospital in Ponoka. Her Magistrate's Notebook includes numerous memos to herself, sometimes written years after she disposed of cases, reporting on news of particular individuals. Her files reveal that she sometimes engaged in extensive correspondence with those whom she had incarcerated.

Emily Murphy had no qualms about mixing her day-to-day life on the bench with public service and advocacy.[31] She believed that her role as a magistrate gave her unique insights into human problems and how to resolve them. It was her mission, she felt, to carry the message to the broader community and in particular to the province's and country's leaders. Her deep concern about the offenders who came before her who were victims of drug abuse and dependency moved her to become an activist in the campaign for more extensive and vigorously enforced drug laws and to publish the thoroughly propagandist book, *The Black Candle*.[32] Her blame of the Chinese for the problems of drug abuse led her to support efforts to stop further immigration from China.

Murphy's belief that a proportion of offenders, especially women, were feeble-minded or mentally defective was accentuated by her active involvement in the Social Hygiene Council of Canada as its vice president. This relationship resulted in Murphy's espousal of proposals for the sterilization of mental defectives, proposals that were translated into legislative form in Alberta in 1928.[33] Judge Murphy clearly helped create a climate of opinion in which this avowedly eugenicist initiative became possible.[34]

Her abiding interest in women's issues and in furthering women's rights is evident in her active role as an executive member of the National Council of Women. It was that same interest and her continuing advocacy of the rights of women in marriage that led to Murphy's appointment by the United Farmer's Government of Alberta, in 1926, to a Special Committee to report on the matrimonial property rights of women.[35] Murphy also contributed to the cause of child welfare through her work in the Canadian Council of Child Welfare and as vice president of the Canadian Association of Child Protection Officers. She wrote on all of these topics in professional journals and mass-circulation newspapers and magazines, and she was invariably ready to be interviewed by the press. Moreover, she felt no compunction about expressing her views to the most powerful politicians and highest officials in the land, especially on matters of social policy. Through this quite remarkable record of public service, Murphy developed a high national profile and became one of Canada's most well-known feminists and social activists. In all of this she seems to have earned and maintained widespread respect. Public criticism of her stances was rare.

For Emily Murphy herself, perhaps her crowning achievement was her campaign with four other female activists (Nellie McClung, Henrietta Edwards, Irene Parlby and Louise MacKinney) to establish the right of women to sit in the Canadian Senate, a right recognized finally and definitively by Lord Chancellor Sankey in the Privy Council in 1929, in the *Persons* case.[36]

Emily Murphy retired from the bench on November 21, 1931, an event accepted with regret by the many people she had worked with in the justice system.[37] She died in her sleep on October 26, 1933.

## ACHIEVEMENTS AND CONTRIBUTIONS

Historians of the feminist movement of the late nineteenth and early twentieth century have referred to the thinking of that era as maternal or social feminism. It is true that, among feminists of that era, some of radical sentiment believed that securing political, social, and economic equality for women was important because it allowed them to realize their individual and personal goals, including careers, independent of men. However, the mainstream feminists believed that women's claim to participate in the political process derived from their moral superiority to men, a superiority that came from the unique feelings and insights they had gained as wives and mothers.[38] There was overlap and identification between maternal feminism and both the social purity and social gospel movements. All three groups embodied the energetic commitment of evangelical Christianity to reproducing the heavenly kingdom on earth through the politics of moral uplift and of social justice respectively. The combination of impulses meant that these reformers, including maternal feminists, often found it difficult to identify with working-class people, especially "fallen women," and to be highly judgmental in matters of class, race, and religion.[39] As inspired amateurs, they also betrayed a tendency to place great store in scientific solutions to social problems.

Emily Murphy's conception of her role and her conduct as a police magistrate and social activist fits the model of the committed maternal feminist. She wrote and said on a number of occasions that women were morally superior to men.[40] Her views on female criminality reflect a developing belief in the view that "feeble-mindedness" was at the root of much female deviance, and demonstrate the deference that she paid to scientific and medical opinion. Her remarkable record of involvement in advocating major changes in Canadian social policy bears testimony to her place in progressive reform.

In both her public advocacy and her work as a magistrate, Murphy sent a strong message that the key to a better society lies in the family and its strengthening. Murphy's record as a magistrate suggests that her personal frame of reference was that of the intelligent, successful maternal figure who through her familial role, strength of character, and moral insight could lead the less fortunate to a recognition of the error of their ways and personal reformation, and thus, lead society to a new and more moral tomorrow. This mission was carried through with a strong belief in the superiority of white, Anglo-Saxon, Protestant values and institutions and of the need, if those values and institutions were to be preserved, for all Canadians, whatever their social, economic, ethnic, or cultural background, to conform. In some instances (as in the case of the Chinese and blacks), this belief system caused Murphy to develop a deep and unreasoning antipathy to immigrant communities that she perceived were incapable of complying with the dominant moral order.

Although Emily Murphy fits the mold of maternal feminism to a significant degree, certain facets of her character and her beliefs suggest that, in some respects, she was atypical. Her strong belief in herself as a woman and her independence of thought caused Murphy occasionally to question the assumptions and some of the panaceas of her colleagues. She also entertained some doubts about the view, which was strong among maternal feminists, that a woman should not carve out an independent career for herself. Although an appointment as a lay magistrate, especially one with jurisdiction over women and children for which the remuneration was modest in the extreme, was seen as a permissible extension of the notion of "good works" in the community, Emily Murphy made her magistracy very much her own and seems to have seen it as her "career." In that sense, her work provided a role model to women who might wish to take the further and more dramatic step of training in the legal profession. Murphy also encouraged women who had entered or were contemplating entering the legal profession—women such as Rosa Ginsberg, the first woman to seek admission to the Palestinian bar.[41]

While Emily Murphy labored under the biases and mental blocks that afflicted both maternal feminists and the advocates of social purity and the social gospel, she had observed with interest the pattern of life within a number of different Canadian communities. As a result, she could be less judgmental and more cosmopolitan than some of her colleagues in dealing with Canada's growing cultural mosaic. At a time when Eastern Europeans were often viewed with suspicion, she wrote with enthusiasm about them and their culture.[42] She also came to the support of the Mormons who were the victims of episodic criticism, much of which she saw as stemming from ignorance and unsubstantiated rumor.[43] For her, any group that was prepared to work hard and maintained a strong sense of family and community was to be applauded and encouraged, and had a place in the Canadian family.

Emily Murphy was also more urbane than many of her colleagues. Unlike Nellie McClung, for instance, who viewed urbanization with despair, Murphy was more comfortable with urban life and somewhat more optimistic about the ability of reformers to work change within the country's cities. As someone who had traveled in Britain and observed slum life and who, as a magistrate, was well aware of the conditions in which many of those who came before her had grown up and now struggled, she was perhaps somewhat more understanding of the impact of environment on behavior.[44] It would be wrong to claim that Judge Murphy had a strong sense that the problems that were the daily fare of her work in magistrate's court were susceptible to solutions and strategies developed in those communities. Nonetheless, her approach to individual offenders and her attempts to work out solutions *with* them rather than *for* them suggests that she did not fully subscribe to the view that abstract and highly directive middle-class solutions were appropriate. To some extent, Murphy's responses reflect the view that it is not some ideal of virtue that is the answer, but a mending or healing that takes account of individual circumstance and social and economic environment.

Murphy seems to have felt that this approach had the merit of engaging the individual's sense of responsibility. Insofar as this approach was adopted more generally in family and juvenile courts after 1920, it constitutes one of Murphy's more enduring contributions to Canada's concepts of justice.

Emily Murphy's professional life, like her private life, was marked by complexities and often contradictions of thought, ideology, and bias. On the one hand, her commitment to the greater individualization of justice, her campaigns for greater access to the courts for the poor, and her more flexible and sensitive approach to sentencing were positive contributions to the discourse and practice of Canadian justice and corrections. On the other hand, her selective racism and adherence to the more extreme tenets of the social hygiene movement and active espousal of eugenic solutions were most decidedly not. But she proved beyond doubt that women were more than a match for the challenges of judicial office and were perfectly capable of taking on a career in the law, while maintaining a commitment to family life. In that sense, Murphy's judicial career provides an intriguing bridge between the maternal feminism of that era and the rights-based and collectivist theories of feminism that are current today.

## NOTES

1. John McLaren, ''Maternal Feminism in Action—Emily Murphy Police Magistrate,'' 8 *Windsor Yearbook of Access to Justice* (1988): 234.

2. Ibid.; E. McGill, *My Mother the Judge* (Toronto: Peter Martin and Associates, 1981); and D. Chunn, ''Maternal Feminism, Legal Professionalism and Political Pragmatism: The Rise and Fall of Magistrate Margaret Patterson, 1922–1934,'' in Wes Pue and Barry Wright, eds., *Canadian Perspectives on Law and Society: Issues in Canadian Legal History* (Ottawa: Carleton University Press, 1988).

3. C. Mander, *Emily Murphy: Rebel* (Toronto: Simon and Pierre, 1985), 15.

4. Ibid., 22 and 25.

5. Ibid., 26–29.

6. Ibid., 29–37 and 54–77.

7. Ibid., 38–53.

8. Emily Murphy, *Janey Canuck in the West* (Toronto: McClelland and Stewart, 1975, reprint of 1910 original).

9. Mander, 78–92.

10. C. Cavanaugh, ''The Women's Movement in Alberta as Seen Through the Campaign for Dower Rights 1909–1928,'' (M.A. Thesis, Department of History, University of Alberta, 1986), 43–44.

11. B. H. Sanders, *Emily Murphy Crusader (''Janey Canuck'')* (Toronto: Macmillan of Canada, 1945), 130.

12. Ibid., 139–41.

13. Edmonton City Archives (hereinafter, ECA), ''Emily Murphy Papers,'' M.G. 2, Box 1. The letter from Cross is not in the papers, but its gist is contained in Mrs. Murphy's response dated June 24, 1916.

14. *Edmonton Morning Bulletin* (June 14, 1916).

15. See letter from Judge Murphy to A. Browning, deputy attorney general, dated December 2, 1916, complaining of the failure of the chief of police to appoint a court orderly to her court, despite earlier instructions to that effect from the department; letter dated March 3, 1920, to Browning complaining about the practice of the police in sending liquor charges involving women to Men's Court. ECA, ''Emily Murphy Papers,'' M.G. 2, Box 1.

16. ''Magistrate's Notebook,'' Vol. 2, *R v. Nora Holt*, Case no. 151 (October 24, 1917). ECA, ''Emily Murphy Papers,'' M.G. 2, Box 3.

17. Letter dated October 25, 1917, Judge Murphy to E. Jackson. ECA, ''Emily Murphy Papers,'' M.G. 2, Box 1.

18. Ibid.

19. Sanders, 142–43.

20. Emily Murphy, ''A Straight Talk on Courts,'' *Maclean's Magazine* (October 1, 1920): 10.

21. Sanders, 155.

22. ''Magistrate's Notebooks,'' Vol.1, ECA, ''Emily Murphy Papers,'' M.G. 2, Box 3.

23. ''Children's Protection Act,'' S.A. 1909, ss. 22, 23, as amended.

24. Mander, 99.

25. Emily Murphy, ''The Womens' Court,'' *Maclean's Magazine* (January, 1920): 27.

26. Emily Murphy, ''Equality of Justice for the Poor,'' *Western Home Monthly* (July, 1931): 4.

27. Murphy, ''The Women's Court,'' 27.

28. Letter dated September 29, 1918, from Judge Murphy to Alice McCallum of the Alta. WCTU, ECA. M.G. 2, Box 1.

29. Murphy, ''A Straight Talk on Courts,'' 57.

30. Letter dated January 2, 1923, from Judge Murphy to Rt. Hon. W. L. MacKenzie King, prime minister of Canada. I am indebted to Professor Wilbur Bowker of the Faculty of Law, University of Alberta, for bringing this letter to my attention.

31. Sanders, 345–48.

32. Emily Murphy, *The Black Candle* (Toronto: Coles Books, 1973, reprint of 1922 original).

33. ''Sterilization Act,'' S.A. 1928, c. 37.

34. T. Christian, ''The Mentally Ill and Human Rights in Alberta: A Study of the Alberta Sexual Sterilization Act'' (unpublished study, University of Alberta), 10–12.

35. Cavanaugh, 79–94.

36. *Edwards v. Attorney-General for Canada* [1930] Appeal Cases. 124 (P.C., Can.).

37. Mander, 130–34.

38. Naomi Black, ''Introduction'' in E. MacGill, xix–xxiv.

39. John McLaren, ''White Slavers: The Reform of Canada's Prostitution Laws and Pattern of Enforcement, 1900–1920,'' 8 *Criminal Justice History* (1987): 53; and H.

Palmer, *Patterns of Prejudice: A History of Nativism in Alberta* (Toronto: McClelland and Stewart, 1982).

40. Emily Murphy, "Women," *Canadian Home Journal* (March, 1931): 6–7, 93–94.

41. Sanders, 304–5.

42. "*Janey Canuck*—Communing with Ruthenians," 40 *Canadian Magazine* (1913): 403.

43. Emily Murphy, "Mormonism in Western Canada," (undated pamphlet republishing short article from *Canadian Courier*, October 28, 1911).

44. Emily Murphy, "The Dual Problem of Modern Social Organization: The City—the Problem of Congestion; the Country—the Problem of Isolation," 3 *Social Welfare* (1920): 38.

## REFERENCES

Black, Naomi. "Introduction." In *My Mother the Judge*. E. MacGill. Toronto: Peter Martin and Associates, 1981, xix–xxiv.

Cavanaugh, C. "The Women's Movement in Alberta as Seen Through the Campaign for Dower Rights 1909–1928." Master of Arts Thesis. Department of History, University of Alberta, 1986.

Christian, T. "The Mentally Ill and Human Rights in Alberta: A Study of the Alberta Sexual Sterilization Act." Unpublished study. University of Alberta.

Chunn, D. "Maternal Feminism, Legal Professionalism and Political Pragmatism: The Rise and Fall of Magistrate Margaret Patterson, 1922–1934." In *Canadian Perspectives on Law and Society: Issues in Canadian Legal History*. Eds. Wes Pue and Barry Wright. Ottawa: Carleton University Press, 1988, 91–117.

"*Janey Canuck*—Communing with Ruthenians." *Canadian Magazine* 40 (1913): 403–10.

Mander, C. *Emily Murphy: Rebel*. Toronto: Simon and Pierre, 1985.

McGill, E. *My Mother the Judge*. Toronto: Peter Martin and Associates, 1981.

McLaren, John. "Maternal Feminism in Action Emily Murphy Police Magistrate." *Windsor Yearbook of Access to Justice* 8 (1988): 234–51.

McLaren, John. "White Slavers: The Reform of Canada's Prostitution Laws and Pattern of Enforcement, 1900–1920." *Criminal Justice History* 8 (1987): 53–119.

Murphy, Emily. *Janey Canuck in the West*. Toronto: McClelland and Stewart, 1975 (reprint of 1910 original).

Murphy, Emily. *The Black Candle*. Toronto: Coles Books, 1973 (reprint of 1922 original).

Murphy, Emily. "Equality of Justice for the Poor." *Western Home Monthly* (July 1931): 4, 41, 44–45.

Murphy, Emily. "Women." *Canadian Home Journal* (March 1931): 6–7, 93–94.

Murphy, Emily. "The Dual Problem of Modern Social Organization: The City—the Problem of Congestion; the Country—the Problem of Isolation." *Social Welfare* 3 (1920): 38–40.

Murphy, Emily. "A Straight Talk on Courts." *Maclean's Magazine* (October 1, 1920): 9–10, 55–57.

Murphy, Emily. "The Womens' Court." *Maclean's Magazine* (January 1920): 27–28, 73–75.

Murphy, Emily. "Mormonism in Western Canada." Undated pamphlet republishing short article from *Canadian Courier* (October 28, 1911).

Murphy, Emily. Papers of Emily Murphy. Maintained at Edmonton City Archives.

Palmer, H. *Patterns of Prejudice: A History of Nativism in Alberta.* Toronto: McClelland and Stewart, 1982.

Sanders, B. H. *Emily Murphy Crusader ("Janey Canuck").* Toronto: Macmillan of Canada, 1945.

*JOHN McLAREN*

# ELEANOR HOLMES NORTON (1938– )

Eleanor Holmes Norton has dedicated a lifetime to the struggle to ensure that a fair and just interpretation of the United States Constitution is applied to all Americans, regardless of race, gender, ethnicity, economic status, and other categories which serve to create separation and division. From her early involvement in the civil rights movement to her current office as the congressional delegate for the District of Columbia, Norton has worked to end discrimination. She is nationally recognized for her expertise on a wide range of issues, including labor, employment, antidiscrimination, and education policy, and has published many articles and provided commentary through various media. Most interesting, however, Ms. Norton has worn various hats throughout her career. She has been law clerk, university professor and lecturer, assistant legal director, senior fellow, scholar, author, and most recently, legislator. Through her multiple activities, she has raised the consciousness of a nation on the issues of legal, political, racial, gender, and social equity.

## FAMILY BACKGROUND AND EDUCATION

Eleanor Holmes was born on April 8, 1938. She was one of the fourth generation of her family to call the nation's capital "home." She was the eldest of three girls, and her parents were college educated. Her father, a civil servant, returned to school to earn a law degree when Eleanor was a child. Eleanor's mother was a school teacher, and her grandfather served as a District of Columbia fire fighter. Holmes Norton has said that she inherited her resolve from her parents: "My father gave me this sense of boundlessness, and my mother gave me an existential sense of struggle."[1] As a descendant of a family with a legacy of public service, it is not surprising that her career choices have traditionally been oriented to the public sector.

Holmes completed her elementary and secondary school education in Washington, D.C. schools. She received a Bachelor of Arts degree from Antioch College, and earned her Masters of Arts in American History and a Bachelor of Laws from Yale University in 1963 and 1964. The following year, Eleanor Holmes married Edward Norton who was also a lawyer. They have two children, John and Katherine.

## CAREER DEVELOPMENT

Norton's first position after graduation from law school was as a clerk for Federal District Court Judge A. Leon Higginbotham of the Third Circuit. Upon completing her clerkship, she joined the American Civil Liberties Union (ACLU) as a practicing attorney in 1965.

During her tenure at the ACLU, Norton specialized in cases involving the First Amendment, specifically those rights involving freedom of speech. In this capacity, she defended the right of the American Independent party's presidential candidate, Governor George Wallace, to present a public forum in New York City. Some may question how Norton, a woman who has built a legacy of involvement in the black civil rights struggle, could represent an avowed racist. But they need only examine her reputation as a staunch supporter of legal and constitutional rights and principles. The ACLU won the case for Wallace, and the decision was appealed. In the interim, however, Wallace moved the site of the rally in the interest of time and the expense of litigation. But it was this case that merited Norton national attention, and shortly thereafter, she became the assistant legal director for the ACLU.

In fulfilling her responsibilities as assistant legal director, Norton also represented alleged criminals, members of the Ku Klux Klan, individuals who were civil rights activists, and feminists. She contributed extensively to the development of litigation related to maternity benefits, equal access for female reporters, abortion rights, regulation of worker's compensation, and minimum wage law.

In 1970, Norton became the first woman to head the New York City Commission on Human Rights. She was appointed by Mayor John V. Lindsay, and the appointment was renewed by Mayor Abraham Beame in 1974. Norton also served as Lindsay's executive assistant from 1972 to 1974. As chairperson of the commission, Norton focused on the efficiency and productivity of her agency, and she ultimately established a system in which 60 percent of the cases were completed within three months of filing. She implemented a wide-ranging management and accountability system that centered on rapid charge processing and early settlement. As a result, the Commission became the first agency in city government to win decentralized authority over significant personnel and budget decisions. One analyst wrote that Norton rescued the Commission from its "bureaucratic blundering and transformed it into one of the most responsive and sensitive agencies of its kind."[2]

Norton's focus on the necessity for management accountability has been a recurring theme throughout her career and is, perhaps, one of the reasons why she has earned a reputation for being able to "get the job done." When her efficiency as a manager is combined with her sensitivity and dedication to human concerns, the results are nothing less than success.

During her tenure as chair of the New York Commission on Human Rights, Norton was instrumental in advancing the cause of equal rights and protection for women in both labor and politics, and she presided over what was one of the first comprehensive inquiries into the problems faced by women in the quest for equality and parity across all arenas. Under Norton's leadership, the agency worked to find jobs and urge promotions for minorities and women. The success rate of the agency, particularly with respect to employment, was noteworthy.

In 1977, Norton was appointed by President Jimmy Carter as the seventh person to head the United States Equal Employment Opportunity Commission (EEOC). With four other commissioners, Norton was responsible for enforcing the provisions of Title VII of the Civil Rights Act of 1964 and the Equal Employment Act of 1972. Once again, Norton walked into an organization that suffered from backlog and inefficient management of caseloads. At the time of her appointment, the EEOC had 130,000 cases pending. The Commission was created in 1965, under Title VII of the 1964 Civil Rights Act, and Norton's predecessors at the Commission had experienced various problems and difficulties with their colleagues, Congress, the president, labor, and the public. In all likelihood, President Carter, who appointed Norton, was probably the first president committed to ensuring that the agency seriously tackle the policy reform for which it was charged.

On the day Norton took office, she initiated the process of resolving the separate and competing federal selection guidelines and set in motion steps to produce unified guidelines that would facilitate the ability of employers to meet governmental standards related to equal opportunity. Norton described her goals for the Commission before the House Subcommittee on Equal Employment Opportunities in 1977 as the "most extensive overhaul of the agency structure and processes since the establishment of the Commission in 1965." With Norton serving as chief administrative officer and policymaker, increased emphasis was placed on the career development of lawyers and investigators who worked for the EEOC. She also oversaw the development of an improved financial system. Finally, she initiated a more collegial system among the members of the Commission, which encouraged the commissioners to be more involved in the decision-making processes.

As a result of Norton's leadership, the productivity of EEOC area offices increased by 65 percent, and the entire organization was transformed into an effective agency. As one might expect, Norton used her experience and the successes gained from her tenure at the New York City Commission on Human Rights to tackle the problems that plagued the EEOC.

As chair of the EEOC, Norton was instrumental in focusing attention on the necessity for protecting women's rights in the workplace. She initiated a set of federal guidelines on sexual harassment, stating that sexual activity as a condition of employment or promotion was a violation of Title VII of the 1964 Civil Rights Act.[3]

Norton has also established a distinguished career and reputation in the legal profession and in the arena of legal education. She has successfully argued before the Supreme Court and has represented a wide range of individuals and groups. From 1970 to 1971, she worked as an adjunct assistant professor of law at New York University Law School, and she served as professor of law at Georgetown University Law Center beginning in 1982. Professor Norton was also a visiting fellow at Harvard's John F. Kennedy School of Government in 1984, and the Ralph E. Shikes Bicentennial fellow at Harvad Law School in 1987.

From 1981 to 1982, Professor Norton was a senior fellow at the Urban Institute. In this capacity, she was appointed resident fellow in order to work on a book that focused on the development and impact of anti-discrimination and affirmative action remedies and their legal, economic, and social rationale. She has also written articles for the *Tulane Law Review*, *Howard Law Journal*, *Yale Law Journal*, *Public Law Forum*, and *New York University Law Review*.

It was only natural, given her personal commitment to human rights and public service, that Norton would enter the realm of electoral politics. In 1988, she was designated by Reverend Jesse Jackson to handle platform discussions during his presidential campaign. And only two years later, she made her own bid for political office.

After Walter E. Fauntroy, the congressional delegate for the District of Columbia, decided to run for mayor of the district, Eleanor Holmes Norton declared herself a candidate for the vacant seat on Capitol Hill.[4] Although Norton had to overcome last-minute obstacles related to her husband's failure to file the family's income tax, she won a narrow victory in the Democratic primary and went on to win the delegate seat.

As a delegate, Norton has been praised for winning the confidence, respect, and even high marks of those who initially opposed her election by consistently developing and applying an organized and structured approach to problem-solving in a non-partisan manner.

In 1992, Norton easily won reelection, receiving 85 percent of the vote. As a fourth-generation Washingtonian, it is obvious that Norton's love for the district as well as her no-nonsense attitude motivates her to achieve excellence in her representation of her constituents. She has earned the respect and admiration of many along the Beltway with her resourcefulness, energy, and accomplishments in her representation of the district, including her efforts related to passage of legislation that allowed limited voting rights to the District, American Samoa, Guam, Puerto Rico, and the Virgin Islands.

Norton has also introduced a bill that would allow the District of Columbia to become the fifty-first state. While the proposal has the broad support of working-class individuals who live in the District on a full-time basis, it has been persistently opposed by those part-time residents who are generally elected politicians as well as those who believe the District ought to maintain its unique status as the nation's capital. In light of the Congress's control over the District of Columbia, Norton has also advocated for stronger and more autonomous District governance.[5]

In 1994, Norton was reelected with an overwhelming 89 percent of the vote. She currently serves on the Committee on Government Reform and Oversight, the Committee on Transportation and Infrastructure, and the Subcommittee on Public Buildings and Economic Development, the Subcommittee on Water Resources and Environment, and she is the ranking minority member of the Subcommittee on the District of Columbia. Norton is also a member of the Democratic Congressional Campaign Committee and the Congressional Black Caucus, and serves as the vice chair of the Congressional Caucus for Women's Issues.

## ACHIEVEMENTS AND CONTRIBUTIONS

Eleanor Holmes Norton has dedicated her life to improving the situation of others. While the major focus of her work has been in the area of civil rights and most especially, the rights of women and minorities, her political activity as a delegate to the United States House of Representatives is a continuation of her personal commitment to enhancing the rights of all citizens. This attribute was seen very early on in her career when she assumed the responsibility of providing legal representation to those whose political activities and ideologies were clearly out of the mainstream of American consciousness. Norton's defense of Governor Wallace, members of the Ku Klux Klan, and the National States Rights party is indicative of her very staunch commitment to upholding constitutional rights.[6]

Norton has always been involved in the struggle for civil and human rights. In her youth, she participated as a member of the Student Nonviolent Coordinating Committee, worked as an attorney advising the Mississippi Freedom Democratic party, and served as a member of the national staff of the March on Washington.[7] Norton was also a founder of the National Black Feminist Organization and was an early supporter of the Free South Africa movement.

Eleanor Homes Norton has been described as a champion of equality and the rights of the poor and working people. She has been recognized by *Washington Magazine* as "One of the Most Powerful Women in Washington" and by the *Ladies Home Journal* as one of the magazine's "One Hundred Most Important Women."[8]

In reflecting on the evolving black agenda, Norton has argued that success in moving the black agenda forward beyond the achievement of the civil rights laws has led to a rethinking and retooling of the black agenda. The gains made in the 1950s and 1960s, such as integration and obtaining the unfettered right to vote, were goals that were clear and singular. But, according to Norton, these successes now dictate the need for a carefully crafted and more urgent agenda designed for an increasingly diverse population.[9] In a *Life* magazine article, Norton was quoted as saying, "the greatest success of the civil rights period was the achievement of legal equality—the laws, the courts and the legislation all moved to the side of equality."[10]

Norton has contributed a significant portion of her time and expertise to many organizations, serving as both a trustee and a board member. She is a trustee of the Rockefeller Foundation and serves as a board member for the Carter Center; the Metropolitan Life Insurance Company; the Pitney Bowes Corporation; the Urban Institute; the Southern Christian Conference; the Martin Luther King Jr., Center for Social Change; and the Stanley Works. She is a member of the Council on Foreign Relations and the United States Committee to monitor the Helsinki Accords. She also serves on the Judicial Panel of the Center for Public Resources and the American Arbitration Association Commercial Panel.[11] She has received 37 honorary degrees, including honorary doctorates from Howard University and Georgetown University.[12]

Professor Norton has written several books and many articles on civil rights as well as her personal experiences from within governmental bureaucracies. Of particular interest is her assessment of those government agencies that she directed. In "Public Assistance, Post–New Deal Bureaucracy, and the Law: Learning from Negative Models," Norton suggests that what the government agencies she headed had in common were seriously flawed bureaucratic mechanisms. Because of the crisis situations that existed upon her arrival, she enjoyed a rare opportunity to rethink and redesign both the structural organization and standard operations.[13] Her track record as an agency director is evidence of Norton's success in incorporating the traditional bureaucratic values of efficiency and effectiveness, which seem to be unattainable in many bureaucratic scenarios.

Perhaps Eleanor Holmes Norton's most important contribution has been as an educator. While she merits accolades as a scholar and professor within the academic world, her most significant work may be her willingness to reach out to the citizens of this nation and provide them with the basic insights into law, human rights, and politics. Blending her political experiences and scholarly knowledge, Norton has toured the nation as a lecturer and has served as a commentator on National Public Radio. By explaining in simple terms the controversies that take place in the nation's capital and in the mean urban streets, Eleanor Holmes Norton has managed to bring to life the necessity of constitutional law and human rights for the public citizen. She has, indeed, built a career of service to the nation.

## NOTES

1. Tonya Whitfield, ''A Voice for the District,'' 25 *National Journal* 10 (March, 1993): 579.

2. Jacob Wortham, ''The Equal Employment Opportunity Commission,'' *Black Enterprise* (September, 1977).

3. Susan Brownmiller and Dolores Alexander, ''From Carmita Wood to Anita Hill,'' 2 *Ms. Magazine* 4 (January–February, 1992): 70.

4. The District of Columbia does not enjoy full representation in the United States Congress. Rather than selecting representatives or senators, the District is entitled to a nonvoting delegate. While the delegate may participate in floor discussions and committee meetings in the House of Representatives, the delegate may not cast votes on issues pending before that body.

5. Karen DeWitt, ''District's Delegate to Congress Builds Bridge Between Capital and Capitol,'' 143 *The New York Times* (July 29, 1994): A8, A16.

6. Jo Ann Lahmon, ''Eleanor Holmes Norton,'' in Jessie C. Smith (ed.), *Notable Black American Women* (Detroit: Gale Research, 1992).

7. Mecca Nelson, ''Eleanor Holmes Norton,'' in Darlene Clark Hine (ed.), *Black Women in America: An Historical Encyclopedia* (New York: Carlson Publishing, 1993), 886–87.

8. Lahmon, 1992.

9. Eleanor Holmes Norton, ''On Black Initiative and Governmental Responsibility,'' *Focus* (March, 1988).

10. Eleanor Holmes Norton, ''Tough Talk on the Crippling of a Noble Cause and Breaking Through Today's Barriers,'' 11 *Life Magazine* (Spring, 1988): 42.

11. ''State Delegations—District of Columbia,'' *Congressional Staff Directory* (Washington, D.C.: Staff Directories, Ltd., 1995).

12. Lahmon, 1992.

13. Eleanor Holmes Norton, ''Public Assistance, Post New Deal Bureaucracy, and the Law: Learning from Negative Models,'' 92 *Yale Law Journal* (1983): 1287.

## REFERENCES

Breslow, Marc. ''A View from the Hill: Congresswoman Eleanor Holmes Norton on Women and the Economy.'' *Dollars and Sense* 182 (December, 1992): 14–16.

Brown, Frank. ''A New Era in D.C. Politics.'' *Black Enterprise Magazine* 21 (November, 1990): 17.

Brownmiller, Susan, and Dolores Alexander. ''From Carmita Wood to Anita Hill.'' *Ms. Magazine* 2 (January–February 1992): 70–71.

DeWitt, Karen. ''District's Delegate to Congress Builds Bridge Between Capital and Capitol.'' *The New York Times* (July 29, 1994): A8, A16.

Lahmon, Jo Ann. ''Eleanor Holmes Norton.'' In *Notable Black American Women*. Ed. Jessie C. Smith. Detroit: Gale Research, 1992, 809–12.

Lawrence, Christine. ''D.C.'s Norton: Non-Voting Clout.'' *Congressional Quarterly Weekly Report* 50 (December 12, 1992): 3779.

London, Paul. ''A Conversation with Eleanor Holmes Norton.'' *Employee Relations Law Journal* 3 (1977/1978): 313–35.

McCoy, Frank. ''Freshmen on the Hill.'' *Black Enterprise* 21 (April 1991): 25.

Nelson, Mecca. ''Eleanor Holmes Norton.'' In *Black Women in America: An Historical Encyclopedia* Ed. Darlene Clark Hine. New York: Carlson Publishing, 1993, 886–87.

Norton, Eleanor Holmes. ''On Black Initiative and Governmental Responsibility.'' *Focus* (March 1988): 3–7

Norton, Eleanor Holmes. ''Tough Talk on the Crippling of a Noble Cause and Breaking Through Today's Barriers.'' *Life Magazine* 11 (Spring 1988): 42–44.

Norton, Eleanor Holmes. ''Public Assistance, Post New Deal Bureaucracy, and the Law: Learning from Negative Models.'' *Yale Law Journal* 92 (1983): 1287–99.

Norton, Eleanor Holmes. ''Overhauling the EEOC.'' *Labor Law Journal* (November, 1977): 683–95.

''State Delegations—District of Columbia.'' *Congressional Staff Directory*. Washington, D.C.: Staff Directories, Ltd., 1995, 47, 610.

Watts, David. ''The American Dilemma Has Not Been Solved.'' *Black Enterprise* 20 (October, 1989): 26.

Whitfield, Tonya. ''A Voice for the District.'' *National Journal* 25 (March, 1993): 579.

Williams, Lillian S.''Eleanor Holmes Norton.'' In *African American Women: A Biographical Dictionary*. Ed. Dorothy Salem. New York: Garland Publishing, 1993, 375–76.

Wortham, Jacob. ''The Equal Employment Opportunity Commission.'' *Black Enterprise* (September 1977): 21–24.

*VALERIE L. PATTERSON*

# SANDRA DAY O'CONNOR (1930– )

On the first Monday in October of 1981, the Supreme Court of the United States forever changed. For the first time in the nation's history and the 191 years of the Court, a black-robed woman assumed her place at the dais that had previously seated only men. Joining the ranks of the 101 justices who had come before her, Sandra Day O'Connor secured yet another "first" as a woman in American history. As Senator Edward M. Kennedy noted during O'Connor's confirmation hearings, "Americans can be proud of this day as we put one more 'men only' sign behind us."[1]

Justice O'Connor brought with her to the bench a unique mix of experiences. She was schooled during a time when women were expected to be wives and mothers, not politicians or judges. Like many of her generation, she bore the burden of juggling family and career just as women were beginning to break down the social and professional barriers that had kept them out of the workplace. Despite this era of transition, O'Connor managed to garner a wealth of skills in all three branches of government in her home state of Arizona and had a long record of community service. O'Connor was no avid feminist; while she had supported the Equal Rights Amendment as a politician, she was not a frontline advocate for women's causes in the 1960s and 1970s. But by her works and her accomplishments, Sandra Day O'Connor proved that women could break the glass ceiling if given the opportunity.

## FAMILY BACKGROUND AND EDUCATION

Sandra Day was born on March 26, 1930, in El Paso, Texas, one of three children born to Harry and Ada Mae Day.[2] Home was a large, 162,000-acre cattle ranch in Arizona that her grandfather had started near the border of southeastern Arizona and New Mexico in 1881, near the town of Duncan. Because the schooling opportunities were not to the liking of the Day parents, Sandra spent most of the year with her maternal grandmother in El Paso, Texas, where she attended school, and returned home in the summers and on holidays to the ranch.

The young Ms. Day exhibited academic prowess early in her education. In 1946, she graduated from high school ahead of her class at the age of 16 and enrolled at Stanford University. While many of her female colleagues were immersed in the traditional education-oriented courses, O'Connor pursued a rigorous course of study in economics. One of her former roommates recalled Ms. Day as even-tempered, "She never got upset. She never went into a panic about anything. She was easy to get along with and she was fun."[3] Again, she managed to complete the majority of her degree requirements ahead of her class and graduated with distinction in just three years.

Before she had even graduated, Day had been accepted for admission to the law school at Stanford. She earned a place on Law Review and met her future husband, John Jay O'Connor III, the son of a prominent San Francisco doctor. The soon-to-be Mrs. O'Connor completed her degree in 1952, third in her class. Ahead of her in the class rankings was none other than a future colleague on the Supreme Court and chief justice, William Rehnquist.

John and Sandra married after graduation. Sandra, expecting to enter her chosen profession through an offer from a prestigious law firm, found nothing but roadblocks. The only offer she received was for a position as a legal secretary. Dismayed but undaunted, O'Connor investigated the possibility of public service and was hired as a deputy county attorney for San Mateo County in their civil division.

Both John and Sandra's legal careers were put on hold when John was drafted into the military. Assigned to Germany, Sandra accompanied her husband and again gained employment in the public sector, reviewing contracts for the military's Quartermaster Corps. During their stay in Germany, the young Mrs. O'Connor also began her lifelong commitment to volunteerism and community service, assisting Germans who were still suffering the long-term effects of war. When John's tour was up in 1957, the O'Connors debated their next step and settled on a move to Arizona. Phoenix was a growing city and one in which the O'Connors felt they could be successful both professionally and socially.

While waiting to take the Arizona bar examination, Mrs. O'Connor found that the same doors to major law firms that were closed to women in California were also shut tight in Arizona. Undeterred, she opened a private practice in the suburban town of Maryvale with a friend she had met while studying for the bar. Her practice was diverse, and she handled everything from small business issues to landlord/tenant disputes and other civil litigation, as well as some criminal matters.

The sudden expansion of the O'Connor family, however, made it difficult for Sandra to maintain her practice. In 1960, feeling torn between caring for her two young sons (a third was born in 1962) and managing her growing career, she made the decision to leave her practice to dedicate her time solely to her children and family. It was a difficult decision, "I didn't know how I would be able to get back to the law."[4] But, in reality, she never left the law.

During her five-year hiatus from traditional practice, Sandra Day O'Connor kept her hand in the field by doing volunteer work. For the state bar association, O'Connor wrote examination questions and did grading. She also established a lawyer-referral service for the local bar association. She served as a juvenile court referee, making recommendations to the judge in juvenile cases, and sat as chairperson of a juvenile home-visit board that evaluated home treatment centers. O'Connor was also appointed as a bankruptcy trustee for the bankruptcy court. And it was during this time that Mrs. O'Connor made her first foray into the political arena. She first became a precinct committee member for the Republican party and was subsequently named as the legislative district chairperson.[5]

By 1965, when her youngest son was three, it was clear that O'Connor was working as hard at her volunteer work as she had at her professional practice. Her time management skills had improved so much that she could maintain her home and develop a career simultaneously. After discussions with her husband, O'Connor returned to the public sector as an assistant attorney general with the state government. In this capacity, she served as a legal adviser to various state agencies.

O'Connor managed to keep her hand in party politics throughout her employment, and the reward came in 1969, when she was appointed to a vacancy in the state senate. She subsequently won her first election and was reelected, serving two full terms in the senate. More importantly, however, in 1972, Mrs. O'Connor became the first woman to serve as majority leader in any state senate. She also served as co-chairman of the Arizona Committee to Re-elect the President in 1972 and was an alternate delegate to the Republican National Convention.

When her interest in electoral politics waned, she decided to pursue a position in the only branch of government in which she had not yet served. In 1975, Sandra Day O'Connor ran for a judicial seat in Maricopa County. Despite opposition, her name recognition and reputation resulted in her election as a trial judge. Four years later, the Democratic governor of Arizona, Bruce Babbitt, named Sandra Day O'Connor to the Arizona Court of Appeals, an intermediate appellate court.

How Sandra Day O'Connor found her way to the Supreme Court in 1981, is a classic example of electoral politics. In October of 1980, with the presidential campaign in full swing, Ronald Reagan's advisers realized that support by women for the Republican nominee was soft. In a strategic move to bolster his appeal to "the ladies," Reagan vowed to name a woman to the Supreme Court upon a vacancy.[6] Only four months into the Reagan presidency, Justice Potter

Stewart announced his impending retirement, and the search for a nominee began.

Attorney General William French Smith, recalling the campaign pledge to appoint a woman, began to assemble the names of potential candidates. But White House Counsel Fred Fielding had also developed a list of potential nominees in advance of Stewart's retirement and independent of the attorney general. Both lists had three categories: prominent conservative lawyers and jurists, old friends who fit the Reagan philosophical mold, and women. Sandra Day O'Connor's name appeared on both the Smith and Fielding lists. It has been suggested that her connections to William Rehnquist, then an associate justice on the Court, and her friendship with Chief Justice Warren Burger resulted in her subsequent nomination.

On July 7, 1981, President Ronald Reagan announced that his nominee to the Supreme Court would be Sandra Day O'Connor. In his statement, Reagan recalled his promise to the American people.

> During my campaign for the Presidency, I made a commitment that one of my first appointments to a Supreme Court vacancy would be the most qualified woman I could possibly find. That is not to say I would appoint a woman merely to do so. That would not be fair to women, nor to future generations of Americans whose lives are so deeply affected by the decisions of the court. Rather, I pledged to appoint a woman who meets the very high standards I demand of all court appointees.[7]

Immediately upon his announcement, the press brought up the topic that would be the single controversy surrounding O'Connor's nomination: her position on abortion. O'Connor, holding a press conference in Arizona that same day, also found herself confronted by the abortion issue and gracefully avoided the question, a tactic that she was to employ throughout her Senate confirmation hearings.

On September 9, 1981, the opening day of the Senate hearings, Sandra Day O'Connor acknowledged the honor of being nominated as the first woman justice of the Supreme Court. "But I happily share the honor with millions of American women of yesterday and today whose abilities and conduct have given me this opportunity to service."[8] The O'Connor nomination virtually sailed through the Senate Judiciary Committee. She received the committee's 17–0 endorsement after three days of hearings and the full Senate's unanimous confirmation on September 21, 1981.[9] She was sworn in as the first woman to sit on the United States Supreme Court on September 25, in time for the opening of the Supreme Court's new term.

## ACHIEVEMENTS AND CONTRIBUTIONS

Sandra Day O'Connor brought with her to the Supreme Court a wealth of experience in state politics. Having held a position in each of the three branches of government in Arizona, it is no surprise that she clearly understands the separation of powers philosophy embedded in the Constitution of the United States. As a result, O'Connor, like many of her conservative brethren, exhibits a healthy dose of judicial restraint on policy matters that she believes are best left to legislative decision makers. In addition, her state-based experiences have influenced her decisions in that she tends to grant state governments more latitude in policy making when possible, thus, recognizing the role that states play in the larger federal scheme.

As a state senator and majority leader, O'Connor was well-respected by her colleagues for her diligence, fairness, and honesty in political brokering. What she lacked, however, was the charisma typical of most popular elected leaders. As Bill Jacquin, who was president of the Arizona Senate at the time of O'Connor's selection as majority leader, noted,

> Sandra possessed all the attributes—she does her homework, she knows how to get the proper things out of her staff. She has a very precise and concise mind and was able to do that very well. She does not have the charisma, in the sense of stirring speeches, that kind of thing. . . . She does have the ability to make an articulate speech that is founded on fact, and that's what I was looking for.[10]

Sandra Day O'Connor's tenure as a state senator is marked by her clear independence from ideological ties. Although a loyal Republican, her voting history reflects an issue-focused record. As a new state senator in 1970, O'Connor had allegedly supported a bill in committee that would have overturned Arizona state statutes forbidding abortions.[11] Four years later, Senator O'Connor voted against two pieces of legislation designed to restrict abortion availability. The first would have prohibited the use of public funds for abortions, and the second would have restricted the University of Arizona hospital from performing abortions. In addition, O'Connor was on record as opposing a resolution to the United States Congress seeking a constitutional amendment recognizing fetal rights to life, and she had co-sponsored legislation to make birth control information more accessible.

Senator O'Connor also supported the feminist agenda of the early 1970s. She voted in favor of the Equal Rights Amendment (ERA) as a senator (it failed by one vote on the Senate floor) and later co-authored a resolution to put the ratification question on ERA to a popular vote. She also worked to amend state laws that discriminated against women in the workplace and in child custody disputes. On the social service and governmental affairs fronts, she also tried to implement a Medicaid program for the poor and disadvantaged citizens of Arizona, established regular reviews of commitments to mental health institutions, effected probate code and no-fault divorce reforms, and successfully advocated open, public meetings of governmental agencies.

Despite these votes, Senator O'Connor was not an ardent feminist by any measure, and she was clearly in the conservative camp on most issues. She opposed gun control, supported legislation to limit state spending, worked to restore the state death penalty, and opposed school busing as a means of integration. But it was her work in the state senate on women's issues that spawned the most serious criticism of her nomination to the Supreme Court by anti-abortion activists who felt abandoned by President Reagan.

As a judge, O'Connor had a reputation for doing her homework, but she was not considered brilliant by the attorneys who practiced before her. In fact, her ratings by the Arizona Bar Association were dismal; in 1978, after nearly three years on the trial bench, she was rated lowest of the eight judges evaluated. And as an appellate judge, she ranked eighth out of a field of ten during her first year on the appellate court. While bar rankings may not fully reflect the abilities of a judge and can arguably be seen as popularity contests, O'Connor's poor rating did not seem to have much of an impact on her later nomination to the highest court in the nation. In contrast, it should also be noted that as an appellate judge, 90 percent of the Arizona bar had recommended that she be retained, and as a trial judge, 85 percent had supported her retention.[12]

Once her nomination was announced, O'Connor's judgeships on the Arizona courts provided the press and potential critics with few clues as to how she would vote if confirmed as a justice of the Supreme Court. She had not had the opportunity in her short tenure as an appellate judge to address the most salient issues likely to come before the nation's highest courts. While the American Bar Association's evaluation found O'Connor to be qualified for the bench, it noted her lack of "extensive or challenging" experiences as a judge.[13] However, most appraisals of her judicial work suggested that she was "a sometime conservative with a moderate, even progressive streak, a determined woman but not a dogmatic one."[14] Regardless of her political stances, as one newspaper noted, "Any Supreme Court nomination is special, and President Reagan's nomination of Sandra Day O'Connor was so special as to all but doom any opposition that was not based on the discovery of personal or political scandal."[15]

While O'Connor's nomination provoked the ire of anti-abortion organizations who felt she was more liberal than conservative on the issue, she assured both the president and the Senate Judiciary Committee, "I am opposed to abortion as a matter of birth control or otherwise." She also expressed personal support for the death penalty, opposed school busing, and indicated that she had some difficulty with the breadth of the exclusionary rules. But O'Connor consistently refused to disclose how she would vote as a member of the Court when and if these issues came before her as a justice, noting that personal views "have no place in the resolution of legal issues."[16] She enjoyed the support of a range of women's organizations, including the National Organization for Women, the National Association of Women Judges, and the National Women's Political Caucus. The major legal associations, the American Bar Association and the National Bar Association, also testified in support of her confirmation.

As a justice of the U.S. Supreme Court, Sandra Day O'Connor has continued her tradition of moderate independence. While she has sided with the conservative bloc of the Court more often than not, early on she exhibited her penchant for not fitting into a specific ideological box. An analysis of her first term on the bench indicated that she voted with Chief Justice Warren Burger and Justices Lewis Powell and William Rehnquist nearly 77 percent of the time.[17] While she was a typical ''freshman'' on the Court, receiving the fewest number of majority opinion writing assignments that first term, O'Connor did not shy away from participating in the Court's outcomes, ranking fourth in the number of concurring opinions authored.[18]

There has been a healthy scholarly debate over whether Justice O'Connor provides a ''feminine voice'' on the Court.[19] Her break with Chief Justice Rehnquist on two major reproductive rights cases suggested that gender may indeed play a role in O'Connor's decisions.[20] It has also been found that O'Connor's alliance with the conservative bloc varies according to the issue. For example, over her first ten years on the Court, O'Connor voted with Rehnquist more often on criminal procedure cases (87.2 percent) than on civil rights issues (62.2 percent) or matters concerning the First Amendment's establishment clause (52.9 percent).[21]

With the slow change in the Court's membership over the past 15 years, Justice O'Connor has become a pivotal member of the Rehnquist Court. Her alliance with the conservative justices weakened with the appointments of Justices Antonin Scalia and Clarence Thomas, ideologues who staunchly advocate theories of original intent, limited national government, and judicial conservatism when it fits their needs. It appears that their avid conservatism has pushed O'Connor more to the middle of the judicial spectrum; as a result, her power now rests in her ability to bridge the moderate conservatives and more liberal justices to build majority voting blocs on the Court. If this trend continues, Justice O'Connor's substantive contributions to American legal history will be seen largely in her ability to temper the Court's decisions during an era of potential radical change.

## NOTES

1. Linda Greenhouse, ''Senate Confirms Judge O'Connor,'' *New York Times* (September 22, 1981): A1.

2. Sources for this section include John Crewdson, ''Nominee for High Court: A Record Defying Labels,'' *New York Times* (July 12, 1981): A1; B. Drummond Ayres, Jr., ''Woman in the News: Reputation for Excelling,'' *New York Times* (July 8, 1981): A1; Stuart Taylor, Jr., ''Rather an Unknown,'' *New York Times* (July 9, 1981): A13; and Denie S. Weil, ''Personal Priorities,'' *Working Woman* (January 1986).

3. Crewdson, A1 (quoting Marilyn Brown).

4. Weil.

5. Ibid.

6. Aric Press, ''A Woman for the Court,'' *Newsweek* (July 10, 1981): 16.

7. ''Transcript of Remarks by Reagan and Nominee to High Court,'' *New York Times* (July 8, 1981): A12.

8. Linda Greenhouse, ''O'Connor Hearings Open on a Note of Friendship,'' *New York Times* (September 10, 1981): B14.

9. Senator Jeremiah Denton (Republican, Alabama) voted ''present,'' citing the fact that he could not get O'Connor to directly criticize the 1973 Supreme Court decision legalizing abortion (*Roe v. Wade*) or commit to overturning the precedent.

10. Quoted in Crewdson, A1.

11. Since committee votes were not recorded, there is no confirmation that Senator O'Connor did support the measure, but recollections of colleagues seem to support the fact. The bill eventually failed in the Rules Committee. Ibid.

12. Ayres, A1.

13. Michael Wright and Caroline Rand Herron, ''A Judicious Nominee Keeps Her Own Counsel,'' *New York Times* (September 13, 1981): D2.

14. Crewdson, A1.

15. Special, ''New Right Loses on Judge But Gains New Zeal,'' *New York Times* (September 17, 1981): A20.

16. Wright and Herron, D2.

17. John M. Scheb, II, and Lee W. Ailshie, ''Justice Sandra Day O'Connor and the 'Freshman Effect','' 69 *Judicature* (June–July, 1985): 11.

18. Ibid., 10.

19. See, for example, Sue Davis, ''The Voice of Sandra Day O'Connor,'' 77 *Judicature* (November–December, 1993): 134–39; Suzanna Sherry, ''Civic Virtue and the Feminine Voice in Constitutional Adjudication,'' 72 *Virginia Law Review* (1986): 543–615; Comment, ''The Emerging Jurisprudence of Justice O'Connor,'' 52 *University of Chicago Law Review* (1985): 389–459; and Jilda M. Aliotta, ''Justice O'Connor and the Equal Protection Clause: A Feminine Voice?'' 78 *Judicature* (March–April, 1995): 232–35.

20. *Webster v. Reproductive Health Services*, 492 U.S. 490 (1989), and *Planned Parenthood of Southeastern Pennsylvania v. Casey*, 112 S.Ct. 2791 (1992).

21. Davis, 137.

## REFERENCES


Aliotta, Jilda M. ''Justice O'Connor and the Equal Protection Clause: A Feminine Voice?'' *Judicature* 78 (March–April, 1995): 232–35.

Ayres, B. Drummond, Jr. ''Woman in the News: Reputation for Excelling.'' *New York Times* (July 8, 1981): A1.

Comment. ''The Emerging Jurisprudence of Justice O'Connor.'' *University of Chicago Law Review* 52 (1985): 389–459.

Crewdson, John. ''Nominee for High Court: A Record Defying Labels.'' *New York Times* (July 12, 1981): A1.

Davis, Sue. ''The Voice of Sandra Day O'Connor.'' *Judicature* 77 (November–December 1993): 134–39.

Greenhouse, Linda. ''O'Connor Hearings Open on a Note of Friendship.'' *New York Times* (September 10, 1981): B14.

Greenhouse, Linda. ''Senate Confirms Judge O'Connor.'' *New York Times* (September 22, 1981): A1.

''New Right Loses on Judge But Gains New Zeal.'' *New York Times* (September 17, 1981): A20.

Press, Aric. ''A Woman for the Court.'' *Newsweek* (July 10, 1981): 16.

Scheb, John M., II, and Lee W. Ailshie. ''Justice Sandra Day O'Connor and the 'Freshman Effect.' '' *Judicature* 69 (June–July, 1985): 11.

Sherry, Suzanna. ''Civic Virtue and the Feminine Voice in Constitutional Adjudication.'' *Virginia Law Review* 72 (1986): 543–615.

Taylor, Stuart, Jr. ''Rather an Unknown.'' *New York Times* (July 9, 1981): A13.

''Transcript of Remarks by Reagan and Nominee to High Court.'' *New York Times* (July 8, 1981): A12.

Weil, Denie S. ''Personal Priorities.'' *Working Woman* (January, 1986).

Wright, Michael, and Caroline Rand Herron. ''A Judicious Nominee Keeps Her Own Counsel.'' *New York Times* (September 13, 1981): D2.

*REBECCA MAE SALOKAR AND MICHAEL WILSON*

# SADAKO OGATA (1927–    )

In today's global arena at the intersection of law and politics and in the overlap of norm making and practical implementation, the United Nations High Commissioner for Refugees (UNHCR) occupies a special place. Uprooted people engaged in forced migration throughout the world are often enough not just video bytes on a television screen but actually new neighbors for many people. The UNHCR must bring bureaucratic resources, understanding, and perhaps even preventive vision to the task of assisting such people. Sadako Ogata, high commissioner since 1991, brings these aspects of the UNHCR's role, as well as personal diplomatic experience, academic credentials, and compassion to her activities as advocate for such people in international politics and as administrator of the particular organization established for their protection under the United Nations system. Her high global visibility has made Sadako Ogata a well-known figure in the institutional and human dimensions of the contemporary world of law at the international level.

Sadako Ogata is a Japanese woman with a cosmopolitan upbringing and strong family ties, who has been engaged in public and private spheres both within Japan and internationally.[1] She has contributed to education and scholarly research, the content of which will be examined later in this article. In addition, Ogata has held several posts in the diplomatic service of the Japanese government and at the age of 63 became an international civil servant as high commissioner.

## FAMILY BACKGROUND AND EDUCATION

Sadako Ogata (nee Nakamura) was born in Japan on September 16, 1927, into a family with a background in diplomatic and political life. Her father,

Toyoichi Nakamura, served in several overseas posts for the Japanese Foreign Ministry as she was growing up. Her mother was the eldest daughter of Kenkichi Yoshizawa, who held prominent positions in the Japanese Foreign Ministry from the 1920s through the 1950s. Sadako's maternal grandfather, Yoshizawa, was married to a daughter of Tsuyoshi Inukai, who was prime minister when he was assassinated in 1932.

The young Sadako grew up in a cosmopolitan environment, learning English as a child along with her mother tongue of Japanese. She listened to family talk about politics and foreign affairs and knew first hand of the effects of militarism and war. Because of her father's travels, Sadako spent about five years in San Francisco, California, and Portland, Oregon, as a small child, and three years in China (Guangdong and Hong Kong), before returning to Japan for the fifth year of elementary school. She continued her education through high school in Japan while her father continued to serve in China and awaited posting to Finland as World War II ended. Sadako attended the University of the Sacred Heart in Tokyo during and just after the Second World War, and was baptized in the Roman Catholic Church.

Sadako Nakamura's family was not only conscious of politics but also acutely aware of the importance of education, and her parents encouraged and supported her in a liberal fashion in her academic and personal pursuits. She received a Rotary Foundation Fellowship in 1951, permitting her to attend Georgetown University in Washington, D.C., where she obtained a master's degree in international relations in 1953. During those years, she also worked as a guide and translator for Michiko Fujiwara, a Japanese woman politician who was on tour in the United States. That experience served to introduce Sadako to the social welfare issues that Fujiwara was examining and brought her into contact with such prominent people as Mrs. Eleanor Roosevelt.

The theoretical study of international relations that Sadako completed at Georgetown served to whet her appetite for history, particularly Japanese diplomatic history, which she pursued as a research student at the University of Tokyo from 1953 to 1956 (under Professor Yoshitake Oka). In 1956, she returned once more to the United States, this time to obtain a doctorate in political science at the University of California, Berkeley. She worked as research assistant to Robert Scalapino during these years. Because of her father's declining health, Sadako Nakamura returned to Japan in 1958, where she carried out the research for her doctoral dissertation on the making of Japan's foreign policy during the years leading up to the full outbreak of the Second World War. The events had profoundly affected her and her family, and as a research theme, they constituted an intellectual puzzle for Sadako because of the apparent irrationality of Japan's course of action.

Sadako Nakamura plunged into the study of primary sources (both public and private, written and oral) related to Japan's military involvement in Manchuria. She submitted a first draft of her dissertation in 1960, the same year that she married Shijuro Ogata. Her husband's father, Taketora Ogata, was a famous journalist and influential statesman. Since Shijuro's father and Sadako's grandfather were close friends, the future husband and wife had already known each other through family connections; though in different years, they had also attended Professor Oka's seminar at the University of Tokyo. Shijuro Ogata was beginning what would become a prominent career in the Bank of Japan and later in other banking circles. As a result, the newlyweds found themselves transferred to various locations in Japan (Osaka) and abroad (Britain and the United States), even as Sadako Ogata was putting the finishing touches on her doctoral dissertation. She received her Ph.D. in political science in 1963, and her dissertation was published in 1964 as *Defiance in Manchuria: The Making of Japanese Foreign Policy 1931–1932*.[2]

## CAREER DEVELOPMENT

After returning to Japan, Ogata became active in academic and public life while raising her own family (one son and one daughter) and caring for her elderly parents (her father died in 1971, her mother in 1986). From 1965 to 1974, she was a part-time lecturer at the University of the Sacred Heart and at International Christian University in Tokyo, and from 1974 to 1979, she was associate professor at International Christian University, where she taught diplomatic history and international relations theory.

In the summer of 1968, Ogata was approached by Fusae Ichikawa, an important figure in promoting women's role in public life in Japan, to join the Japanese delegation at the twenty-third Session of the United Nations General Assembly in New York. Ogata's formal involvement with international organizations begins with this appointment. She also attended sessions in 1970 and 1975, before being appointed minister, Permanent Mission of Japan to the United Nations (1976–1978) and Envoy Extraordinary and Minister Plenipotentiary (1978–1979). In 1978 and 1979, Ogata served as chairperson of the UNICEF Executive Board. Her husband's assignment to posts in the Bank of Japan in New York in 1975 made for convergence of family life and professional life during these years. Ogata was notable for moving back and forth between academe and public service, a rarity in Japanese career trajectories.

Because of her assignments with the Japanese Foreign Ministry at the United Nations and her extended leave of absence from International Christian University, Ogata resigned her academic position in 1979. Returning to Japan in 1980, she became professor of international relations at Sophia University in Tokyo, where her teaching was primarily in the fields of foreign policy decision making and international organizations. In the months between her appointment at the United Nations and her professorship at Sophia University, Ogata served as head of the Japanese Government Mission to Extend Relief Measures to Cambodian Refugees (with rank of ambassador), when the Indochinese refugees had suddenly recaptured the world's attention as "boat people" engaged in a mass exodus.

While continuing her full-time role at Sophia University (she served variously as head of the undergraduate program in international relations, the director of the Institute of International Relations, and the dean of the Faculty of Foreign Studies), Ogata continued a vigorous involvement in public service and engagement in activities with a wider society, both nationally and internationally. For example, she participated in various advisory panels to government agencies on a wide range of issues, including women, diplomatic personnel, budget, and the economy. She was also the Japanese government's representative on the United Nations Human Rights Commission from 1982 to 1985, the first years of Japan's full involvement with the Commission. Within Japan, her varied activities included her association with the National Institute of Research Advancement, the Japan Association of International Relations, the Japan Foundation, and the Mitsubishi Bank Foundation. Internationally, she has been engaged in the activities of such diverse groups as the Trilateral Commission, the Pontifical Commission on Culture, the Independent Commission on Humanitarian Issues, and more recently, the Commission on Global Governance.

Shortly after returning to Japan from Myanmar in November, 1990, where she had gone as Special Rapporteur to examine conditions on behalf of the United Nations Human Rights Commission, Ogata learned that the incumbent United Nations High Commissioner for Refugees (UNHCR) would be leaving the post to return to Norway. This began a rapid sequence of events that led to her selection as high commissioner by the United Nations General Assembly in December. Quickly bringing her university responsibilities to a close, Ogata began full-time work as High Commissioner in Geneva in February, 1991. She completed the remaining three years of that term (1991–1993) and is now in the middle of a full five-year term (1994–1998).[3] She was named professor emeritus at Sophia University in 1994.

## ACHIEVEMENTS AND CONTRIBUTIONS

Sadako Ogata's scholarly writings span three decades, during which her own experiences expanded significantly and vast changes occurred in global politics, particularly in Japan's relations with the rest of the world. Not surprisingly, a number of themes recur in her work, but her work also reflects continuous development of previous topics and examination of new circumstances with new analytical tools. Her career as a scholar and diplomat blends well with the major subjects of her research: Japan's historical and contemporary involvement in international relations; the politics of international organizations; the role of nonstate actors in global affairs, including economic and humanitarian fields, and their interaction with political actors both domestic and abroad. Although it is not easy to categorize her writings either by content or by methodology over time, many of her early works are historical studies, a number of writings from the 1970s and 1980s have a more analytical bent, and attention to policy issues becomes prominent in later pieces. Several of the major questions that she examines are discussed below.

Her doctoral dissertation, published originally as *Defiance in Manchuria: The Making of Japanese Foreign Policy, 1931–1932*, and revised and expanded for publication in Japan,[4] went beyond stereotypical views of Japan's pre-World War II foreign policy. It demonstrated the system of irresponsibility in which junior Japanese military officers defied not only the civilian authorities but their own military leaders as well. Their radical role in the disintegration of the decision making structure was an underlying current in the long sequence of events from Japan's expansion in China, through its withdrawal from the League of Nations, to its ever deeper international isolation, and ultimately full-scale war and disastrous defeat. Ogata considers her dissertation to be her best piece of research.[5]

The historical impact of public opinion and nongovernmental groups on Japan's foreign relations—particularly in regard to the League of Nations—is examined in several of Ogata's early studies.[6] Her scholarly interest branches out to a number of related questions: the interaction of domestic and international politics, the place of multilateral/international organizations in the overall conduct of a nation's foreign policy, and the international organizations themselves. These themes come back over and over in the whole corpus of Ogata's scholarly writings.[7]

The substance of Japan's relations with two great countries on either side of the Pacific Ocean—China and the United States—tells a great deal of the story of Japan's foreign policy before, during, and after the Second World War, up to the present day. This alone is sufficient justification for Ogata's frequent return to these themes.[8] Her personal and her family's experiences are also reflected in her choice of these research topics.

Japan's relations to China,[9] the United States' relations with China,[10] and the United States' relations with Japan[11] are all taken up separately. This traditional form of foreign policy analysis is necessary but not sufficient for understanding the dynamics of global politics involving these actors. Ogata's analytical focus shifts over time to a comparative perspective and then to a triangular and systemic approach in later writings; China, Japan, and the United States relate to each other not one by one, but in a three-sided, mutual set of interactions.[12]

Ogata's interest in Japan's proper role in the world—whether vis-à-vis the United States or China or within international organizations—is a theme that emerges naturally from her studies of diplomatic history. Her treatment of the matter, however, is influenced by developments in the field of political science: decision-making analysis, interest group politics, the impact of nongovernmental actors, new questions about political economy, and humanitarian issues. Her discussion of the role of the Japanese business community in Japan's decision-making processes regarding capital liberalization and normalization of relations with China is particularly innovative.[13] With regard to capital liberalization, Japan's close relationship with the United States provided more scope for initiatives by the governmental bureaucracy, while private business groups took the lead in the matter of relations with China, affecting the domestic sociopolitical environment and encouraging governmental policy change.

Ogata's scholarly analysis of international organizations and of national policies toward them occupies a central place in her writings.[14] These studies cover a broad range of topics, including political and security issues, the relationship between economic power and political responsibility in global politics, the dynamics of political currents within the organizations, and the question of public and governmental support for the organizations. Her treatment of human rights[15] often takes the perspective of international organizations as well. And her reflections on broader issues of international inequality,[16] humanitarian concerns,[17] and refugees[18] show a perspective linked to addressing such questions through the organized efforts of the international community.

In regard to human rights issues, Ogata has outlined the long-term, broad lines of international promotion and protection of human rights through the 1960s and 1970s.[19] But her approach is an objective one, which recognizes how cold war politics and the different stages of national development have led to the politicization of what otherwise might be considered an idealist or merely humanitarian question.[20] Furthermore, her work with the Independent Commission on Humanitarian Issues informs her perspective on the nongovernmental as well as intergovernmental or international organizational aspects of the protection of human rights.[21]

As a Japanese and a diplomat, her analysis of the United Nations has been affected by the particular relationship which the Japanese people and their government have had with the organization. As the ''enemy states'' of World War II, Japan and Germany were considered somewhat suspect by the Allies, who formed the core of the United Nations organization. Although that historical context has changed in the half-century since its founding, the United Nations is still in the process of working out a proper *modus vivendi* with these resurgent former enemy powers. The Japanese people reacted strongly against the militarism of the 1930s and 1940s; in that post–World War II environment, an idealistic, somewhat simplistic reliance on the United Nations as a replacement for national military strength (sometimes called pacifism in Japan) received widespread support in Japan. Ogata herself took a more realistic position,[22] which recognized the changing political currents in the world body over the years and the political necessity for a United States committed to its effective functioning.

The longstanding question of Japan's admission to the United Nations Security Council highlights the dilemma of Japan's multilateral diplomacy. Rather than considering the issue in a principled, strategic manner relating to Japan's contribution to its own and its neighbors' security, much of the domestic debate on the question has centered on the prestige of an economic superpower. Japan's ''resource diplomacy'' of the 1970s highlighted a similar ambiguity in Japan's foreign policy. Ogata's numerous contributions to the discussion of these questions in the 1980s show her concern that the United Nations continue to play an active international role, one that would maintain the United States' interest in the organization, and thus provide a realistic venue for Japan's own policies.

In fact, the 1980s were years in which Japan itself (and Ogata herself, as Japan's first representative on the United Nations Human Rights Commission) started to act more vigorously in the humanitarian and development fields in which the United Nations was involved. While this did not solve the dilemma of Japan's involvement in the organization's security functions, it helped to reorient the country to a more cooperative relationship with the organization rather than its previous dependency relationship.[23] After a long and sometimes rancorous public debate, Japan finally adopted a law in 1992 permitting members of its Self-Defense Forces to participate in cooperative roles as part of the United Nations peacekeeping forces. This represents an important shift in Japanese public and governmental attitudes toward the United Nations (and toward foreign relations more generally). The United Nations was and continues to be a kind of safety net for Japan's diplomacy. However, this need not be understood in a merely escapist sense, but as a genuine act of trust in the world body's potential as forum and actor. The new peacekeeping functions in which Japan may participate symbolize a more positive contribution to such a body.[24] For Ogata, the framework provided by the United Nations is a liberal one of tolerance for global diversity, based on a broad humanist perspective seeking compromise where conflicting forces clash.[25]

Sadako Ogata's personal education and career development point to her identity as both a Japanese woman and an international actor. She has stepped into the role of United Nations High Commissioner for Refugees at a dramatic moment in world history and in the life of the organization for which she is responsible. As events in Cambodia and Iraq show, international action on behalf of refugees is intricately involved with high politics and even military force, as well as with traditional legal protection and humanitarian assistance. Bosnia and Somalia have made the world aware of the radically new problems of internally displaced people in the post–cold war era. The Rwandan crisis indicates how massive and instantaneous forced migrations can become, as well as how intractable ethnic conflicts are.

In the face of these new circumstances, Sadako Ogata has led an organization whose budget has more than tripled in the few short years of her incumbency.[26] The range of questions facing the high commissioner and the world community has become vast and complex, with the old definitions of "refugee" seeming very inadequate to the realities of people whose situations of displacement and uprootedness are generated by underdevelopment, violence, human rights abuses, and ecological disasters. As high commissioner, Sadako Ogata has attempted to adapt her office to a flexible and realistic understanding of her mandate and responsibilities, while bringing a fresh analytical focus to long-range needs and tasks.[27] As high commissioner, Sadako Ogata's biography continues as it becomes intertwined with the lives of forced migrants throughout the world and with the still unanswered question of how our world will treat them.

## NOTES

1. Many details concerning Ogata's family and education are reported in an extensive interview with a Japanese journalist. See Fuyuko Kamisaka, ''Gemba ni tatsu no wa 'Ima shika nai': gakkyuu seikatsukara kokusai butai ni deta kokuren nammin kootoo bemmukan, Ogata Sadako'' ('' 'Now is the time' for action: Ogata Sadako, the United Nations High Commissioner for Refugees, from academic life to the international stage''), in *Minami no shima no Maria: gendai ni choosen shita onnatachi* (*Mary of the Southern Isles: Women Who Have Challenged Our Era*) (Tokyo: Bungei Shunju, 1994), 123–58.

2. Sadako Ogata, *Defiance in Manchuria: The Making of Japanese Foreign Policy 1931–1932* (Berkeley: University of California Press, 1964).

3. A diary of her activities as high commissioner may be found in Sadako Ogata, ''Kokuren nammin kootoo bemmukan boochuu nikki'' (''Diary of the United Nations High Commissioner for Refugees''), *Gaiko Forum* (monthly series, August, 1993–December, 1994).

4. Sadako Ogata, *Manshuu jihen to seisaku no keisei katei* (*The Manchurian Affair and the Process of Policy Formulation*) (Tokyo: Hara Shoboo, 1966).

5. Sadako Ogata, Personal communication to David Wessels, dated March 20, 1995.

6. Sadako Ogata, ''Gaikoo to yoron: renmei dattai wo meguru ichikoosatsu'' (''Diplomacy and public opinion: reflections on the withdrawal from the League of Nations''), 41 *Kokusai seiji* (1970):140–55; Ogata, ''Kokusaishugi dantai no yakuwari'' (''The role of internationalist groups''), in C. Hosoya (ed.), *Nichibei kankei shi* (*The History of Japanese-American Relations*), Vol. 3 (Tokyo: University of Tokyo Press, 1971), 307–53; and Ogata, ''The Role of Liberal Nongovernmental Organizations in Japan,'' in D. Borg and S. Okamoto (eds.), *Pearl Harbor as History: Japanese-American Relations 1931–1941* (New York: Columbia University Press, 1973), 459–83.

7. Sadako Ogata, ''Jinken no kokusaiteki yoogo to kokunaiteki shoseisaku'' (''The international protection of human rights and domestic policies''), 46 *Kokusai seiji* (1972): 132–41; Ogata, ''Kokusai rengoo ni okeru jinken yoogo katsudoo'' (''Activities for human rights protection within the United Nations'') in *Jinken hakusho* (*Human Rights White Paper*) (Tokyo: Nihon Hyooron Sha, 1972), 380–404; Ogata, *Kokuren kara no shiten* (*Vantage Point from the United Nations*) (Tokyo: Asahi Evening News Publications, 1980); Ogata, *Nihon ni okeru kokusai soshiki kenkyuu* (*Survey of International Organization Studies in Japan*) (Tokyo: National Institute for Research Advancement, 1982); Ogata, ''Kokusai soshiki kenkyuu to kokusai taisei ron'' (''International organization research and international regime theory''), 76 *Kokusai seiji* (1984):1–10; Ogata, ''The Changing Role of Japan in the United Nations,'' in J. Katz and T. Friedman-Lichtschein (eds.), *Japan's New World Role* (Boulder, Colo.: Westview, 1985), 29–42; Ogata, ''Amerika kokuren seisaku no hensen'' (''Changes in American policy toward the United Nations''), in C. Hosoya (ed.), *Amerika gaikoo: Nichibei kankei no bummyaku no naka de* (*American Diplomacy in the Context of Japanese-American Relations*) (Tokyo: Nihon kokusai mondai kenkyuujo, 1986), 171–204; Ogata, ''Kokuren ni okeru jinken yoogo kinoo'' (''The human rights protection function in the United Nations'') and

''Nihon no kokuren gaikoo no hensen'' (''Changes in Japan's United Nations diplomacy''), in *Satoo Eisaku kinen kokuren daigaku kyoosan zaidan* (ed.), *Kokuren wo kaizoo suru* (*Restructuring the United Nations*) (Tokyo: Sekai no ugoki sha, 1986):141–51, 281–300; Ogata, ''Kokusai seiji to ningen no hogo'' (''International politics and the protection of people'') 36 *Sophia* (1987): 60–73; Ogata, ''Japan's United Nations Policy in the 1980s,'' 27 *Asian Survey* (1987): 957–72; Ogata, ''Shifting Power Relations in Multilateral Banks,'' 22 *The Journal of International Studies (Kokusaigaku Ronshuu)* (1989): 1–25; and Ogata, ''Japan's Policy Toward the United Nations'' in C. Alger, et al., (eds.), *The United Nations System: The Policies of Member States* (Tokyo: United Nations University Press, 1995), 231-70.

8. Sadako Ogata, ''Japanese Attitudes Toward China,'' 5 *Asian Survey* (1965): 389–98; Ogata, ''The Business Community and Japanese Foreign Policy: Normalization of Relations with the People's Republic of China,'' in R. Scalapino (ed.), *The Foreign Policy of Modern Japan* (Berkeley: University of California Press, 1977), 175–203; Ogata, ''Nihon no taigai seisaku kettei katei to zaikai: shihon jiyuuka / Nitchuu kokkoo seijooka katei wo chuushin ni'' (''The Japanese foreign policy making process and big business: the cases of capital liberalization and Sino-Japanese normalization''), in C. Hosoya and J. Watanuki (eds.), *Taigai seisaku kettei katei no Nichibei hikaku* (*A Comparison of Foreign Policy Making Processes in Japan and the United States*) (Tokyo: University of Tokyo Press, 1977), 213–41; Ogata, ''Some Japanese Views on United States–Japan Relations in the 1980s,'' 20 *Asian Survey* (1980): 694–706; Ogata, ''Booeki masatsu: Sono Amerikateki bummyaku'' (''Trade friction: the American context''), *Chuuoo kooron* (August, 1987): 102–11; Ogata, *Normalization with China: A Comparative Study of U.S. and Japanese Processes* (Berkeley: Institute of East Asian Studies, 1989); Ogata, ''Regional and Political Security Issues: The Sino-Japanese-U.S. Triangle,'' in R. Scalapino, et al., (eds.), *Asian Security Issues: Regional and Global* (Berkeley: Institute of East Asian Studies, 1989), 142–64; Ogata, ''Chiikiteki, seijiteki anzen hoshoo mondai: Chuunichibei no sankoku kankei'' (''Regional and political security issues: relations among China, Japan, and the United States'') in *Jiten Ajia Taiheiyoo* (*Dictionary of Asia and the Pacific*) (Tokyo: Chuuoo keizai sha, 1990), 53–73; and Ogata, trans. by Y. Soeya, *Sengo Nitchuu Beichuu kankei* (*Postwar Sino-Japanese and Sino-American Relations*) (Tokyo: University of Tokyo Press, 1992).

9. Ogata, ''Japanese Attitudes Toward China'' (1965); Ogata, ''The Business Community and Japanese Foreign Policy'' (1977); and Ogata, ''The Japanese Foreign Policy Making Process and Big Business'' (1977).

10. Sadako Ogata, ''Beikoku ni okeru Chuugoku seisaku no hensen'' (''Changes in American foreign policy toward China''), 75 *Kokusai mondai* (1966): 10–17.

11. Ogata, ''The Role of Internationalist Groups'' (1971); Ogata, ''The Role of Liberal Nongovernmental Organizations in Japan'' (1973); Ogata, ''Some Japanese Views on United States–Japan Relations in the 1980s'' (1980); and Ogata, ''Trade Friction: The American Context'' (1987).

12. Sadako Ogata, ''Tai-chuu kokkoo seijooka no Nichi-bei hikaku'' (''A comparison of Japanese and U.S. normalization with China''), 254 *Kokusai mondai* (1981): 62–77; Ogata, *Normalization with China* (1989); Ogata, ''Regional and Political Security Issues: The Sino-Japanese-U.S. Triangle'' (1989); Ogata, ''Regional and Political Security Issues: Relations Among China, Japan and the United States'' (1990); and Ogata, *Postwar Sino-Japanese and Sino-American Relations* (1992).

13. Ogata, ''The Business Community and Japanese Foreign Policy'' (1977); and Ogata, ''The Japanese Foreign Policy Making Process and Big Business'' (1977).

14. Ogata, ''Diplomacy and Public Opinion'' (1970); Ogata, ''The Role of Internationalist Groups'' (1971); Ogata, ''Vantage Point from the United Nations'' (1980); Ogata, ''Survey of International Organization Studies in Japan'' (1982); Ogata, ''International Organization Research and International Regime Theory'' (1984); Ogata, ''The Changing Role of Japan in the United Nations'' (1985); Ogata, ''Changes in American Policy Toward the United Nations'' (1986); Ogata, ''Changes in Japan's United Nations Diplomacy'' (1986); Ogata, ''Shifting Power Relations in Multilateral Banks'' (1989); Ogata, ''The United Nations and Japanese Diplomacy'' (1990); and Ogata, ''Japan's Policy Toward the United Nations'' (1995).

15. Ogata, ''The International Protection of Human Rights and Domestic Policies'' (1972); Ogata, ''Activities for Human Rights Protection Within the United Nations'' (1972); Ogata, ''The Human Rights Protection Function in the United Nations'' (1986); and Ogata, ''Japan's United Nation's Policy in the 1980s'' (1987).

16. Sadako Ogata, ''Hookatsu kooshoo wa gensoo na no ka'' (''Are comprehensive negotiations an illusion?''), in S. Ookita (ed.), *Namboku mondai* (*The North-South Problem*) (Tokyo: Chuuoo Kooron Sha, 1984), 163–85.

17. Sadako Ogata, ''Jinken to jindoo: kokusai jindoo mondai dokuritsu iinkai hookoku to no kankei ni oite'' (''Human rights and humanitarianism, in relation to the report of the Independent Commission on Humanitarian Issues''), 1 *Kokusai jinken* (1990): 19–23.

18. Sadako Ogata and A. Mataix (eds.), *Sekai no nammin* (*The World's Refugees*) (Tokyo: Akashi shoboo, 1984).

19. Ogata, ''The Human Rights Protection Function in the United Nations'' (1986).

20. Ogata, ''The International Protection of Human Rights and Domestic Policies'' (1972); and Ogata, ''Activities for Human Rights Protection Within the United Nations'' (1972).

21. Ogata, ''Human Rights and Humanitarianism'' (1990).

22. Ogata, ''Changes in American Policy Toward the United Nations'' (1986).

23. Sadako Ogata, ''The United Nations and Japanese Diplomacy,'' 4 *Japan Review of International Affairs* (1990): 141–65.

24. Ogata, ''Japan's Policy Toward the United Nations'' (1995).

25. Ogata, ''Vantage Point from the United Nations'' (1980).

26. Gil Loescher, ''The International Refugee Regime: Stretched to the Limit?'' 47 *Journal of International Affairs* (1994): 351–77.

27. Gil Loescher, Personal communication to David Wessels, dated April 21, 1995.

## REFERENCES

Kamisaka, Fuyuko. ''Gemba ni tatsu no wa 'Ima shika nai': gakkyuu seikatsukara kokusai butai ni deta kokuren nammin kootoo bemmukan, Ogata Sadako'' ('' 'Now is the time' for action: Ogata Sadako, the United Nations High Commissioner for Refugees, from academic life to the international stage''). In *Minami no shima no Maria: gendai ni choosen shita onnatachi* (*Mary of the Southern Isles: Women Who Have Challenged Our Era*). Tokyo: Bungei Shunju, 1994, 123–58.

Loescher, Gil. ''The International Refugee Regime: Stretched to the Limit?'' *Journal of International Affairs* 47 (1994): 351–77.

Ogata, Sadako. ''Japan's Policy Toward the United Nations.'' In *The United Nations System: The Policies of Member States*. Eds. C. Alger et al. Tokyo: United Nations University Press, 1995, 231–70

Ogata, Sadako. ''Kokuren nammin kootoo bemmukan boochuu nikki'' (''Diary of the United Nations High Commissioner for Refugees''). *Gaiko Forum*. Monthly series, August, 1993–December, 1994.

Ogata, Sadako. *Sengo Nitchuu Beichuu kankei* (*Postwar Sino-Japanese and Sino-American Relations*). Translated by Y. Soeya. Tokyo: University of Tokyo Press, 1992.

Ogata, Sadako. ''Chiikiteki, seijiteki anzen hoshoo mondai: Chuunichibei no sankoku kankei'' (''Regional and political security issues: relations among China, Japan, and the United States''). In *Jiten Ajia Taiheiyoo* (*Dictionary of Asia and the Pacific*). Tokyo: Chuuoo keizai sha, 1990, 53–73.

Ogata, Sadako. ''Jinken to jindoo: kokusai jindoo mondai dokuritsu iinkai hookoku to no kankei ni oite'' (''Human rights and humanitarianism, in relation to the report of the Independent Commission on Humanitarian Issues''). *Kokusai jinken* 1 (1990): 19–23.

Ogata, Sadako. ''The United Nations and Japanese Diplomacy.'' *Japan Review of International Affairs* 4 (1990): 141–65.

Ogata, Sadako. *Normalization with China: A Comparative Study of U.S. and Japanese Processes*. Berkeley: Institute of East Asian Studies, 1989.

Ogata, Sadako. ''Regional and Political Security Issues: The Sino-Japanese-U.S. Triangle.'' In *Asian Security Issues: Regional and Global*. Eds. R. Scalapino et al. Berkeley: Institute of East Asian Studies, 1989, 142–64.

Ogata, Sadako. ''Shifting Power Relations in Multilateral Banks.'' *The Journal of International Studies (Kokusaigaku Ronshuu)* 22 (1989): 1–25.

Ogata, Sadako. ''Booeki masatsu: Sono Amerikateki bummyaku'' (''Trade friction: the American Ogata, Sadako context''). *Chuuoo kooron* (August, 1987): 102–11.

Ogata, Sadako. ''Japan's United Nations Policy in the 1980s.'' *Asian Survey* 27 (1987): 957–72.

Ogata, Sadako. ''Kokusai seiji to ningen no hogo'' (''International Politics and the Protection of People''). *Sophia* 36 (1987): 60–73.

Ogata, Sadako. ''Amerika kokuren seisaku no hensen'' (''Changes in American policy toward the United Nations''). In *Amerika gaikoo: Nichibei kankei no bummyaku no naka de* (*American Diplomacy in the Context of Japanese-American Relations*). Ed. C. Hosoya. Tokyo: Nihon kokusai mondai kenkyuujo, 1986, 171–204.

Ogata, Sadako. ''Kokuren ni okeru jinken yoogo kinoo'' (''The human rights protection function in the United Nations'') and ''Nihon no kokuren gaikoo no hensen'' (''Changes in Japan's United Nations Diplomacy''). In *Kokuren wo kaizoo suru* (*Restructuring the United Nations*). Ed. Satoo Eisaku kinen kokuren daigaku kyoosan zaidan. Tokyo: Sekai no ugoki sha, 1986, 141–51, 281–300.

Ogata, Sadako. ''The Changing Role of Japan in the United Nations.'' In *Japan's New World Role*. Eds. J. Katz and T. Friedman-Lichtschein. Boulder, Colo.: Westview, 1985, 29–42.

Ogata, Sadako. ''Hookatsu kooshoo wa gensoo na no ka'' (''Are comprehensive negotiations an illusion?''). In *Namboku mondai* (*The North-South Problem*). Ed. S. Ookita. Tokyo: Chuuoo Kooron Sha, 1984, 163–85.

Ogata, Sadako. ''Kokusai soshiki kenkyuu to kokusai taisei ron'' (''International organization research and international regime theory''). *Kokusai seiji* 76 (1984): 1–10.

Ogata, Sadako. *Nihon ni okeru kokusai soshiki kenkyuu* (*Survey of International Organization Studies in Japan*). Tokyo: National Institute for Research Advancement, 1982.

Ogata, Sadako. ''Tai-chuu kokkoo seijooka no Nichi-bei hikaku'' (''A Comparison of Japanese and U.S. Normalization with China''). *Kokusai mondai* 254 (1981): 62–77.

Ogata, Sadako. *Kokuren kara no shiten* (*Vantage Point from the United Nations*). Tokyo: Asahi Evening News Publications, 1980.

Ogata, Sadako. ''Some Japanese Views on United States–Japan Relations in the 1980s.'' *Asian Survey* 20 (1980): 694–706.

Ogata, Sadako. ''The Business Community and Japanese Foreign Policy: Normalization of Relations with the People's Republic of China.'' In *The Foreign Policy of Modern Japan*. Ed. R. Scalapino. Berkeley: University of California Press, 1977: 175–203.

Ogata, Sadako. ''Nihon no taigai seisaku kettei katei to zaikai: shihon jiyuuka/Nitchuu kokkoo seijooka katei wo chuushin ni'' (''The Japanese foreign policy making process and big business: the cases of capital liberalization and Sino-Japanese normalization''). In *Taigai seisaku kettei katei no Nichibei hikaku* (*A Comparison of Foreign Policy Making Processes in Japan and the United States*). Eds. C. Hosoya and J. Watanuki. Tokyo: University of Tokyo Press, 1977, 213–41.

Ogata, Sadako. ''The Role of Liberal Nongovernmental Organizations in Japan.'' In *Pearl Harbor as History: Japanese-American Relations 1931–1941*. Eds. D. Borg and S. Okamoto. New York: Columbia University Press, 1973, 459–83.

Ogata, Sadako. ''Jinken no kokusaiteki yoogo to kokunaiteki shoseisaku'' (''The international protection of human rights and domestic policies''). *Kokusai seiji* 46 (1972): 132–41.

Ogata, Sadako. ''Kokusai rengoo ni okeru jinken yoogo katsudoo'' (''Activities for human rights protection within the United Nations''). In *Jinken hakusho* (*Human Rights White Paper*). Tokyo: Nihon Hyooron Sha, 1972, 380–404.

Ogata, Sadako. ''Kokusaishugi dantai no yakuwari'' (''The role of internationalist groups''). In *Nichibei kankei shi* (*The History of Japanese-American Relations*), Volume 3. Ed. C. Hosoya. Tokyo: University of Tokyo Press, 1971, 307–53.

Ogata, Sadako. ''Gaikoo to yoron: renmei dattai wo meguru ichikoosatsu'' (''Diplomacy and public opinion: reflections on the withdrawal from the League of Nations''). *Kokusai seiji* 41 (1970): 40–55.

Ogata, Sadako. ''Beikoku ni okeru Chuugoku seisaku no hensen'' (''Changes in American foreign policy toward China''). *Kokusai mondai* 75 (1966): 10–17.

Ogata, Sadako. *Manshuu jihen to seisaku no keisei katei* (*The Manchurian Affair and the Process of Policy Formulation*). Tokyo: Hara Shoboo, 1966.

Ogata, Sadako. ''Japanese Attitudes Toward China.'' *Asian Survey* 5 (1965): 389–98.

Ogata, Sadako. *Defiance in Manchuria: The Making of Japanese Foreign Policy 1931–1932*. Doctoral dissertation. Berkeley: University of California Press, 1964.

Ogata, Sadako, and A. Mataix, eds. *Sekai no nammin* (*The World's Refugees*). Tokyo: Akashi shoboo, 1984.

*DAVID WESSELS WITH YOSHIHIDE SOEYA AND MASATSUGU NAYA*

# CECILIA MUÑOZ PALMA (1913–    )

''Pro God, pro people, pro poor.'' That is how Cecilia Muñoz Palma, president of the Constitutional Commission of the Republic of the Philippines, characterized the 1987 constitution, which mapped the country's transition back to hopeful democracy after the long, authoritarian, and economically disastrous rule of President Ferdinand Marcos and his wife, Imelda Marcos. That also encapsulates the exceptional life and legal career of Justice Palma, a mixture of passionate commitment to social justice and the rule of law, in service to God and her island country of 60 million. In 1986, over 2,000 distinguished and politically diverse citizens were nominated for the 48 places on the Constitutional Commission. The Commission's unanimous election of Cecilia Muñoz Palma to its presidency accurately reflects the special regard in which she is held by most Filipinos.

## FAMILY BACKGROUND AND EDUCATION

With the Filipino custom of nicknaming, Cecilia is known as ''Celing.'' Celing was born on November 22, 1913, in Bauan, Batangas Province. Her academic distinction began early. She was class valedictorian at St. Scholastica College (secondary school), Manila, in 1931, and went on to receive her Bachelor of Laws degree from the College of Law, University of the Philippines in 1937. That year she placed first (''bar topnotcher'') in the national bar examinations. Palma also began, in 1937, an enduring marriage to Rodolfo C. Palma. On their wedding day he encouraged her to pursue her legal career, and even to dare to dream of a Supreme Court appointment; but he added, ''please, no politics.'' During the Second World War, Rodolfo survived the Bataan Death March and was cited for bravery. Since then, he has had a distinguished career as an attorney and law professor. They have three children, 15 grandchildren, and a great grandson.

In 1947, Palma received a Master of Laws degree from Manila University, and in 1954, she earned a Master of Laws degree from Yale University while on a scholarship from the American Association of University Women. Beginning in 1974, Celing has received numerous honorary doctorates, including one from Ewha Women's University, Seoul, Korea, the world's largest woman's university. The list of her awards for public and community service has grown long, as has the record of her ''firsts'' for a woman and her leadership positions.

## CAREER DEVELOPMENT

At the University of the Philippines, Palma was the first woman president of the Law Student Council. She vigorously participated in the successful national movement in 1936 and 1937 to give women the right to vote. After the Philippines gained its independence in 1946, she became the country's first woman prosecutor (Quezon City, 1947–1954) and later its first woman district judge (Negros Oriental, 1954–1968). Palma was the second woman to rise to the position of Associate Justice of the Court of Appeals (1968–1973), and in 1973, became the first woman associate justice of the Supreme Court (1973–1978).

The constitutional law of the Philippines fuses indigenous elements with the European civil law tradition, and America's common law and emphasis on the power of courts to review the constitutionality and legality of laws and other official acts. The Supreme Court has enjoyed special prestige among national institutions since its beginnings under the 1935 Constitution of the Commonwealth of the Philippines, approved by the U.S. government. The court's power and prestige continue today, although its integrity was compromised at times during the Marcos era. After independence came on July 4, 1946, the Commonwealth Constitution continued in effect until the 1970s. While a Constitutional Convention was drafting a new, more fully Filipino democratic constitution in 1971 and 1972, President Marcos intervened, declared martial law on questionable grounds, and thereafter put in place a constitution that gave him extraordinary powers until the ''People's Revolution'' of 1986, led by President Corazon Aquino.

In 1973, on the recommendation of Secretary of Justice Vicente Abad Santos, Marcos appointed Cecilia Muñoz Palma the first woman justice of the Supreme Court of the Philippines. While some colleagues on the Court were cowed into conformity with the wishes of the legally astute Marcos in sensitive cases, she took a courageous stand against human rights violations of the regime. As former Chief Justice Marcelo Fernan said, ''Her stint was marked by exemplary courage. She never wavered in raising a dissenting voice against a regime that cleverly manipulated the law to legitimize its disregard of the fundamental rights and freedoms of the citizen.'' A commentator noted after the difficult Diokno case (discussed later in this article): "The only man in the Supreme Court happens to be a woman."

After reaching the compulsory retirement age of 65 in 1978, Justice Palma became a persistent voice in the peaceful movement to lift martial law and restore individual rights and democracy, which culminated in the 1986 election of President Corazon Aquino. The stage was set for the rebellion and the subsequent establishment of Palma's Constitutional Commission by the 1983 assassination of Benigno S. Aquino, Jr., Aquino's husband, former senator, and leading Marcos opponent. The airport shooting death involved people close to Marcos. In 1984, representing the capital Quezon City, Justice Palma became one of only three prominent opposition leaders elected to the National Assembly (*Batasang Pambansa*).

As head of the National Unification Committee (NUC), which united opposition political parties, and as a supporter of Corazon Aquino's peaceful People's Revolution, Palma played an important role in the demise and departure from the Philippines of President Marcos. Backed by the Catholic Church and broadly representative, the People's Revolution of 1986 was a remarkable religiopolitical rebellion that shocked and inspired the oppressed around the world. It overcame military and police power by including them. Soldiers sent to deal decisively with the rebellion found their tanks and trucks surrounded by civilians pleading and praying for their peaceful support; instead of killing them, they accepted their sandwiches and joined the revolution.

As a devout Catholic, Justice Palma has been driven not by political or economic ambition but by Christian concern for just law and relief for the poor and violated. She sees her considerable abilities as gifts from God entailing unavoidably heavy social responsibilities, and her strength as coming from prayer, the Mass, and the Bible. She has won respect by her unequivocal consistency on human rights issues and her special empathy for those who suffer most from the abuse of power, the poor.

Under the more democratic governments of President Aquino (1986–1992) and President Fidel Ramos (1992–), her blunt criticism of public and private violations of human rights continued. For example, in a December, 1988, speech, Justice Palma noted that during the Marcos regime there were 2,501 political murders, 132 community massacres, tens of thousands improperly imprisoned (many of them tortured), and an estimated 100,000 killed and 2 million displaced during the Muslim rebellion on Mindanao. However, she also attacked the failure of the Aquino regime to stop deaths, disappearances, torture, the violent private armies of propertied regional lords, and the assassination of five human rights lawyers. Typically, Palma gave due credit to government efforts to rein in and bring to justice military and other perpetrators, but said:

> I am sure that I shall be castigated by those in government for the grim picture given on the human rights situation today. But facts are facts, and events are events, and they must be brought out in the light of day in order that fair and impartial investigations

may be made by the proper government agencies and the guilty persons brought to the bar of justice. Otherwise the Philippines Human Rights System will be a mere mockery of the rule of law.

In 1990, in the face of severe poverty and other economic problems, attempted military coups, political fractiousness, and continued insurgencies, President Aquino established the National Peace Conference. The NUC united 250 organizations in 17 sectors of society to develop a vision of peaceful approaches to solving national problems over time, and to propose strategies and action plans to end violence and to promote political and cultural development based on civilian supremacy and constitutional democracy. In 1994, Justice Palma became president of the NUC as well as a leader of President Ramos's Moral Recovery Program. Like Thomas More, whom she is fond of quoting, she is a person ''for all seasons,'' in her 80s as in her youth.

## ACHIEVEMENTS AND CONTRIBUTIONS

For decades, Palma represented women, the government, or the legal profession of the Philippines at international conferences. Her awards, which number about 100, single her out for her exceptional service as citizen, woman, lawyer, and judge. Typical is the ''Outstanding Citizenship Award'' from the Community Chest of Greater Manila as ''leader of the community, servant of the people, friend of the needy.'' In 1977, Pope Paul VI honored her with the *Pro Ecclesia et Pontifice* Cross for courageously upholding the cause of human rights, truth, and justice. The Philippines Junior Chamber of Commerce named Palma one of the ''Ten Outstanding Filipinos'' in 1989. She received the Women's Lawyers Association's first Golden Achievement Award in 1990, ''for her unequalled achievement and service to her country and people—the epitome of greatness in her simplicity and humility, moral integrity, passionate sense of justice tempered with compassion.'' As one of its founders and early leaders, Palma began a free legal aid program for the poor in 1946, especially for women affected by the postwar chaos and for ''G.I. babies'' left by American fathers.

Justice Palma has held many leadership positions in civic, professional, and Catholic associations, for example, the National Committee on Human Rights and Due Process of the Integrated Bar of the Philippines (Chair, 1988–1990), the Community Chest, the Philippine Tuberculosis Society (President, 1992–present), the National Council for Women, Boards of Trustees of educational institutions, the Family Rights Movement of the Philippines, and the Zonta Club (first district governor for Asia). (Zonta International is an international service organization of executive women in business and the professions.) Her concern for the poor is illustrated by the Zonta Manila Tondo Feeding Project. Through Justice Palma's leadership, Zonta Manila learned of a Jesuit project fighting malnourishment among children and assumed full responsibility for the program.

Less widely known is her longstanding practice of bringing solace and conversation to the inmates of the Correctional Institution for Women (*Mandaluyong*).

Faced with the great range of Cecilia Muñoz Palma's other community services, one can forget she has been primarily a jurist. As for Thomas More and for most judges, attorneys, and legal scholars, the critical tests of character and lifelong performance arise rarely and within contexts of technical judgment opaque to the general public. Justice Palma met such tests well in her dissenting opinions on the Supreme Court. The 1974 *habeas corpus* case involving Marcos's opponent, Senator Jose Diokno, provides an example from early in her tenure on the bench when the first *habeas corpus* cases were filed after martial law Proclamation No. 1081, September 21, 1972. Diokno had been held under martial law without charges for almost two years when Justice Palma issued her dissenting opinion favoring his release, to the great displeasure of some fellow justices and the president. Her opinion was a major reason for Diokno's eventual release. She held:

> [The detention of Jose Diokno] has reached a point where it can be adjudged by this Court as arbitrary and oppressive. I invoke: (1) the principles of humane justice so eloquently espoused by this Court in [precedents involving Second World War and other political prisoners] . . . ; (2) the rules of natural justice which among other things uphold the dignity of man and his inviolable right to freedom, so eloquently expressed . . . in the General Assembly of Bishops in Rome in 1971; (3) the Universal Declaration of Human Rights . . . , Articles 1, 3, 8, and 9 . . . ; (4) the physical condition of petitioner Diokno, not to mention his mental anguish and suffering . . . ; (5) there is nothing in the record of this case to show some good reason for withholding [a release order].

In other cases, Palma challenged the regime's detention under martial law of Benigno S. Aquino. For example, on September 17, 1974, she concluded:

> To recapitulate: (1) Is the constitutional sufficiency of a proclamation of martial law by the President a political question? I hold that it is not a political, but it is a justiciable one. (2) Did the proclamation of martial law automatically suspend the privilege of the writ of *habeas corpus*? No, is my answer. (3) Did . . . Transitory Provisions of the 1973 Constitution foreclose judicial inquiry into the validity of all decrees, orders, and acts of the incumbent President executed after the proclamation of martial law . . . ? I say NO, because these acts are still subject to the power of judicial review if and when they are shown to be arbitrary, oppressive, or unjust, in violation of the Constitution and/or the generally accepted principles of International Law.

In remarks made upon her retirement from the Supreme Court, she humanely praised colleagues and friends of the Court at the banquet, but then sharply attacked the "weakening of the judiciary" under martial law for replacing the ordinary courts with military tribunals, for rendering insecure judges' tenure, and for "sepulchral silence on a matter which affects the very institution of the

Rule of Law.'' The reason, she said, was ''the lack of militant leadership'' from ''the Supreme Court of the land,'' for which she appealed.

Her dissents were sometimes written with personal and professional anguish, not with calm ease but with a clear understanding of consequences. Palma felt that faith enabled her to follow principle. For many of her years on the bench, she played the organ for noon weekday Mass at St. Thomas More Chapel with other court personnel in attendance; but after offering soothing music, she would return to the court to write what some might consider politically incorrect, disturbingly unpleasant opinions against her peers in government, law, and politics. Palma is a woman for all seasons, to be admired in all cultures.

*LAWRENCE W. BEER*

# TAMAR PELLEG-SRYCK (1926– )

Tamar Pelleg-Sryck, a human rights lawyer and an Israeli Jew, has devoted her legal career to the defense of Palestinians under Israeli occupation. While her early education was not in the area of law, her political activism prompted her to seek such a degree at the age of 60, and she has used this education to challenge the human rights abuses of the Israeli occupation. Pelleg-Sryck has helped to enlarge the scope of the occupation officials' accountability and narrowed the gap between the law and its practice in the Occupied Territories. Through her tireless efforts, she has sought to improve both prison conditions and the treatment of Palestinian prisoners. In addition, methodologically, her unique practice of "being there"—being present when human rights violations were occurring; her cooperative work with Palestinian lawyers, organizations, and individuals; her regular publications in the Hebrew press; her cooperation, advice to, and reports to human rights organizations around the world; and her infinite filing of complaints with the Israeli authorities—have been hallmarks of Pelleg-Sryck's work to alleviate human rights abuses against the Palestinians.

## FAMILY BACKGROUND AND EDUCATION

Tamar's mother, Lydia Unkovskaya, was a Russian Christian from Moscow who converted to Judaism when she met her husband, Jacob Eliasberg, from Pinsk. After marrying, they settled in the Jewish *shtetel* in Pinsk, then part of Poland. Tamar, the only child of this union, was born in 1926. Religion played no part in Tamar's home life, yet both Christian and Jewish holidays were observed in a rather idiosyncratic way. While Zionism was not stressed at home, Jewish consciousness, pride, and values were strongly advocated. Tamar recalls that in her youth she felt alienated from her schoolmates and friends because she was the only child in the community who did not speak Yiddish; because in this exclusively Jewish enclave, her family had a Christmas tree and painted eggs at Easter; and because her family was well-to-do, owned a large house and summer home, and had one of the two existing automobiles in Pinsk. As Tamar described it, she was, "a minority inside a minority. . . . All through my life I have been exposed to seemingly conflicting norms and values."[1]

She adored her father, and he apparently returned the sentiment.

> Father has been my beloved hero and protector, the only authority I accepted besides my own. He did not make compromises when his moral principles were involved . . . and yet he was a man of status, highly valued in the community. He was also a true humanist, very considerate, sociable, and admittedly charming, witty, and wise. From my father, I learned the lesson that has been the guiding creed of my life: that principles must be taken seriously and lived by, and that life *per se* is nothing, it is how you live it that matters.

In September of 1939, Tamar's young life was severely disrupted by the events of World War II when the family was deported to Kazakhstan. There, in order to attend school, Tamar had to live with a strange family. The experience involved many deprivations and was not pleasant: "What made me [most] miserable and unhappy was the sudden and so complete absence of love." But in June of 1941, her family began a complex three-year journey that took them through Yangi-Yul, Batumi, Teheran, Abadan, Karachi, and Port Tawfic before they finally arrived in Palestine in 1943. Of her arrival, Tamar recalled, "I felt like I was coming home. My only wish, which reached the point of obsession, was to become assimilated, to belong. . . . I refused to speak anything but Hebrew . . . and also I wanted to make up the time I had lost in studying."

With regard to the Palestinians, Tamar recalled that she was simply unaware of them; it was as though they did not exist. "Of course, I went to war with them in 1948, but as an abstraction, they didn't have faces. This is so typical in Israel and in the beginning, I wanted to be more typical than typical. . . . The Zionist spirit and ideology were all that I knew and it took a long time for the realities to penetrate."

In 1945, Tamar joined the *Haganah* (the regular Zionist underground military), and when hostilities broke out in Jerusalem in November, 1947, she became actively involved in secretly transporting arms to *Haganah* outposts. Later, Tamar became a company welfare and culture sergeant stationed in the mountains outside Jerusalem. "These were absolutely my cups of tea, and very much so, due both to my feelings for the cause (Zionism) and to my temperament."

In the mid-1940s, Tamar began her collegiate education at the Hebrew University. She studied history, psychology, and philosophy and received a Master of Arts degree, *magna cum laude*, in history, with psychology as a second area. On graduating in December, 1950, she was awarded a scholarship from the

French government at the *Institut de Paris* where she chose to pursue a year of studies in psychopathology and clinical psychology.

In 1951, Tamar married Eli Pelleg, an envoy of the Jewish Agency in Paris on behalf of *Mapam* (a leftist political party in Israel), and in 1952, she gave birth to their daughter, Orna. Five years later, their son, Danny, was born.

While studying in Paris, Tamar came into contact with a number of leftists and radicals—students and others. Her husband, Pelleg, became a communist and Tamar joined the Communist party in 1953, remaining a member for 12 years. The party was legal in Israel and tended to attract mainly Israeli Arabs and dissident Jews. Within the party, Tamar was active in the Association of Democratic Teachers, an Arab-Jewish organization within the National Teachers Union. Of her experience with the Communist party, Tamar recalled that she hated the discipline, but that the episode gave her a "rare and practically non-existent opportunity in Israel to meet the Arabs as equals. (They did not call themselves Palestinians at the time.) My contacts with the Arabs went beyond the party. We worked together, visited each other, and friendships developed on a personal basis some of which have survived until the present." After Tamar quit the party, she joined a loosely organized movement, the New Israeli Left (SIAH), whose main focus was on the Palestinian issue. That was her last organizational involvement; later, she became what she describes as a "free lance leftist."

The same year that Tamar married Eli, he was thrown out of the *kibbutz* (agricultural collective), of which he was a founding member, as a consequence of his political views. Eli took a party job but was so poorly paid that Tamar essentially became responsible for the financial well-being of the family. "I had to take a job, any job." Eli died in 1965, and for a short time, Tamar truly had full responsibility for their two children.

In 1966, Tamar married the Czech film critic, Joseph Sryck, and had a daughter, Aya, in 1967. In 1970, she again entered a psychology program (psychohistory) at Tel Aviv University where she earned high honors and a scholarship. However, after three years of intense study and reading and just as she was preparing to begin writing her dissertation, differing theoretical and intellectual perspectives between Tamar and her major professor left her without a dissertation sponsor and as a result, without the much-desired doctoral degree.

Tamar's first full-time position, in the early 1950s, was teaching mentally retarded children; in addition, she began teaching psychology at night at a teachers training college. Some years later this college became an important institution for the study of art—the State Art Teachers Training College—and Tamar became a full-time teacher there. The school was very humanistic and liberal, and Tamar found the work rewarding. In 1975, she was appointed vice headmaster and remained in the position until 1983, when she chose early retirement. During her tenure at the college, Tamar was active in sponsoring, organizing, and encouraging political events—lectures, demonstrations, exhibitions—many with emphasis on the Palestinians. Between 1979 and 1983, Tamar both worked at the Teachers College and studied psychohistory at Tel Aviv University. Joseph, her second husband, died in 1982.

In 1979, Tamar entered law school at Tel Aviv University and passed the bar examination in February, 1986, at the age of 60. She did her practicum with Avigdor Feldman, a highly respected Israeli lawyer dedicated to human rights. When Tamar received her attorney's license, she practiced for a short time in her own office representing Bedouins, leftist demonstrators, workers, and other similarly disenfranchised persons. While these were, for the most part, very important civil and human rights cases, the work did not provide an adequate living. Subsequently, in October, 1987, Tamar joined the staff of the Association for Civil Rights in Israel (ACRI). The *Intifada* (Palestinian uprising) erupted two months later, and she became exclusively absorbed in defending Palestinian human rights, even though this was not ACRI's principal focus. As a salaried employee for ACRI, her services to the Palestinians were always without charge.

## ACHIEVEMENTS AND CONTRIBUTIONS

Consider the obstacles faced by an attorney defending Palestinians under Israeli occupation, an occupation where military commanders legislate Military Orders (MOs) to suit any situation they come up against (there are more than 1,000 such MOs), where they have the right to change any law that they feel contradicts "security," and where, in practice, there is virtually no rule of law. What can one realistically accomplish in the practice of human rights law in such a situation? According to Tamar Pelleg-Sryck,

> Legal practice is needed because you do improve the lot of these individuals. How much so is for them to judge. But if you can get a permit for a sick child to go to a hospital or if you can shorten the length of administrative detention, I think this not only justifies but obliges you to practice law. Law is never a way to improve society but it can certainly make individuals less miserable.

Pelleg-Sryck has been basically a "field lawyer," working primarily in the Gaza Strip and at Ketziot prison (in Israel's southern Negev), but also in other prisons and in other places in the West Bank. For the most part, her work has not been in the formal courtroom setting except for those occasions when she has filed petitions in the military courts for releases on bail and appealed administrative detentions and deportations. Because of the intensity of her fieldwork, Pelleg-Sryck rarely appeared before the Israeli High Court of Justice, preferring to leave such appeals to her colleagues at ACRI.

Pelleg-Sryck opted to be where things were "happening"—torture, deportations, arrests, shootings, house searches, and house demolitions. She felt that it was important "to see with my own eyes the jails, the jailed, and the jailers; to meet the beaten and the shot; to bear witness to the haughtiness and brutality of the occupier and to the humiliation and suffering of the occupied; to see and listen and to have the immediate knowledge of the effects of the occupation.'' As a result of her constant presence in the field, individual cases gave birth to projects that were part of her larger struggle against specific human rights violations.

While working for and out of ACRI, Pelleg-Sryck initiated a variety of interventions to help her clients that have enlarged the scope of ACRI's activity. For example, ACRI policy had been to take only test cases to court. Thus, if there were 15 cases of men denied a lawyer, ACRI took only one and tried to get a favorable ruling. But even when they succeeded in obtaining a positive outcome, it would never be known by the Palestinians. Someone, specifically an Israeli, had to implement the ruling and had to make the Palestinians and most especially their lawyers, aware of it. The test case approach simply did not solve the unique problems in the Occupied Territories. As a consequence of Pelleg-Sryck's wide-ranging fieldwork, ACRI expanded its conception of appropriate interventions in the Occupied Territories beyond the test case approach.

I think that my role in changing ACRI was in part due to the extent I got involved and was in such close touch with so many cases and so many Palestinian lawyers, and so many Palestinian organizations. It's a question of being persistent, persistence of will, not intelligence. The situation is that after eight years of constant, relentless involvement, I have learned a lot and have become relatively effective. Of course, everything is relative!

Pelleg-Sryck's primary focus has been on administrative detention (the practice of arresting and holding individuals in preventive detention without charge or trial), and on Ketziot prison (Ansar 3) in the Negev (southern Israel). Administrative detention allows the incarceration of thousands of individuals without any due process, and Ketziot was opened in March of 1988, explicitly to accommodate such prisoners. Although administrative detainees in the Occupied Territories are granted the right of appeal, the appeal is heard *in camera* by a military judge in the prison; there is no privilege of reviewing the evidence, and there are no witnesses. A General Security Services (GSS) representative brings the secret file of the appellant, but the contents remain hidden from the appellant and his lawyer. Most of the questions asked of the state by the appellant's lawyer remain unanswered on grounds of ''security.'' According to Pelleg-Sryck, ''These are very frustrating proceedings. And yet, quite a few terms of detention are reduced by the judge. Also, physically being there makes it possible to supervise the proceeding and to insist that the law, harsh as it is, be observed.''

During the *Intifada,* there could be as many as 3,000 prisoners at Ketziot at any given time. Pelleg-Sryck has represented over 200 administrative detainees a year. She has traveled once each week from her home in Tel Aviv to Ketziot to represent detainees at their appellate hearings, and to attend to the problems and regular complaints of her clients and the general prison population.[2] While most of her work has centered on filing appeals for administrative detainees, additional problems often arise, such as the health of a person in prison, general problems relating to the conditions of incarceration, or the problems a released prisoner faces, for example, in the matter of his identification permit, his freedom of movement, or harm to his family. Pelleg-Sryck has consistently intervened on behalf of Palestinian prisoners on all these issues. ''All of this [representation and intervention] does not change the system of administrative detention but it changes peoples' fate. And I think I have made a difference here, by being there every week for eight years.''

At one point, ACRI doubted the necessity of continuing administrative detainee appeals, but Pelleg-Sryck persuaded the organization otherwise:

> I need these representations for two reasons: (1) to supervise prison conditions. That's how I get information. That's how I know—how I can take care of human rights issues like health, torture, and prison conditions. (2) Also, with regard to the proceedings themselves, I may improve them by being there and constantly intervening and complaining in detail. Palestinian lawyers are, by definition, under occupation like everyone else and often, because of curfews and closures, they cannot reach the prison. In addition, they are treated as inferiors and without respect.

ACRI relented, and Pelleg-Sryck continued her work at Ketziot.

Pelleg-Sryck has been very involved in the issue of prison conditions for the administrative detainees. She has written extensive reports on the deplorable conditions and distributed them widely.

> This [Ketziot] is a prison in which people live in tents, sleeping on a narrow, thin piece of mattress, close to the ground, and around the tent are more and more tents, and beyond them is a paved plot with no greenery and that's all. There are no tables and no chairs. Each tent has between 24 and 28 people so that the bunks are very close together. This past winter was very severe and cold. People didn't sleep nights as there were no heaters. Tents leaked, tents were inundated, conditions were very difficult. In winter there is also the problem of light. Because of the cold, it's necessary to shut the tent, and then it's dark inside. It is almost impossible to function under such circumstances. People aren't able to sit and read or write. The prisoners have no transistors, they have no radio. They do not have easy access to books. Getting a book into Ketziot is like crossing the Red Sea. Newspapers arrive after a long intentional delay; letters arrive after a long delay and after being censored; and basically the food is inedible.[3]

After observing these conditions, Pelleg-Sryck stated:

> It was my responsibility to follow through. In the beginning, I was so shocked that I had to get it out of my system and so I wrote many reports and mailed them to as many people as possible including government and military officials. Some were published in the Hebrew press. I believe that if I had not been there, if I had not published things, the situation would have been much worse. Also, the deprivations were so severe, so extreme, perhaps my work speeded up somewhat the improvements, maybe it was more

than that. You never know, you really never know. But I feel in my heart that I made a difference—judging by concrete changes and by the way the administrative detainees and also the establishment treated me.

Pelleg-Sryck also worked on the issue of deportations, representing three groups of deportees from Gaza before the Appeal Committees. Additionally, she has been involved and concerned over the matter of torture.

Raji Sourani, a Palestinian lawyer who later became the director of the Gaza Center for Rights and Law, and I started a project on torture. We began interviewing people recently incarcerated who had been subjected to interrogation. I did this in close cooperation with many Palestinian lawyers and other Palestinian individuals and organizations. But with the Gaza Center it was more than cooperation; it was genuine teamwork. That's one of the differences between me and other lawyers who work at ACRI—my receiving information and being approached by Palestinian lawyers, individuals and organizations. We were mutually dependent and complimented one another. None of us working alone could have achieved the results we did by working together.

Indeed, Pelleg-Sryck's collaboration with Palestinians has been a highly significant strategy to her work. Because of the estrangement between Israelis and Palestinians, it is very unusual for an Israeli to ask a Palestinian for assistance in helping another Palestinian. But for Pelleg-Sryck, ''It never occurred to me to treat Palestinian lawyers as less than equal. As a matter of course, on certain issues they know more than I do. I never think of them as 'them' and I believe the joint work that I have done with Palestinian lawyers—the common front we've sometimes been able to face the authorities with—has enhanced the outcome of several cases.'' Because of her willingness to work with Palestinian legal counsels, she has managed to enhance the access that the Palestinian lawyers have to their clients. ''In one particular case, a miracle happened. The Palestinian lawyer and I spent four hours with the prisoners. It was without precedent—so far from what a Palestinian lawyer could do alone, not because he is incompetent, but because as an Israeli I can approach and am tolerated by the authorities in a different manner. Of course, it does not always work for me either.''

Consider the following example that illustrates Pelleg-Sryck's point about the innovations that come from cooperation. A 22-year-old man who had just finished his studies in Jordan had returned home and was ordered to present himself to the Civil Administration. Twenty-fours hours later he died in Tulkarim (in the West Bank) prison. Pelleg-Sryck heard of the death from a lecturer at a local university who took her, a fieldworker from the Palestine Human Rights International Center (PHRIC), and a lawyer from *Al Haq* (Law in the Service of Man, the West Bank Affiliate of the International Commission of Jurists) to the village where the young man had lived. Together, they began an investigation of his death.

I had reliable information from a confidential source who trusts me. I wrote the initial report and the formal complaint in such a way that no one would ever know my source. PHRIC took care of the forensic pathology, arranging to have the body taken to the Israeli Forensic Pathologic Institute. Everyone did what he/she could without a formal organization. We all met with the pathologist following the examination and then PHRIC organized a press conference. The night before, we had a meeting on how to present the case publicly. I tried to set the tone in a factual, objective, nondefensive manner. We never received any real answer to our complaint but I assume from general reports about subsequent incidents of deaths under interrogation, that our work had an impact.

Pelleg-Sryck has continued monitoring and writing reports about maltreatment and torture, disclosing the General Security Services (GSS) methods of interrogation. For instance, some of the methods include keeping detainees for long periods in a ''cupboard,'' a tiny, suffocating, stinking, closed space; denying sleep; playing unbearably loud music to which detainees are exposed for days and nights on end; and putting detainees in ''frigidaires'' where they are held for extensive periods in extremely low temperatures, being allowed to wear only a cotton overall. Pelleg-Sryck takes affidavits from the prisoners who have been subjected to these conditions, and in turn they have been included in the torture reports of *Bet Ts'elem*, an Israeli human rights organization.

Pelleg-Sryck has also provided data and information on torture and other human rights abuses to Amnesty International, Human Rights Watch/Middle East Watch, the Lawyers Committee for Human Rights, the Israeli press, the foreign press, Cable News Network, and other fact-finding commissions coming from abroad. Regrettably and with no justification, some organizations are much more likely to believe an Israeli than a Palestinian source, and thus, Pelleg-Sryck's efforts in this regard have been very important. She has also written numerous articles for the Hebrew press.

The policy of destroying houses with mortars, rockets, grenades, and machine guns, initiated in the summer of 1992, gave rise to multiple human rights violations. (The Israeli authorities allege that there were wanted people inside and destroying the houses facilititates their capture.) For Pelleg-Sryck, the experience was unforgettable.

When I saw it for the first time, it was one of the worst experiences of my life—11 houses in Khan Yunis. Usually when I write letters to the authorities, I do so politely and without agitation and it usually works very well. This time, I just couldn't. I didn't know it was official policy. I wrote a letter demanding to investigate, to charge people, and to punish those who planned the operation, carried out the attack, everyone involved. I wrote details—how many windows, how many this, how many that. . . . Maybe this is my invention, to write, to complain, in such detail that even the GSS say I am a credible person; it has come back to me that my complaints are credible. When you are in a minority position you must bring facts. And here I am in a terrible position, I represent the enemy. And the enemy lies (by definition, in the view of the Occupation Authorities), so I have to prove my credibility. Thus, I sent extremely detailed letters to everybody—the Judge Advocate or Attorney General of the Army, to everyone.

Actually, Pelleg-Sryck's practice of writing reports and complaints to the authorities has been quite important. Israelis and the Israeli authorities like to present a positive face to the outside world; thus, the constant complaints and reports had some effect. The officials could not ignore facts and continually feign ignorance. Quite often, they would attempt to do something, to change practices, within the limits of their power. This is how the rule of law—the Military Law of the occupation—could be sporadically enforced.

Pelleg-Sryck believes that style is always important in dealing with the authorities. "I remember the first time I wanted to visit the prison in Gaza (Ansar 2), they tried to fool me. I got from the authority, 'He's not there, he's there,' . . . all those tricks. When I went to the prison there was another order that forbade me from meeting with other lawyers—everything they do to every Palestinian lawyer and to inexperienced Israeli lawyers." But her persistence and experience have paid off. "They won't do it to me now; they cannot fool me. But, after so many experiences I know that with some prison authorities, I can be humorous, polite, even friendly. One develops a style of work. And it should perhaps be mentioned that Israelis perceive Israelis as Israelis—we are one, we are together." Pelleg-Sryck has even managed to earn the respect of those who imprison her clients. "A year ago I received a *Rosh Ha'shannah* (New Year's) greeting from the commander of Ketziot and he wrote: 'I learned to know you and I wish you to continue with your humanistic work.' This kind of relationship makes all kinds of things possible."

Pelleg-Sryck received a prestigious award in December, 1991, from the New York-based Human Rights Watch for her legal work in human rights. Together with 15 other human rights monitors from around the world, she was invited to New York and Washington, where she met with officials from the State Department, Congress, and the media to discuss the human rights situation in the Occupied Territories.

On a different, but equally important level, a Muslim Arab from Gaza, who spent years in prison and was very active in resisting the Israeli occupation, named his only daughter Tamar, a distinctly Hebrew name. When I asked him why, he replied that he wanted to honor in some way Tamar Pelleg who had helped him greatly and whose work on behalf of the Palestinians was unparalleled.

Pelleg-Sryck's work with the Palestinians began with the *Intifada* in 1987. At this writing, the political situation is very different, with a Palestinian "Authority" sitting in Gaza. This has meant something of a change in the demand for Israeli human rights lawyers. Nevertheless, as Pelleg-Sryck notes, "My phone keeps ringing and people keep asking for help. Lately, it has been mainly for the arrested, administratively detained, and imprisoned. There is a change in my work but so far I have no reason to fear unemployment. It is too early to analyze the new political situation and predict future developments.''

## NOTES

1. Interview with Tamar Pelleg-Sryck over two days, September 14–15, 1994, Tel Aviv, Israel in Tamar's home. All subsequent quotations, unless otherwise annotated, come from this interview.

2. Maya Rosenfeld, ''Interview with Tamar Pelleg: 'I Now Have a New Identity,' '' 3 *Challenge* (Winter, 1992): 8.

3. Ibid., 10.

## REFERENCES

Brenner, Elie Brenner. ''A Human Rights Watch Dog'' (in Hebrew). *Davar* (Hebrew daily) (December 6, 1991).

''The Civil Rights Enforcers of Israel.'' *The American Lawyer* (June 1990).

Cohen, Amiram. ''The Incorrigible'' (in Hebrew). *al-Hamishmar* (Hebrew daily) (February 26, 1988).

Cohen, Oren. ''Out of 4,414 Appeals Against Administrative Detention, 747 Were Received—ACRI's Report'' (in Hebrew). *Hadashot* (Hebrew daily) (March 12, 1989).

Dagan, Amihai. ''She Does Not Turn a Blind Eye'' (in Hebrew). *HaAretz* (Weekly supplement) (August 12, 1988).

''Gal Ochowsky Speaks with Tamar Pelleg, the ACRI Lawyer Who Was Forbidden to Pass over a Book by Amos Oz [an Israeli writer]: A List of Permitted Books Hanging on the Wall'' (in Hebrew). *Hadashot* (Hebrew daily) (August 9, 1989).

Hanokh-Filosof, Miri. ''She was a Psychologist, now a Lawyer: What Makes a Person Change Professions, a 180 Degree Turn?'' (in Hebrew). *Yediot Ahronot* (Hebrew daily) (January 13, 1993).

Kadosh, Orna. ''Helping the Underdog: Tamar Pelleg, 61, Lawyer for Two Years and Has No Time to Make Money'' (in Hebrew). *Ha'eer* (Hebrew weekly) (December 12, 1987).

Kadosh, Ruthie. ''This Story Could Not Have Been Made up But Neither Could it Have Happened'' (in Hebrew). *al-Hamishmar* (Hebrew daily) (May 6, 1990).

Paychere, Francois. ''Israel et les Territoires Occupes, La Fin du non-droit?'' (in French). *Pladoyer* Nr. 4/94: 41.

Pelleg, Tamar. ''The Limits of Defense'' (in Hebrew). *HaAretz* (Weekly supplement) (May 6, 1994).

Pelleg, Tamar. ''Of Rights and Men: A Human Rights Lawyer's Dilemma.'' *News from Within* (Israeli monthly) (August, 1994).

Pelleg, Tamar. ''Not for Love of the High Court of Justice'' (in Hebrew). *HaAretz* (February 2, 1993).

Pelleg, Tamar. ''No Hope in Gaza.'' *American-Israeli Civil Liberties Coalition*. Volume 14, no. 1 (Summer 1992).

Pelleg, Tamar. ''The Situation in Gaza Is Deteriorating and Who Knows If We Can Keep Up with the Pace?'' *News from Within* (Israeli monthly) (March 1991).

Pelleg, Tamar. ''The Labyrinth of Administrative Detention'' (in Hebrew). *HaAretz* (Hebrew daily) (December 18, 1990).
Pelleg, Tamar. ''In the Prison of Ketziot After the High Court of Justice'' (in Hebrew). *Davar* (Hebrew daily) (January 4 and 5, 1989).
Pelleg, Tamar. ''A Lawyer's Diary from Ketziot Prison'' (in Hebrew). *Gesher* (Hebrew weekly) (July 5, 1989).
Pelleg, Tamar. ''A Net for the Law'' (in Hebrew). *al Hamishmar* (Hebrew daily) (October, 25, 1989).
Pelleg, Tamar. ''The Duty Gone with the Right'' (in Hebrew). *al-Hamishmar* (Hebrew daily) (March 29, 1987).
Pelleg, Tamar. ''A Short Course in the Laws of Discrimination'' (in Hebrew). *al-Hamishmar* (Hebrew daily) (May 5, 1987).
Rieker, Francine. ''Tamar Pelleg, Avocate a Gaza'' (in French and German). *Pladoyer: Revue Juridique et Politique*, 5 (1990), 49.
Rosenfeld, Maya. ''Interview with Tamar Pelleg: 'I Now Have a New Identity.' '' *Challenge* 3 (Winter, 1992): 8.
Rosenthal, Eddo. ''Aftsluiting Gazastrook is belangrijkste oorzaak Geweld'' (in Dutch). *de Volkskrant* (Dutch daily) (May 22, 1993).
''Tamar Pelleg, Attorney, Defends Human Rights'' (in Hebrew). *Kol Ha-eer* (Hebrew weekly) (Special issue devoted to the second anniversary of the *Intifada*) (December 8, 1989).
''Tamar Pelleg, Israeli Attorney and Human Rights Activists—'Situation in Ansar 3 Detention Camp Critical' '' (in English). *al-Fajr* (Weekly) (September 9, 1991).
Yoeli, Romit. ''The Nature of the State and Not Somebody's Destiny Is at Stake: Interview with Tamar Pelleg Who Dealt in the Past with the Petitions of Deportees'' (in Hebrew). *Hadashot* (Hebrew daily) (December 23, 1992).
Zelig, Yaron. ''Pelleg's Report'' (in Hebrew). *Tel-Aviv* (Weekly supplement of *Yediot Aharonet*) (May 13, 1988).

*CHERYL A. RUBENBERG*

# JANET RENO (1938–    )

Janet Reno has enjoyed a successful career as a lawyer in public service to her hometown community of south Florida and to her nation. A graduate of Harvard Law School, she began her legal career in south Florida and worked in both private and public practice. While her national fame stems from her appointment to the post of attorney general of the United States, she will always be fondly remembered by south Floridians as a native daughter. Reno's dominating presence and her often disheveled appearance combined with a gentle yet adamant voice of concern for this nation's children has allowed her to capture the attention of the nation. Perhaps no other contemporary attorney general has enjoyed such recognition and popularity as Attorney General Janet Reno.

## FAMILY BACKGROUND AND EDUCATION

Janet Reno was born on July 21, 1938, to Jane Wood and Henry Ramissen. Tiring of having his name mispronounced, Ramissen changed his Danish surname to Reno (like Reno, Nevada).[1] Janet is the eldest of four children. Her brother, Bob, is a columnist for *Newsday*; her sister, Maggie, is a county commissioner in central Florida; and her brother Mark, is a tugboat captain.

Janet's father was a police reporter for the *Miami Herald* for more than 43 years, and it was through him that Janet received her earliest introduction to the law and legal system. Reno's mother was an investigative reporter who married Henry at age 24. She was a strong-minded woman who was known for her powerful will, for her taste for alcohol, and for wrestling alligators.[2] But Mother Reno could also don "white gloves and sip tea with the best of them,"[3] as Janet recalls. Janet Reno comes "from a long line of memorable women."[4] According to Bob Reno, "Mother's mother and Father's mother were absolutely indomitable . . . all the women in the family were. The men were strong too. They just had no talent for marrying spineless women.''[5]

Janet Reno knew she wanted to be a lawyer at 15 years of age.[6] She received her bachelor's degree in chemistry from Cornell University in 1960 and in 1963, earned her law degree from Harvard Law School as one of 16 women in a class of 400 at Harvard. While studying, Reno would return to Miami in the summers to work as a clerk typist for the Dade County Board of the County Commissioners.

After her studies were complete, she returned to Miami to live with her parents and begin her legal career. Although she has never married nor has she raised children, Janet Reno has been a front-line advocate for children's rights.[7] The welfare of children, along with family matters and women's rights, has been a preeminent concern throughout her professional career.

## CAREER DEVELOPMENT

In 1963, Reno began her career with the firm, Brigham & Dence, where she specialized in eminent domain law. From 1967 to 1972, Reno was a partner in the law firm Lewis and Reno. Her first foray into electoral politics was in 1972, when Reno, a fervent Democrat, ran for the state legislature. She lost, however, to the Republican candidate.[8]

Shortly, thereafter, Reno entered public service. She became assistant state attorney for the Eleventh Judicial Circuit, Magistrate and Juvenile Court, in the State Attorney's Office in Dade County. In 1973, she served as a consultant to the Criminal Justice Committee of the Florida Senate, where she helped revise the Criminal Code. From 1973 to 1976, Reno was the administrative assistant to the state attorney and was responsible for the administration of the state attorney's office. Finally, in 1976, Reno returned for a short stint to private practice as a partner of the prestigious firm, Steel, Hector & Davis. But public service was to be her calling.

When Richard E. Gerstin, the state attorney for Dade County, contemplated retirement, he sought out and supported Janet Reno as his hand-picked successor. He had groomed her for the position, and she was ultimately appointed to complete Gerstin's term of office, taking the reins of the largest law office in the state of Florida. The Eleventh Judicial Circuit, which includes all of Dade County, had a $30 million budget in 1993 and employed 238 attorneys who prosecute over 40,000 felony cases a year.[9] The post is a nonpartisan elected position with a tenure of four years. In 1980, Reno won her first election as state attorney for Dade County and continued to be successful in three subsequent reelection efforts (in 1984, 1988, and 1992). Reno held this position for 15 years and only resigned in 1993, when President Bill Clinton nominated her as attorney general of the United States.

While Clinton was on the campaign trail, he expressed a commitment to making government more representative of the people and promised to appoint an increased number of women and minorities to significant posts in his administration. Thus, while it was ground breaking, it was no real surprise that Clinton's list of possible nominations to the position of attorney general contained the names of a number of women. But when President-Elect Clinton first considered his list of candidates for attorney general in late 1992, Reno relayed the message that she was not interested in the position. A move to Washington, D.C., was not an option given her mother's failing health and Reno's need to remain at her side in Dade County. But the failed nomination of Zoe Baird for the position and the subsequent delays in finding the "squeaky clean" candidate for the position provided time for Janet Reno's personal situation to change. Reno's mother passed away in the interim, and Janet's obligation to remain in south Florida dissolved.

Reno's high ethical standards and integrity, as well as her penchant for initiating innovative programs, made her the perfect nominee for the post, and a relatively easy Senate confirmation proceeding followed. She was sworn in on March 12, 1993, becoming the first woman to serve as the attorney general of the United States. As attorney general, Janet Reno oversees 98,000 employees and a Department of Justice that has an annual budget of $13 billion.

## ACHIEVEMENTS AND CONTRIBUTIONS

Janet Reno is a determined woman who has developed her own philosophy on law and crime. She strongly believes that individual social conditions directly affect crime and that the early education of youth can play a major role in reducing and deterring later criminal behavior. A strong advocate for Head Start programs, she believes in teaching children how to be good citizens as early as three years of age.[10] Reno also believes that solutions to the national crime problem in the United States can be found in the community and by those who are closest to the problems. Consequently, Reno thinks that the government should "trust, respect and empower the individual to act, respect the family unit, whatever it is; and empower the community to act and solve the problems."[11]

Clearly, not all public officials share her view. Reno received mixed reviews and criticism for focusing on protecting the rights of the innocent instead of convicting the guilty.[12] However, criticism has never swayed Reno from what she believes is right. She has worked to find alternatives to incarceration for crimes related to juvenile delinquency, drugs, and child abuse. Since she believes that these crimes are products of the community and the family, she has worked to involve the community at large in the search for solutions.

Reno has made many contributions to the development of law at the local, state, and national levels. Early in her career, she drafted a revision of the Florida constitution, which included a resolution to reform the court system into a uniform two-tier trial court system. She also worked on the development of a new criminal code for the state of Florida. When named state attorney, she searched for solutions to the multitude of complex problems confronting Dade County and south Florida, especially those related to the drug trade, the influx of legal and illegal immigrants from the Caribbean and Central and South America, and the never-ending racial and ethnic tensions that pervade the south Florida social landscape. While serving in what is typically viewed as a conservative post, Reno brought her liberal political beliefs to bear. The results were often, as Temple University Professor John Glodkamp put it, too "radical for a prosecutor."[13]

One of Reno's innovative approaches was the creation of a special drug court within the Dade County judicial system.[14] Working with the Public Defender's Office and court administrators, Reno successfully established a judicial arena that dealt solely with first-time, nonviolent drug offenders, offering defendants a year of rehabilitative programming in lieu of imprisonment or traditional penalties. The program, as Reno explained, was designed to "entice drug abusers into treatment and return them to society as productive citizens."[15] The success rate was phenomenal; nine out of ten defendants completed the program, and as a result, the paradigm has been adopted by other jurisdictions across the nation.[16]

Reno also created one of the first sexual battery units of any prosecutor's office in Florida and the first Domestic Violence Unit in Florida. Working with the medical establishment, state social workers, and the court system, and dedicating a team of assistant state attorneys from her office, Reno developed a rapid response team for incidents of rape and sexual abuse, and created an expedited process for obtaining restraining orders against those who perpetuate domestic violence. Reno also established a one-stop child support center for the prosecution of sexual abuse cases against children that also provides medical and psychological assistance to the young victims.

Reno's concern for children and family issues led her to use the powers of her office to force, if necessary, parental responsibility. She vigorously prosecuted fathers who did not pay child support, and in 1986, she created a task force to enforce child support in Dade County. From 1986 to 1993, the task force collected more than $42 million on behalf of 173,000 single parents.[17] She has continued this work as attorney general, supporting national legislation that would allow law enforcement agencies to reach across state lines to ensure that child support orders are enforced. Interestingly, Reno has also advocated shortened workdays so that parents can be home and supervise their children after school hours.[18]

As part of her delinquency prevention approach, Reno created a rehabilitation program for juvenile offenders. Similar to the Drug Courts, this program also provides an alternative to imprisonment for nonviolent first-time offenders. Annually, more than 7,000 offenders enroll in this program in lieu of jail time.[19]

But Janet Reno's role as state attorney for Dade County was not without difficulty. During her first years, Reno lost three significant drug cases due to inexperienced prosecutors.[20] She was also criticized for being slow to hire minorities, and the allegation of racism by her office in its prosecutions was raised repeatedly. One of the first major prosecutions of a public official involved the case of Johnny Jones, the first African American to serve as superintendent of the Dade County Public School System, who was tried and convicted for theft of school board property. But perhaps most difficult was the persistent perception that prevailed in the community that her office was not vigorous enough in prosecuting incidents of police brutality against African Americans. Two particular cases, the McDuffie case and the Lozano case, involved the issue of excessive force by local police departments and were highly charged by racial and ethnic overtones. Both incidents resulted in major civil unrest in the 1980s.

The McDuffie case stemmed from the beating of an African-American salesman, Arthur McDuffie, in 1980. Five police officers beat McDuffie to death during a purported traffic stop. Despite Reno's prosecution of the officers, Miami exploded into riots when the officers were found "not guilty," leaving hundreds of businesses destroyed, 16 people beaten or shot to death, and ultimately, forcing the activation of the National Guard to restore order. Nine years later, riots erupted again when Miami police officer William Lozano shot and killed a black motorcyclist and his passenger. While Lozano was found guilty, thus appeasing the African-American community, the Hispanic population balked at the verdict.

Because of the events of the early 1980s, Reno's relationship with the African-American community was "strained."[21] However, Reno learned from her mistakes and worked hard to regain the confidence of that community. She became personally involved in issues that affected African Americans and was known to walk the streets in the blighted, downtown areas, talking to citizens and listening to their complaints. Ultimately, it was this personal touch and her close work with the church ministers of the area that earned her their respect.

In 1992, Janet Reno served as chairperson of the statewide Social Service Task Force, which recommended solutions for housing, health care, and other human services issues salient to Floridians. Reno also worked with community leaders to encourage coordinated activities to achieve common goals, bringing together leaders of the triethnic and at times, deeply divided metropolitan area. She urged various housing programs serving Dade County to correct deficiencies in public housing. Her attacks on human service delivery focused on the systemic problem inherent in bureaucratic solutions: "We spend more money trying to determine whether people are eligible for services than we do serving them. We've got to figure out how to take the federal bureaucracy and weave it together as a whole, so that we can reweave the fabric of society around our children."[22] Reno was more than willing to seek a grand jury presentment on the ineffective operations of a dismal district office of Health and Rehabilitative Services office in Dade County.

Reno was active in several local organizations that had less to do with her legal career and more to do with her love of Dade County and the outdoors. She belonged to the major garden society, and supported the Historical Museum of Southern Florida Society and the Zoological Society of Florida, as well as other environmentally oriented organizations. Her professional career ensured her memberships in the various local Chambers of Commerce, the Association of Chiefs of Police, and of course, the American Bar Association. Through the bar, Reno worked diligently on issues related to juveniles, namely, the Joint Commission on Juvenile Justice Standards and the Institute for Judicial Administration. In 1970, the Joint Commission developed a 20–volume Juvenile Justice System, which is considered the bible for juvenile justice workers. Reno also chaired the Committee on Overcrowded Jails of the Judicial Administration (1983) and was a member of a Task Force on Minorities and the Justice System (1992).

Because of her deep, longstanding commitment to south Florida, Reno has received many awards. In recognition of outstanding dedication and service to victims of crime, she received The Fogarty Award from the Florida Network of Victim/Witness Services in 1989. In 1990, she received the Public Citizen of the Year Award from the National Association of Social Workers, Miami Dade Unit, and in 1990, the Medal of Honor Award from the Florida Bar Foundation.

As the attorney general of the United States, Reno has already faced a variety of crises such as the bombing of the World Trade Center in New York, the appointment of an independent counsel for the Whitewater investigation, the passage of the Crime Bill, and the bombing of the Oklahoma Center Federal Building. Janet Reno was catapulted into the limelight when as the newly appointed attorney general, she gave the order to invade the Branch Davidian compound with Bradley tanks and tear gas on April 19, 1993.

As Reno was sworn in as attorney general in March of 1993, David Koresh and his Branch Davidian followers were already barricaded in their religious commune near Waco, Texas, with federal law enforcement officials on the perimeter. The Bureau of Alcohol, Tobacco and Firearms had attempted to serve the Branch Davidians with a search warrant, but shooting ensued and a standoff had begun. Attorney General Reno had inherited a volatile problem, and after days of waiting, information-gathering and strategy sessions, Reno made the decision to attempt a resolution. Her motivation hinged on information obtained by the Federal Bureau of Investigation that child abuse and psychological abuse of the occupants were taking place within the compound while the federal forces stood guard. In authorizing the paramilitary action, Reno had hoped to force Koresh to surrender. Instead, the Branch Davidians set fire to the housing unit in an act of suicide, resulting in the deaths of 86 people, including 17 children.

In a manner uncharacteristic of political officeholders and to the surprise of a highly critical media, Reno took full responsibility for the attack saying, "I made the decision. I am accountable. The buck stops here."[23] While the disaster could have ended her short career as attorney general, her willingness to assume responsibility made her a "national hero."[24] As a result, her national recognition and reputation skyrocketed.

While reform, government reorganization, and enhanced bureaucratic efficiency have been themes of the Clinton administration, Reno's efforts to reorganize the Department of Justice have been difficult largely because of differences with the White House. When Vice-President Al Gore proposed consolidating the Drug Enforcement Agency with the Federal Bureau of Investigation, Reno nixed the idea. The decision was summarized by a *New York Times* headline: ''Bureaucracy one, Gore 0.''[25] As a result, Reno's reorganization of Justice has largely been superficial and has not resulted in the massive changes that the White House desired.

Reno has not only had differences with the White House. Conservatives have attacked her for being ''soft on crime at a moment of unparalleled public concern over violence.''[26] Early on, even her staff criticized her micro-management style, which ''hinders her capabilities to look at the larger picture.''[27] But the level of respect that she has earned from many of the Justice Department employees stems from her unprecedented access to those who often never encountered their boss. Reno is known for regularly taking her meals in the employee cafeteria and for avoiding the accoutrements generally associated with her office, like the private dining facility and chauffeured limousines. Often, Reno can be seen in the early morning hours walking from her apartment in the Connecticut Avenue area of the District of Columbia to her office.

A recent event that tested Reno's ability to deal with terrorism was the April 19, 1995, bombing of the Oklahoma federal building. Many believe that this tragic incident may have been somehow linked to the Waco disaster. Prime suspect Timothy MacVeigh ''was said to be obsessed with the federal government's 1993 assault on the Branch Davidians.''[28] The investigation is still under way, and although Reno does not advocate the death penalty, she said that Justice will pursue such a sentence in this case.

Throughout her public career, Reno has taken women under her tutelage and served as a role model and mentor. It was only natural, then, that her handpicked successor to the position of state attorney for Dade County was none other than a woman. And within the southeast Florida community, numerous women have watched and learned that they, too, can break the glass ceilings of the legal profession.

Throughout her long and distinguished career, Janet Reno has shown the courage to face the problems of our society and act decisively. Even though she has often been criticized for not being harsh enough on criminals and ''soft'' on crime, her dedication to those values given her by her family, her honesty and frankness, and her firm style have taken Reno to the highest law enforcement position in the United States. In searching for the social causes and solutions to crime, Reno has chosen to be innovative and proactive in her approaches. But it is her integrity that has made Attorney General Janet Reno one of President Clinton's most popular appointments.

## NOTES

1. Nancy Gibbs, ''Truth, Justice and the Reno Way,'' *Time* (July 12, 1993): 20.
2. Ruth Marcus, ''Clinton Nominates Reno at Justice,'' *The Washington Post* (February 12, 1993): A1.

3. Stanley W. Cloud, "Standing Tall," *Time* (May 10, 1994): 46.
4. Ibid.
5. Ibid.
6. Judith Graham (ed.), *Current Biography* (New York: H. W. Wilson, 1993), 485.
7. Gibbs, 20.
8. Maya Bell, "Reno Has a Passel of Boosters in Dade," *Orlando Sentinel Tribune* (February 12, 1993): A1.
9. Gibbs, 20.
10. Ibid.
11. Anne Groer, "Floridian of the Year. Janet Reno: Justice, Compassion, True Grit," *Orlando Sentinel Tribune* (January 2, 1994): E1.
12. Jeff Leen, "Miami Nice: Janet Reno's Other Record," *The New Republic* (March 21, 1994): 19–22.
13. Ibid.
14. Marcus, A1.
15. United States Senate, Committee on the Judiciary, "Confirmation Hearing for the Attorney General Janet Reno" (Washington, D.C.: Government Printing Office, 1993).
16. Gibbs, 20.
17. Ibid.
18. Ibid.
19. Chris Wood and Louisa Huband, "America's Top Cop: Vice Still Thrives in Miami, Where the New U.S. Attorney General Janet Reno Cut Her Teeth," *MacLean Hunter Limited* (April 5, 1993).
20. Marcus, A1.
21. Ibid.
22. Gibbs, 20.
23. Peter Boyer, "Children of Waco," *The New Yorker* (May 15, 1995).
24. Ibid.
25. James Rowley, "Reno Won't Take Stand on Merging FBI, DEA," *Chicago Sun-Times* (September 10, 1993): 29.
26. Gordon Witkin and Ted Gest, "Can Janet Reno Get a Grip on her Job?," *U.S.News & World Report* (February 14, 1994): 25.
27. Ibid.
28. "Law Woman of the Week," *Time* (May 1, 1995): 21.

## REFERENCES

Anderson, Paul. *Janet Reno: Doing the Right Thing*. New York: John Wiley and Son, 1994.

Bell, Maya. "Reno Has a Passel of Boosters in Dade." *Orlando Sentinel Tribune* (February 12, 1993): A1–4.

Boyer, Peter. "Children of Waco." *The New Yorker* (May 15, 1995): 38–45.

Cloud, Stanley W. "Standing Tall." *Time* (May 10, 1994): 46–47.

Gibbs, Nancy. "Truth, Justice and the Reno Way." *Time* (July 12, 1993): 20–29.

Graham, Judith (ed.). *Current Biography*. New York: H. W. Wilson, 1993.

Groer, Anne. "Floridian of the Year. Janet Reno: Justice, Compassion, True Grit." *Orlando Sentinel Tribune* (January 2, 1994): E1, 15.

"Law Woman of the Week." *Time* (May 1, 1995): 21.

Leen, Jeff. ''Miami Nice: Janet Reno's Other Record.'' *The New Republic* (March 21, 1994): 19–22.

Marcus, Ruth. ''Clinton Nominates Reno at Justice.'' *The Washington Post* (February 12, 1993): A1, 4.

Rowley, James. ''Reno Won't Take Stand on Merging FBI, DEA.'' *Chicago Sun-Times* (September 10, 1993): 29–30.

United States Senate, Committee on the Judiciary. ''Confirmation Hearing for the Attorney General Janet Reno.'' Washington, D.C.: Government Printing Office, 1993.

Witkin, Gordon, and Ted Gest. ''Can Janet Reno Get a Grip on Her Job?'' *U.S. News & World Report* (February 14, 1994): 25–27.

Wood, Chris, and Louisa Huband. ''America's Top Cop: Vice Still Thrives in Miami, Where the New U.S. Attorney General Janet Reno Cut Her Teeth.'' *MacLean Hunter Limited* (April 5, 1993): 18–20.

*GISELLE DE BRUNO JAMISON*

# MARY ROBINSON (1944– )

One of the most remarkable stories in modern Irish politics traces how Mary Robinson, a liberal and independent woman, became both the president and "the most subversive force in the country."[1] Robinson's political and personal beliefs did not augur well for success in law or politics in a nation that is steeped in conservative Catholicism, a culture that values traditional family and social structures. Her political agenda invariably set her against the dominant political parties and the Catholic Church. As a member of the Irish Senate (*Seanad*), a body of marginal influence on public policy, Robinson proposed some of the most far-reaching legislative reforms on social policy and saw each proposal defeated, if only in the short term. She later failed to win election to the more powerful lower house of parliament (*Dáil*). And in the 1980s, her stand on two highly controversial constitutional amendments was soundly rejected by the electorate.

Yet for all the evidence of a political career doomed to frustration, Mary Robinson's story is one of remarkable success. In 1990, she successfully ran for election as the Labour party's nominee for president, the first woman to achieve such a position in Irish politics. She has become a source of national pride, and her once-doomed political agenda is now a font of important legislative and social change.

## FAMILY BACKGROUND AND EDUCATION

Mary Robinson was born Marie Terese Winifred Bourke in western Ireland in 1944.[2] Both parents were trained as medical doctors, but her mother was a homemaker while her father was the breadwinner. Mary Bourke is the third of five children, and the only girl. Her upbringing was the product of "well-to-do professionals who afforded their children a superior education coupled with a strong sense of noblesse oblige.''[3] After private schooling in her hometown, Bourke was sent to an exclusive Dublin boarding school where she maintained an impressive record as a diligent and talented student. At the age of 17, she went to Paris to attend a finishing school for girls, a practice not unusual for ''upper middle class Irish Catholic families.''[4]

On her return to Ireland, Bourke began undergraduate work at Trinity College in Dublin. This step in her career is more complicated than it appears; at the time, the Catholic Church had forbidden Catholics to enroll there because of Trinity's long association with the Protestant faith. Exceptions to the rule were occasionally permitted, and in the case of the Bourke family, special authorization was obtained from the archbishop of Dublin. Trinity College is the best known and most elite of Ireland's universities, drawing substantial enrollment from outside the Republic. When Mary Bourke enrolled, she was one of only three women in the undergraduate law class. She is remembered as serious about her studies and uninterested in politics, but Bourke was active in the student community, serving as auditor of the law society, editor of a law review, and secretary of a student council. In 1967, Bourke graduated with first-class honors, and, equally important, won a Harvard scholarship.

Mary Bourke was ''transformed by her American experience.''[5] She recalls, ''There was intense questioning then. . . . I had a law degree, but I hadn't really been encouraged to think. And Harvard was just facing up to the fact that there were inequalities of sex and race.''[6] Being at Harvard during the throes of the 1960s, an era of protest in the United States, also had a lasting impact on Robinson. ''I found there was a great questioning of the values of society. It was the period of the Vietnam war and the civil rights movement in the south. There was even questioning of the teaching of the law and values of a legal education. Everything was up for examination.''[7] While earning her Master of Laws degree at Harvard, Mary Bourke also witnessed some of the more activist and progressive decisions of the American courts. It was in this context that Ireland's future president developed her vision of law's positive role in promoting social change.

The first truly remarkable event in her career came at the end of her Harvard studies: Mary Bourke was offered the Reid Professorship of Law at Trinity College. The opportunity was extraordinary, and even her Harvard credentials had to be weighed against her youth. In the conservative world of Irish academia, her gender was another liability. Whatever the rationale of her appointment, it began a series of record-breaking achievements on her part. At age 25, Mary Bourke was the youngest professor of law in a university whose history spanned 350 years.

In 1970, Mary married Nicholas Robinson, another Trinity law graduate. It was, in Irish terms, a mixed marriage (a union of Catholic and Protestant) and one that evidently distressed her family. Neither her parents nor her brothers attended the ceremony.

## CAREER DEVELOPMENT

To understand Mary Robinson's political career, a snapshot of the Irish political system is necessary. Three parties dominate contemporary parliamentary politics in Ireland: *Fianna Fáil*, *Fine Gael*, and Labour. The two largest parties, *Fianna Fáil*, and its close rival, *Fine Gael*, forged their identities on the issues of partition, civil war, and republicanism, while the Labour party takes pride in its commitment to trade unionism and socialist politics. Because Ireland's representational system is based on proportional representation, small parties such as Labour can play a pivotal role in the parliamentary democracy. Accordingly, Labour has become a coalition partner in government when either of the major parties has failed to garner a majority at the polls.

The Irish Constitution explicitly reflects a Catholic culture. Until 1972, the Roman Catholic Church was recognized as having a "special position" in the state (Article 44.1). Even an antiquated view of the role of women has been constitutionally embedded; divorce was expressly prohibited (Article 41.3) until 1995, and in 1983, the prohibition of abortion, already established by statute, was lifted to constitutional status by a pro-life amendment (Article 40.3). Finally, another constitutional provision "recognizes that by her life within the home, woman gives the State a support without which the common good cannot be achieved. . . . The State shall, therefore, endeavour to ensure that mothers shall not be obliged by economic necessity to engage in labour to the neglect of their duties in the home" (Article 41.2).

Like its American counterpart, the Irish constitution provides for a president, a bicameral legislature, and an independent judiciary. But there the similarities end. The president is largely a figurehead, performing symbolic functions at the request of the government. The president is not allowed to participate in political debate, and his or her speeches and travel plans are subject to the government's approval. The upper house of the legislature, the *Seanad*, is extremely limited in power and influence. As with most parliamentary democracies, the party or parties that dominate the lower house (*Dáil*) run the government and encounter few obstacles to their policy programs. The most unusual aspect of the *Seanad* is its vocational representation scheme; of its 60 members, 6 are elected by university graduates alone, 11 are appointed by the prime minister (*Taoiseach*), and the last 43 represent five groups (Labour, Agriculture, Industry, Administration, and Culture/Education).

As Mary Robinson began teaching law, her position at Trinity afforded her a unique opportunity to begin a political career. Because of the peculiar configuration of the *Seanad*, a well-known Trinity graduate could, if she was daring, land a seat in the Irish Parliament. Thus, in 1969, Robinson ran for one of the three Trinity seats in the *Seanad*. Chronically low turnout gave her reasonably organized campaign some chance of success, and she won with only 1,300 votes. In doing so, Robinson set two records: she was the first Catholic ever elected by Trinity graduates and "the youngest woman ever elected to the senate."[8]

She was one of six women in the *Seanad* in 1969, while only two women held seats in the more powerful *Dáil*.

Senator Robinson believed that the *Seanad*, given its limited powers, should be a "forum for new and possibly unpopular views."[9] Her time there was difficult; she was an activist in a body devoted to avoiding the exercise of power. By 1971, Robinson's desire for change had a distinctly feminist tone—she described the women's movement as the only radical force in the "stagnant pool of Irish life."[10] At the time, women were not allowed on juries, were paid less for equal work, and suffered various disadvantages in welfare and family law. Her liberal approach to issues long avoided in Irish politics surfaced quickly.

Robinson also supported highly controversial constitutional reforms. She wanted to remove the prohibition of divorce and the claim that the six counties of Northern Ireland are part of the "national territory" (Article 2.1). She sought to secularize the constitution in order to accommodate and promote a pluralistic society. As for government policy, Robinson advocated radical changes in family law that included the reform of adoption laws to allow partners in a mixed marriage to adopt, and she decried "blatant discrimination" against women in welfare law. Robinson's agenda for a new Ireland meant liberalizing current law on family planning, illegitimacy, equal pay, married women's domicile, family courts, civil legal aid, prison administration, the protection of the mentally ill in criminal proceedings, and child support enforcement.

Robinson's most significant crusade began in 1971, when she helped introduce a bill to decriminalize the distribution of contraceptives. Though the bill failed, it is remembered as the first major public policy initiative undertaken by Senator Robinson, and it marked the beginning of a long three-way struggle between liberal/progressive forces, the Roman Catholic Church, and the major political parties. In 1973, Robinson introduced yet another family planning bill. The government responded with its own proposal, sinking any hopes for Robinson's more liberal proposal. In a conclusion fitting to the perverse ways of Irish politics, the government's bill was also defeated. Family planning reform in Ireland proved to be a Herculean task.

Throughout her travails in the *Seanad*, Robinson maintained a vision of a progressive liberal Irish state where laws functioned to ensure freedom of the individual. "Justice was important to Mary because justice flowed from the law, properly applied. Equality was a matter of justice. But her approach when she entered the Senate was academic rather than militant. It was her experience in the Senate that changed her, rather than any ideology she brought with her into that chamber."[11]

After seven years in the upper house, Robinson was frustrated. She once told the *Irish Times* that the *Seanad* "was too expensive, met too rarely and used too few of its powers to justify the amount of money and space it took up."[12] To be effective, she had to run for the *Dáil*. In 1976, Robinson joined the Labour party—perhaps because it was more amenable to change than either of its rivals. Nevertheless, it remained the weakest of the main parties. With Labour backing, she launched two unsuccessful campaigns (1976 and 1981) for a *Dáil* seat, running on her commitment "to a socialist and democratic state."[13] Various reasons might account for her defeats. Robinson may have been deserted by the Labour machine, her constituents might have viewed her as too liberal or lacking in the style of a "real politician," or she might have been rejected because of her gender.

These defeats did not signal an end to Mary Robinson's political career. Reelected to the *Seanad* in 1983, she quickly engaged in the debate over a pro-life amendment that was to be decided by popular referendum. While maintaining her own personal disapproval of abortion, she opposed the amendment, arguing that it would invite litigation and make the law less, not more, clear. The amendment also explicitly reflected Catholic policy and was thereby a rejection of a pluralistic society. Finally, it would not change the reality of Irish abortions; an estimated 5,000 Irish women travel to Britain for abortions each year. Ultimately, Robinson lost the battle—the amendment passed with the support of 54 percent of the voters.

In 1985, Robinson faced yet another setback. Her uneasiness with the Labour party was brought to a head by the Anglo-Irish Agreement signed that year. The agreement gave the Dublin government a limited consultative role in the affairs of Northern Ireland, and Labour supported the proposal. Senator Robinson broke with the party's line since the agreement was premised on the exclusion of Northern Ireland's Unionists, thus offending her desire for a politics of reconciliation. Robinson believed that any arrangements worked out between London and Dublin would prove unworkable and she subsequently resigned from the Labour Party.

The following year brought Robinson into yet another struggle for political reform important to women. She supported a referendum on divorce—a reform that would provide an opportunity for some divorces to be granted in Ireland. Robinson had been one of the first to urge this reform in the *Seanad* some ten years earlier. But this referendum failed as well, by a two to one majority. After 20 years of continuous struggle on behalf of Ireland's powerless and disenfranchised in both the legislature and the courts, Robinson decided to resign her seat in 1989.

Leaving politics, Robinson devoted her energy to the Irish Center for European Law, which she administered at Trinity. At this point in her career, she had learned precisely how to use the courts, Irish and European, to promote a liberal agenda.

> [T]he constitutional cases in which she participated were many and varied . . . she represented a wide cross-section of people and views ranging from a man who sought the decriminalisation of homosexual acts, a wife who sought to obtain a judicial separation from her husband, a couple who sought equality of social welfare benefits or the illegitimate child who sought equality of treatment with a child born within marriage.
>
> She devoted a considerable part of her legal career to liberalising what were arguably

some of the most reactionary laws on the statute books of any country in the industrialized world. She established a reputation as one of the leading authorities on social welfare law, and as one colleague observed, "her contribution in the area of public law has been substantial." As an academic lawyer she made European law her special interest and used it to good advantage for many of her clients.[14]

Robinson argued and won two path-breaking privacy cases: one involving a government wiretap of a journalist's phone, and the other involving Ireland's sodomy law. Other notable successes in her legal career include establishing the right of women to serve on juries, abolishing censorship of family planning materials, and guaranteeing the state's obligation to provide civil legal aid to the indigent. Robinson also won important cases before the European Court of Justice on pay equity. One assessment of her impact on the plight of women in Ireland reads: "No one has shouted less and achieved more."[15]

Robinson's career as a legal advocate was short-lived. In the spring of 1990, the leader of the Labour party persuaded Robinson to run for the presidency. The idea, prompted by a secretary's comment,[16] was courageous for several reasons. First, Robinson refused to rejoin the Labour party, the party that was encouraging her candidacy. Second, no woman had run for the presidency in Ireland and moreover, the office of the presidency was traditionally viewed as a reward for loyal service to one of the two major parties. However, Robinson and her Labour allies saw an opportunity to invigorate the office and to create an activist presidency. Historically, "[g]olf figured prominently in what people most remembered the President doing."[17]

With some important assistance from the Labour machine, Robinson ran an innovative campaign. She toured Ireland for six months (prior campaigns had lasted three weeks), remade her image to downplay her lawyerly ways, and asserted her independence from the political status quo. Robinson appealed for a working presidency that would promote a new, pluralistic, and tolerant Ireland. Political pundits were unanimous in the view that she had no hope of getting over 25 percent of the vote; the *Fianna Fáil* candidate was considered a sure bet. But Robinson's campaign disrupted the status quo, drawing women's interest and votes like no other. She put her campaign at risk when she complained about the "whole patriarchal, male-dominated presence of the Catholic Church [that] sought to do down [sic] women."[18]

A month before the election, Robinson was projected as second in a three-person race, with about 32 percent of the voters committed to her.[19] But the front runner, a *Fianna Fáil* nominee, became embroiled in a Watergate-style fiasco that proved he was a less-than-accomplished liar. As a result, Robinson's momentum increased dramatically. *Fianna Fáil* then made a bad situation worse when one of its ministers made this late and desperate attack on Robinson: "She has to have new clothes and her new look, and her new hairdo and she has the new interest in family, being a mother and all that kind of thing. But none of us you know, none of us who ever knew Mary Robinson very well in previous incarnations ever heard her claiming to be a great wife and mother.''[20]

The minister later apologized, but it was too late. Robinson took the presidency with 53 percent of the vote. On her victory night, she reveled in the upset and paid tribute to her most important supporters:

> I want to be a President for all the people. Because I was elected by men and women of all parties and none, by many with great moral courage who stepped out from the faded flags of the Civil War and voted for a new Ireland. And above all by the women of Ireland—*Mná na hÉireann!*—who instead of rocking the cradle rocked the system, and who came out massively to make their mark on the ballot paper, and on a new Ireland.[21]

## ACHIEVEMENTS AND CONTRIBUTIONS

Mary Robinson has fulfilled her promise of a working presidency. Halfway through a seven-year term she has, despite the formidable constraints of her office, been visible, assertive, influential, and relentlessly political. One of her first gestures was to attend Mass in one of Dublin's poorest neighborhoods, avoiding the usual ceremony in the president's private chapel. Her many visits to Great Britain and Northern Ireland are unprecedented for an Irish president. Robinson's meeting with the Queen was, in the world of Anglo-Irish politics, comparable to the collapse of the Berlin Wall. She also made clear her support for the dialogue that ultimately brought an IRA cease-fire in the fall of 1994. Robinson has traveled extensively in Africa, and argued strenuously before the United Nations and in her book on Somalia for increased aid to the Third World.[22]

President Robinson has been honored by the International League of Human Rights and awarded a ''Feminist of the Year'' prize by the Feminist Majority Foundation. She consistently asserts a feminist credo: ''Equality between the sexes is seen to be a woman's issue. It is not. It is said to be a marginal issue. It is not. It is perceived as a threat to the traditional structures of society. And it is not.''[23] ''In a society where the rights and potential of women are constrained, no man can be truly free. He may have power, but he will not have freedom.''[24]

Robinson's election effectively realigned both of the major parties, thus changing the direction of public policy in a variety of arenas, but most especially as it concerns women and family planning. The government has liberalized contraception regulations, and the prohibition on divorce is under review again with popular support for reform estimated at about 60 percent. In a 1992 referendum on abortion, voters supported freedom of travel for abortion (formally recognizing an Irish tradition) and free access to abortion information (a longtime Robinson crusade). The voters rejected limited access to abortion in Ireland; pro-choice voters thought it too meager, whereas pro-life voters thought it too liberal. Also, in response to a European Court of Justice ruling (which Robinson had argued), Ireland repealed its sodomy laws. In 1992, the Labour party doubled its representation in the *Dáil*, while women increased their representation by 50 percent, now holding 20 of the 166 seats.

In a land where change comes ''dripping slow'' (to borrow a phrase from Yeats), these are astounding developments. But unemployment, emigration, and poverty rates are high in Ireland and will continue to present grave challenges to successive governments. Irish women, with the highest birthrate in the European Community (though now in decline), are particularly at risk. Although it is not clear that much can be done by an activist president to cure those ills, what is clear is that President Mary Robinson can be relied on to battle for the weakest. As she said of her visit to Somalia, ''I was conscious of a weight of responsibility: they had asked me to be a voice.''[25] Despite her many political disappointments and struggles over the years, President Robinson is now in a position where she can be the voice of those who cannot be heard.

## NOTES

1. A. Phillips, ''A Woman of Substance,'' 105 *Maclean's* (October 19, 1992): 47.
2. Much of the information in this and the following section is drawn from Michael O'Sullivan, *Mary Robinson: The Life and Times of an Irish Liberal* (Dublin: Blackwater Press, 1993).
3. E. O'Reilly, *Candidate: The Truth Behind the Presidential Campaign* (Dublin: Attic Press, 1991), 33.
4. O'Sullivan, 21.
5. Ibid., 31.
6. Ibid., 33.
7. Ibid., 30.
8. F. Finlay, *Mary Robinson: A President with a Purpose* (Dublin: O'Brien Press, 1990), 25.
9. O'Sullivan, 38.
10. Ibid., 42.
11. Finlay, 28.
12. O'Sullivan, 120.
13. Ibid., 95.
14. Ibid., 163–164.
15. Finlay, 99.
16. Ibid., 16.
17. O'Reilly, 18.
18. R. Mahoney, *Whoredom in Kimmage* (New York: Anchor Books, 1993), 283.
19. A. Smyth, ''A Great Day for the Women of Ireland . . . The Meaning of Mary Robinson's Presidency for Irish Women,'' 18 *Canadian Journal of Irish Studies* (1992): 67.
20. Cited in Finlay, 135.
21. Smyth, 61.
22. Mary Robinson, *A Voice for Somalia* (Dublin: O'Brien Press, 1992).

23. *The Irish Times* (February 28, 1992).
24. Cited in Mahoney, xv.
25. Robinson, 24.

## REFERENCES

Finlay, F. *Mary Robinson: A President with a Purpose*. Dublin: O'Brien Press, 1990.

Mahoney, R. *Whoredom in Kimmage*. New York: Anchor Books, 1993.

O'Reilly, E. *Candidate: The Truth Behind the Presidential Campaign*. Dublin: Attic Press, 1991.

O'Sullivan, Michael. *Mary Robinson: The Life and Times of an Irish Liberal*. Dublin: Blackwater Press, 1993.

Phillips, A. "A Woman of Substance." *Maclean's* 105 (October 19, 1992): 46–47.

Robinson, Mary. *A Voice for Somalia*. Dublin: O'Brien Press, 1992.

Smyth, A. "A Great Day for the Women of Ireland . . . The Meaning of Mary Robinson's Presidency for Irish Women." *Canadian Journal of Irish Studies* 18 (1992): 61–75.

*JEROME O'CALLAGHAN*

# FLERIDA RUTH P. ROMERO (193?–  )

Teacher, scholar, community and political activist, and adviser to the Philippines' first woman president, Corazon Aquino, Flerida Ruth Pineda Romero is the fifth woman appointed to the Supreme Court of the Philippines. In sharp contrast to the usual situation surrounding the appointment of justices to that Court, the appointment of Romero produced, for a time, a hot controversy. Viewed from the perspective of the desirability of representing women in a nation's top judicial body, the furor over Romero's appointment to the Philippine Supreme Court was ironic. In many ways, her career pattern had been remarkably similar to that of Irene Cortes,* the third woman appointed to the Court, whose appointment in February, 1987, had not been controversial. In addition, if Cortes and Romero were objectionable because they, like many male appointees, lacked judicial experience, the same could not be said of the other three women to serve on the Court; Cecilia Muñoz Palma,* Ameurfina Melencio-Herrera, and Carolina Grino-Aquino—all of whom had extensive judicial careers terminating with service in the Court of Appeals.

## CAREER DEVELOPMENT

Prior to her appointment as special assistant to President Aquino, Flerida Ruth Romero had been a career academic. She received her Bachelor of Laws degree from the prestigious University of the Philippines (UP) College of Law in 1952, and followed that with a Bachelor of Arts in Arts and Law from the UP a year later. She then embarked for the United States and Indiana University, where she completed a Master of Laws degree in 1955. Upon her return to the Philippines, she began a long career in labor relations and labor law when she became assistant to the director of the Asian Labor Education Center (ALEC).

Romero continued as a labor educator with ALEC until 1964, when she became a professor of law at the University of the Philippines and head of the Division of Continuing Education at the newly inaugurated UP Law Center.

Romero taught a variety of civil and labor law subjects in the regular curriculum of the UP College of Law. But beyond these, her continuing education responsibilities involved supervising and conducting seminars and public forums on legal practice, administrative law, trial techniques and procedures, and legal aspects of business, among others. Romero was also responsible for organizing conferences and courses for judges, organizing bar reviews, and coordinating a variety of conferences on legal education. She continued as director of the Division of Continuing Education in the Law Center until 1979, when she was named the Center's director, replacing Irene Cortes, who moved on to become law school dean.

Romero remained as director of the UP Law Center until 1985. While in that capacity, she was perhaps best known for her efforts to popularize the law. These included educational programs, conducted mostly in Filipino, the national vernacular, for high school students, members of nongovernmental organizations, and local government officials, and a Filipino radio show with a question and answer format.[1]

Romero's role as director of the UP Law Center provided numerous opportunities to serve as a representative to legal education conferences and seminars around Southeast Asia and the world. She was well known as a leader in the continuing legal education field, and also began to develop a reputation as the person largely responsible for the development of the Philippines' new family code. As a legal scholar, she was active primarily as an editor of annual symposia on labor relations law.

Romero might have remained an academic but for the chain of political events that led to the "People Power Revolution" that overthrew Ferdinand Marcos in early 1986. Her position as a responsible administrator in the government-sponsored University of the Philippines no doubt placed restrictions on Romero's ability to participate in the developing middle-class opposition to the Marcos dictatorship, an opposition in which women played a prominent role. This opposition developed upon his return to the Philippines in 1983, in the wake of the assassination of Benigno "Ninoy" Aquino, Marcos's principal political opponent and the husband of Corazon Aquino. The middle-class opposition combined with other strands of opposition—and pressure on Marcos exerted by the United States—to force the president to attempt to demonstrate his democratic tendencies and popularity by declaring, in late 1985, a "snap" presidential election to be held in February, 1986.

Marcos calculated that he would easily be able to win such an election because his fractured opposition would not have time to unify and organize well enough to defeat his well-oiled political organization. But he miscalculated. At the last hour, the opposition forces were able to unite behind a ticket with Corazon Aquino and Salvador Laural as presidential and vice-presidential candidates, respectively. Faced with an effective opposition, Marcos tried to win by fraud what he feared he would not be able to win at the ballot box. But, again, he miscalculated. His attempts to steal the election were transparent, even to teams of official election observers from the United States and elsewhere, and shortly led to the combined military uprising and mass revolt that became known as the People Power Revolution. This revolution drove Marcos, his family, and principal supporters from the country and installed Corazon Aquino as the new president.

## ACHIEVEMENTS AND CONTRIBUTIONS

When the new president sought to consolidate her administration, Corazon Aquino looked for an able, legally trained personal assistant, and settled on Romero. Over her five years in the Aquino administration, Romero served as secretary-general of the Constitutional Commission that drafted the new constitution. She also assumed the role of executive director of the Education Campaign that urged the ratification of the 1987 constitution. Her regular duties included service as presidential legislative liaison to the Senate, a member of the Cabinet Cluster concentrating on National Security and Development, the Task Force on Law Enforcement, and the Board of Regents of the University of the Philippines, and a commissioner of the Presidential Commission on Culture and the Arts.[2]

By 1991, her service had earned her a Judicial and Bar Council nomination for a Supreme Court vacancy, a nomination that became an appointment after President Aquino named her to the Court, effective October 16, 1991. But when the president announced on October 9, 1991, that Romero would fill one of two then vacant seats of the Supreme Court, 29 (of 49) incumbent justices of the Philippines' second highest court, the Court of Appeals, "fired off" a telegram to Aquino protesting:

> Beyond question is the presidential power of appointment. Regrettably, however, on four occasions, not one justice of Court of Appeals has been promoted to Supreme Court. Hence, we, the undersigned justices, in order to abort complete demoralization in judicial career service, respectfully recommend that the remaining Supreme Court vacancy be filled up by one from appellate court.[3]

It was clear that the judicial reaction to Romero's appointment did not result entirely, perhaps not even principally, from her own qualifications. At least as much, it reflected the fact that the overwhelming majority of the new justices Aquino had named to the Supreme Court since her accession to the presidency in February, 1986, had been "outsiders," people who had not made their careers in the judiciary. Specifically, only 3 of the 16 (including Romero) had held the most common position from which Supreme Court justices had historically been appointed, presiding justice of the Court of Appeals, and only five (including a court administrator, who holds an official rank identical to that of the presiding justice of the Court of Appeals) could be described as career members of the judicial hierarchy.

The lack of judicial experience that made her appointment objectionable to the members of the career judiciary was one pillar of the controversy over Romero's appointment to the Supreme Court. Her close political ties to President Aquino were clearly another. As special assistant to the president of the Republic of the Philippines from 1986 to 1991, few lawyers appeared to have a closer working relationship with Corazon Aquino than Romero. Even before Aquino won the presidency, Romero had reportedly been her legal adviser and confidante. But while serving as special assistant, Romero had been ''self-effacing and publicity shy,'' rarely talking to reporters, even though she had written a regular column for the *Philippine Star* newspaper.[4]

Under the current (1987) constitution of the Philippines, appointments to the Supreme Court are made by the president from a list submitted by the Judicial and Bar Council, a constitutional body with members representing the Supreme Court, the Department of Justice, the legislature, the judiciary, the bar, academic lawyers, and the private sector. When the Judicial and Bar Council announced its nominees for the position to which Romero would be appointed, a prominent senator claimed that Romero had not even been on the original list from which the nominees were chosen, implying that the president and her supporters had manipulated the nomination process to ensure that her political ally could receive the appointment. While the senator's claim proved incorrect, the implication remained.

Partisan critics of Aquino's choice of Romero suggested that it was just one more in the line of ''political'' appointments that had given Aquino a Supreme Court that was overwhelmingly favorable to her interests. The suspicion they tried to fan was that Aquino wished to retain firm control over the Court because, contrary to her frequent public announcements, she intended to run for reelection in the presidential elections that were forthcoming in 1992. Shortly after Romero's appointment, it became clear that this suspicion was also unfounded, and that Aquino would not run for reelection, and so, much of the political furor over her appointments quieted. The remainder of the controversy dissipated when Aquino named to the next two Supreme Court vacancies career judges who held the rank of presiding justice of the Court of Appeals.

Whether or not Corazon Aquino and her supporters in the Judicial and Bar Council wished to maintain in the Supreme Court a majority favorable to her political interests, the president's appointment of Romero ensured that the representation of women on that august body, compared to other Supreme Courts and at least for a time, would remain substantial. When she was appointed, Romero restored the number of active female Supreme Court justices to its maximum, three. Had she not been appointed, and had subsequent appointments continued to be all male, as they have been, there would now once again be no woman on the Philippine Supreme Court. It seems probable that Aquino's understandable desire to appoint her valuable aide and political adviser to the Supreme Court may also have reflected a desire to maintain a feminist presence at the top of the judicial hierarchy.

## NOTES

1. Flerida Ruth P. Romero, ''Curriculum Vitae'' (1994).
2. Ibid.
3. Aquino (1991), 15.
4. Dana Batnag, ''Women of the High Court,'' *Philippine Graphic* (March 9, 1992): 42; and Romero.

## REFERENCES

Aquino, Mikael G. ''Revolt in the Courts.'' *Phillippines Free Press* (November 2, 1991): 15–16, 33, 36.

Batnag, Dana. ''Women of the High Court.'' *Philippine Graphic* (March 9, 1992): 42.

Romero, Flerida Ruth P. *The Constitution and the Legal System of the Philippines.* Bloomington, Ind.: Indiana University School of Law, 1994.

Romero, Flerida Ruth P. ''Curriculum Vitae'' (1994).

Romero, Flerida Ruth P. *Family Law in the Philippines*. Quezon City: University of the Philippines Law Center, 1982.

Romero, Flerida Ruth P. *Women's Status in Philippine Society*. Quezon City: University of the Philippines Law Center, 1982.

*C. NEAL TATE*

# SIMONE ROZÈS-LUDWIG (1920– )

Simone Rozès-Ludwig is one of the most outstanding figures in French judicial history, and she has served as a respected adviser to the French legislature. Her contributions have extended beyond her national home of France, owing to her curiosity about the law and legal traditions of other nations, and stemming from her prestigious assignment at the European Court of Justice. To date, no other woman in France has attained her legal stature.

## FAMILY BACKGROUND AND EDUCATION

Simone Ludwig was born on March 29, 1920, in Paris. Although she did not grow up among jurists (her father was a commercial director), she was fascinated by them and considered them to be men and women of peace. After succeeding at the *baccalaureat*, she decided to begin legal studies. She had no intention of becoming a lawyer, even though the profession had been open to women in 1900 after Jeanne Chauvin's energetic fight to obtain that right (the judiciary was still reserved to men); instead, she was gratifying her own personal satisfaction. At the same time, she enrolled at *l'Institut des Sciences Politiques* and admits having worked harder for that diploma.

When she graduated from the university, one of her professors regretted that Ludwig could not enter the *Conseil d'Etat* (Counsel of State), for she would have been an excellent recruit. Indeed, Simone Ludwig showed more concern for public law and the quest for an equilibrium between public and private interests. Participating in the *grand corps de l'Etat* would have corresponded perfectly to her concerns.

In 1942, Simone Ludwig married Gabriel Rozès, an *administrateur civil* at the Ministry of Finances who was engaged in a promising career. One day in

1946, he came home with the *Journal Officiel* under his arm. He had just read about the law authorizing women to enter the judiciary and handed the paper to his wife, suggesting she might be interested. Simone Rozès found the idea appealing. Thus began the most magnificent judicial career of any French woman.

## CAREER DEVELOPMENT

Simone Rozès plunged into her books and prepared for the competitive exam. To this day, she remembers how hard it had been to study again. She also had to submit to another requirement of the law, a two-year probationary term as a lawyer, which she accomplished from 1947 to 1949.

Rozès entered the judiciary in 1950. These were the pioneer years, and women were regarded with enmity at the concourse or when they took up their functions. Nominated as assistant-judge at the Court of Appeals in Bourges, Rozès had no choice but to accept. This assignment meant leaving her family when her first child was only two years old, but her husband was supportive and encouraged her to accept. For Rozès, the appointment was a sacrifice, but she confesses that it was not the only one she would make during her career. Simone Rozès was the first woman affected in the circumscription of this court, for her superior was very strict. He insisted that she adhere to the obligation of residing in the town, so she rented an apartment. To see her family, she traveled ten hours by train each weekend.

In 1953, Rozès was assigned to the Ministry of Justice in Paris, where she would spend most of her career, which is quite exceptional. She worked in the Ministry until 1962, and because it was a period of great governmental instability, she served under 17 different ministers of justice. In 1962, Rozès returned to a jurisdiction in the *tribunal de grande instance* in Paris, first as judge, then as vice president from 1969 to 1973. She then returned to the Ministry of Justice as *directeur de l'Education surveillée*. It was the first time a woman had served as a director.

In 1975, Rozès marked another first for women in France when she was appointed president of the *tribunal de grande instance* in Paris. Although it is not the highest position in the judiciary, it is considered the most interesting. But Rozès left this post six years later for another exciting experience she had not anticipated. In 1981, Simone Rozès was asked to become the French *avocat general* (public prosecutor) at the European Court of Justice. Once again, it was not a position that she had aspired to (since a woman had never held this office), but she accepted promptly because of the opportunity to explore new legal systems and the difficulties of legal application. The family obstacles of earlier years had disappeared; her two children were grown, and modern transportation linked Luxembourg and Paris, allowing quick trips between the cities for her and her husband.

Rozès thought that the European Court assignment would be her last and was surprised when she was called back to France in 1984, to assume the position of first president of the *Cour de cassation* (the Supreme Court), where she remained until she retired in 1988. This appointment was the most significant for it was the first time a woman rose to the rank of first magistrate in France. Rozès was selected because of her talents as a jurist, and not on the basis of intrigues or political allegiances. On that point, Simone Rozès has always manifested great independence, and this was obvious during her five years as president of the seventeenth chamber of the *tribunal de grande instance* in Paris, with competency for cases concerning the press. At times, for example, Rozès's decisions prompted some to label her a *juge rouge* (red judge, favorable to left-wing ideas), but at other times, she was considered an instrument of the conservatives.

As first president of the *Cour de cassation,* Simone Rozès had diverse responsibilities. She assumed jurisdictional functions that could have allowed her to determine the jurisprudence of the court if the magistrates split evenly (which is extremely rare). This happened only once during her four years as first president in a labor case. The first president also administers the court and presides over the *bureau de la Cour de cassation*, which, until the reforms of 1994, played an important part in the determining composition of the *Conseil supérieur de la magistrature* (CSM). In addition, the first president has a fundamental role in the judiciary by presiding over the CSM for disciplinary cases concerning judges of the bench and over the *Collège des magistrats* that designates the commission for advancement and integration. Finally, the first president presides in the *conseil d'administration* of the *Ecole nationale de la magistrature*, the body that trains future generations of judges.

Rozès's zeal, talent, and personal qualities, such as her firm character, intelligence, talent for administration, and interest in young people have been publicly acknowledged. She was awarded the Medal of Education *surveillée et administration pénitentiaire*, and she received the *Légion d'honneur* (actually *commandeur*) and the *ordre national du Mérite (officier*).

## ACHIEVEMENTS AND CONTRIBUTIONS

Simone Rozès-Ludwig served in the judiciary of France for 38 years. During that time, she held the positions of judge of the bench, member of the prosecution, and participant in the central administration (ministry), often as the first woman to achieve such appointments. Her experiences allowed her to engage in nearly all fields of law, but Rozès showed particular interest in criminal law. Perhaps her early interest in the balance between public and private interests led her to this particular specialization.

Rozès, unlike many of her compatriots, was determined not to limit her horizons to French frontiers. She showed great interest in other legal systems and did not wait for her appointment to Luxembourg to establish contacts with jurists of other countries. She began her international contacts early in her judicial career. In 1950, the *Association pour les échanges entre juristes français et allemands* was founded, and Rozès joined because she believed that it was impossible to build a future if antagonisms between France and Germany continued. Years later, she was rewarded with the distinction of *commandeur du Mérite* of the Federal Republic of Germany. Rozès also attended sessions in the courts of England and Scotland, and gave a conference at the University of Edinburgh where she received the title of doctor *honoris causa*.

Her knowledge of American legal practice is probably even more developed. Rozès was a member of the United Nations committee to fight delinquency and prevent crime for 14 years (1977–1991), holding the chairmanship at one point. She was able to assume this task in tandem with her main activities because it only required a trip to Vienna, Austria or a two weeks' stay in New York from time to time. As she knew the English language well, she took advantage of those stays to observe American practices and to draw a number of conclusions that she would later explain in a book written during her retirement.

Her *ouverture* to others structured her way of thinking and led her to firm European convictions. She foresees, in the distant future, the international exchange of judges, but only if there is a harmonization of legal systems and cultures. Rozès has not been reluctant to share her views of the law with international colleagues. Thus, in November of 1994, she flew to Italy to discuss anticorruption measures with Italian authorities.

Retirement is nonsense to a person like Simone Rozès. She continues giving conferences and presided over a court of arbitration. In collaboration with lawyer Paul Lombard, she has written a book, *Le juge et l'avocat. Dialogue sur la justice* (1992), in which she addresses major contemporary legal themes. She has acknowledged the feminization of the judiciary and regrets that it has contributed to the depreciation of the office. On this matter, Rozès believes the essential question is not why there are so many women in the ranks of the judiciary, but why there are so few men?

Rozès has also criticized the phenomenon of unionization among the judiciary since 1968 because it provides a mechanism to introduce politics into the judiciary; it is a disturbing element and infringes on the principle of independence. She also considers the position of *juge d'instruction* too ticklish to be left to novices. Rozès has also insisted on the secrecy of the investigation and admits that it is difficult to harmonize the well-established presumption of innocence with the right to inform.

Other remarks result from her comparisons with the American system. During her trips to the United States, Rozès had the opportunity to assist in court sessions, to witness judicial election campaigns, and to discover the great liberty with which journalists would make announcements, yet be punished when they transgressed ethical boundaries. It was during these travels that Rozès came to the conclusion that it would be impossible to import the American system to France, as some French jurists have proposed. Rozès rejects elections for judges and the accusatory procedure. She has even taken a position against the maintenance of the criminal jury based on the fiction developed during the French Revolution that the people are sovereign and cannot be mistaken. On this point, hers is an isolated opinion. On the other hand, Rozès admires the proceedings against untimely journalistic declarations.

Rozès's skill in wielding legal concepts, her accuracy of judgment, and her solid common sense prompted Prime Minister Edouard Balladur to call on her in September, 1994 to head a commission to explore solutions to two vigorously debated questions: corruption and the secrecy of criminal investigations. Rozès was on vacation in Brazil, but she was contacted with the help of the French embassy. Here again, fate served her well; she ended her holiday abruptly and returned to Paris.

The *Commission Rozès* was composed of experts from business, labor unions and the judiciary. Under Rozès's leadership, the emphasis rested on a moral approach. The commission tried to determine the means to ensure better morality in public political activities, and their proposals appear to be a reaction to the scandals involving ministers and political parties. The commission suggested that private enterprise be forbidden to give financial support to political activities (parties and electoral campaigns). The relationship between private enterprises and public authorities should be as clear as possible, banishing all intermediates in contracts for public works, for example. The commission further suggested that all persons elected on a local or national level be obligated to declare their financial situation in the *préfecture*. If an elected official yielded to corruption, sold his influence, meddled in business, or embezzled, he should automatically be ineligible for office. To limit such risks, the commission advocated enforcement of parliamentary incompatibilities. Parliament subsequently enacted the reforms suggested by the commission but limited the obligation to declare one's financial situation to members of Parliament.

The main judicial question raised during the commission's work was that of the secrecy of a criminal investigation. Rozès had expressed her ideas on this issue in her book, reminding the reader that the presumption of innocence is consecrated in French law and, as such, that the secrecy of the investigation proceeds from it. She does not reject the right of citizens to be informed, but an equilibrium must be found to harmonize both rights. Rozès suggests that the public prosecutor could give primary information without divulging important elements, and at the same time, she criticizes journalists who try to obtain major information on criminal investigations and urges the sanction of this practice.

As the pioneer woman in the French judicial system, Simone Rozès-Ludwig serves as a role model for other women. Her interest in the development of international law and the transference of legal lessons between nations is indicative of her global vision for the future of law. Even as her work continues, Simone Rozès has left her mark on French judicial and legal history.

**ACKNOWLEDGMENT**

I wish to express my sincere gratitude to Madame Simone Rozès-Ludwig who agreed to receive me at her home and answer my questions despite her very heavy schedule in December, 1994.

**REFERENCE**

Rozès, Simone, and Paul Lombard. *Le juge et l'avocat, Dialogue sur la justice*. Paris: Robert Laffont, 1992.

*JACQUELINE LUCIENNE LAFON*

# WILTRAUT RUPP-VON BRÜNNECK (1912–1977)

Wiltraut Rupp-von Brünneck was an associate justice of West Germany's Federal Constitutional Court from 1963 to 1977. She was the only woman among the Court's 16 members during her 14 years on the German Federal Republic's highest court of constitutional review. Elected to fill the seat on the First Senate vacated by Justice Erna Scheffler,[1] the only other woman to have been appointed to the Court in the first 26 years of its existence, she distinguished herself as an independent-minded judge of enormous talent and sensitivity. Rupp-von Brünneck was also a controversial judge and the author of some of the Court's most notable dissenting opinions during her tenure of office. As noted below, several important areas of German constitutional law bear the imprint of her influence. Succumbing to cancer, she died in office at the age of 65, three years prior to her scheduled retirement. Looking back on her career at the time, *Das Parlament* described her as "one of the most important women in the public life of the Federal Republic."[2]

## FAMILY BACKGROUND AND EDUCATION

Wiltraut von Brünneck was born on August 7, 1912, in Berlin-Lankwitz. Descended from a noble family of ancient lineage, she was the granddaughter of Wilhelm von Brünneck (1839–1917), a noted professor of law at Halle University, and the daughter of Dr. Werner von Brünneck, a high official in the Prussian Ministry of Justice. Her mother, Margarita Schmidt, was the daughter of the president of Berlin's Superior Court of Justice. With this family background, she was almost surely headed for a career in Germany's judicial establishment. Indeed, after passing her school-leaving *Abitur* examination with high honors in 1931, followed by a year of residence in an agricultural college for women, she embarked on the study of law at the universities of Berlin, Königsberg, Göttingen, and Heidelberg.

Her commitment to the defense of women's interests appeared early. At Berlin and Heidelberg, she helped to organize a group of women law students dedicated to defending women academicians and lawyers against the National Socialist effort to keep them out of the professions. After finishing her university studies in 1936, she went on to pass her first state bar examination with distinction. In 1937, she embarked on the practical phase of her training, apprenticing in the courts of Berlin and Sangerhausen.

Interrupted by two years of compulsory military service in an aircraft warning unit, she ended this phase of her legal training in 1941. At a time when women were encouraged to toil at the hearth and bear children for the Fatherland, she was determined to press on with her legal studies, eventually earning the right to sit for her second state bar examination. Once again, she passed with high honors, an unusual accomplishment for one of her sex who had chosen to defy an all-male bar hostile to the admission of women.

## CAREER DEVELOPMENT

Wiltraut von Brünneck started her professional career in 1941 as a research assistant in Berlin University's Labor Law Institute, where she was working on her doctoral dissertation. Her plan to secure a doctoral degree, however, ended abruptly in 1943, when a bombing raid destroyed her collected materials and notes. For the remainder of the war, von Brünneck worked as a legal adviser in the *Reich* Ministry of Justice, mainly in divisions on inheritance and real estate law. Immediately after the war, she returned to her family's estate in Oberröblingen, located in the Soviet Zone of Occupation. Shortly thereafter, she served as a judge on Sangerhausen's District Court and later on Merseburg's Regional Court, presiding over cases dealing mainly with probate, inheritance, and guardianship law.

Her legal career in the Soviet Zone soon ended, however, when she was removed from her position and dispossessed of her property because of her family background and "bourgeois" legal education. She left the Soviet Zone in 1947 to set up a law office in Wiesbaden where she met Georg-August Zinn, minister of justice for Hesse and well-known for his anti-Nazi record before and during the war. Zinn, who would later become one of the Social Democratic party's leading members of West Germany's constitutional convention (known as the Parliamentary Council [*parliamentarische Rat*]), recognized her talents immediately. He appointed her to a post in the Justice Ministry's public law division, the position that placed her on an upward trajectory into the highest echelon of Germany's legal profession.

Wiltraut von Brünneck was present at the creation of the West German Federal Republic. As Georg-August Zinn's personal assistant in his capacity as chairman of the Parliamentary Council's Constitutional Court Committee and member of its Committee on Basic Rights, she was among the "insiders" behind the scenes who had the rare privilege of witnessing and contributing to the Council's work as the Basic Law was being debated and drafted. After its entry into force in 1949, she continued as Zinn's assistant during his brief term of office in the *Bundestag*. When he resigned his parliamentary seat to become Hesse's minister-president in 1951, he brought Wiltraut von Brünneck into his circle of advisers at the state chancellery office. Over the next ten years, she remained one of Zinn's closest associates and a leading figure in his administration.

In addition to her work as legal adviser and senior official in the executive branch of the Hessian state government, von Brünneck served in several other capacities, both public and private. She was an active member of the constitutional and administrative tribunals of the Evangelical Church in Hesse and Nassau, and a member of the executive committee of Germany's Federation of Women Lawyers. She was also active in the German-French Women Lawyer's Association. In 1960, she became an elected member of the Congress of German Lawyers where she remained an active participant until her election to the Constitutional Court. While engaged in these and other activities, she managed to write numerous articles in specialized legal journals, including a major treatise on the origin and principles of Hesse's constitution. She also collaborated with George-August Zinn and Erwin Stein—another justice-to-be of the Federal Constitutional Court—in publishing an authoritative commentary on the Hessian constitution.

Wiltraut von Brünneck's most important responsibilities, however, were carried out in the name of Hesse's state (*Land*) government. She headed Hesse's Office of *Bundesrat* Affairs and represented Hesse on the *Bundesrat*'s Legal Affairs Committee. (The *Bundesrat*, i.e., the Council of State Governments, represents the various states [*Länder*] in the national legislative process.) She also played a prominent role in formulating Hesse's broadcasting policy, an area of law constitutionally reserved to the *Länder*. As a member of the Council of the Hessian Broadcasting Station, she negotiated numerous radio and television contracts with the Federal government and with other German states. She also served as Minister-President Zinn's top adviser at numerous national conferences of state ministers-president. Finally, in 1963, Zinn named her assistant director of the state chancellery office.

It was from this position that she was elected, again with George-August Zinn's support, as associate justice of the Federal Constitutional Court. As chairman of the *Bundesrat*'s Committee on Selection of Constitutional Judges, he exercised enormous influence over the *Bundesrat*'s appointments to the Federal Constitutional Court, particularly when it was the Social Democratic party's (SPD) turn to produce the nominee. Von Brünneck was the SPD's unanimous choice to fill the open seat on the First Senate. Reporters often remarked that von Brünneck's career spiraled along with Zinn's own, but they hastened to add that her intelligence, integrity, competence, and devotion to duty—an unswerving commitment often attributed to her upbringing in the Prussian tradition of state service—would have propelled her into the highest echelons of whatever branch of government she might have chosen to enter. Given her governmental experience and background in constitutional law, no one doubted that she was supremely qualified for a position on the nation's highest tribunal.

Shortly after taking her seat in 1963, she met Justice Hans Rupp, a distinguished member of the Constitutional Court's Second Senate. They married in 1965, she for the first time, and he—a widower—for the second. Honored and toasted inside the Court, the two justices by their membership on different senates were able to avoid even the appearance of impropriety. Henceforth, the esteemed wife of an equally esteemed groom would go by the name of Wiltraut Rupp-von Brünneck.

## ACHIEVEMENTS AND CONTRIBUTIONS

Rupp-von Brünneck soon established herself as an extremely able jurist who would combine enormous legal competence with compassion in the interpretation of the constitution. She would also steer an independent course in important areas of constitutional law. Dedicated particularly to the cause of equal rights for women, nonmarital children, and orphans, she played a crucial role in ridding national statutes of their discriminatory provisions against these groups. She was also the official rapporteur in numerous cases involving welfare and social security recipients.[3] Perhaps the most important of the cases in which she took the leading role as rapporteur was a 1969 judgment resulting in the repeal of all legal provisions discriminating against nonmarital children. In addition, Rupp-von Brünneck was widely recognized as the First Senate's leading authority on constitutional issues relating to the protection of marriage and the family under Article 6 of the constitution. In this context, she fought for the equality of women within marriage.

The opinion in the *Spanish Marriage* case (1971), largely the result of her work as rapporteur, was a resounding vindication of the right to marry under Article 6 of the Basic Law,[4] and the decision laid the groundwork for the subsequent reform of West Germany's marriage and divorce law. *Spanish Marriage* involved a Spanish national who applied for a license to marry a German woman divorced in a German court pursuant to German law. Spanish authorities, however, refused to grant him the necessary certificate of eligibility for marriage required under German law because his fiancee's divorce was not recognized under Spanish law. In applying international private law to this case, the German courts sustained the denial of the marriage license, and it was this decision that Rupp-von Brünneck was instrumental in overruling. The Constitutional Court accepted her view that Spanish law, which did not recognize divorce, could not be enforced in Germany in the light of the special protection bestowed upon marriage under the Basic Law.

Occasionally portrayed as the "conscience of the First Senate," Wiltraut

Rupp-von Brünneck envisioned the Basic Law as an instrument for achieving social justice. In her view, individual rights could be effectively exercised only within a genuinely communal social structure. Thus, the principle of the social welfare state (*Sozialstaatsprinzip*) laid down in Article 20 of the Basic Law, particularly when seen in tandem with the guarantee of equality, imposed affirmative obligations on government to create such a structure. In one of her landmark dissents, Rupp-von Brünneck argued that the principle of the social state (*Sozialstaatsprinzip*) requires government to do more than provide for the minimal needs of socially disadvantaged groups. Adequate housing, education, medical care, and social security were, in her view, entitlements that all persons should enjoy as a matter of constitutional right.

The dissenting opinions for which she was most noted appeared in the *Mephisto* case (1971) and *Abortion* case (1975), two of the Constitutional Court's most controversial decisions. Her dissents in both cases were popular as well as carefully crafted. In *Mephisto*,[5] the Court sustained a ban on the distribution of a satirical novel because it injured the reputation of a deceased actor who flourished on the German stage during the Nazi era. Rupp-von Brünneck's dissent was a ringing declaration in favor of artistic freedom, a view that would eventually gain increasing favor in the First Senate.

Her dissent in the *Abortion Case*, however, rebuked the First Senate for exceeding its proper authority in holding a liberalized abortion law unconstitutional. The law permitted a woman to procure a legal abortion within the first trimester of pregnancy following mandated and nonbinding counseling. In a 6–2 decision, the Senate struck down the law on the ground that it violated the right to life in light of the principle of human dignity.[6] The Court defined abortion as "an act of killing" whose criminalization is required unless an abortion can be justified for serious reasons specified by law. Rupp-von Brünneck had no quarrel with the proposition that the state had an obligation to protect the fetus under the "right to life" provision of the Basic Law. She maintained, however, that in requiring counseling and providing public support to any woman who would carry her child to term, the state had struck a permissible balance between the fetus's right to life and the woman's right to the development of her personality. Years later, in 1993, the essential core of her dissent would prevail when the Second Senate reviewed a post-reunification abortion statute passed by the newly elected, all-German parliament.[7]

In a memorial ceremony in the presence of her colleagues and other high government officials, the President of the Federal Constitutional Court, Ernst Benda, with whom Rupp-von Brünneck had been in frequent disagreement, recounted Rupp-von Brünneck's many contributions to Germany's developing constitutional law. He also paid tribute to the industry, collegiality, and the awesome sense of responsibility she brought to her role as a constitutional court justice. Even in the presence of great physical pain and in the face of certain death, she insisted on doing her normal share of the Court's work. "We take leave of her today,'' said President Benda, ''thankful to have been associated with a great judicial personality.''

## NOTES

1. The Federal Constitutional Court consists of two panels called senates. The First and the Second Senates, each made up of eight justices, exercise mutually exclusive jurisdiction. Most constitutional complaints involving claims to substantive rights under the Basic Law, or *Grundgesetz* (Germany's constitution), are decided by the First Senate.

2. *Das Parlament* (September 3, 1977).

3. There is a specialized division of labor on the Federal Constitutional Court. Each justice serves as the rapporteur in areas of jurisdiction in which he or she is the acknowledged authority. After receiving a given case, the rapporteur is responsible for preparing a report (*Votum*) on the case for his or her colleagues. The report includes a detailed summary of the facts of the case, a restatement of arguments on all sides of the dispute, and a recommended solution. When finished, the report is sent to the rapporteur's colleagues prior to its being taken up collectively in conference. The rapporteur nevertheless plays a critical role in this process, and his or her judgment prevails more often than not, particularly if he or she is a respected colleague and performs his or her role with competence and good judgment.

4. Judgment of May 4, 1971, 31 BVerfGE 58 (1971).

5. Judgment of February 24, 1971, 30 BVerfGE 173, 218–227 (1971).

6. Judgment of February 25, 1975, 39 BVerfGE 1 (1975). Rupp-von Brünneck's dissenting opinion appears at 68–95.

7. Judgment of May 28, 1993, 80 BVerfGE 203 (1993).

## REFERENCES

*Das Parlament* (September 3, 1977).

Judgment of February 25, 1975. (*Abortion* case.) 39 BVerfGE 1 (1975) (dissent with Judge Helmut Simon at 69–95).

Judgment of February 24, 1971. (*Mephisto* case.) 30 BVerfGE 173 at 218–27 (1975).

Judgment of May 1, 1971. (*Spanish Marriage* case.) 31 BVerfGE 58 (1971).

Rupp von-Brünneck, Wiltraut.''Verfassungsgerichtsbarkeit und gesetzgebende Gewalt.'' 102 *Archiv des öffentlichen Rechts* (1977): 1–26.

Rupp von-Brünneck, Wiltraut.''Admonitory Functions of Constitutional Courts.'' 22 *American Journal of Comparative Law* (1972): 387–403.

Rupp von-Brünneck, Wiltraut. ''Darf das Bundesverfassungsgericht an den Gesetzgeber Appellierent?'' *Festschrift für Gebhard Müller*. Tübingen: Mohr, 1970, 355–78.

Rupp von-Brünneck, Wiltraut. *Die Grundrechte im Juristischen Alltag*. Frankfurt a. M: Metzner, 1970.

Rupp von-Brünneck, Wiltraut.''Die Verfassung des Landes Hessen vom 1.12.1946.'' 3 *Jahrbuch des öffentlichen Rechts*. N.F. (1954): 213–70.

*DONALD P. KOMMERS*

# HELGA SEIBERT (1939– )

Helga Seibert is a justice of Germany's Federal Constitutional Court, the highest tribunal in the country and one of the world's most powerful and prestigious constitutional courts. Germany's council of state governments (*Bundesrat*) elected her to a seat on the Court's First Senate in 1989. (The Court consists of two senates, the First and Second, with mutually exclusive jurisdiction.) The 16 justices (8 on each senate) are elected for nonrenewable terms of 12 years. Thus, Justice Seibert's term will expire in 2001. The seat she occupies on the First Senate was earmarked for a female appointee since the Court's beginning in 1951. She is the fourth woman to hold this seat and at the time of her election, the fifth woman overall to have been selected to this most prestigious body.[1]

## FAMILY BACKGROUND AND EDUCATION

Helga Seibert was born in Witzenhausen on January 7, 1939. Her parents were teachers. At the age of 19, looking toward an international career, she embarked on two years of foreign language training at the well-known Language Training Institute in Germersheim. In 1960, however, she switched to the study of law. After spending a year at Marburg University, she went to the Free University of Berlin, in part to observe life in Berlin first hand and to familiarize herself with the special condition of the city as a flash point in the troubled relationship between East and West. She returned to Marburg to finish the university phase of her legal studies in 1964.

Having passed her first major state examination in law, Seibert served briefly as an assistant to Professor Gerhardt Hoffmann in Marburg's Institute of Public Law. After that, still very much interested in foreign affairs, she spent a year (1965–1966) at the School of Advanced International Studies of Johns Hopkins

University in Bologna, where she took courses on American constitutional law, European law, and the Atlantic Alliance. In 1966, she entered the Yale Law School, graduating with a Master of Laws degree in 1967. While at Yale, she studied and worked with some of the luminaries of American constitutional law and jurisprudence, including Robert Bork, Alexander Bickel, Thomas Emerson, and Ronald Dworkin.

After completing her studies abroad, Seibert returned to Germany to begin the practical phase of her legal education, during which time she also served as a research assistant to Professor Dietrich Pirson at Marburg University's Public Law Institute. While at Marburg, she also met and worked with Peter Häberle who in time would become one of Germany's leading constitutional scholars and the editor of the distinguished *Jahrbuch des Öffentlichen Rechts*. As for Professor Pirson, he had at the time written an authoritative commentary on provisions of the Basic Law (Germany's constitution), dealing with the protection of marriage, family and motherhood, and the rights of illegitimate children, the field of legal research that Helga Seibert herself would soon cultivate in various professional capacities and later as a justice of the Federal Constitutional Court. She started the practical phase of her training in the District (*Land*) Court of Giessen. There she met the president of the Giessen Court who would later become the permanent secretary in the Federal Ministry of Justice. (She would spend much of her later career in the Justice Ministry.) In addition, and along the way, she joined the Social Democratic party (SPD) and was an active member of its working group of Social Democratic jurists.

## CAREER DEVELOPMENT

Shortly after passing her second major state law examination in October 1970, and upon the recommendation of Professor Häberle, Seibert spent a year as a special adviser to the SPD's Legal Affairs Working Group in the national Parliament (*Bundestag*). There she participated in drafting proposals for reforming West Germany's marriage and divorce law, a process in which Martin Hirsch, an SPD parliamentary leader, was also deeply engaged. One of the SPD's esteemed experts on legal policy, Hirsch recognized in Helga Seibert a young legal professional of considerable talent and commitment. And so, when Hirsch himself became a justice of the Federal Constitutional Court in January of 1971, she accompanied him to Karlsruhe (the location of the Court) as one of his legal clerks, working in that capacity from February of 1972 until September of 1974. She would be one of several clerks over the years who would later return to the Constitutional Court as one of its elected members.

Upon leaving her clerkship, Seibert joined the legal staff of the Federal Ministry of Justice in Bonn, where she remained as a high-level civil servant until her election to the Constitutional Court. During her first four years in the Justice Ministry, she worked in sections dealing with constitutional matters. One of her tasks was to assist in screening government-prepared bills for possible constitutional deficiencies. She also worked in a section concerned with the legal aspects of government organization, and for several months, she devoted her attention to international human rights law. Later in her career in the Justice Ministry, Seibert was preoccupied for two years with matters relating to European Community law. During this time she took a five-month course of studies at the Federal Academy for Civil Servants, which included a four-month internship with the legal office of the Council of Ministers of the European Communities. With this background and experience, not to mention her command of foreign languages, Seibert was fully qualified and poised to enter the field of international civil service.

In 1982, however, she was placed in charge of the Justice Ministry's section on basic rights, in which capacity she was responsible for seeing that government bills conformed to the Basic Law. Over the next seven years, she would develop and sharpen her expertise in German constitutional law, especially in the field of fundamental rights and liberties. The work required her to read and master the relevant decisions of the Federal Constitutional Court, and one of her tasks was to prepare legislation required by the Constitutional Court's directives and admonitions. A case in point was the well-known *Federal Census Act* case (1983) in which the Constitutional Court had declared parts of a federal census statute unconstitutional for violating the personal right to "informational self-determination." Seibert helped to prepare the necessary corrective legislation designed to ensure that census data could not be manipulated in such a way as to reveal personal information about particular individuals. She was similarly involved in drafting legislation having to do with internal security and criminal procedure.

Seibert happened to be in the right spot at the right time when Gisela Niemeyer's term on the Constitutional Court's First Senate expired in 1989. This particular seat would be filled by a person recommended by SPD and chosen by the Council of State Governments (*Bundesrat*).[2] This meant that the nominee would likely be a high civil servant or judge at the federal level or a person of Cabinet rank in state government. Helga Seibert, an unpretentious woman not given to self-promotion and with no prior judicial experience, was not an obvious choice. She was, however, a logical choice. She had all the right personal and intellectual credentials: She was oriented toward the SPD but not slavishly partisan; she held progressive views on social and cultural issues, but respected alternative arguments; she was an expert on family law, but also broadly conversant with the full range of constitutional issues in the field of human rights; she was clearly her own person, but also known for her collegiality. In addition, she enjoyed the firm support of Minister of Justice Hans A. Engelhard, who applauded her "brilliant expertise," her "constitutional honesty and objectivity," and her "precise argumentation." The vote in the *Bundesrat* was unanimous, and with her election, she became the second member of her immediate family to make it to one of the high federal courts. Her brother, Dr. Gerhard Seibert, is a judge of the Federal Administrative Court in Berlin.

## ACHIEVEMENTS AND CONTRIBUTIONS

As a member of the First Senate, Justice Seibert has served as the rapporteur in a number of jurisprudential areas,[3] but she appears to have been most influential in cases arising under Article 6 of the Basic Law which, as indicated above, deals with marriage, family, motherhood, and illegitimate children. A quiet revolution has been taking place in this field of law, the changes being directed toward more and greater equality in marriage, toward expanding the protection of Article 6 to nonmarital partnerships, and toward securing equal rights for illegitimate children. Numerous Article 6 cases have reached the Court in recent years and Seibert's hand has been visible in the disposition of most of them, including a 1995 decision recognizing the ''parental rights'' of biological fathers in adoption proceedings. In this landmark case, the father of a child born out of wedlock must be consulted before the natural mother who marries another person can adopt the child. Prior to this case, the biological mother's parental right over the child born out of wedlock was exclusive.

In some of her off-the-bench writings, Justice Seibert has begun to explore the constitutional implications of artificial insemination, surrogate motherhood, and other issues of reproductive technology. She has approached these issues with caution and with due appreciation of the protections that the Basic Law bestows on motherhood and the rights of parents. In fact, she has raised serious questions about the validity of forcing any surrogate mother to surrender the child pursuant to a contractual agreement. As this and related issues begin to work their way into the Constitutional Court, she can be expected to play an increasingly important role. As noted earlier, her term expires in the year 2001. It seems clear that Justice Seibert will be found to have contributed substantially to the Court's jurisprudence on marriage and family issues as it continues to unfold in the years remaining in this century.

## NOTES

1. The other justices who preceded her on the First Senate seat to which she was appointed were Erna Scheffler (1951–1963), Wiltraut Rupp-von Brünneck* (1963–1977), and Gisela Niemeyer (1977–1989). Karin Grasshof, who was the first woman to be appointed to the Second Senate, took her seat in 1986. Since Helga Seibert joined the Court in 1989, three additional women have been elected to the Federal Constitutional Court. Renate Jäger, nominated by the SPD, and Evelyn Haas, nominated by the CDU, joined Helga Seibert on the First Senate in 1994. Jutta Limbach,* an SPD nominee also selected in 1994, was appointed vice president and, a few months later, president (''chief justice'') of the Constitutional Court. Thus, in 1995, five of the Court's 16 members were women. Three were members of the First Senate, two of the Second.

2. One-half of the justices in each Senate are elected by the *Bundesrat*, and the other half by the *Bundestag*, or the national Parliament. The *Bundestag* has delegated its electoral authority to a 12–member committee whose party membership is proportionate to

the strength of each party in the full house. Since a two-thirds vote is required to elect a justice in both houses, candidates need the support of the main political parties.

3. There is a specialized division of labor on the Federal Constitutional Court. Each justice serves as the rapporteur in areas of jurisdiction in which he or she is the acknowledged authority. After receiving a given case, the rapporteur is responsible for preparing a report (*Votum*) on the case for his or her colleagues. The report includes a detailed summary of the facts of the case, a restatement of arguments on all sides of the dispute, and a recommended solution. When finished, the report is sent to the rapporteur's colleagues prior to its being taken up collectively in conference. The rapporteur nevertheless plays a critical role in this process; his or her judgment prevails more often than not, particularly if he or she is a respected colleague and performs his or her role with competence and judgment.

## REFERENCES

Seibert, Helga. ''Verfassungsrecht und Befruchtungstechniken.'' In *Embryoneneschutz und Befruchtungstechnik.* Munich: J. Schwietzer Verlag, 1986, 62–79.

Seibert, Helga. ''Prüfung der Verfassungsmässigkeit.'' In *Praxis der Gesetzgebung* (1983): 81–99.

*DONALD P. KOMMERS*

# ELISABETH SELBERT (1896–1986)

Elisabeth Selbert's achievements were many, and her 90 years spanned four eras of German political life. She was born under the German empire, raised during the Weimar Republic, worked through the Nazi regime, and helped to write the constitution of the Federal Republic of Germany (GFR). She was a wife, mother, lawyer, activist in the Social Democrat Party (SPD) and champion of women's rights. She is largely responsible for the equal rights provision, paragraph 2, in Article 3 of the GFR constitution:

1. All persons shall be equal before the law.
2. Men and women shall have equal rights.
3. No one may be prejudiced or favored because of his sex, his parentage, his race, his language, his homeland and origin, his faith, or his religious or political opinions.[1]

Selbert was one of only three women who participated directly in writing the 1948 constitution and is regarded as a ''mother'' of the German Republic. Her contributions continued, however, through the 1960s.

## FAMILY BACKGROUND AND EDUCATION

Elisabeth Rohde was born in 1896, in Kassel, the second of four daughters.[2] Her father was in the legal profession, and her mother was an independent-minded and active woman. Both parents believed strongly in educating their daughters for professions. Her father fell into heavy debt and was unable to support those ambitions for his daughters, but Elisabeth worked to enter middle school. She was a gifted student and successfully passed her examinations before the commission. At that time, only girls had to endure the scrutiny of commission exams.

Elisabeth did not immediately enter the university to undertake her legal studies. Instead, she took a job with an export company and, at the outbreak of World War I, began as a clerical worker in the post office. She was drawn to politics, even without role models for inspiration. At age 22, she joined the Social Democrat Party and, through her party work, met the man whom she would marry and who would be her political mentor, Adam Selbert. Selbert was a printer working in her neighborhood who was active in the Kassel Workers and Soldiers Movement. His political passions attracted her, and the two were married in 1920.

Elisabeth and Adam Selbert regarded their marriage as an emancipated partnership. They shared responsibilities for family, profession, and politics. It was Adam Selbert who encouraged Elisabeth to complete her high school education and later to pursue her legal studies. When she was 30, and the mother of two, she entered the university and finished her law degree in the absolute minimum time possible—three years. Her husband and her parents had, during that time, assumed total responsibility for the household and children. Selbert's dissertation was written in a mere four months on the topic of irreconcilable differences as a ground for divorce ("Zerrüttung als Ehescheidungsgrund"). Although her theory was not treated seriously at the time of its writing (1929), its concepts were eventually incorporated into the reform of the West German divorce law in 1977.

## CAREER DEVELOPMENT

Elisabeth Selbert passed her examination to practice law in October, 1934. When the National Socialists assumed power in 1933, they ended political opposition and revoked what legal rights women had been granted. One month after Selbert received her law license, the regime ceased issuing licenses to women. Adam Selbert was, at this time, the mayor of Kassel and was arrested by the Gestapo. As a result, Elisabeth became the sole support of the family while he was imprisoned. She managed two law firms and maintained close contact with the remaining members of the SPD. She was prohibited from representing any political prisoners and was under close surveillance by the Gestapo until the defeat of the Nazis. Even so, she maintained connections with a small SPD opposition group.

At the end of World War II, Elisabeth was among the first to work actively to rebuild the Social Democrat Party. Her political affiliations took her first to the constitutional convention in the state of Hesse in 1946 and then to the national constitutional convention in 1948. Women's equality was not initially on the agenda of the national constitutional body, but she made it part of the convention's work. Selbert was one of only four women delegates, and not surprisingly, the first initiative for a statement of women's equality was defeated in the spring of 1948. Subsequently, the convention devoted 42 sittings to discussions of Article 3, and paragraph 2, and eventually, the provision recognizing legal gender equality was passed.

## ACHIEVEMENTS AND CONTRIBUTIONS

Elisabeth Selbert returned to Kassel, where she was active in the government of Hesse and in the leadership of the SPD until 1958. She continued to strive for implementation of genuine rights for women, but she also was an advocate for the rights of minorities, the mentally ill, prisoners, and illegitimate children. Another element of her efforts, in conjunction with social scientists and feminists, was devoted to trying to achieve sociological equality for women in both the home and the workplace.

Unlike many feminists, Selbert argued that women should not gain equality by imitating men. Her strategy was to encourage and facilitate women's achievements through their own individuality; she opposed making comparisons between men and women. Selbert left the center of political life in 1958 and died on June 9, 1986, at age 90.

Elisabeth Selbert was born the same year that the German Civil Code was enacted, a code that embodied all of the assumptions of a patriarchal society, or what she referred to as "seeing with only one eye, the male one." The German Women's party was two years old at the time of her birth and advocated better education and employment opportunities for women, the right to vote for women, and the end of double standards of morality. During Selbert's lifetime, many of those goals were attained. She was a thinker and writer ahead of her time, proposing no-fault divorce in 1929. She was also a political activist who accomplished her ends through the political process. The gender equality provision in the 1949 constitution was included largely through her efforts. Even with that guarantee, however, full women's rights were not achieved until much later, and Selbert was a tireless advocate for them throughout her life.

## NOTES

1. Quoted in Donald P. Kommers, *The Constitutional Jurisprudence of the Federal Republic of Germany* (Durham, N.C.: Duke University Press, 1989), 505.

2. Much of the information in this article is from Birgit Meyer, "Elisabeth Selbert (1896–1986): *Gleichberechtigung ohne Wenn und Aber*." In Thomas Blanke, (ed.), *Streitbare Juristen*. (Baden-Baden: Nomos Verlagsgesellschaft, 1990), 427–38.

## REFERENCES

Kommers, Donald P. *The Constitutional Jurisprudence of the Federal Republic of Germany*. Durham, N.C.: Duke University Press, 1989.

Meyer, Birgit. ''Elisabeth Selbert (1896–1986): ''Gleichberechtigung ohne Wenn und Aber.'' In *Streitbare Juristen*. Ed. Thomas Blanke. Baden-Baden: Nomos Verlagsgesellschaft, 1990.

*MARY L. VOLCANSEK AND LUBA DEWITT*

# MARGARET A. SOMERVILLE (1942– )

Margaret Anne Ganley Somerville is Gale Professor of Law in the Faculty of Law of McGill University, Montreal. She was the first woman to hold a named chair in law in Canada. Professor Somerville is also Professor in McGill's Faculty of Medicine and the founding director of the McGill Centre for Medicine, Ethics and Law. She has made her scholarly contributions to the development of law by employing a "transdisciplinary" approach in her work. Professor Somerville's research in contemporary health-oriented legal issues is the result of her academic interests in law, medicine, and ethics combined with a genuine personal concern for the well-being of others.[1]

## EDUCATION AND CAREER DEVELOPMENT

Margaret Somerville was born in 1942 and raised in Australia. She graduated with distinction in pharmacy from the University of Adelaide in 1963 and is a registered pharmacist in Australia and New Zealand. After years with a large pharmaceutics firm preparing special-order medicines for physicians and hospitals in Adelaide, Somerville practiced pharmacy in Melbourne, New Zealand, and later in Sydney, Australia, while attending law school.

In 1973, Somerville graduated in law from the University of Sydney with First Class Honors and received the coveted University of Sydney Award for placing first over the four-year course with unusually high merit. She passed the New South Wales bar examinations in 1974 and worked for a leading Sydney law firm (Mallesons) on litigation and advisory work involving a medical element. In 1978, Somerville received her doctorate in civil law from the Postgraduate Institute of Comparative Law at McGill University. Since then, she has been a major contributor to world dialogue on medicolegal education and bioethics.

Among the many honors received for her contributions are honorary doctorates from the University of Windsor, Ontario (1992), and Macquarie University, New South Wales (1993), the Distinguished Service Award of the American Society of Law and Medicine (1985), the *Pax Orbis ex Jure* Gold medal of the World Jurists Association (1985), and the Order of Australia (1989). Somerville became a Fellow of the Royal Society of Canada in 1991.

Professor Somerville is an active consultant and member of many professional associations. For example, she has advised the Global Programme on AIDS of the World Health Organization, the United Nations Human Rights Secretariat in Geneva, and Law Reform Commissions in Canada and Australia. She has also been a speaker (including keynote) at UNESCO conferences in Paris. In addition, Somerville is chairperson of the Ethics Committee of the National Research Council of Canada and a member of the Board of Directors of the Canadian Anti-Doping Council and of the American Society of Law, Medicine, and Ethics. She also serves on clinical ethics committees and as a consultant to teaching hospitals. Since 1986, Somerville has served on the National Advisory Committee on AIDS of Canada's Ministry of Health and Welfare. She is a member of the Canadian Bar Association, the Canadian Pharmacists Association, the World Association for Medical Law, the Society for Health and Human Values, and the International Academy for Comparative Law.

## ACHIEVEMENTS AND CONTRIBUTIONS

Dr. Somerville's dissertation topic was titled "Medical Experimentation on the Person: A Comparative Survey of Legal and Extra-Legal Controls." This work is an analytical fusion of law, medicine, and ethics comparing the United Kingdom, Common Law Canada, the United States, and Australia with the civil law jurisdictions of France and Quebec. This ambitious geographic and intellectual reach typifies Margaret Somerville's bold and imaginative responses to some of the most profound challenges facing humankind at the juncture of law, medicine, religion, ethics, and philosophy in the late twentieth century. However daunting or controversial the issue may be, Professor Somerville has urged "transdisciplinary" study balanced by a sense of awe before nature's mysteries, and a kindly sense of humor in the face of human complexity.

Somerville has published a book, *Cases and Materials on the Law of Torts* (second edition, 1981), but it is her many articles, speeches, and book chapters that better reflect the range of her concerns regarding older persons, human rights in medicine and health care, reproductive technology, AIDS, abortion, genetics, medical malpractice, the allocation of medical resources, public health, and the pharmaceutical industry. Samples from some titles are: "causation"; "human experimentation in Canada"; "sex sterilization of mentally incompetent people"; abortion "head-turning conduct"; informed consent; pregnant minors; the law of pain treatment in hospitals; medical or family intervention in Canadian abortion law; dying, aging, and the elderly; birth technology; the definition of euthanasia; the right to refuse treatment; organ transplant access; defining human life (law, ethics, medicine); psychiatric treatment and confinement; "determinations of competence as a mechanism for control of persons"; and "nurses' participation in medical research."

In communicating about such profundities and technicalities with people of varied backgrounds and cultures in professional contexts or on radio and television, Professor Somerville shows special qualities of respect, clarity, and honest concern for all affected individuals and societies. With this writer and others, Dean Richard Cruess of the McGill Faculty of Medicine recognizes Professor Somerville as "one of the truly creative intellects with whom I have come in contact. . . . She has been a major force in Canada and throughout the world in delineating both the rights of patients with AIDS and the rights of society. . . . She is quite capable of being a positive and creative force in any area where medicine, law and society interface."

Exceptional intellects may be rare, but rarer still is the gifted mind that can build a working institution that lends concreteness to a genuinely original vision. Dr. Somerville has recognized the inadequacy of unidisciplinary and interdisciplinary study as approaches to issues linking ethics, medicine, and law. Scientific and ethical truth, and correct law will not succeed without a fusion of disciplinary focuses in what she calls "transdisciplinary" research, "essentially creating a new discipline out of multiple partners."[2] She conceptualized and built the McGill Centre for Medicine, Ethics, and Law, which is jointly sponsored by the Faculties of Medicine, Law, Religious Studies, and Arts (because of philosophy's relevance). "It is financially supported by our teaching hospitals, who in return receive the services of clinical ethicists at a level that would not be possible if each one of them was working independently. We have extended this concept to the graduate level and offer a graduate degree in which there are multiple academic portals of entry (i.e., medicine, nursing, law, religious studies, philosophy, etc.)."[3] However sensibly responsive to need, reorganizing quite diverse academic disciplines into a center for a research, educational, and service project proved difficult but possible. The McGill model for multidisciplinary reflection and community service has been successful. Professor Somerville's approach has helped not only hospitals, practitioners, and researchers, but also policy analysts seeking informed and balanced guidance in Canada and in other countries.

A distinctively inspiring quality marks Margaret Somerville: behind all the particulars of her work in medicolegal ethics are an enthusiastic hope and set of humane, evocative institutions, attitudes, and principles. Her primary focus might be called transcultural medical human rights law, which invokes an appreciation not only for the admirable values of each social culture but also for the rights of each person within each society. The worldwide "search for ethics" with a "new consciousness" is ultimately the greater enterprise than science.

Lending seminal perspectives in this endeavor may be Professor Somerville's single most important contribution.

Somerville views both awe and humor as essential for "establishing a healing culture." In a 1993 speech at Macquarie University in Australia, "Leaving Home(s): Awe, Humor and Australian Culture," Professor Somerville asks: "Is this combination itself particularly important, in that awe without a sense of humor is overwhelming, even paralyzing, and a sense of humor without one of awe, superficial and in danger of being contentless? Could it also represent a combination of intuition and 'examined emotions?' . . . I believe that right now the world urgently needs this combination of characteristics."

In this same speech, Somerville linked an aboriginal practice with a call for openness to "other ways of knowing" in addition to science:

> Recently, I was asked to do a consultation on whether it was acceptable for Canadian hospitals to sell placentas to be used for medical research, or for the manufacture of pharmaceutical products or even of cosmetics. In considering whether the placenta is simply waste and can be disposed of in any reasonable way that we dispose of waste, or, whether because of its human origins, it may or should be disposed of only under certain restricted conditions (for instance, does it belong to the mother, the parents, the baby, the hospital or to no one?) I came across an article in a book called "Voices of the First Day." In this, it was explained that for the Australian aborigines, traditionally, the placenta has sacred significance and is buried at the spot where the child is born, with certain rituals surrounding this. From then on that person is deeply connected to that place, including at the time of death. I felt that in some small way, I understood this. I wondered whether maybe . . . something causes even us later arriving Australians to respond in a similar way to the original Australians.
>
> In saying this, I should perhaps explain that I believe that we are only starting to recognize the depth of the mystery of both our "ways of knowing" and of the knowledge that is potentially open to us (which include intuition and "examined emotions") and give access to more than scientific knowledge. . . . The incredible combination of realities that we now need to hold in our individual and "collective" psyches (society also has a psyche): on the one hand, we are just one tiny, temporary individual . . . [in a vast universe]; and, on the other hand, the feeling of and need to recognize the extraordinary importance of each of us. We can probably only handle this if we recognize that an integral part of us as humans is a space for spirit and a sense of the sacred. These are often closely connected with a sense of awe; are not necessarily connected with religion; and are needed even in a secular society.

In short, Somerville seems to suggest that to achieve sound moral judgments on the great issues of life, death and health, individuals and communities might well emulate the spirit of the McGill Centre. Such an approach would require taking into account not only medical science and technology, but that which can be learned by examining a number of diverse sources like customary and clinical practice, the reflections of legal scholars and moral philosophers, and beliefs about the sacred and visions of the universe as defined by the cultural and religious context of human life.

What drives Margaret Somerville's intellectual and service explorations?

> I perceive my professional life as having unfolded . . . [through] serendipity . . . almost entirely on occasions where I was highly curious (usually in an intellectual sense) and excited by the 'hunt'. . . . [A] criterion by which I judge what I want to do is very much an aim of not being bored in doing it. Another criterion . . . is whether I am pursuing something for its own importance or for some secondary gain for myself. It is only if it is important itself that one can actually be fully immersed in it, which I believe is crucial to experiencing the type of intellectual excitement that I have referred to above. Consequently, this is not necessarily an unselfish aim.[4]

Somerville's professional recommendations on specific issues are likely to be informed, balanced, and cautious, with empathy for the individual's rights. She sees her work as a "searching for the purple-pink middle," as she put it in a speech at the University of Windsor, Ontario.[5] Along with "the journey into vast outer space," she says, we are beginning "the journey into vast inner space—through genetics and biotechnology, in particular, mapping the human genome." To appropriately link these journeys in our studies and judgments, we need to get away from the metaphors of "black and white" and "gray" and stress the imagination more by using "red and blue and purple-pink . . . the colors of imagination . . . one of the most important and enjoyable attributes that we have as humans." Incidentally, this preference for the purple-pink middle in ethical judgments extends to her office decor! "Everything in my office that can be purple-pink is purple-pink or is chosen to enhance this color—couches, paintings, walls, etc."[6]

With "transgenesis," genetics is doing the unthinkable, intervening "to achieve outcomes that could never occur in nature," "impossible combinations." For example, bright blue roses have been created by inserting a blue gene from delphiniums. The baked potato has been protected "by the insertion of a gene from flounder—perhaps we could regard this as 'twenty-first century fish and chips.' " Organs are transplanted; "a grandmother gives birth to her grandchildren; or a woman gives birth to a child genetically unrelated to her." Radical shifts in the paradigms of science and society are occurring, and these demand more, not less, nuanced emphasis on virtue, the family, and community. "I propose to you that we are currently . . . evolving a new societal paradigm . . . and that we should all make it part of our life journey . . . to help to give shape to this new paradigm. . . . It will require many attributes . . . [including] courage, wisdom, good judgment, optimism, integrity, trustworthiness, and honesty."

Somerville notes that at present the need for such virtues is not so often taken for granted, but is more explicitly recognized in professional discourse (for example, as "virtue ethics"). She calls for "more nuanced definitions" of virtues, which guide understanding and judgment in challenging medicolegal contexts. More courage, even heroism, may be required to choose a middle ground than a black or white position as a doctor, attorney, politician, businessman, involved patient, or pregnant teenager. ''Moreover, such courage or heroism when it occurs, occurs at a pole.'' Sometimes we need to start at the middle, she suggests, rather than at the end. Purple-pink is not a ''wishy washy'' color.

In considering the pros and cons of ''possible 'impossible combinations,' '' she urges imaginative awe and humor: ''A true sense of humor will provide us with both the capacity to experience the wonder and awe of our own individuality and how very important each of us is to ourselves and to one another, and, at the same time, the capacity to experience, fully, as my father once described it, 'living with the universe.' ''

As professor, lawyer, pharmacist, globalist, and humane leader, Dr. Margaret Somerville generates hope for a colorful and principled future in inner and outer space.

## NOTES

1. Sources for this article include interviews and correspondence with Professor Margaret Somerville and Dean Richard Cruess of McGill University.
2. Statement of Dean Richard Cruess.
3. Ibid.
4. Correspondence (August 15, 1994).
5. (June 6, 1992).
6. Correspondence (August 15, 1994).

## REFERENCES

Correspondence with Professor Margaret A. Somerville. August, 15, 1994.

Interview with Dean Richard Cruess of McGill Faculty of Medicine.

Somerville, Margaret A. ''The Song of Death: The Lyrics of Euthanasia.'' *Journal of Contemporary Health Law Policy* 9 (1993): 1–76.

Somerville, Margaret A. ''Law as an 'Art Form' Reflecting AIDS: A Challenge to the Province and Function of Law.'' In *Fluid Exchanges: Artists and Critics in the AIDS Crisis*. Ed. James Miller. Toronto: University of Toronto Press, 1992, 287–304.

Somerville, Margaret A. Speech given at the University of Windsor, Ontario, on June 6, 1992.

Somerville, Margaret A. ''Weaving 'Birth' Technologies into the 'Value and Policy Web' of Medicine, Ethics and Law: Should Policies on 'Conception' be Consistent?'' *Nova Law Review* 13 (1989): 515–608.

Somerville, Margaret A. ''Transdisciplinary Teaching and Learning: The Role of Bioethics.'' Final Report on the Bioethics Forum sponsored by the National Film Board of Canada. November 6–7, 1986 at Montreal, Canada, (1986): Volume II Appendices.

Somerville, Margaret A. "Access to Organs for Transplantation: Overcoming 'Rejection.' " *Canadian Medical Association Journal* 132 (1985): 113–17.

Somerville, Margaret A. "Birth Technology, Parenting and 'Deviance.' " *International Journal of Law and Psychiatry* 5, no. 2 (1982): 123–53.

Somerville, Margaret A. "Inadequate Treatment of Pail in Hospitalized Patients." Correspondence. *New England Journal of Medicine* 307 (1982): 55.

Somerville, Margaret A. "Therapeutic and Non-Therapeutic Medical Procedures—What are the Distinctions?" *Health Law in Canada* 2, no. 4 (1981): 85-90.

*Somerville, Margaret A.* "Abortion: Head-turning Conduct." *Health Law in Canada* 1, no. 1 (1980): 426.

Somerville, Margaret A. "Medical Interventions and the Criminal Law: Lawful or Excusable Wounding?" *McGill Law Journal* 26, no. 1 (1980): 82–96.

Somerville, Margaret A. "The Pregnant Minor: Contraception and Abortion under Canadian Law." *Medico-Legal News* 8 (now published as *Law, Medicine and Health Care*) (1980) 4–9.

Somerville, Margaret A. "Human Experimentation in Canada." *Canadian Doctor* 45, no. 5 (1979): 52, 58.

Somerville, Margaret A. "Informed Consent." *Canadian Doctor* 45, no. 5 (1979): 68, 70.

Somerville, Margaret A. "Sexual Sterilization of Mentally Incompetent Persons in Canadian Civil and Common Law." Proceedings of the 5th World Congress on Medical Law, Ghent, Belgium, Volume 1 (August 1979): 77–102. Reprinted at *Jus Medicum* 7 (1982): 95–114.

*LAWRENCE W. BEER*

# HELENE STÖCKER (1869–1943)

Helene Stöcker was not formally trained in law but rather studied literature. Nonetheless, she is remembered for her contributions to the reform of German family law and not for her literary work. She was a scholar and an activist, and her writing in several forums is voluminous. Although some of the changes she advocated were not adopted as law until the decades after World War II, Stöcker was an early advocate of no fault divorce, equality of the sexes, and the rights of illegitimate children. She was also a proponent of homosexual rights and of a woman's right of choice in unwanted pregnancies. One of her major contributions was provision of a philosophical basis, grounded in her reading of Friedrich Nietzsche, for gender equality. Her advocacy for women's and homosexuals' rights made it impossible for her to stay in Germany after the National Socialists came to power in 1933. Stöcker fled into exile in Switzerland at age 64 and died of cancer ten years later in New York in 1943.

## FAMILY BACKGROUND AND EDUCATION

Helene Stöcker was born on November 13, 1869, in Elberfeld, Prussia, the oldest of eight children.[1] Her upbringing followed strict Calvinism, and her father aspired to be a missionary. Instead, like his father before him, he became the proprietor of a repair shop. Helene always recalled her father as an exemplary man and her mother as overworked and burdened with too many pregnancies and too large a household. These images likely helped to form her later position on abortion. Helene shared in the household work and as the oldest child, was responsible for aiding in the rearing of her younger siblings.

Helene moved to Berlin in 1892, where she attended a teachers' institute and gymnasium (high school), but at that time women in Prussia were denied entrance into universities except as auditors. In 1896–1897, the University of Friedrich-Wilhelm Berlin admitted women, and she was among the 40 who enrolled immediately; by 1898, the number of women had risen to 238. Stöcker studied the history of literature, philosophy, and economics, and in 1897, she made her first public address linking Nietzsche's work to women's struggles.

In 1899, Stöcker studied for one semester in Glasgow, where she met and fell in love with Alexander Tilly, a German lecturer in literature. Tilly, however, was married with four children. His wife died suddenly in 1902, and Helene returned to Scotland to study and to take care of his children. She tried to continue her work, as Tilly did his, but she found that being "wife," stepmother, and professional was too difficult. She returned to Berlin, where she sank into a serious depression.

After her initial studies in Glasgow, Stöcker returned to Berlin and then moved to Bern, Switzerland, where she wrote her dissertation, "Artistic Views of the Eighteenth Century" ("Zur Kunstanschauung des 18. Jahrhunderts"). She took up residence again in Berlin after her graduation and became active in the Union of Progressive Women. In that context, Stöcker worked with some of the most vocal feminists of her time, including Minna Cauer, Marie Stritt, Anita Augsburg,* Lida Gustava Heymann and Maria Lischnewska. They proposed a number of radical reforms for the family and marriage. Stöcker argued for a spiritual conception of the "motherhood" of a country and for equal rights for women.

In 1905, Helene Stöcker met a lawyer, Bruno Springer, with whom she had a lifetime arrangement that endured until his death in 1931. The two never married, but resided in two apartments on the same floor for a long time. Springer served as her legal adviser on both private and political questions.

## CAREER DEVELOPMENT

In 1891, Stöcker read August Bebels's *Women and Socialism*, which had a profound effect on her subsequent intellectual life. She attempted to connect Bebels with Nietzsche's *Re-evaluation of Values* and thereby locate a place for the development of women's rights and female values. These linkages were to form the recurrent themes in her writing, wherein she expounded on the need for relationships between men and women that were sanctioned on an ethical and moral plane. She wrote that men were capable of achieving higher values only with women beside them. She advocated a new ethic, opposite to government policy, that placed women's sensuality and intelligence at the forefront and allowed women to control their own destinies. Women would escape men's repression, Stöcker said, not through active employment and political engagement, but through sexual and intellectual independence; only through independence in these spheres could a woman exercise her own free will and change both the culture and herself. She argued that only if women were free would men be able to view them as more than whores. Under such circumstances, both sexes could experience emancipation. Men and women could then pursue relationships that were harmonious and fulfilling, in which women would be treated with respect as individuals rather than as mere possessions.

In 1893, Stöcker wrote in *Modern Woman* (*Die Moderne Frau*) about the inequality of rights for women in family law. Her proposal was for economic independence as the base for women's freedom, which should be condoned and supported by law. She further suggested that the law should do more than not bar women from the freedom of decision; it should affirmatively support women's pursuit of aspirations beyond marriage and motherhood. Stöcker was also among the first to champion no fault divorces, requiring only that irreconcilable differences be necessary to find that a marriage was irretrievably broken.

Stöcker founded a magazine, *The New Generation* (*Die Neue Generation*), in which the fundamental roles of wife and mother, as practiced at the time, were challenged. Through that vehicle, she expressed many of her ideas for changes in government policy. She argued, for example, for the state to pay alimony after a divorce, so that the woman could be fully freed from her relationship with the man. Stöcker advocated reform of German family law, which under the 1876 civil code denied a married woman's independent action and placed her under the direction of her husband. She also used the magazine to agitate for educational freedom for women and for their entrance into universities. Stöcker continued publishing *New Generation* until 1933, and in its pages discussed changes in morality and culture. She argued for the connection of theory with practice, on the grounds that government policies could not be cohesive without broad theoretical foundations.

Her notions of relationships between men and women formed the theme of her novel, *Love* (*Liebe*), published in 1922. Her heroine, Irene, becomes romantically involved with a man who is incapable of breaking with middle-class double standards and, although in love with Irene, cannot bring himself to seek a divorce. Irene is a woman growing in self-confidence and independence, who believes that her love will enable him to find his own independent personality. Ultimately, his weakness prevents him from joining her.

Stöcker was also an early advocate for abortion, arguing that it be provided by the state at the woman's request during the first trimester of pregnancy. Perhaps in anticipation of later events in Germany, the corollary to that proposed policy was that no woman should ever be forced to have an abortion against her will. The campaign of Stöcker and her compatriots in the 1927 and 1931 sessions of the *Reichstag* adopted the slogan, "No woman should become a mother against her will."

Along with her advocacy of no-fault divorce and abortion was her campaign for the rights of illegitimate children. Stöcker proposed that fathers of children born out of wedlock should be financially responsible for child support and that the children should be entitled to their fathers' names and inheritance. Such a law was not even seriously discussed in the German Federal Republic Parliament until 1969.

Stöcker's political causes were not limited solely to those of women's rights. She also opposed the law that prohibited homosexual relationships. Even though the law of 1910–1911 specifically addressed male homosexuality, she attacked it as potentially damaging to women's living arrangements. Her arguments were applicable, however, to any form of government interference in or regulation of sexual conduct. Love between adults, she contended, is the most private part of life and is or should be totally independent of any state or any law; it is spiritual and emotional as well as physical. She used her magazine *New Ethics* to call for the creation of a scientific and humanitarian committee on homosexuality, and Magnus Hirschfeld subsequently established what became the first homosexual organization in Germany. Sexual counseling offices were created first in Hamburg in 1924, and then in Berlin and other places.

The other strand of Stöcker's efforts for political change was pacifism. She wrote in *Lexicon* in 1922, in opposition to war, any war. She argued that World War I had been the result of differences in race, religion, social class, and gender, but that use of state power for those purposes rested on erroneous interpretations of the authority of the state. Bad government was what led to war. She advocated draft evasion in the event of another war.

Not surprisingly, Helene Stöcker did not find Germany a safe place to live once the National Socialists assumed power. After she left for Switzerland in 1933, all of her belongings were confiscated, and in 1937, her German citizenship was revoked. She continued to support herself in Switzerland through her publications and her lectures, but by 1935, health problems interfered and in 1938, Germany, Austria, and Czechoslovakia closed the markets for German literature.

Stöcker moved to Sweden, where she was in 1939, when the war broke out and when the Germans invaded Denmark. She traveled to Moscow and took the Trans-Siberian Railroad to Japan. From there, she made her way to California, where she was treated for cancer. She died in February, 1943 in New York.

## ACHIEVEMENTS AND CONTRIBUTIONS

Helene Stöcker did not achieve immediate results from her agitations over more than four decades beginning in the nineteenth century. Her ideas were ahead of her time, and only after her death were some of the legal reforms that she sought enacted. In 1957, the law of equal rights passed the West German Parliament, and the marriage and family law was enacted in 1977. The rights of illegitimate children were addressed to some extent in 1969 legislation. Abortion remains a thorny question in Germany, particularly after unification in 1990.

Stöcker's accomplishments lie in her readiness to champion unpopular causes and to think beyond the boundaries of her contemporary world. She also tried to find a philosophical basis for equality between the sexes and for privacy in sexual relationships. She sought to locate the nexus between theory and policy.

Although she never practiced law, she was a vocal and visible force pushing for legal change.

## NOTE

1. Much of the information for this article is from Christl Wickert, ''Helene Stöcker (1869–1943): Leben und Arbeit für die Gleichstellung der Frau,'' in Thomas Blanke (ed.), *Streitbare Juristen* (Baden-Baden: Nomos Verlagsgesselschaft, 1990), 104–16.

## REFERENCE

Wickert, Christl. ''Helene Stöcker (1869–1943): Leben und Arbeit für die Gleichstellung der Frau.'' In *Streitbare Juristen*. Ed. Thomas Blanke. Baden-Baden: Nomos Verlagsgesselschaft, 1990, 104–16.

*MARY L. VOLCANSEK AND LUBA DEWITT*

# HELEN SUZMAN (1917– )

Helen Suzman was a member of the South African Parliament for 36 years (1953–1989) during the apartheid era. She was a vigorous opponent of apartheid and a forceful proponent of human rights. For 13 years (1962–1974), she was the only member of the liberal opposition party, the Progressive party, to be elected to the all-white Parliament. During this time, Suzman waged a solitary battle within Parliament against discriminatory race laws and repressive security laws. At a time when blacks were denied representation in Parliament or in government, she was regarded as the voice of the millions of disenfranchised black South Africans. Although not a lawyer by profession, Helen Suzman laid the foundations for a rights culture in South Africa by her courageous advocacy of human rights during the bleak apartheid years.

## FAMILY BACKGROUND AND EDUCATION

Helen Gavronsky was born on November 7, 1917, in Germiston, a town ten miles southeast of Johannesburg. Her parents were Samuel Gavronsky, a Lithuanian Jew, who had immigrated to South Africa in 1904, and Frieda David, the daughter of another Lithuanian immigrant family. Her mother died two weeks after she was born. When Helen was five, Samuel Gavronsky moved the family, Helen and her sister, Gertrude, to Johannesburg. In 1927, her father remarried.

Helen attended school at the Parktown Convent in Johannesburg. At the age of 16, she went to the University of the Witwatersrand where she studied for the degree of Bachelor of Commerce, with the intention of later proceeding to a postgraduate degree in law. Her university career was academically unsuccessful, and she did not graduate.

When she was 19, she married Moses Meyer (''Mosie'') Suzman, a physician from a well-known Jewish family. They had two daughters, Frances and Patricia. Mosie, who became one of South Africa's leading physicians, died in 1994.

During the war, Helen Suzman returned to the university and completed her degree with first-class passes in economics and economic history. Soon after, she was appointed as a tutor and later as a lecturer in economic history at the University of the Witwatersrand, a post she held until she entered Parliament in 1953.

While a lecturer at the University of the Witwatersrand, Helen Suzman became interested in politics. She was active in the South African Institute of Race Relations, a body of liberal South Africans committed to the promotion of good race relations through research and public education. In 1948, General Jan Smuts' United party government was defeated by the National party, and the paternalistic racial policy of the United party was replaced by the racist policy of apartheid, which sought to entrench white racial domination and segregation through the instrument of the law. Suzman's political life now commenced in earnest. She was active in the party structures of the United party, the main opposition party, and despite her youth and sex, soon made her mark. In 1952, she won a three-cornered nomination contest for the safe opposition constituency of Houghton, and, in 1953, she was elected to Parliament.

## ACHIEVEMENTS AND CONTRIBUTIONS

When Helen Suzman entered Parliament in 1953, the National party had been in power for five years, and the foundations of apartheid had been firmly laid. The population of South Africa had been classified along racial lines; interracial marriages had been prohibited; steps had been taken to remove the remaining nonwhite voters from the voters' roll; and the ''pass laws,'' which restricted the free movement of Africans outside the African ''reserves,'' had been extended. In addition, draconian security laws had been passed to suppress opposition to apartheid.

The United party had opposed these laws with a measure of equivocation. Smuts was now dead and the new leader, J.G.N. Strauss, was unable to prevent the United party from splitting into a liberal faction, which believed that apartheid should be vigorously opposed, and a conservative faction, which preferred a more cautious approach that would not alienate the conservative, rural white voter.

In her early years in Parliament, Suzman was the United party spokesperson on economic affairs. Although her speeches attacked racial discrimination and displayed a sense of justice that was already becoming rare in Parliament, legal matters remained the preserve of the many lawyers in her party.

In 1958, Helen Suzman was returned to Parliament unopposed. Tension between the liberal and conservative factions in the United party continued to grow, and in 1959, 11 liberal members of Parliament, including Suzman, left the United party to found the Progressive party. This group refused to resign their parliamentary seats and continued in office until the next general election of 1961. With one exception, these liberal parliamentarians were rejected by the white electorate. The one exception was Helen Suzman, who won her seat of Houghton in a bitterly contested election.

In 1962, Helen Suzman returned to Parliament as the sole Progressive party member. Opposite her sat a new minister of justice, B. J. Vorster, whose terms of office as minister of justice (1961–1966) and prime minister (1966–1978) were to be characterized by a series of security laws and repressive police action that would transform South Africa into a police-dominated state. Although Helen was now required to address every issue that came before Parliament, it was inevitable that the defense of human rights and due process of law (the rule of law) would be elevated to positions of top priority. This time was undoubtedly Helen's "finest hour." But it was an "hour" that was to continue for 13 years.

During this period, a number of laws were passed that provided for detention without trial for the purpose of interrogating political opponents of the National party regime in police custody. In 1963, the police were empowered to detain a person for 90 days; in 1965, this was extended to 180 days; and in 1967, all limits were removed by a law permitting indefinite detention without trial. Other laws enacted during this time permitted house arrest and the deprivation of the most basic civil liberties (freedom of speech, assembly, and association) by executive decree; McCarthy-style parliamentary investigations were held to inquire into the activities of political opponents.

These laws were enforced with vigor. From 1963 to 1965, 1,095 persons were held under the 90-day detention law and from 1965 to 1967, over 400 persons were held under the 180-day detention law. Between 1967 and 1985, some 4,700 persons were held under the law permitting indefinite detention without trial. To aggravate matters, suspicious deaths in detention under these laws became a common occurrence, and allegations of torture were widespread.

These laws were introduced by lawyers of the governing National party who dismissed notions of the rule of law and due process of law as obstacles in the fight against "communism," and complained that human rights were getting out of hand. To make matters worse, they were acquiesced in by lawyers in the official opposition party—the United party. It therefore fell to a nonlawyer, Helen Suzman, to defend human rights and the legal values of the South African common law.

Helen Suzman used every opportunity to oppose these laws and their implementation. She boldly opposed the laws in Parliament, while the official opposition prevaricated; she lectured Parliament on the rule of law and the laws that undermined it; she raised innumerable questions about detention and police brutality; she brought instances of gross injustices to the attention of an embarrassed Parliament; and she campaigned ceaselessly outside Parliament in protest meetings across the country. Her critics responded by resorting to personal abuse. Suzman was accused of being unpatriotic, pro-communist, and sympathetic to terrorists. Strong convictions, courage, and a sense of humor helped her to survive these lonely years.

On its formation, the Progressive party had committed itself to a Bill of Rights for South Africa. It was Suzman's vigorous defense of human rights, however, that made this the party's chief concern. She rightly saw attitudes toward human rights as the great divide in South African politics and was determined that the Progressive party should not compromise its principles as the United party had done. As the sole member of the parliamentary caucus, it was easy for her to keep this resolve.

Helen Suzman's defense of human rights was not confined to Parliament. No meeting to protest against injustice was complete without her on the platform. Membership in Parliament enabled her to obtain permission to visit South Africa's prisons. She visited Nelson Mandela and other political prisoners on Robben Island and in Pretoria; and she visited nonpolitical prisoners in other jails throughout the country. Complaints from prisoners conveyed by her to the authorities were frequently heeded. The white South African poet, Breyten Breytenbach, who served a long prison sentence for his political activities, wrote of Helen Suzman: "I don't think it will be excessive to say that the prisoners, both political and common law, consider her as Our Lady of the Prisoners. She is indeed a living myth among the people inhabiting the world of the shadows."[1]

Victims of racial discrimination also received Suzman's attention. She attended the notorious pass courts where blacks were summarily tried and sentenced to prison for not having their documents in order; and she visited the areas where blacks were forcibly "relocated" by the thousands to satisfy the demands of territorial segregation. Helen Suzman thus became a spokesperson for the politically voiceless black majority who suffered the full hardships, brutality, and indignity of apartheid. In name, she remained the member of Parliament for Houghton, but, in fact, her constituency encompassed the whole of South Africa with supporters from all racial groups.

In the parliamentary elections of 1966 and 1971, Suzman was again the only Progressive party member to be elected to Parliament. In 1974, however, the party succeeded in winning seven parliamentary seats. This was the beginning of the end for the United party. The Progressive party began to grow in elections and by coalition with other opposition groups until it became the official opposition (under the name of the Progressive Federal party). Although Suzman sought no leadership position in any of these new coalitions, her moral leadership was assured. She was the person who had kept the torch of liberalism burning in Parliament through the dark years of Verwoerd and Vorster, and the sole member to have set an example of determined opposition to future parliamentarians. Although she was now surrounded by lawyers in Parliament, Suzman remained the principal spokesperson on human rights issues.

After 1974, the apartheid state was consolidated by new measures. While the laws entrenching white domination and segregation remained in place, new laws were enacted to give "independence" to four African reserves, or *Bantustans*, as part of the Grand Design of territorial apartheid. In order to further populate these "states," Transkei, Bophuthatswana, Venda, and Ciskei, removals of the black population were intensified. On the security front, the revolt of black school children against apartheid education in 1976 led to new forms of police repression and to amendments to the security laws. When these measures failed to stop the tide of opposition to its policies, the National party government declared emergency rule from 1985 to 1989.

Suzman took the lead in opposing these measures. With recourse to the courts largely excluded and *habeas corpus* a distant memory, constant public exposure and condemnation of the system remained the only redress. Suzman used both the forum of Parliament and the protest platform to great effect. She was in the forefront of the public protests that followed the deaths in detention of the black consciousness leader, Steve Biko, the white trade unionist, Neil Aggett, and other detainees. On these occasions, her message was clear and unequivocal: the security laws providing for detention without trial authorized torture and were to blame for the deaths of those who died in detention. At a public protest over Neil Aggett's death, she stated:

> He died under a law that kept him in solitary confinement, in the hands of the security police, away from public scrutiny and denied the protection of the courts. He is among the more than 40 people who have died in detention under security law. Laws that are a travesty of justice. Laws that are not to be found on the statute book of any Western country other than South Africa.

Emergency rule was condemned with equal force. Suzman condemned the decision to resort to emergency rule and the measures employed to enforce it; she disclosed the startling statistics of detention under the emergency laws: 8,000 people detained for more than 30 days in the first emergency (July 1985 to March 1986), 11,000 in the second emergency (1986–1987), and 3,000 in the third emergency (1987–1988). She condemned the detention of children, drew attention to the failure of the police to inform the relatives of detainees about their detention, and revealed the methods of torture employed to extract statements from detainees. Her judgment of emergency rule was severe. It had "taken South Africa from the ranks of countries with Western democratic values into the ranks of Third World countries in which people go missing and their relatives are left in agonizing uncertainty and anxiety."

Other causes also received the attention of Suzman, the Parliamentarian. She campaigned passionately for the abolition of the death penalty during the years when it was not uncommon for over 100 persons to be executed annually. Her pleas were to no avail, however, and Parliament refused even to accept her repeated requests that a commission of inquiry be established to investigate the need for retaining the death penalty.

Suzman saw the advancement of women's rights as part of the advancement of human rights. She played a major role in the nearly all-white, male Parliament in opposing the legal disabilities imposed on women, particularly African women. She called for the abolition of the laws that prohibited marriage and sexual relations between persons of different races and, from a pro-choice perspective, she sought, unsuccessfully, to reform the restrictive abortion laws.

In 1989, Helen Suzman retired from Parliament, but not from public life. In 1990, she was elected president of the South African Institute of Race Relations. She participated in the Convention for a Democratic South Africa (CODESA) in 1991, which preceded the final negotiations for a democratic South Africa. In 1994, Suzman served as a member of the Independent Electoral Commission, which was responsible for administering and supervising South Africa's first democratic elections. In 1995, she was appointed to the Human Rights Commission established under the democratic constitution of 1993.

Helen Suzman has been widely acclaimed at home and abroad. She is the recipient of 22 honorary degrees from some of the leading universities in the world, including Oxford and Harvard. In 1989, she was appointed an Honorary Dame Commander of the Civil Division of the Order of the British Empire, but because she is not a British citizen, she is not entitled to be called ''Dame Helen.'' President Mandela, speaking for the new democratic South Africa, has repeatedly acknowledged the important role Helen Suzman played in the struggle against apartheid.

While Suzman holds several honorary doctorates in law, she has no formal legal qualifications. Nevertheless, she probably spoke more seriously and more frequently about the nature and function of law in her 36 years in Parliament than any other person in the history of the South African Parliament. The rule of law, or due process of law, was Suzman's standard for good civilized government. While many jurists have sought to depict the rule of law as a legal standard by which laws are judged, she was content to view it as a value concept, as a concept containing a cluster of basic Western values by which the morality or decency of laws are to be measured. The notion of justice was at the center of this cluster of values. Law and order must be preserved, she would say, but if order is to be preserved the law must be just.

Suzman measured the laws of apartheid against the rule of law. Again and again, she condemned apartheid as a violation of the rule of law. It was the simplicity of her standard and the stubbornness with which she clung to it, that gave Suzman strength. Unlike the government, the official parliamentary opposition, or the white electorate, she was not prepared to compromise on the rule of law and human rights.

Although Suzman's standard for measuring evil laws was simple and straightforward, her speeches were not lacking in depth. She realized that if she, a nonlawyer, was to challenge a Parliament comprised of many trained lawyers on legal grounds, she would be obliged to protect herself against charges of ignorance and lack of understanding. So she set out to be better prepared and more informed than her opponents. Suzman studied legislative history, read the law reviews, examined the implementation of the laws in practice and researched the laws and practices of other countries. Consequently, she spoke with knowledge and authority of the violations of human rights in South Africa and of the legal mechanisms employed in other countries to advance human rights. She compared detention-without-trial in South Africa with the experiences of Northern Ireland and Israel; contrasted the homicide rate in South Africa with rates in countries that had abolished the death penalty; and explained how the American Bill of Rights and the European Convention on Human Rights protected human rights. Although she occasionally sought advice from lawyers on these matters, Suzman was largely self-taught.

The people of South Africa suffered under apartheid. So did the law. Within Parliament, both the National party government and the official opposition party were prepared to destroy the foundation of the legal system in order to preserve white supremacy. Outside Parliament, the law fared little better. The judges, with few exceptions, enforced the abhorrent laws of apartheid without question. And the legal profession was largely silent. It was therefore left to a nonlawyer, Helen Suzman, to defend the law itself. It was left to her to remind South Africans that law is not simply an expression of the will of the legislature, but that it is a body of rules and principles, infused with values and traditions, with an integrity of its own and above all, with a purpose to achieve justice by the promotion of equality and liberty.

Suzman's recipe for restoring the rule of law in South Africa was a Bill of Rights that would provide judicial protection for the basic civil and political rights and, at the same time, stimulate a rights culture in South Africa. This was heresy to the National party government, which preferred the unlimited powers that flowed from the doctrine of parliamentary supremacy that South Africa had inherited from British constitutional law. It was also rejected by the government as a "humanist" institution that had no place in South Africa. Other political groups, apart from Suzman's own Progressive party, were also unenthusiastic about a Bill of Rights. The African National Congress (ANC) declared that its prime concern was liberation and not the advancement of civil rights. In the late 1980s, however, attitudes began to change. Both the ANC and the National party began to see the advantages of a Bill of Rights in a postapartheid South Africa.

The 1993 constitution of South Africa, which provides the foundation for the new democratic South Africa, contains a Bill of Rights protecting basic civil and political rights that the courts are empowered to enforce. Many factors contributed to the inclusion of a Bill of Rights in this constitution. But Helen Suzman's contribution is perhaps the most significant. It was she who repeatedly reminded South Africa during the years of apartheid that there could be no law without justice, and that this could best be achieved through a Bill of Rights.

## NOTE

1. Breyten Breytenbach, *The True Confessions of an Albino Terrorist* (New York: Farrar, Straus and Giroux, 1983): 182.

## REFERENCES

Breytenbach, Breyten. *The True Confessions of an Albino Terrorist*. New York: Farrar, Straus and Giroux, 1983.

Dugard, John. *Human Rights and the South African Legal Order*. Princeton, N.J.: Princeton University Press, 1978.

Lee, R. (ed.). *Values Alive: A Tribute to Helen Suzman*. Johannesburg: Jonathan Ball Publishers, 1990.

Lewsen, P. *Helen Suzman's Solo Years*. Johannesburg: Jonathan Ball Publishers, 1991.

Strangwayes-Booth, J. *A Cricket in the Thorn Tree: Helen Suzman and the Progressive Party*. Johannesburg: Hutchinson of South Africa, 1976.

Suzman, Helen. *In No Uncertain Terms: Memoirs*. Johannesburg: Jonathan Ball Publishers, 1993.

*JOHN DUGARD*

# LEAH TSEMEL (1945– )

Leah Tsemel is a pioneer in the practice of human rights law. As an Israeli Jew, she has been recognized internationally for her 23 years of tireless and innovative work on behalf of Palestinians under Israeli occupation. Leah Tsemel can be credited with numerous legal achievements, but it is her pioneering work in human rights law that is exceptional.

A woman of courage, Tsemel was the first to challenge the deportation of Palestinians before the High Court of Israel. She secured the ruling that deportations can be reviewed and are not final, and she was responsible for the only known cancellation of a deportation order. Tsemel, through her legal work, established the process that compels the state to institute preliminary reviews of cases, and she was the first to challenge the right of the Israeli government to maintain the Ansar I prison in Lebanon. Tsemel also exposed the existence of a secret cemetery, a mass grave, of unidentified corpses of Palestinian and Lebanese individuals in Northern Israel. She has collected thousands of affidavits of families of disappeared Lebanese and Palestinian persons, presented them on appeal to the Supreme Court, and, as a consequence, secured the release of many of these people. With Mubarak Awad, she founded the first public campaign on family reunification. And finally, she was the first woman to challenge the dress code for Israeli lawyers.

While Tsemel's legal efforts have not always been successful, her persistence in defending and advancing human rights in the occupied lands, and the global attention she has brought to the Palestinian situation merit recognition. It is a rare person who vigorously defends those people perceived by her homeland as the enemy.

## FAMILY BACKGROUND AND EDUCATION

Leah Tsemel was born in Haifa, Palestine, in 1945. Her mother, Fanya Sternberg, was originally from Russia and her father, Tswi Tsemel, from Poland. They both came to Palestine in 1933, where they met and married. Theirs was a comfortable life: Tswi was an architect for the municipality in Haifa, and Fanya also worked. They had two children, a son, Samuel, the oldest, and Leah. Fanya's parents lived with them—her father (Leah's grandfather) was a rabbi who had been stabbed in the back by an Arab in 1948. Leah recalled that memory only much later in life when she was defending Arabs who were accused of stabbing Jews during the *Intifada* (Palestinian uprising).

Leah described her childhood as typically middle class, very felicitous, and fascinating because her neighborhood was populated by Jews who came from widely differing places, with a variety of cultures and experiences. Her home life was happy, and her parents allowed her freedom to think and grow as an individual. At the same time, they taught her positive values, for example, that racism was wrong and honesty was of cardinal importance. During her formative years she was strongly socialized, both at home and at school, in the ideology of Zionism. Tsemel recalls that she had been taught that Zionist ideas and the Israeli state were the best in the world. The whole thrust of her education was "putting into us, very deeply, the importance of building up the 'New Israel' and the 'New Jew.' I think it was a very interesting youth."[1]

With regard to the Palestinians, whose defense was to become her life's work, Tsemel reflected that in her adolescence, they were simply invisible. The psychological blind spot was so strong that even those Palestinians who lived and worked in Haifa were unseen or simply not noticed. Yet Tsemel recalls her early concerns about the blacks in South Africa; crying when she read *Uncle Tom's Cabin*; her deep sentiments about the Holocaust and Jews in the diaspora; and strong feelings about injustice in general. But with respect to the Palestinians, she had "a total blindness" as a young woman.

In 1963, Tsemel joined the Israeli army as obligated but did not enjoy the experience, even though her superiors urged her to join the officer corps. She recounted creating some "dilemmas" for her commanders and as a consequence, was discharged honorably after one year of service (rather than the usual two). But it was during her military service that Tsemel began to study law at night at Tel Aviv University. Her interest in the law stemmed from her perception of it as a way to pursue social justice: "I had such a strong feeling that injustice was intolerable that I had to do something about it." After her discharge, she moved to Jerusalem and continued her law studies full time at the Hebrew University. There were a few Israeli Arabs in her classes whom she related to as equals, even dating one quite seriously with the blessing of her family.

Still, politics and the Palestinian issue were not part of her consciousness. Then the 1967 "Six-Day War" occurred in which she was a volunteer near the border in Jerusalem. When the war was over, Tsemel was one of the first Israelis to visit the Old City and the first Israeli woman to see the Wailing Wall. The army, in appreciation, took the volunteers around the West Bank on a victorious tour, and it was on this excursion that Tsemel witnessed several events that affected her tremendously, drawing her attention to the issue of the Palestinians.

The first incident took place in a Bethlehem cinema where soldiers and Israeli civilians were celebrating raucously. In the middle of this triumphant jubilee, 20 Palestinian notables were brought in by the Israeli army to "share" in the festivities. Tsemel recalls that her first reaction was to feel sorry for them, but that this emotion was quickly displaced by a feeling of utter shame as the Palestinians were humiliated by the victors. She realized then that there could never be peace between Israel and the Palestinians, "because this great victory for us was a complete disaster for them."

Her second disturbing experience on the victory tour took place on the road to Jericho where she saw endless lines of people carrying their belongings and fleeing the Israeli occupation—a whole new generation of refugees. Tsemel recalls: "I couldn't bear it. It was directly a picture of the Jews in Europe and it was clear that they were being forced to leave. The feeling in me was horrible." She also witnessed the Israeli army's destruction of a Palestinian neighborhood near the Wailing Wall and learned of an incident at the Damia Bridge where many Palestinians were trying to swim across the Jordan River to return to their homes when the Israeli army opened fire on the defenseless population. A final episode, shortly after the war, involved the destruction of three villages in the Latrun area near Ramla. "So I was shocked, really, really shocked. I couldn't believe that we were doing these things."

At the Hebrew University after the war, Tsemel took an interest in politics and joined a radical movement, *Matzpen*, whose main tenets were anti-Zionism and socialism. The organization was very active throughout Israel—demonstrating, giving speeches, issuing pamphlets, and engaging in other forms of political activity. "We were extremely isolated in Israeli society. We faced incredible opposition. I knew I was not accepted—people would see me and call me a traitor—but I never felt isolated in a personal way, the *Matzpen* circle was very supportive of each other. It was very satisfying."

Very quickly, however, Tsemel's views became widely known, and when she finished her formal studies in 1968, she was unable for some time to find a practicing lawyer who would accept her for the required two-year practicum. Eventually, she did locate someone to supervise her practicum, and she completed her legal apprenticeship. She took her law exams in 1970, after having also obtained a certificate in criminal law from the Hebrew University.

In 1972, Leah Tsemel married Michel Warchevsky, a French Jew who came to Israel to attend Yeshiva (religious) School. Subsequently, he abandoned his religious studies and became a journalist for several French and Israeli publications. They have two children—a son, Nissan, born in 1972, and a daughter, Talila, born in 1982.

## CAREER DEVELOPMENT

Leah Tsemel's first job as a lawyer was working for someone else. But in that position she defended two famous cases—the Black Panthers (underprivileged Oriental/Sephardic Jews who were demonstrating for better treatment in Israeli society) and a group of feminists (Israeli Jews) who were charged with breaking public order when they demonstrated against the intrusion of religion in personal affairs.

Then came what Tsemel considers the turning point in her career. In 1972, the Israeli authorities exposed a Jewish-Arab network which believed that talking and diplomacy were useless and that a common struggle should really be a common struggle. The individuals had joined an illegal Palestinian organization, some had gone to Syria for training, and one of the Jews gave the Syrians some sensitive information. In this affair, Tsemel defended the Israeli Arabs all the way to the High Court. Of the experience, Tsemel recalls:

> To represent these people you had to have a lot of public courage because we were attacked physically and socially. I was called a quisling. My mother was totally isolated because she didn't denounce me. It was a witch hunt; life was really difficult—being attacked everywhere you went, in the newspapers, being called a traitor and so on. The trial was totally unfair. It is not acceptable, it's not done—for a Jew to defend Arabs and Jewish turncoats. But as a natural outcome I came to know many more Palestinian political prisoners in the military courts and in the civil courts.

After this trial, Tsemel began to practice law on her own from a tiny office in Jerusalem where she had many poor Palestinian clients from the West Bank, Gaza, and East Jerusalem who could pay only a pittance for her services. When a compelling issue was involved, Tsemel accepted clients who could pay nothing. To make ends meet, she had to work enormously hard—two or three times harder than any other lawyer. And for many years, Leah Tsemel was the only Israeli lawyer (with the exception of Felicia Langer who has recently left the country) defending the Palestinians. "You should be sure enough of yourself to do this kind of work—to have fights all day long, every day, with every soldier, every policeman, every judge, every prosecutor. When I was pregnant with my daughter, settlers attacked me physically and beat me. One said, 'You are going to bear a satan.' "

Only after the Israeli invasion of Lebanon in 1982 did attitudes begin to change in Israel, albeit, very slowly. Today, Leah Tsemel enjoys the respect of many of her countrymen—even those who do not agree with her—for her courage, integrity, and unceasing dedication to human rights law. Until very recently, there were no support groups in the area of human rights, and it is only within the past five or six years that the Association for Civil Rights in Israel (ACRI), the Committee Against Torture, Israeli Women for Palestinian Political Prisoners, and a few others formed. Thus, during most of the 20 years of her work,

Leah Tsemel fought lonely battles without support. Now, in addition to these organizations, there are also a few other lawyers practicing human rights law with the Palestinians.

## ACHIEVEMENTS AND CONTRIBUTIONS

What can one realistically accomplish in the practice of human rights law when two nations, Israel and Palestine, are engaged in a longstanding war, when the Palestinians exist in a state of total dependency on the Israeli authorities—even to the point of having to obtain a permit to plant a tomato, and when it is always an Israeli judge who judges the Palestinians that come before him? Success in this environment is measured incrementally and often, gratification is found in the seemingly minor accomplishments in a court of law. As Leah Tsemel explained,

> Success is something other than winning. You almost never win a case but you may be able to change the charges; you may be able to improve the conditions of incarceration; sometimes you can limit the length and intensity of the torture; instead of a death sentence you may be able to get life; instead of 20 years you may be able to get eight or instead of eight, maybe three. You can try to give some legitimacy to their struggle. You try to show the human face of the prisoners, their personal tragedies, the chain of circumstances—always initiated by Israel—that led them to undertake an operation or throw a stone. It has always been important to me to show the relationship between the occupier and the occupied, and its logical consequences—to show that there is an historical background in which Israel has played a major role in causing their actions.

Despite her modesty, Tsemel has introduced numerous innovations in the practice of human rights law and has been able to help many Palestinians. Much of her work has been focused on the practice of torture, and she has written numerous articles that have been published all over the world, providing enormous amounts of data to groups like Amnesty International. More recently, she worked with the Committee Against Torture in Israel. "In Israel, the only state I know of in the Western world, torture against Palestinians is legitimized by the decision of the Landau Commission which was nominated by the Government and headed by one of the ex-High Court Justices. Permission was given to the Security Services to exercise what they call 'moderate physical pressure.' And from this many prisoners died."

Tsemel has worked to document the interrogations of Palestinians by the Israeli Security Services. In one of her published articles, she wrote:

> Almost without exception a lawyer gets access to a client only after the client has broken down and confessed, or when the security services have abandoned interrogation. The reason for this is simple. The interrogation has one simple purpose: to extract a confession. In order to achieve that purpose, the authorities subject the prisoner to isolation, torture, and humiliating physical conditions. The detainee undergoes a preliminary period

> of starvation, sleep deprivation, and prolonged periods of standing with his hands cuffed and his head covered with a sack. The prisoners frequently complain of physical abuse—being dragged about, beaten and kicked—during this initial period. Often a prisoner is stripped and thrust under a cold shower. Verbal abuse, psychological pressure, and humiliation—such as spitting in the prisoner's face or forcing him to crawl around a cell—are also frequently reported.[2]

While Tsemel worked diligently to prove cases of torture, often the Security Services and medical staff would simply lie to the court, denying any involvement in the physical abuse of Palestinian prisoners. While it has not always worked, Tsemel's exposure of systematic torture to gain a confession has been successful in some cases in substantially reducing the prisoner's sentence, particularly when the interrogator fails to appear in court. Tsemel has also been able to reduce the sentences of some severely tortured prisoners by taking the case to another court—a civilian court or the High Court of Justice.

Family reunification is another issue on which Tsemel has worked very hard. Because of Israeli policies, if a Palestinian from the West Bank marries a woman from Amman, Jordan, she is prohibited from joining him. In such cases, Tsemel's strategy is to plead the case before the Israeli High Court, although, as she emphasized, not every case can be taken there for fear of a backlash by the Court. But when a case is brought to the High Court, it obliges the authorities to review their policies, and very often, just because the case has been brought before the Court, it is won. Tsemel's intuitive knowledge of both the limits and flexibility of the system clearly serves her well.

In the same vein as family reunification is the issue of travel from and return to the Occupied Territories and the rights of individuals in transit. "Often laws are changed and people are not informed. . . . Palestinians are intentionally kept ignorant. When they return they sometimes have to wait weeks or months to see the civil administration to get information, and they must pay enormous sums of money. And still it is often the case that their I.D. will not be restored." Tsemel has been able to reestablish the status of numerous individuals through the argument that families have a right to be together. On the other hand, Tsemel believes that her prominent public campaign on the issue of family reunification undertaken with a Palestinian proponent of nonviolence, Mubarak Awad, may have been a major factor in his deportation.

This raises the issue of deportation—a problem on which Tsemel has been very active. She worked on the cases of several hundred individuals who were deported between 1967 and 1972. "These individuals were deported completely arbitrarily—they were 'suspected' of opposing the occupation but they had no due process—no charges, no hearing. They were picked up in the middle of the night, hooded, and dropped over the border in Lebanon (and occasionally, Jordan). They were not politically active either before or after they were deported." Tsemel spent seven years, beginning in 1985, struggling to have the cases opened for review. As a consequence, the Court agreed to review them, and

Tsemel managed to bring back 23 individuals before the authorities suspended the reviews.

In 1978, Tsemel was able, for the first time, to temporarily stop a deportation and to invoke judicial review of the action. A Palestinian from the West Bank was accused of "collaborating" with a legal organization of Israeli–Palestinian students at the Hebrew University. He was charged with attempting to mobilize the organization and make it more militant on the Palestinian issue. He was considered a member of an illegal organization in the West Bank and was allegedly recruiting Israeli Arabs for this group.

> We brought it to court and although we lost the case, we established the precedent that people cannot just be thrown out of the country without some due process. Since then, each case of deportation has taken anywhere from one to eight months. . . . Once you have a legal process, you have time to mobilize people and time for political education. I still keep a clipping citing a complaint by Yitzak Rabin saying that it is so difficult to deport Palestinians these days that the tool of deportation has become almost irrelevant.

Tsemel has worked on every deportation case since 1978. But perhaps the most publicized cases took place in December, 1992, when Israel attempted to deport some 400 alleged Hamas supporters *en masse*. Tsemel intervened in the middle of the night to get a court order to stop the deportations and succeeded in getting a hearing scheduled for 5 A.M. the following morning. As a result, the buses carrying the Palestinians were stopped at the Lebanese border, and the deportees remained on board. The Court ordered the Chief of Staff to justify the deportations, and they were subsequently upheld. "But by then all the world knew about it. . . . So this possibility I had, and I see it as an achievement, was to stop the busses for 24 or 36 hours, get everyone awake and working on the subject. And these people who were deported for an unlimited period came back after a year or so. And I hope this incident, with all its publicity, ended the policy of deportations. . . . This small act made a big difference."

Another issue that has consumed a great deal of Tsemel's time and energy has been the demolition of Palestinian homes by the Israelis. The Association for Civil Rights in Israel (ACRI) has helped facilitate her work over recent years. In practice, when a Palestinian is *accused* of a security offense, before he is tried or convicted, the house of his family can be demolished by an order of a military commander. This is a form of collective punishment and was carried out without any warning to the family, typically in the middle of the night. Tsemel worked to prevent this destruction by filing cases before the High Court of Justice. "I managed to save a number of houses . . . but once the occupation authorities realized that I had succeeded, they tightened their policy on alerting people as to what they were intending to do." While Tsemel was seeking the court's review on these individual cases, ACRI was fighting to establish the right to a due process hearing in advance of the residential demolitions.

We won, and the fact that I was able to work with ACRI on this issue was very helpful. At the time we were cooperating, I took it upon myself to apply to the High Court for each of *my* clients . . . Sometimes I literally flooded the Court with cases saying that since they do not tell us ahead of time what houses they are going to demolish then every house of every prisoner may be demolished. So every case, every case, I would go to the High Court and say: ''My client was arrested, maybe the IDF will demolish the whole house; in order to prevent it, I want an order.'' . . . So at least in the case of house demolitions, we managed to force them to alert the families although still they gave only 24 hours notice. But, most important, now we have a process by which this issue is clearly determined (although in some cases there is still arbitrary military action).

Tsemel has also expended considerable energy attempting to obtain compensation from the state of Israel for the deaths and injuries of Palestinian civilians who were not involved in any political activity, but were shot by the Israeli Defense Forces.

You have to file a civil case and you have to bring in expert opinions. Palestinian experts do not count so you have to bring an Israeli expert. For example, I have cases where a soldier shot and killed small children—two year olds, four year olds, five year olds, etc. The compensation for death is very small, but if a person is crippled for life—left a paraplegic or quadriplegic—then he/she should get compensation for his/her rehabilitation if we are successful. But to be victorious I have to prove that the army did it without reason, that the person was not participating in a demonstration, and that there was absolutely no danger from that person.

While Tsemel's efforts have been largely unsuccessful in this area of litigation, she remains hopeful that this legal strategy will eventually compensate some of the victims of the violence. ''We consider such civil actions as a major duty of human rights work although the authorities now want to change the law that permits the bringing of such cases.''

Administrative detention, a core element of occupation policy, allows the state to arrest individuals and hold them without charge or trial for a period of six months; the detention may be extended for another six months, then another, *ad infinitum*. During the first years of the *Intifada*, there were 12,000 to 15,000 administrative detainees at any given time. Tsemel's work on this issue has been multifaceted. She established a Committee of Lawyers Against Administrative Detention; raised money from various sources in order to organize it and to supply every prisoner with a proper lawyer and an opportunity to appeal; and opened a special office to support the lawyers and supplied every lawyer with background information on prisoners and information to facilitate their visits. ''Supplying a lawyer to every detainee was essential. From this experience we learned that if you badger the authorities on specific cases they tend to attack less because they don't want to be bothered.'' While a Palestinian lawyer would not have been able to initiate this project, Tsemel's groundwork legitimized the organization, which was eventually turned over to the Palestinian Lawyers Association.

Tsemel also does monumental work on trying to improve prison conditions, considered to be among some of the worst in the world. "I have taken dozens of cases of prisoners who weren't my clients before their imprisonment but who called me in because of the deplorable conditions. I approach such cases by threats or demands or appeals to the authorities. I do daily work on specific cases of individuals who don't get mail, water, exercise, space, books, etc." While her success in improving prison conditions has been limited, Tsemel did what no Palestinian lawyer could possibly do; she persuaded the High Court justices to visit the Ansar 3 prison in the Negev (Southern Israel). "We dragged the High Court justices there to see for themselves and as a result, we were able to improve some of the conditions." With the Palestinian-Israeli Doctors for Human Rights, she also managed to persuade the authorities to allow prisoners the right to access private doctors.

Most recently, Tsemel was working on a new case to assert the religious right of a person under interrogation. Specifically, she is arguing that Palestinians should have their Koran and their carpet, and be allowed to pray five times a day. The arguments have been submitted to the minister of religion and eventually Tsemel will take the case to the High Court.

Tsemel has employed many legal strategies to assist her clients; one tactic is to use different courts within the judicial system. For instance, when the issue is a matter of a civilian against the State apparatus, it is possible to seek the desired remedy in the High Court. Tsemel is not a great believer in the justice of the High Court, and she has won many cases by not bringing litigation before the Court. "Sometimes just by addressing the Court but not actually going for a hearing brings a better remedy. The authorities do not know how the Court will rule and thus they will compromise with me. . . . There is a need to maneuver and be creative all the time."

Tsemel sees advantages and disadvantages in being an Israeli woman practicing human rights law on behalf of the Palestinians.

> On the one hand its easier for a man to meet and deal with the authorities simply because he is a man and no one questions him. But sometimes a woman throws harder, she will not give up as easily, she will be more persistent, and fight harder. Still, at times there is a real isolation in being a woman . . . So there can be hatred and anger—but there may also sometimes be a grudging respect and sometimes I can use that to my advantage. But not because I am a woman, but because of who I am.
>
> The strongest weapon I have in dealing with the authorities is courage. They know they cannot break me. Sometimes they make me angry but they cannot break me. Also, they cannot bribe me. And, it's very, very clear who I am and what I stand for. They cannot alter my commitment to the Palestinian people. I think that the most important role I have played has been by speaking as an Israeli Jew and *being there*—I think that made the most impact, the most important contribution in the legal defense of the Palestinians.

Of Leah Tsemel, the well-known and highly respected Israeli writer, David Grossman, had this to say: ''In her relations with Arabs there is something you don't come across very often—straight forwardness and equality, without a trace of sanctimony; she places herself neither above nor below her clients, and there is no soft and self-effacing paternalism. Very rare.''[3]

Despite the recent positive political developments and guarded optimism regarding the Palestinian situation, Leah Tsemel continues her work. ''The new political developments [the Oslo Accord and the establishment of the Palestine Authority in Gaza and Jericho] have not solved the basic problems, and we are far from resting. I still see a great need for legal struggle until the last settlement is dissolved and the last Israeli soldier leaves the Occupied Territories.''

## NOTES

1. Personal interview with Leah Tsemel, Jerusalem (September 17, 1994). All subsequent quotations from Leah Tsemel, unless otherwise indicated, came from this lengthy, eight-hour, interview in her home.
2. Leah Tsemel, ''Personal Status and Rights,'' in Naseer Aruri (ed.), *Occupation: Israel over Palestine* (2nd ed.) (Belmont, Mass.: Association of Arab American University Graduates Press, 1989), 129.
3. David Grossman, *The Yellow Wind* (trans. by Haim Watzman) (New York: Farrar, Straus and Giroux, 1988), 79.

## REFERENCES


Aburish, Said K. ''Profiles in Courage: Leah Tsemel.'' In *Cry Palestine: Inside the West Bank*. Boulder, Colo.: Westview Press, 1993.

Ambrosino, Michael, and Gillian Barnes. ''Journey to the Occupied Lands.'' *Frontline*. Documentary Consortium of Public Television, 1992.

''Attorney Leah Tsemel Wants to be Heard.'' *Kol Ha'ir* (Hebrew weekly) (December 10, 1993).

''Death Behind Closed Doors.'' *Ha'artz* (Hebrew daily) (November 25, 1988).

''Embattled Lawyer: An Israeli Jew Courts Insults by Defending Palestinian Protesters.'' *Wall Street Journal* (European Edition) (March 21, 1988): 1.

''En Israel Ils Tenden La Main Aux Arabs.'' *La Vie* (French weekly) (June 18–24, 1992): 20–27.

Grossman, David. ''Report from Israel.'' *The New Yorker* (February 8 and February 15, 1988).

Grossman, David. *The Yellow Wind*. Translated by Haim Watzman. New York: Farrar, Straus and Giroux, 1988.

''Integrity Under a Death Threat.'' *Yorkshire Post* (England) (June 22, 1987).

''Israeli Roots, Palestinian Clients.'' *Los Angeles Times* (April 27, 1988).

''A Summer Day on Gaza Beach.'' *L'autre Journal* 16. Paris, France: September, 1991.

''I Support Attacks on the Settlers: They Say to Go Out to the Occupied Territories with Leah Tsemel Is Like Going Around with Yasser Arafat.'' *Ma'ariv* (Hebrew daily) (February 4, 1993).

Tsemel, Leah. Interview with Cheryl Rubenberg. Jerusalem, September 17, 1994.

Tsemel, Leah. ''Personal Status and Rights.'' In *Occupation: Israel over Palestine*, 2nd ed. Ed. Naseer Aruri. Belmont, Mass.: Association of Arab American University Graduates Press, 1989.

Tsemel, Leah. ''Double Standard of Justice in Israel: The Case of the Jewish Terrorist Organization.'' *The Palestine Yearbook of International Law* II (1985).

Tsemel, Leah. ''Open Letter to Itzhar Nafsu.'' *Ha'olam Hazeh* (Hebrew weekly) (1985).

Tsemel, Leah. *Zionism, Feminism and Women's Liberation.* Tel Aviv, Israel: Red Pages Publishers, 1980.

Tsemel, Leah. *You Have the Right to Remain Silent Tel Aviv.* Israel: Key Publishing, 1978.

Tsemel, Leah. *Monthly Report on the Conditions for Political Prisoners in Israeli Jails.* Published by Leah Tsemel and distributed monthly to local and international human rights organizations, 1975–1982.

Tsemel, Leah. ''Know Your Rights.'' *Civil Rights Primer for Civil Disobedience in Israel.* Tel Aviv, Israel: Red Pages Publishers, 1974.

''Violent Acts Were Committed Under the Rubric of the Law.'' Report on Lawyer's Conference of Israeli Bar. *Ha'artz* (Hebrew daily) (September 24, 1988).

*CHERYL A. RUBENBERG*

# AGATHE UWILINGIYIMANA (1953–1994)

The biography of Agathe Uwilingiyimana, Rwanda's first woman prime minister, is as tragic as the recent history of the small African nation which she briefly led as head of government. At the same time, Uwilingiyimana's relatively short political career was a triumph for women's rights in Africa, if not for the idea of democracy itself in a politically fragile continent. Though she was prime minister for less than one year before being assassinated in an abortive coup attempt in April, 1994, her precedent-setting career is certainly noteworthy in African political history. Since her career was an attempt to transcend the entrenched boundaries of ethnic hatred in Rwanda, some mention must be made of the political context in which she worked and lived.

## FAMILY BACKGROUND AND EDUCATION

The late prime minister's family and educational background is somewhat sketchy. Agathe Uwilingiyimana, a Tutsi, was born to peasant farming parents in 1953, in the village of Nyaruhengeri, some 140 kilometers southeast of Kigali, Rwanda's capital city. She taught high school science for ten years after earning a master's degree in chemistry.[1] In the African context, this achievement itself is quite extraordinary, since those with advanced scientific educations often leave the continent altogether or teach in the national universities. Uwilingiyimana was married to a university employee and had five children.[2] Unfortunately, this is all the early background available.

## CAREER DEVELOPMENT

It is difficult to appreciate Agathe Uwilingiyimana's political career without an understanding of the conditions under which she worked, lived, and ultimately died; it was a context of ethnic politics and genocide. Rwanda and neighboring Burundi are small nations, both about the size of New Jersey. Both countries, however, are Africa's most densely populated nations, with Rwanda having about 7.5 million residents. Rwanda has two major ethnic groups: the Tutsi, who are about 10 percent of the population and who ruled Rwanda for centuries as a monarchy (before colonization by the Germans and later by the Belgians), and the Hutus, who make up over 85 percent of Rwanda's population. In this context, minority Tutsi rule can be found at the roots of Rwanda's frequent genocides. The death of Agathe Uwilingiyimana, a Tutsi, is partly attributable to this history of ethnic rivalry and bloodshed.

Traditionally, the Tutsi, a Nilotic people (also known as the ''Giant Watusi'' in the West because of their tall stature) ruled Rwanda as a small minority. By 1962, when the mountain nation received its independence from Belgium, a Hutu uprising had led to that group's seizure of power from the Tutsi minority. At least 20,000 Tutsi were massacred and over 150,000 fled to neighboring countries.[3] Historically, the ethnic differences between the Hutu and Tutsi had been exacerbated by the Belgian colonial governments, who only educated male Tutsis, a discriminatory practice that Prime Minister Uwilingiyimana would overcome.

Intermittent massacres of Tutsi by the Hutu-dominated government and military continued throughout the next 30 years. By 1990, the Rwandan Patriotic Front (RPF), a Tutsi-dominated movement, invaded Rwanda from neighboring Uganda. And three years later, in late 1993, President Juvenal Habyarimana, a Hutu, and RPF Commander Kagame signed an agreement to end the war, which had led to the flight of over 1 million Rwandans to neighboring countries. Unfortunately, this agreement never came to fruition, and the ethnic killing in Rwanda continues at the time of this writing.

Uwilingiyimana's brief political career was during this time of negotiations between the Hutu-dominated government of Juvenal Habyarimana, president of Rwanda for almost two decades, and the Tutsi-dominated RPF. As such, her tenure as prime minister came at one of the most crucial times in Rwandan history. Uwilingiyimana joined the Republican and Democratic Movement (MDR), an opposition party, in January of 1992, and four months later was appointed minister of education by Dismas Nsensiyaremye, the first opposition prime minister under a power-sharing scheme negotiated between President Habyarimana and the five major opposition parties.[4] Previously, she had been director of small and medium-sized industries in the Ministry of Commerce and Industry.[5]

## ACHIEVEMENTS AND CONTRIBUTIONS

On July 17, 1993, after a meeting between President Habyarimana and the five opposition parties, Agathe Uwilingiyimana became the first woman prime minister of Rwanda, replacing Dismas Nsensiyaremye, the man who had appointed her minister of education. His candidacy had been rejected by all five opposition parties except his own MDR. On the day of her appointment, Nsensiyaremye and other members of the MDR immediately suspended Uwilingiyimana's membership in the party.[6]

Uwilingiyimana's new government had the daunting task of bringing the talks with the rebel Rwandan Patriotic Front (RPF), the Tutsi-dominated guerrilla movement, to a successful conclusion with the signing of a peace accord. The accord was to have included a transitional coalition government and security guarantees. The MDR had opposed the formation of any new government until the RPF rebels could be brought into an interim government.[7]

An agreement between President Habyarimana, the five opposition parties led ostensibly by Uwilingiyimana, and the rebel RPF was finally reached on August 4, 1993. This agreement called for the president to form a new government within 30 days under a power-sharing agreement between all parties. Under the agreement, Habyarimana's ruling National Movement for Democracy and Development (MRND) was supposed to take 6 of the 22 Cabinet posts in the interim government, including the presidency. The MDR, the party that had suspended Prime Minister Uwilingiyimana's membership, was to take five Cabinet posts, including that of prime minister. And the rebel RPF was to have five posts, including those of deputy prime minister and minister of the interior.[8] As a result, President Habyarimana officially dismissed Agathe Uwilingiyimana as prime minister less than 30 days after her appointment to the office, replacing her with Faustin Twagiramungu of the MDR, a man who had been instrumental in suspending Uwilingiyimana from her own political party.

Owing to the tenuous nature of transitional politics in a country with more experience in ethnic genocide than in multiparty democracy, Uwilingiyimana stayed on as prime minister in a caretaker capacity for several months until her death in April, 1994. This was despite her being excoriated by all the Hutu-dominated parties, including her own MDR, President Habyarimana's ruling party, and several others. In fact, the president's party held a press conference in January, 1994, in which it blamed Uwilingiyimana for being a ''political trickster.''[9]

The swearing-in of the new transitional government in which Juvenal Habyarimana was to remain president and the parties, including the rebel RPF, were to share power as outlined above, was to have taken place on March 25, 1994. On that day, Agathe Uwilingiyimana was to have stepped down as prime minister in favor of Faustin Twagiramungu. By prior agreement, Uwilingiyimana was guaranteed a lower-level ministerial post in the new transitional government that was to have taken Rwanda in a peaceful, democratic direction. But the Tutsi-dominated Rwandan Patriotic Front did not show up at the swearing-in ceremonies, and the establishment of the new transitional regime was postponed. Prime Minister Uwilingiyimana held talks that day with the RPF and gained an agreement that the new government would be sworn in the following afternoon.[10] That ceremony was also postponed.

The agreement between President Habyarimana, Prime Minister Uwilingiyimana, and the Rwandan Patriotic Front was never culminated. On his way back from talks in Tanzania with Burundian President Cyprien Ntaryamira, also a Hutu, both presidents were killed when their plane was attacked on its final approach to the Kigali Airport on April 6, 1994.[11] It is still unclear who shot down the plane, though most speculation points to factions of the Hutu-dominated Rwandan army who were opposed to Habyarimana's overtures to the Tutsi-led RPF. Others point the finger at the RPF itself, although no concrete evidence exists to support either conclusion.[12]

In an interview with Radio France on the night of President Habyarimana's assassination, Prime Minister Uwilingiyimana announced that there would be an immediate investigation. She also said, in what would be her last recorded words: "There is shooting, people are being terrorized, people are inside their homes lying on the floor. We are suffering the consequences of the death of the head of state, I believe. We, the civilians, are in no way responsible for the death of our head of state."[13]

In the early morning hours, according to reports from Belgian military investigators, the United Nations peacekeeping force in Rwanda sent a Belgian escort to Prime Minister Uwilingiyimana's home to take her to Radio Rwanda from where she planned to broadcast, at dawn, an announcement asking for national calm. Uwilingiyimana's house was being guarded by five Ghanaian U.N. troops on the outside in addition to ten U.N. Belgian troops. But the Rwandan presidential guard was assigned to the inside detail. The presidential gendarmes inside Uwilingiyimana's house disarmed the Belgians and Ghanaians, shot and killed the prime minister and her husband, confiscated their bodies, and then took the Belgians back to a military compound where they were hacked to death with machetes.[14]

The event has led some to speculate that the killing of both President Habyarimana and Prime Minister Uwilingiyimana was a planned coup attempt by the Presidential Guard itself. These two assassinations, within 24 hours of each other, sparked a civil war that lasted throughout the year and led to the deaths of over 1 million Rwandans, nearly 15 percent of the country's population, and a flood of refugees into neighboring countries such as Zaire. This latest and most brutal phase of Rwanda's genocidal history caught the attention of the rest of the world.

Statements condemning the killing of Prime Minister Uwilingiyimana were quickly issued by both the Tutsi-dominated Rwandan Patriotic Front and by several majority Hutu political parties. The RPF viewed her death within the context of a well-planned and orchestrated coup attempt by radical factions of the Hutu-dominated army:

> According to reports reaching us, it is in this context [of Army attacks on civilians and government members] that the prime minister, Mrs Agathe Uwilingiyimana, has been assassinated along with her family. The same is reportedly the case for Mr. Joseph

Kavaruganda, the chairman of the constitutional court; Mr. Landouald Ndasingwa, the minister of labour and social affairs and vice-chairman of the Liberal party [PL]: and Mr. [Faustin] Rucogoza, the minister of information. Cases of kidnapping by the same presidential guards are also noted, notably that of Frederic Nzamurambaho, chairman of the PSD [Social Democratic party], and Mr. Felicien Ngango, first vice-chairman of the PSD, to mention only a couple.[15]

The man who was to have taken over from Uwilingiyimana, Faustin Twagiramungu, managed to flee to Kenya; he himself agreed that the killings of the president and prime minister seemed to have been a well-orchestrated plan by radical factions of the Hutu-dominated army opposed to peace with the Tutsi RPF.[16]

The Liberal party, in a later broadcast, went on to announce:

The Liberal party denounces the massacres in the rest of the country—the massacres perpetrated by presidential guards, MRND youthwingers and some elements of the army. The killings targeted members of the opposition and people of Tutsi origin. They killed the prime minister, Mrs. Agathe Uwilingiyimana, cabinet ministers and opposition leaders. It is clear that the massacres had been planned earlier on.[17]

Agathe Uwilingiyimana, the first woman prime minister of Rwanda, was the victim of political violence in a nation with all too much experience in genocide, coups, and ethnic slaughter. In a tribute to her brief but important political career, the interim president, a Tutsi, announced in October, 1994, that a shrine would be built along with a cemetery containing the bodies of Uwilingiyimana and other heroes of recent Rwandan history.

## NOTES

1. ''Rwanda's Uwilingiyimana Was Crusader for Justice,'' *Reuters News Service* (April 8, 1994) (newswire).

2. ''Rwanda: First Woman Premier Dies,'' *Inter Press Service* (April 8, 1994) (newswire).

3. Frank Smyth, ''The Horror—Rwanda: A History Lesson,'' 210 *The New Republic* (1994): 14–19.

4. ''Rwanda's Uwilingiyimana Was Crusader for Justice,'' *Reuters News Service* (April 8, 1994) (newswire).

5. ''Rwanda: First Woman Premier Dies,'' *Inter Press Service* (April 8, 1994) (newswire).

6. ''Woman Named as Rwandan Prime Minister,'' *Agence France Presse* (July 17, 1993) (newswire).

7. ''Rwandan New Prime Minister Suspended from Party,'' *The Xinhua General Overseas News Service* (July 19, 1993) (newswire).

8. ''Rwandan President Appoints New Prime Minister,'' *The Xinhua General Overseas News Service* (August 7, 1993) (newswire).

9. "Ruling Party Blames Transitional Prime Minister for Delays in Democratization," *BBC Summary of World Broadcasts* (January 4, 1994) (newswire).

10. "Setting up of Transitional Institutions Postponed on Two Consecutive Days," *BBC Summary of World Broadcasts* (March 28, 1994) (newswire).

11. "Civil War Resumes After Rwandan Premier Is Slain," *The Glasgow Herald* (April 8, 1994) (newswire).

12. "Belgian Tries to Learn Who Killed Rwandan President," *Reuters News Service* (November 1, 1994) (newswire).

13. "Civil War Resumes After Rwandan Premier Is Slain," *The Glasgow Herald* (April 8, 1994) (newswire).

14. "Belgian Tries to Learn Who Killed Rwandan President," *Reuters News Service* (November 1, 1994) (newswire).

15. "RPF Radio Reports Death of Prime Minister, Ethnic Killing by Presidential Guards," *BBC Summary of World Broadcasts* (April 9, 1994) (newswire).

16. "Prime Minister-Designate Accuses Hutu Soldiers of Killing Habyarimana," *BBC Summary of World Broadcasts* (April 27, 1994) (newswire).

17. "RPF Radio Broadcasts Liberal Party Faction's Denunciation of Party's Leadership," *BBC Summary of World Broadcasts* (April 15, 1994) (newswire).

## REFERENCES

"Belgian Tries to Learn Who Killed Rwandan President." *Reuters News Service*. Newswire (November 1, 1994).

"Civil War Resumes After Rwandan Premier Is Slain." *The Glasgow Herald*. Newswire (April 8, 1994).

"Prime Minister-Designate Accuses Hutu Soldiers of Killing Habyarimana." *BBC Summary of World Broadcasts*. Newswire (April 27, 1994).

"RPF Radio Broadcasts Liberal Party Faction's Denunciation of Party's Leadership." *BBC Summary of World Broadcasts*. Newswire (April 15, 1994).

"RPF Radio Reports Death of Prime Minister, Ethnic Killing by Presidential Guards." *BBC Summary of World Broadcasts*. Newswire (April 9, 1994).

"Ruling Party Blames Transitional Prime Minister for Delays in Democratization." *BBC Summary of World Broadcasts*. Newswire (January 4, 1994).

"Rwanda: First Woman Premier Dies." *Inter Press Service*. Newswire (April 8, 1994).

"Rwandan New Prime Minister Suspended from Party." *The Xinhua General Overseas News Service*. Newswire (July 19, 1993).

"Rwandan President Appoints New Prime Minister." *The Xinhua General Overseas News Service*. Newswire (August 7, 1993).

"Rwanda's Uwilingiyimana Was Crusader for Justice." *Reuters News Service*. Newswire (April 8, 1994).

"Setting up of Transitional Institutions Postponed on Two Consecutive Days." *BBC Summary of World Broadcasts*. Newswire (March 28, 1994).

Smyth, Frank. "The Horror—Rwanda: a History Lesson." *The New Republic* 210 (1994): 14–19.

"Woman Named as Rwandan Prime Minister." *Agence France Presse*. Newswire (July 17, 1993).

*KEVIN HILL*

# SIMONE VEIL-JACOB (1927– )

In April of 1944, at the age of 17, a young Jewish girl arrived at the concentration camp of Auschwitz-Birkenau. More than 50 years later, in January of 1995, that same woman returned to the site of that camp as a representative of the French government to commemorate the liberation of Auschwitz-Birkenau. Between 1944 and 1995, the woman who had witnessed the pain and horrors of the Holocaust as a young adult never forgot those experiences. ''To forget is to betray.'' With this principle as a guide, Simone Veil's accomplishments and contributions to French politics and her devotion to human rights have been extraordinary.[1]

## FAMILY BACKGROUND AND EDUCATION

Simone Jacob was born in Nice, France, on July 13, 1927, the youngest of four children (three girls and one boy). Her father, André Jacob, had served during World War I and was taken prisoner for a time. He long remembered Maréchal Pétain as the victor of Verdun, and he was profoundly deceived by his attitude during World War II. André Jacob had a very strict attitude toward life, based not on religion, but on republican ethics.

André married the beautiful Yvonne Steinmetz in 1922. Her parents, furriers established in Paris, brought up their daughters in an unusual manner for the time, encouraging them to obtain university diplomas in order to work. Yvonne started studying chemistry and her sister studied medicine, becoming one of the first female doctors in France. Yvonne never worked, but educated her daughters with the intention that they would assume a profession.

André Jacob opened his architectural practice in Nice on the Côte d'Azur and provided a comfortable, cultivated bourgeois life for his family, but the economic crisis of 1929 forced him to curtail his standard of living. In September, 1941, he was forbidden to continue his profession, and times became very hard.

When the German occupation became more threatening, the Jacobs moved out of their apartment and took up the name of Jacquier. Simone went to live with her professor of literature and was determined to succeed at the baccalaureate so she could pursue legal studies and become a lawyer. In November, 1943, the headmistress of the *lycée* notified Simone that she did not think it was suitable for her to remain enrolled. But Simone prepared for her examination in secret with the help of school friends and professors.

On March 28, 1944, Simone courageously presented herself at the *baccalauréat* exam under her real identity. Two days later, she was arrested in the street by the Gestapo. She was not quite 17 years of age. The other members of her family were arrested shortly thereafter with the exception of a sister involved with the *Résistance*, who was arrested and deported later.

Simone was undoubtedly intelligent. She had lived in fear of arrest since the beginning of the war and was, perhaps, unconsciously prepared. She had grown up fast. She was a gay, funny, and very willful child capable of taking fire easily. Surely, the early days of the war helped to develop her intuition, her sense of responsibility (particularly toward her mother), and a quickness in disentangling desperate situations. It was these qualities that served her well during her captivity.

Simone, her mother, and sister, Madeleine, were first sent to Drancy and from there, to Auschwitz-Birkenau on April 13, 1944. Simone's astuteness allowed her to survey and observe the workings of the camp and to figure out a means to survive. Simone felt an overwhelming responsibility for her mother and sister, who lacked the vital aggressiveness indispensable in such circumstances. But Simone never forgot her mother's admonishment to retain her decency whatever happened. In February, 1945, the three women were transferred to the camp of Bergen-Belsen because of the Allies' approach. Simone's mother died of typhus at the camp in March, 1945; Simone and her sister were also sick with typhus when the camp was liberated the following month.

Returning to Paris and reintegrating into life was difficult, and became even harder when she heard of her father's and brother's deaths. She was also offended by the attitude of those French who were interested in persons deported for acts of resistance, but showed little concern for the Jews, despite the fact that they had endured the same horrors of the concentration camps. Nevertheless Simone never envisaged Israel as a possible land of refuge. Most of all, she took as a personal defeat the death of her mother, whom she had not been able to protect and bring back to France. Simone was only 18 years of age, yet she had lived through the two events that would shape her future: the death of her mother and Auschwitz. These memories would prompt her to speak on behalf of prisoners and the defenseless, to advocate for their dignity and to promote peace.

Simone finally decided that life was worth living and that she would fight her way through. When she was told she had passed the *baccalauréat*, she began studying law and took an inscription at the *Institut d'études politiques* (IEP). Her strength of character took over. Those who had known Simone before her captivity acknowledged a profound change in the young woman; she could be very harsh. At the IEP, Simone was distant and never expressed any emotions.

In February of 1946, Simone met Antoine Veil at the IEP. His father directed the family textile industry in the east of France and was *conseiller municipal* (town counselor). Simone and Antoine married in October, 1946, and within the first two years of their marriage had two young sons. Antoine was appointed to the French Consulate in Wiesbaden, Germany, and Simone accepted the necessary concessions to accommodate his professional development. This launched the beginning of a social life for Simone; she met politicians who were to become influential and helpful later on in her own endeavors, people such as Pierre-Henri Teitgen and Alain Poher.[2]

Simone made nearly all of the sacrifices in her married life except one: she wanted to work despite her husband's disapproval. After the birth of their third son in 1954, they managed a compromise. He agreed to allow her to work provided it was not as a lawyer, a profession he considered incompatible with womanhood and motherhood. The judiciary seemed more appropriate and Veil started the two-year preparation for such a position. She completed her preparation in 1956.

## CAREER DEVELOPMENT

Simone Veil entered the judiciary with high marks and thus, the promise of a successful career. However, as a judge she never sat in a jurisdiction and therefore never judged a case. Rather, she occupied diverse and interesting positions. Her initial aspirations of becoming a lawyer surged, and she defended her *dossiers* with the same energy that she would have exerted to plead a case.

Veil was lucky enough to begin her career at the Ministry of Justice in Paris, since her husband did not want her to abandon her family and their Parisian life. She was assigned to the Department of Penitential Administration. In 1959, when the Algerian war was at its peak, Simone Veil was sent on a two-week assignment to inspect the prisons in Algeria. On the whole, her work at the penitential department was very trying because she always felt personally involved, to the point of jeopardizing the harmony in her family life.

In 1964, Minister of Justice Foyer transferred her to the Department of Civil Affairs. At that time the agency was involved in the reform of the Civil Code, and Foyer placed Simone on the commission working on adoption policy. When she presented the final report to the minister, he charged her with writing the project of law that was passed by Parliament. René Pléven, who was then presiding over the Commission on Laws, appreciated her juridical qualities, and when he became minister of justice in 1969, he nominated Simone Veil as *conseiller technique* in his Cabinet. This assignment was an honor for a judge, and Simone Veil was making her mark. But although she was close to power and enjoyed the experience, the job required too much of her time and took her away from her family on many evenings; she soon applied for another assignment.

In March, 1970, the president of the Republic, Georges Pompidou, nominated her to the post of secretary general of the *Conseil supérieur de la magistrature* (CSM). She was the first female judge to hold this position. Her role involved preparing promotions or transfers of judges as well as studying the lawyers' reports for death-sentence clients in order to submit them to the president of the Republic who, once informed, would decide whether or not to grant clemency. During this period, Minister Pléven sent her to Strasbourg as an expert to the Council of Europe. She enjoyed her work on very specific legal questions concerning family law.

May, 1974, marked a turning point in Veil's career, for she entered the political arena. Prime Minister Jacques Chirac nominated her to be a member of the government as the minister of the Health, Social Security, and Family Department and she accepted. The real motivation behind this assignment may have been President Valéry Giscard d'Éstaing's desire to promote women in government. Veil spent five years at that ministry, and became very popular.

In 1979, Veil was elected a deputy to the first European Parliament, and resigned as minister. President Giscard d'Éstaing supported her, and after this electoral success, he used his influence to assure her election to the presidency of the Parliament, a position he considered the most prestigious and symbolic of the oncoming Europe, and one he believed should be held by a French representative. He thought Simone Veil had the necessary qualities to serve as president of that august body, given her devotion to Europe and to the principles of reconciliation. Her personal experiences as a Jew who had lived through deportation would serve her well in this capacity. But d'Éstaing was also aware of the opposition likely to come from conservatives and Christian Democrats because of Veil's defense of the abortion laws.

Simone Veil was elected president of the European Parliament in the second round of balloting, and she occupied this post until January, 1982. The subsequent European elections took place in 1984. She ran again and was obliged, through political pressure, to place on her list Robert Hersant, the owner of several newspapers, one of which was *Le Figaro*. It was a difficult decision because of Hersant's attitude during World War II. But Veil bowed to the pressure and was reelected in 1984, and again in 1989.

Many had considered Simone Veil's political service to France finished when she resigned her position as minister of health in 1979, and shifted her focus to European matters. But in 1993, to the joy of the French citizenry, Prime Minister Edouard Balladur appointed her as *ministre d'État chargé de la Santé, des Affaires sociales et de la Ville*. Veil returned to a department she knew well (health and social affairs), and she insisted on taking on all of the controversial questions related to urban policy. Balladur, in appointing Veil, had set aside his personal opposition to abortion because he knew that Veil would be an asset to his government. She was a woman, Jewish, a politically qualified ''centrist,'' and extremely popular. He gave her the title of minister of state, granting her the first rank in his government. It seems that his political flair served him well, for Balladur and Veil complemented each other.

## ACHIEVEMENTS AND CONTRIBUTIONS

Working with Simone Veil is said not to be an easy task; her character and personality are legendary. As a small child, she was already very determined and would not hesitate to argue with her father. She could easily lose her temper but would compensate immediately with a lovely smile. The young Veil could be a nice companion, witty and happy. During the war, she developed astuteness and a sense of responsibility. When she came back from deportation, some of her manners had faded away; she was no longer carefree, and she could be extremely harsh. Other aspects of her character surfaced, including her sudden fits of humor tempered with a smile and her authoritarianism. During her studies following her liberation, Veil exhibited great independence with regard to men and contempt for the ''establishment.''

These attitudes engendered hostility toward her but did not make her change. Veil became aware of the necessity of compromise in politics, an aspect of her career that she feared and resisted, but learned well. Her great working capacity and her ability to get straight to the crux of issues have allowed her to master diverse questions quickly.

In her long career, Simone Veil lived through several crises in French modern history that have given her the opportunity to express, test, and shape her own political ideas. During World War II, she became Gaullist; later, in 1958, however, when General de Gaulle reappeared on the political scene, she was not an unconditional admirer. She disapproved of his assumption of power in a non-democratic way but approved of his peacemaking policy in Algeria.

It was also during World War II that her anticommunism emerged. Among her family, her mother, and most especially, her maternal aunt and uncle were attracted to left-wing ideas. Veil could have easily adopted these views, if she had not witnessed the animosity of the communist prisoners against Jews and others who had been deported for racial reasons in the concentration camp. When she returned to France, she was astounded to find ''her France'' under communist influence. As a result, her hostility toward communism grew. Although she regarded Pierre Mendes-France's social democratic ideas with interest during the Fourth Republic and even though she joined the *Syndicat de la Magistrature* (left wing) at its creation in 1968, under the Fifth Republic, she never mixed with left-wing politicians. In 1981, for example, she was profoundly opposed to François Mitterand's candidacy for the French presidency because he proposed a political program based on a coalition of socialists and communists. Veil always believed that French socialism was extremely influenced by Marxism. When Socialist Prime Minister Michael Rocard approached her to join his government, she refused.

But Veil did not mingle with the right-wing politicians either. She felt no sympathy for *la droite giscardienne*, composed of men whose lives, unlike her own, had been easy. Nonetheless, she accepted service under President Giscard d'Éstaing in Jacques Chirac's government. She had been impressed by Giscard d'Éstaing's determination to modernize France and begin multiple reforms. She was thankful that he had nominated her as minister and had allowed her to pursue some of her own ideas and policies. Veil served him well on two occasions: the elaboration and defense of the law on abortion, and the 1978 campaign for deputies in which she saved the votes of the citizens in the "center." And it is the "center" that best reflects Veil's ideas. In return for her support, Valéry Giscard d'Éstaing managed her election as president of the European Parliament.

This independence enabled Veil to affirm personal convictions without having to follow party dictates. Hence, she spoke in favor of the independence of Algeria, argued adamantly against the death sentence, and was opposed to the concept of direct universal suffrage for the election of the president of the French Republic.

Over the almost 40 years of her career, Simone Veil occupied important "key" functions in which she assumed engagements that made profound changes in French institutions. Veil's first assignment at the Ministry's Department of Penitential Administration in 1956, was most opportune. She was still haunted by her captivity in Auschwitz, the deprivation of liberty, the promiscuity, and the total negation of human dignity. As soon as she assumed her function, she started inspecting the prisons throughout the country where she witnessed a disastrous situation. She implemented reforms concerning prisoners' health and education by imposing systematic X-rays to track tuberculosis and by creating medical-physiological centers integrated in the jails. Vail was particularly attentive to the prisons for women, demanding that the women be treated as decently as men.

Three years later, close collaborators of Minister of Justice Michelet thought Simone Veil was the appropriate judge to inspect the prisons in Algeria. Her two-week mission allowed her to appreciate the gravity of the Algerian prison situation. As soon as she returned to Paris, she handwrote her report and gave it to the minister herself, for she distrusted some employees. In that report, she concluded that the same rules should be applied in all prisons on Algerian and French soil, and she requested the transfer of numerous *Front de libération nationale* prisoners, those who had fought for Algerian independence, into the metropolitan prisons, for fear that they would be dragged out of prison and summarily sentenced. Veil was constantly attentive to the prisoners' situation. Remembering those who had been defenseless in Auschwitz, she believed she "owed" them that.

In 1964, she was designated secretary of the commission working on reform of adoption. It was Veil who argued that the basic principle governing adoption should be that any policy must be in the best interest of the child. She worked with two nonjurists on the commission: a psychiatrist and a doctor both specializing in children. She also questioned adoptive parents, educators, and managers of the *Assistance publique*. Although the commission's proposals upset the majority of deputies, it received the minister's approval and the law was passed. It has served as a model for many European parliaments grappling with similar issues.

Having defended the cause of children, it might seem inconceivable that Veil would be one of the authors of the law on abortion. However, President Giscard d'Éstaing was convinced that Veil could find the right tactics to present the legislation, and he insisted that she defend it before the National Assembly. The debate opened in November, 1974 and lasted three days and two nights. Veil did not base her argument on a woman's free disposal of her body and convenience. Rather, she insisted on the responsibility and dignity with which the situation should be considered, declaring that abortion must remain the exception, the ultimate recourse for desperate cases, and not a means of regulating births. To appease some opponents, a clause of conscience was included that allowed doctors to refuse to perform abortions. While Veil faced vehement opposition from right-wing deputies and resistance from left-wing deputies because she refused to endorse using public funds for abortions, Veil was successful in seeing the bill through to passage and even managed to obtain unanimous support from the left wing.

Simone Veil is a woman of action and her struggle to build a better world that respected human rights was not limited to France. She was profoundly convinced that Europe, and most especially the European Community, had an extraordinary opportunity to broaden a human rights agenda and develop a policy of reconciliation with Germany. When she followed her husband to Germany in the early 1950s, she at first felt there could be no forgiveness for the German people, but over time, she learned to accept contact and recognized the importance of dialogue. Upon her election to the European Parliament, Veil explained that she had placed all of her hope for peace and humanity in Europe. As long as it had overcome hate and barbarity, the region could enjoy democracy and solidarity.

When Simone Veil joined Prime Minister Edouard Balladur's government, she announced that she wanted to develop a humanitarian mission for France and focus on the everyday way of living. She took specific interest in the disadvantaged members of the population, and this led her to intervene in very different domains. Veil was attentive to the burning question of whether or not to allow the wearing of the Islamic veil in schools, and she suggested delegating the issue to Moslem women mediators. She also advocated for improving the suburban environment. As minister, she was invited to a Cairo conference in September, 1994, where she spoke on women's rights especially in the field of sexuality. Veil also became engaged in the war against illicit drug use and abuse, establishing a commission in 1994 to propose strategies for coping with drugs and toxicomania. She also insisted on governmental action to curtail the spread of Acquired Immune Deficiency Syndrome (AIDS), by proposing preventive measures accepted by the French Council of Ministers in February, 1995, and by hosting international conferences that could lead to the development and adoption of general measures to fight this worldwide epidemic.[3]

Simone Veil's political involvement is comprehensive, not only in France where she supported Balladur's candidacy for the French presidency in spring, 1995, but outside France as well. Thus, in November of 1994, she again met Yasser Arafat in Gaza and expressed her satisfaction with the recently negotiated peace. Peace, as one might expect, was one of Veil's favorite themes, the aspiration of her youth.

Simone Veil has been repeatedly recognized for her contributions. In France, she was conferred the *order national du Mérite (chevalier)*, and she received the medal of *l'Éducation surveillée et de l'ádministration pénitentiaire*. She is doctor *honoris causa* of numerous universities throughout the world, in particular Princeton (1975), the Hebrew University in Jerusalem (1980), Yale (1980), Georgetown (1981), and Yeshiva University in New York (1982). She also received awards from the Onassis Foundation (1986), the Eleanor and Franklin Roosevelt Foundation (1984), the Charlemagne prize, (1981), and the Truman Award for peace in Jerusalem in 1991.

Besides these official honors, Veil enjoys an enduring popularity among her fellow citizens that has little to do with her race or political opinions. Rather, it is an acknowledgment and tribute to her lifelong concern for humanity and her commitment to improving the human condition.

## ACKNOWLEDGMENT

I wish to express my gratitude to Madame Simone Veil who took the time to review this chapter and added personal comments notwithstanding her very heavy agenda.

## NOTES

1. A major source for this article is Maurice Szafran, *Simone Veil: Destin* (Flammarion, 1994).
2. Teitgen was vice president of the Council of Ministers, presided over by Paul Ramadier in January, 1947. Poher served as secretary of state for budget in 1948, and under the Fifth Republic, became president of the Senate.
3. Two conferences have been held. In June, 1994, the health ministers of 40 countries, North and South, came to Paris for a conference on AIDS. And on December 1, 1994, a similar conference was attended by the heads of those governments.

## REFERENCES

Szafran, Maurice. *Simone Veil: Destin.* Flammarion, 1994.
Veil-Jacob, Simone, in collaboration with Clement Launay and Michel Soul. *L'adoption: donnees médicales, psychologiques et sociales*, 7th edition. Paris: ESF, 1980.

*JACQUELINE LUCIENNE LAFON*

# BERTHA WILSON (1923– )

Bertha Wilson's contribution to Canadian law has been both symbolic and substantive. As the first woman lawyer in her law firm, and the first woman appointed to the Ontario Court of Appeal and to the Supreme Court of Canada, she has been an important symbol of women's aspirations, especially women lawyers'.

Beyond her pioneering role as a woman who became a lawyer and then a judge, Wilson's intellectual contribution to the substantive development of law in Canada has also been significant, particularly in relation to the principles of interpretation for the Charter of Rights and Freedoms. Since her retirement from the Court in 1991, she has continued to demonstrate her commitment to challenging intellectual work in her role as chair of the Canadian Bar Association's (CBA) Task Force on Gender Equality in the Legal Profession and as co-chair of the Royal Commission on Aboriginal Peoples.

## FAMILY BACKGROUND AND EDUCATION

Bertha Wilson was born in Kirkcaldy, Fife, Scotland, on September 18, 1923, the daughter of Archibald and Christina Wernham, and attended secondary school in Aberdeen. She received the Master of Arts degree from the University of Aberdeen in 1944 and the Teaching Parchment from the Aberdeen Training College for Teachers in 1945. In that year, she married the Reverend John Wilson, and they moved to Macduff, a small town on the coast of Scotland, where the congregation included mostly fishermen and farmers. In 1949, John and Bertha Wilson immigrated to Canada and settled first in Renfrew, a small community in the Ottawa Valley, where Reverend Wilson became the United Church minister. Three years later, John became a naval chaplain during the Korean War, and Bertha worked briefly as a dentists' receptionist in Ottawa. In

1954, Reverend Wilson was posted to Halifax, and Bertha Wilson joined him there.

After arriving in Halifax, she decided to continue her education by enrolling in law school. At her interview at Dalhousie Law School, Bertha encountered Dean Horace Read's now well-known admonition to her as a woman law student: "Have you any appreciation . . . of how tough a course the law is? This is not something you can do in your spare time. We have no room here for dilettantes. Why don't you just go home and take up crocheting?" Bertha Wilson's reflections on Dean Read's comments show her sense of law as a fundamental part of a liberal education: "It was hard for me to persuade him that I was a serious student; that to me a knowledge of the law was an essential part of a liberal education and that while crocheting might be a very pleasant way to spend one's leisure hours, it could not be the be-all and end-all of one's productive years."

Wilson graduated from Dalhousie Law School in 1957, and after a period of articling, was admitted to the bar of Nova Scotia in the same year.

## CAREER DEVELOPMENT

In 1958, the Wilsons moved to Toronto when John accepted a job with the national office of the United Church of Canada. Bertha eventually obtained another articling position and was admitted to the Ontario bar at the firm of Osler, Hoskin and Harcourt in 1959. She became the first woman lawyer and then the first woman partner ten years later at this firm. At Osler, Hoskin and Harcourt, Bertha developed special expertise as a legal researcher and established the first "research department" at a major Canadian law firm, attracting several other bright young lawyers to work with her.

In 1975, she was appointed to the Ontario Court of Appeal and in 1982, to the Supreme Court of Canada. From 1984 to 1990, she also served on the Permanent Court of Arbitration. She retired as a member of the Supreme Court of Canada in 1991.

Wilson was involved in the Canadian Bar Association as a member of the Ontario and National Councils in the early 1970s. She also served on the Board of Trustees of the Clarke Institute of Psychiatry, the Toronto School of Theology, the Canadian Centre for Philanthropy, and the Board of Governors of Carleton University.

She has received 18 honorary degrees from Canadian universities and a similar honor from the University of Aberdeen. She was elected to the Royal Society of Canada in 1991, and appointed a Companion of the Order of Canada in 1992. These honors reflect the substance of her contribution to law, not simply the symbolism of her pioneering role. As former Chief Justice Dickson stated:

> The sheer quality of her analysis and the depth of her thinking has ensured that her place in history will not only be secure by virtue of her having been the first woman appointed

to the Supreme Court of Canada. Nor will it depend solely on the many ways in which her leadership had advanced the position of women in law. In my view, her place in history is assured because her legal scholarship has been of the highest order.[1]

## ACHIEVEMENTS AND CONTRIBUTIONS

An examination of Wilson's achievements and contributions as a lawyer and judge for more than 30 years reveals her excellent ability for rigorous and cogent legal analysis of the "traditional" kind and, at the same time and especially in cases involving the interpretation of the Charter, an imaginative ability to reconceptualize and revitalize traditional legal principles. More recently, in her work as chair of the CBA Task Force on Gender Equality in the legal profession, she has also demonstrated vision and perseverance in recommending institutional change within the legal profession and the judiciary.

Wilson's demonstrated ability for cogent legal analysis has been described as an achievement of "rationality and logic that sweep one along to an acceptance of her conclusions."[2] Perhaps as a result of her work for 17 years at the law firm, years in which she honed her excellent talents for careful research and analysis, her facility for decision making in the common law tradition was especially resourceful. As "a lawyer's lawyer" at Osler, Hoskin and Harcourt, she developed problem-solving skills that demonstrated both technical proficiency and the importance of the factual context. Especially in complex cases, her analysis rigorously probed competing arguments, examining both historical lines of authority and the context of underlying assumptions and values.

These analytical strengths resulted in her important contributions in the Ontario Court of Appeals in cases that recognized, for example, a tort of discrimination[3] and the availability of the constructive trust remedy at the end of a cohabiting relationship.[4] A similarly rigorous approach to traditional legal doctrines was fundamental to many of her decisions in the Supreme Court of Canada, including her decision to admit expert evidence of the battered woman's syndrome in relation to a plea of self-defense in *Lavallee*.[5]

Innovation in her decision making thus emanated from her ability to analyze legal principles and a strong belief in the inherent flexibility at the heart of the common law tradition. Wilson has been described as someone who was willing to "make new and better law," by contrast with an approach that would simply "add another exception to an unjust rule."[6] In this way, her work both as a lawyer and later as a judge demonstrated her commitment to the vitality of the common law tradition: a tradition that requires a facility for technical legal analysis, but also a sensitivity to the need to shape intellectual ideas in the context of the human condition. Indeed, it has been suggested that as a judge, Bertha Wilson's "most marked characteristic [was] an intense concern for the civil society, the humane society."[7]

In this way, Wilson's intellectual abilities and her enjoyment of the process of legal analysis and argument in the common law tradition resulted in bold innovation in several cases she decided, but her reasoning remained firmly grounded in the framework of the common law tradition. As was suggested at the time of her appointment to the Supreme Court of Canada:

> Madame Justice Wilson has indeed been bold and innovative in her years on the Court of Appeal for Ontario, but it is important to record that her innovations result from carefully reasoned legal analysis—meticulously researched and scrupulously fair. She has evinced a deep respect for the rule of law, and an appreciation for the stability which characterizes the common law at its best.[8]

Wilson's respect for the common law tradition also provided the starting point for her interpretation of the Charter. Appointed to the Supreme Court of Canada less than one month before the proclamation of this new legal development in Canadian law (the constitutional entrenchment of fundamental rights), she faced new intellectual challenges as a Supreme Court justice involved in the process of (re)defining the relationship between the courts and Parliament in the Canadian legal system. As she herself defined this new role, "The judicial role under the Charter . . . has effected a major change in the relationship between the three branches of government. It challenges the right of government to enact certain laws at all and makes the courts the watchdogs over the rights of the citizen."[9]

Yet, although Wilson recognized an enlarged scope for judicial decision making,[10] it was also her view that the process of interpreting Charter guarantees required a principled approach, taking into account both the purpose of the Charter's guarantees and the context in which rights are asserted. According to former Chief Justice Dickson:

> Bertha Wilson struck a finely tuned balance that elegantly sidesteps the increasingly sterile debate between advocates of judicial restraint and . . . judicial activism. . . . The courts can hardly pretend that they have no mandate to effect change in the law when the legislature has itself given them this very mandate in enacting the Charter. And yet, this mandate does not mean that courts can ignore the way in which they fit into our democratic system and the limits that their position in that system [requires].[11]

In addition to a purposive and contextualized approach, however, her judgments evidenced a concern for those members of society who might be excluded by democratic majoritarian processes, and for whom Charter guarantees might thus be more significant. In early cases such as *Singh*, for example, she held that a legislative scheme for refugee determination was invalid because its procedural requirements failed to meet the Charter's guarantee of fundamental justice.

Wilson's contribution to the interpretation of the equality guarantee in Section 15 of the Charter also shows her commitment to these principles of purpose and context, and the need to protect members of minority communities. Her reasoning in *Andrews* in 1989,[12] reinforced by her subsequent decision in *Turpin*,[13] showed her rejection of a simple linguistic approach to defining equality and discrimination. In her view, Section 15 was designed to advance the purposes of "remedying or preventing discrimination against groups suffering social, political and legal disadvantage in our society." Such an approach clearly requires a claimant to show, not just that there has been a denial of equality, but also that there has been discrimination. As Lynn Smith has argued, "the Canadian Supreme Court's approach to constitutional equality rights can be seen as three-dimensional, seeing and taking into account not only comparisons between persons and treatment, but also the comparative disadvantage experienced by particular groups in society."[14]

Wilson's approach has been characterized as a "persistent effort to make justice both equal and accessible," an approach that required her to "search for new frameworks for understanding and celebrating difference."[15] Such an approach, though rooted in the common law tradition of analyzing legal principles in terms of purpose and context, also challenges these concepts in fundamental and important ways:

> Justice Wilson's decisions consistently refuse to obscure the systemic nature of inequality, and the participation of the structures of legal discourse in those systems. As a result, the questions she raises are complex and difficult, and yet they are never presented as impossible. On the contrary, by pushing us to re-examine assumptions, by bringing voices at the margins into the center, and by demanding answers that respond to the logic of context as well as the logic of principle, she has made available to us a new array of possibilities.[16]

In this way, Wilson's judgments reflected her belief that the Charter provided a legislative mandate for a new role for courts in Canada. Although her intellectual commitment to the common law tradition remained evident, her judgments also recognized the new challenges presented by the Charter and the new role for courts, especially in the protection of rights fundamental to disadvantaged groups in Canadian society. Along with other justices, she embraced the test in *Oakes*, which required governments to meet a high standard (under Section 1 of the Charter) to justify legislative enactments that limited the rights and freedoms protected by the Charter.[17] In subsequent cases, she consistently held to this high standard, "because in her eyes any violation of a Charter right was so serious that it could be accepted by the courts only if the government's justification was overwhelming."[18] For her, moreover, the Charter also required new approaches to legal education and advocacy, a responsibility for members of the legal profession as well as for judges:

> I don't believe that counsel have yet realized the importance of taking a broader approach to Charter litigation. . . . We are all in the business now of weighing competing values and values have an emotional and spiritual as well as an intellectual content. So counsel must educate themselves on what it is about a free and democratic society that is so precious. . . . When should the rights of the individual or the minority be sacrificed for

what the government, i.e. the majority, perceives to be the common good? These are not easy questions . . . and the Court needs all the help it can get. So please don't treat Charter cases as if you were dealing with mechanics' liens. Approach them with a bit of imagination.[19]

Wilson's pioneering role as a woman lawyer and judge has been an important model for other women in the legal profession and in Canadian society generally. Beyond her own role, however, she has also contributed to ideas about the nature of sex equality in law and society.[20] In her celebrated speech in 1990 on the topic of women and judging, she emphasized the need for judges to place litigants and their problems in context, both as a feature of good judging and as a means of taking gender into account as part of the human experience. "If women lawyers and women judges through their differing perspectives on life can bring a new humanity to bear on the decision-making process, perhaps they will make a difference. Perhaps they will succeed in infusing the law with an understanding of what it means to be fully human."[21]

Similarly, her judgment in *Lavallee*[22] has been described as one that conveys the "radical message that women's lives are valuable and entitled to be protected. . . . It also raises the question of the connection between what it means to be a woman and what it means to be reasonable."[23] More recently, she has suggested that the issue of domestic violence is one that requires "a critical review of accepted social norms and institutions, [and] being open to the possibility that some traditions would be better deposited on the scrap-heap of history."[24]

The importance of context for legal problems about sex equality was also evident in *Morgentaler*, where Wilson's concurring judgment concluded that the provisions of the Criminal Code concerning abortion infringed the liberty interest of women under Section 7 of the Charter. She was the only justice to decide the case on this basis:

This decision is one that will have profound psychological, economic and social consequences for the pregnant woman. The circumstances giving rise to it can be complex and varied and there may be, and usually are, powerful considerations milling in opposite directions. It is a decision that deeply reflects the way the woman thinks about herself and her relationship to others and to society at large. It is not just a medical decision; it is a profound social and ethical one as well. Her response to it will be the response of the whole person.[25]

In this case, as in others,[26] Wilson linked claims to sex equality to fundamental rights associated with humanity, but imaginatively revisioned legal categories of humanity so as to include "the pregnant woman."[27]

Wilson's contribution to legal concepts of sex equality flowed from her willingness to probe the underlying values of legal principles and to understand the context of legal problems. This approach is also evident in her most recent work on the issue of gender equality in the legal profession and the judiciary.[28] The Task Force recommendations for substantive change within the legal profession and the judiciary demonstrated her commitment to diversity within legal institutions:

> The Task Force believes that the goal of the profession should be diversity. It believes that all "voices" should be heard and all "perspectives" presented. There is no such thing as a neutral perspective. . . . Our profession must be inclusive. It must not deny entry or discriminate at any stage of a lawyer's career on grounds of race, sex, disability or sexual preference. We must discard the white, male, heterosexual image of the lawyer and welcome "the other" to our profession. We must celebrate their achievement as we celebrate our own. . . .
>
> The Task Force accepts as a basic premise that men and women should have an equal opportunity to enter and progress in the profession. It views discrimination on the basis of gender as equally repugnant to discrimination on the basis of race or religion. There is nothing controversial about this assertion. It is the law and must form part of the framework for change in the legal profession.[29]

Wilson's appreciation for the analytical rigor of the common law tradition, coupled with her insights about new possibilities (as well as limits) for courts in the era of the Charter, have continued to inspire her work as a member of the CBA Task Force on Gender Equality and the Royal Commission on Aboriginal Peoples. These recent tasks require all the strengths of her analytical talents at the same time as they engage her commitment to equality in Canada, now and for the future. Like her beloved Scottish compatriot, Sir Walter Scott, Bertha Wilson has shown herself to be dedicated to "the nature of justice as it is in any age."[30]

## ACKNOWLEDGMENT

I gratefully acknowledge the assistance of Ruth Fletcher in the preparation of this article.

## NOTES

1. Brian Dickson, "Madame Justice Wilson: Trailblazer for Justice," in Symposium: "The Democratic Intellect: The Contribution of Bertha Wilson," 15 *Dalhousie Law Journal* (1991): 1.
2. Alan Watson, "Thc Scottish Enlightenment, the Democratic Intellect and the Work of Madame Justice Wilson," in Symposium, 15 *Dalhousie Law Journal* (1991): 23.
3. *Bhadauria v. Board of Governors of Seneca College* (1979), 27 O.R. (2d) 142; [1981] 2 S.C.R. 181.
4. *Becker v. Pettkus* (1978), 20 O.R. (2d) 105; (1980) 19 R. F.L. (2d) 165.
5. *R. v. Lavallee*, [1990] 1 S.C.R. 852.

6. Watson, 23.
7. Ibid.
8. A. Rendall Dick, "Ceremonial Remarks (on the occasion of Justice Bertha Wilson taking the oath of a Justice of the Supreme Court of Canada on 30 March 1982)," *Law Society Gazette* (1982): 172.
9. Bertha Wilson, "Decision-Making in the Supreme Court," 36 *University of Toronto Law Journal* (1986): 227.
10. Bertha Wilson, "Law and Policy in a Court of Last Resort," *Cambridge Lectures* (1989): 219.
11. Dickson, 1.
12. *Andrews v. Law Society of B.C.*, [1989] 1 S.C.R. 143.
13. *R. v. Turpin*, [1989] 2 S.C.R. 1296.
14. Lynn Smith, "Adding a Third Dimension: The Canadian Approach to Constitutional Equality Guarantees," 55 *Law and Contemporary Problems* (1992): 212.
15. Hester Lessard, "Equality and Access to Justice in the Work of Bertha Wilson," in Symposium, 15 *Dalhousie Law Journal* (1991): 35.
16. Ibid.
17. *R. v. Oakes* (1986), 26 D.L.R. (4th) 200.
18. James MacPherson, "Canadian Constitutional Law and Madame Justice Bertha Wilson," in Symposium, 15 *Dalhousie Law Journal* (1991): 217.
19. Bertha Wilson, "Constitutional Advocacy," 24 *Ottawa Law Review* (1992): 265.
20. Bertha Wilson, "Law in Society: The Principle of Sexual Equality," 13 *Manitoba Law Journal* (1983): 221.
21. Bertha Wilson, "Will Women Judges Really Make a Difference?" 28 *Osgoode Hall Law Journal* (1990): 507; *Law Society Gazette* (1990): 261; 14 *Provincial Judges* (1990): 7; and "Est-ce que des femmes juges feront une difference?", 4 *Rev. jur. Femme et Droit* (1990–1991): 359.
22. *R. v. Lavallee*, [1990] 1 S.C.R. 852.
23. Christine Boyle, "The Role of the Judiciary in the Work of Madame Justice Wilson," in Symposium, 15 *Dalhousie Law Journal* (1991): 241.
24. Bertha Wilson, "Family Violence," 5 *Canadian Journal of Women and the Law* (1991): 137.
25. *R. v. Morgentaler* (1988), 44 D.L.R. (4th) 385.
26. Boyle, 241.
27. S. Gavigan, "Morgentaler and Beyond: Abortion, Reproduction, and the Courts," in J. Brodie, S. Gavigan, and J. Jenson, *The Politics of Abortion* (London: Oxford University Press, 1992), 117.
28. Canadian Bar Association, *Touchstones for Change: Equality, Diversity and Accountability* (Report of the Task Force on Gender Equality in the Legal Profession, 1993).
29. Ibid.
30. Bertha Wilson, "The Scottish Enlightenment," 51 *Saskatchewan Law Review* (1986–1987): 251; and 21 *Law Society Gazette* (1987): 185.

## REFERENCES

"Bertha Wilson." *Canadian Who's Who* (1994).
Boyle, Christine. "The Role of the Judiciary in the Work of Madame Justice Wilson."

In Symposium, ''The Democratic Intellect: The Contribution of Bertha Wilson.'' *Dalhousie Law Journal* 15 (1991): 241–60.

Bryden, Philip. ''The Democratic Intellect: The State in the Work of Madame Justice Wilson.'' In Symposium, ''The Democratic Intellect: The Contribution of Bertha Wilson.'' *Dalhousie Law Journal* 15 (1991): 65–80.

Canadian Bar Association. *Touchstones for Change: Equality, Diversity and Accountability*. Report of the Task Force on Gender Equality in the Legal Profession, 1993.

Dick, A. Rendall. ''Ceremonial Remarks (on the occasion of Justice Bertha Wilson taking the oath of a Justice of the Supreme Court of Canada on 30 March 1982).'' *Law Society Gazette* (1982): 172–79.

Dickson, Brian. ''Madame Justice Wilson: Trailblazer for Justice.'' In Symposium, ''The Democratic Intellect: The Contribution of Bertha Wilson.'' *Dalhousie Law Journal* 15 (1991): 1–22.

Gavigan, S. ''Morgentaler and Beyond: Abortion, Reproduction, and the Courts.'' In *The Politics of Abortion*. J. Brodie, S. Gavigan, and J. Jenson. London: Oxford University Press, 1992, 117–46.

Gwyn, Sandra. ''Madame Justice: How Bertha Wilson's Humanity Is Changing the Last Bastion of Male Power–the Supreme Court of Canada.'' *Saturday Night* (July 1985): 13–19.

Lessard, Hester. ''Equality and Access to Justice in the Work of Bertha Wilson.'' In Symposium, ''The Democratic Intellect: The Contribution of Bertha Wilson.'' *Dalhousie Law Journal* 15 (1991): 35–64.

MacPherson, James. ''Canadian Constitutional Law and Madame Justice Bertha Wilson.'' In Symposium, ''The Democratic Intellect: The Contribution of Bertha Wilson.'' *Dalhousie Law Journal* 15 (1991): 217–40.

Maloney, Maureen. ''Economic Actors in the Work of Madame Justice Wilson.'' In Symposium, ''The Democratic Intellect: The Contribution of Bertha Wilson.'' *Dalhousie Law Journal* 15 (1991): 197–215.

Mossman, Mary Jane. ''The 'Family' in the Work of Madame Justice Wilson.'' In Symposium, ''The Democratic Intellect: The Contribution of Bertha Wilson.'' *Dalhousie Law Journal* 15 (1991): 115–95.

Pinard, Danielle. ''The Constituents of Democracy: The Individual in the Work of Madame Justice Wilson.'' In Symposium, ''The Democratic Intellect: The Contribution of Bertha Wilson.'' *Dalhousie Law Journal* 15 (1991): 81–114.

Smith, Lynn. ''Adding a Third Dimension: The Canadian Approach to Constitutional Equality Guarantees.'' *Law and Contemporary Problems* 55 (1992): 211–33.

Watson, Alan. ''The Scottish Enlightenment, the Democratic Intellect and the Work of Madame Justice Wilson.'' In Symposium, ''The Democratic Intellect: The Contribution of Bertha Wilson.'' *Dalhousie Law Journal* 15 (1991): 23–34.

Wilson, Bertha. ''Constitutional Advocacy.'' *Ottawa Law Review* 24 (1992): 265–73.

Wilson, Bertha. ''Women, the Family and the Constitutional Protection of Privacy.'' *Queen's Law Journal* 17 (1992): 5–30.

Wilson, Bertha. ''Family Violence.'' *Canadian Journal of Women and the Law* 5 (1991): 137–41.

Wilson, Bertha. ''Remarks Given at the Call to the Bar Ceremony.'' *Law Society Gazette* 25 (1991): 102–6.

Wilson, Bertha. ''Will Women Judges Really Make a Difference?'' *Osgoode Hall Law Journal* 28 (1990): 507–22; *Law Society Gazette* (1990): 261–74; *Provincial*

*Judges* 14 (1990): 7–13; and ''Est-ce que des femmes juges feront une difference?'' *Rev. jur. Femme et Droit* 4 (1990–1991): 359–72.
Wilson, Bertha. ''Law and Policy in a Court of Last Resort.'' *Cambridge Lectures* (1989): 219–36.
Wilson, Bertha. ''The Scottish Enlightenment.'' *Saskatchewan Law Review* 51 (1986–1987): 251–71; and *Law Society Gazette* 21 (1987): 185–212.
Wilson, Bertha. ''Decision-Making in the Supreme Court.'' *University of Toronto Law Journal* 36 (1986): 227–48.
Wilson, Bertha. ''Law in Society: The Principle of Sexual Equality.'' *Manitoba Law Journal* 13 (1983): 221–33.
Wilson, Bertha. ''Reminiscences of My Years at Dalhousie Law School.'' *ANSUL Magazine* (1977): 2.

*MARY JANE MOSSMAN*

# APPENDIX

## PRACTICING ATTORNEYS AND JUDGES

| | Year of birth | Country |
|---|---|---|
| Myra Bradwell | 1831 | United States |
| Carrie Burnham Kilgore | 1838 | United States |
| Emily Ferguson Murphy | 1868 | Canada |
| Florence Ellinwood Allen | 1884 | United States |
| Helen Kinnear | 1894 | Canada |
| Burnita Shelton Matthews | 1894 | United States |
| Elisabeth Selbert | 1896 | Germany |
| Wiltraut Rupp-von Brünneck | 1912 | Germany |
| Cecilia Muñoz Palma | 1913 | Philippines |
| Soia Mentschikoff | 1915 | United States |
| Miriam Ben-Porat | 1918 | Israel |
| Irene R. Cortes | 1920 | Philippines |
| Simone Rozès-Ludwig | 1920 | France |
| Constance Baker Motley | 1921 | United States |
| Bertha Wilson | 1923 | Canada |
| Tamar Pelleg-Sryck | 1926 | Israel |
| Claire L'Heureux-Dubé | 1927 | Canada |
| Simone Veil-Jacob | 1927 | France |
| Sandra Day O'Connor | 1930 | United States |
| Flerida Ruth P. Romero | 193? | Philippines |

| | | |
|---|---|---|
| Ruth Bader Ginsburg | 1933 | United States |
| Jutta Limbach | 1934 | Germany |
| Barbara Charline Jordan | 1936 | United States |
| Rosalyn Higgins | 1937 | United Kingdom |
| Eleanor Holmes Norton | 1938 | United States |
| Janet Reno | 1938 | United States |
| Helga Seibert | 1939 | Germany |
| Margaret A. Somerville | 1942 | Canada |
| Beverley McLachlin | 1943 | Canada |
| Mary Robinson | 1944 | Ireland |
| Brenda Marjorie Hale | 1945 | United Kingdom |
| Leah Tsemel | 1945 | Israel |
| Mary Arden | 1947 | United Kingdom |

## EDUCATORS AND SCHOLARS

| | **Year of birth** | **Country** |
|---|---|---|
| Helene Stöcker | 1869 | Germany |
| Burnita Shelton Matthews | 1894 | United States |
| Suzanne Bastid-Basdevant | 1906 | France |
| Soia Mentschikoff | 1915 | United States |
| Helen Suzman | 1917 | South Africa |
| Miriam Ben-Porat | 1918 | Israel |
| Irene R. Cortes | 1920 | Philippines |
| Simone Rozès-Ludwig | 1920 | France |
| Bertha Wilson | 1923 | Canada |
| Beverly Blair Cook | 1927 | United States |
| Claire L'Heureux-Dubé | 1927 | Canada |
| Sadako Ogata | 1927 | Japan |
| Takako Doi | 1928 | Japan |
| Flerida Ruth P. Romero | 193? | Philippines |
| Ruth Bader Ginsburg | 1933 | United States |
| Jutta Limbach | 1934 | Germany |
| Barbara Charline Jordan | 1936 | United States |
| Rosalyn Higgins | 1937 | United Kingdom |
| Eleanor Holmes Norton | 1938 | United States |
| Margaret A. Somerville | 1942 | Canada |
| Beverley McLachlin | 1943 | Canada |
| Mary Robinson | 1944 | Ireland |

| | | |
|---|---|---|
| Brenda Marjorie Hale | 1945 | United Kingdom |
| Mary Arden | 1947 | United Kingdom |

## POLITICAL OFFICEHOLDERS AND ACTIVISTS

| | **Year of birth** | **Country** |
|---|---|---|
| Myra Bradwell | 1831 | United States |
| Carrie Burnham Kilgore | 1838 | United States |
| Anita Augsburg | 1857 | Germany |
| Emily Ferguson Murphy | 1868 | Canada |
| Helene Stöcker | 1869 | Germany |
| Florence Ellinwood Allen | 1884 | United States |
| Helen Kinnear | 1894 | Canada |
| Burnita Shelton Matthews | 1894 | United States |
| Elisabeth Selbert | 1896 | Germany |
| Wiltraut Rupp-von Brünneck | 1912 | Germany |
| Cecilia Muñoz Palma | 1913 | Philippines |
| Helen Suzman | 1917 | South Africa |
| Miriam Ben-Porat | 1918 | Israel |
| Irene R. Cortes | 1920 | Philippines |
| Leonilde Iotti | 1920 | Italy |
| Simone Rozès-Ludwig | 1920 | France |
| Tamar Pelleg-Sryck | 1926 | Israel |
| Claire L'Heureux-Dubé | 1927 | Canada |
| Sadako Ogata | 1927 | Japan |
| Simone Veil-Jacob | 1927 | France |
| Takako Doi | 1928 | Japan |
| Sandra Day O'Connor | 1930 | United States |
| Flerida Ruth P. Romero | 193? | Philippines |
| Jutta Limbach | 1934 | Germany |
| Barbara Charline Jordan | 1936 | United States |
| Eleanor Holmes Norton | 1938 | United States |
| Janet Reno | 1938 | United States |
| Helga Seibert | 1939 | Germany |
| Mary Robinson | 1944 | Ireland |
| Leah Tsemel | 1945 | Israel |
| Sylvie Kanigi | 1953 | Burundi |
| Agathe Uwilingiyimana | 1953 | Rwanda |

# SELECTED BIBLIOGRAPHY

Abel, Richard L. *American Lawyers*. New York: Oxford University Press, 1989.

Aliotta, Jilda M. ''Justice O'Connor and the Equal Protection Clause: A Feminine Voice?'' *Judicature* 78 (March–April, 1995): 232–35.

Allen, David W., and Diane E. Wall. ''Role Orientations and Women State Supreme Court Justices.'' *Judicature* 77 (1993): 156–65.

Allen, Florence Ellinwood. *To Do Justly*. Cleveland: Western Reserve University Press, 1965.

Alpern, Sara, Joyce Antler, Elisabeth Israels Perry, and Ingrid Winther Scobie, eds. *The Challenge of Feminist Biography: Writing the Lives of Modern American Women*. Urbana: University of Illinois Press, 1992.

American Mothers Committee, Inc. *Mothers of Achievement in American History: 1776–1976*. Bicentennial Project 1974–1975. Rutland, Vt.: Tuttle, 1976.

Atkins, Susan, and Brenda Hoggett [B. Hale]. *Women and the Law*. London: Basil Blackwell, 1984.

Blanke, Thomas (ed.). *Streitbare Juristen*. Baden-Baden: Nomos Verlagsgesselschaft, 1990.

Bradbrook, M. C. *That Infidel Place: A Short History of Girton College, 1869–1969*. London: Chatto and Windus, 1969.

Canadian Bar Association. *Touchstones for Change: Equality, Diversity and Accountability*. Report of the Task Force on Gender Equality in the Legal Profession, 1993.

Cook, Beverly B. ''Marion Harron.'' In *American National Biography*. New York: Oxford University Press, 1996.

Cook, Beverly B. ''A Critique of the Supreme Court's 1982 Agenda: Alternatives and the NYU Legal Model.'' *Justice System Journal* 17 (1994): 135–51.

Cook, Beverly B. ''Ghosts and Giants in Judicial Politics.'' *PS: Political Science and Politics* 27 (1994): 78–84.

Cook, Beverly B. ''Moral Authority and Gender Difference: Georgia Bullock and the Los Angeles Women's Court.'' *Judicature* 77 (1993): 144–55.

Cook, Beverly B. ''Women Judges: A Preface to Their History.'' *Golden Gate University Law Review* 14 (1984): 573–74.

Cook, Beverly B. ''Women as Supreme Court Candidates: From Florence Allen to Sandra Day O'Connor.'' *Judicature* 65 (1982): 314–26.

Cook, Beverly B. ''The First Woman Candidate for the Supreme Court.'' *Supreme Court Historical Society Yearbook* (1981): 19–35.

Cook, Beverly B. ''The Impact of Women Judges upon Women's Legal Rights: A Prediction from Attitudes and Simulated Behavior.'' In *Women, Power and Political Systems*. Ed. Margherita Rendel. New York: St. Martin's Press, 1981.

Cook, Beverly B. ''Women Judges: The End of Tokenism.'' In *Women in the Courts*. Williamsburg, Va.: National Center for State Courts, 1978.

Cook, Beverly B. ''The Socialization of New Federal Judges: Impact on District Court Business.'' *Washington University Law Quarterly* (1971): 253.

Cott, Nancy F. *The Grounding of Modern Feminism*. New Haven, Conn.: Yale University Press, 1987.

Davis, Sue. ''The Voice of Sandra Day O'Connor.'' *Judicature* 77 (November–December, 1993): 135.

Davis, Sue, Susan Haire, and Donald R. Songer. ''Voting Behavior and Gender on the U.S. Courts of Appeals.'' *Judicature* 77 (November–December, 1993): 129–33.

Drachman, Virginia G. *Women Lawyers and the Origins of Professional Identity in America*. Ann Arbor: University of Michigan Press, 1993.

Duchen, Claire. *Women's Rights and Women's Lives in France, 1944–1968*. London: Routledge, 1994.

Edelman, Martin. *Courts, Politics, and Culture in Israel*. Charlottesville: University Press of Virginia, 1994.

Edward, India. *Pulling No Punches: Memoirs of a Woman in Politics*. New York: G. P. Putnam's Sons, 1977.

Epstein, Cynthia Fuchs. *Women in Law*. New York: Basic Books, 1981.

Friedman, Jane M. *America's First Woman Lawyer: The Biography of Myra Bradwell*. Buffalo, N.Y.: Prometheus Books, 1993.

Gallagher, Michael, Michael Laver, and Peter Mair. *Representative Government in Modern Europe*. New York: McGraw-Hill, 1995.

Gibb, Frances, and Michael Hornell. ''Women Lawyers Freed to Wear Trousers in Court.'' *The Times* (May 17, 1995): 1.

Hellman, Judith Adler. *Journeys Among Women: Feminism in Five Italian Cities*. New York: Oxford University Press, 1987.

Hine, Darlene Clark (ed.) *Black Women in America: An Historical Encyclopedia*. New York: Carlson Publishing, 1993.

Irwin, Inez Haynes. *Amazons and Angels: A Hundred Years of American Women*. Garden City, N.Y.: Doubleday, Doran, and Co., 1933.

Karim, Wazir Jahan. *Women and Culture: Between Malay Adat and Islam*. Boulder, Colo.: Westview Press, 1992.

Kendall, Paul Murray. *The Art of Biography*. New York: W. W. Norton, 1965.

Lebra, Takie Sugiyama. *Japanese Women: Constraint and Fulfillment*. Honolulu: University of Hawaii Press, 1984.

Lippert, Anne. ''Algerian Women's Access to Power: 1962–1985.'' In *Studies in Power and Class in Africa*. Ed. Irving Leonard Markovitz. New York: Oxford University Press, 1987.

Lovenduski, Joni. *Women and European Politics: Contemporary Feminism and Public Policy*. Amherst: University of Massachusetts Press, 1986.

Martin, Elaine. "The Representative Role of Women Judges," *Judicature* 77 (November–December, 1993): 172.

Martin, Elaine. "Women on the Bench: A Different Voice?" *Judicature* 77 (November–December, 1993): 126.

Mather, Lynn. "Introducing a Feminist Pioneer in Judicial Politics: Beverly Blair Cook." *PS: Political Science and Politics* 27 (1994): 77.

McLachlin, Beverley. "Crime and Women—Feminine Equality and the Criminal Law." *University of British Columbia Law Review* 25 (1991): 1.

Olsen, Frances. "From False Paternalism to False Equality: Judicial Assaults on the Feminist Community, Illinois, 1869–1895." *Michigan Law Review* 84 (June, 1986): 1522.

Personal Narratives Group. *Interpreting Women's Lives: Feminist Theory and Personal Narratives*. Bloomington: Indiana University Press, 1989.

Rhode, Deborah L. "Gender and Professional Roles." *Fordham Law Review* 63 (October, 1994): 39.

Rhode, Deborah L. *Justice and Gender: Sex Discrimination and the Law*. Cambridge, Mass.: Harvard University Press, 1989.

Rhode, Deborah L. "Perspectives on Professional Women." *Stanford Law Review* 40 (May, 1988): 1164.

Robinson, O. F., T. D. Fergus, and W. M. Gordon. *European Legal History: Sources and Institutions*. London: Butterworths, 1994.

Salem, Dorothy (ed.). *African American Women: A Bibliographical Dictionary*. New York: Garland Publishing, 1993.

Sanger, Carol. "Curriculum Vitae (Feminae): Biography and Early American Women Lawyers." *Stanford Law Review* 46 (May 1994): 1257.

Sherry, Suzanna. "Civic Virtue and the Feminine Voice in Constitutional Adjudication." *Virginia Law Review* 72 (1986): 543–615.

Smith, Christopher E., Joyce Ann Baugh, Thomas R. Hensley, and Scott Patrick Johnson. "The First-Term Performance of Justice Ruth Bader Ginsburg." *Judicature* 78 (September–October, 1994): 76.

Smith, Jessie Carney (ed.). *Notable Black Women*. Detroit: Gale Research, 1992.

Staudt, Kathleen. "Women's Politics, the State, and Capitalist Transformation in Africa." In *Studies in Power and Class in Africa*. Ed. Irving Leonard Markovitz. New York: Oxford University Press, 1987.

Tuve, Jeanette. *First Lady of the Law: Florence Ellinwood Allen*. Lanham, Md.: University Press of America, 1984.

United States Senate, Committee on the Judiciary. "The Denial of Justice to Women—A Summary of Discriminations." Committee Print, "Equal Rights." 77th Congress, 1st session (August 15, 1941).

United States Senate, Subcommittee of the Committee on the Judiciary. "Hearings on S.J. Res. 65." 75th Congress, 3rd session (February 7, 8, 9, and 10, 1938).

Ware, Susan. *Beyond Suffrage: Women in the New Deal*. Cambridge, Mass.: Harvard University Press, 1981.

Wilson, Bertha. "Will Women Judges Really Make a Difference?" *Osgoode Hall Law Journal* 28 (1990): 507; *Law Society Gazette* (1990): 261; *Provincial Judges* 14

(1990): 7; and ''Est-ce que des femmes juges feront une difference?'' *Rev. jur. Femme et Droit* 4 (1990–1991): 359.

Windschuttle, Elizabeth (ed.). *Women, Class and History: Feminist Perspectives on Australia, 1788–1978*. Auckland: Fontana/Collins, 1980.

# INDEX

# ABOUT THE EDITORS AND CONTRIBUTORS

LAWRENCE W. BEER is the Fred Morgan Kirby Professor of Civil Rights at Lafayette College, Pennsylvania. His major publications include *Constitutionalism in Asia: Asian Views of the American Influence*, *Constitutional Systems in Late Twentieth Century Asia*, and with Hiroshi Itoh, *The Constitutional Case Law of Japan: Selected Supreme Court Decisions, 1969–70* and *The Constitutional Case Law of Japan, 1971 Through 1990*. Beer is currently revising his 1985 treatise, *Freedom of Expression in Japan: A Study of Comparative Law, Politics and Society*.

GREG CASEY is Associate Professor at the University of Missouri—Columbia. He teaches judicial process, state government, and constitutional law. Much of his research bears on public opinion and courts, and public acceptance of controversial judicial rulings. He is currently working on a study of the role and impact of dissenting, concurring, and other opinions not of the court on the decision-making process.

WILLIAM B. CLEARY is Visiting Professor of Law at the College of International Studies of the University of Tsukuba located near Tokyo. He is the author of several comparative law articles that focus particularly on criminal law and procedure. Cleary is also an international commercial attorney and has practiced business law for 15 years in New York, California, Tokyo, and Guam. He is currently "of counsel" to the law firms of Klemm, Blair, Sterling and Johnson in Guam, and Tokyo City Law and Tax Partners in Shinjuku, Tokyo.

DORIS CORBETT is an historian who has taught at Wayne State University, Madonna University, and the Center for Creative Studies in Michigan. She has traveled as a guest lecturer and speaker on women's history to regional and national conferences around the United States. Corbett is currently writing the biography of Judge Helen Kinnear.

MARIE CORBETT is a justice of the Ontario Court of Justice, Toronto, Canada. She was called to the bar in 1970, and practiced administrative law for 16 years. Corbett is the founding president of the Canadian Chapter of the International Association of Women Judges. She has written and lectured extensively on environmental law, family law, pension law, and criminal law.

MARIA ELISABETTA DE FRANCISCIS earned her Ph.D. in political science from the University of Connecticut. She is now *Riceratore* (Assistant Professor) of Political Science at the University of Naples, Federico II. De Franciscis has published extensively on both Italian and American politics with articles and book chapters in both English and Italian.

LUBA DEWITT earned her master in philosophy at Karl Marx University in Leipzig, Germany, and her Ph.D. at Comenius University in Bratislava, Slovakia. Her dissertation was entitled "Zur Auffassung Croces Von der Asthetik als Wissenschaft von Ausdruck" ("Beneddeto Croce's Conception of Asthetics as Science of Expression"). Presently, Dr. DeWitt teaches Russian language at Florida International University in Miami.

JOHN DUGARD is Professor of Law at the University of the Witwatersrand, Johannesburg, South Africa. He is the author of *International Law: A South African Perspective*, *Recognition and the United Nations*, and *Human Rights and the South African Legal Order*. Dugard has been involved in the advocacy of human rights in South Africa for over 30 years.

MARTIN EDELMAN is Professor of Political Science at the Rockefeller College of Public Affairs and Policy at the University at New York, Albany. He is the author of *Democratic Theories and the Constitution* and *Courts, Politics, and Culture in Israel*. In 1987, Professor Edelman taught the first course on Israeli politics in the People's Republic of China at Peking University. He has also been a visiting professor at the University of Liverpool and Tel Aviv University.

LEE EPSTEIN is Professor of Political Science and Resident Fellow in the Business, Law, and Economics Center at Washington University, St. Louis, Missouri. She is the author of *Conservatives in Court*, editor of *Contemplating Courts*, and co-author of *The Supreme Court and Legal Change*, *The Supreme Court Compendium*, and *Constitutional Law for a Changing America*. Epstein's articles on law and courts have appeared in major American political science journals and law reviews.

CYNTHIA HARRISON is Associate Professor of History and of Women's Studies at George Washington University, Washington, D.C. She was formerly the chief historian at the Federal Judicial History Office, Federal Judicial Center. Harrison is the author of *On Account of Sex: The Politics of Women's Issues, 1945–1968*, and has written several articles and chapters on women and politics. Her current research is focused on the policy impact of women presidential appointees.

KEVIN HILL is Assistant Professor of Political Science at Florida International University. Professor Hill completed his doctoral work at the University of Florida in 1993. His dissertation, funded in part by grants from the National Science Foundation and the Fulbright program, explored the interaction between the state and environmental interest groups in Zimbabwe. His current research focuses on American and international use of the Internet by organized political interests.

DONALD W. JACKSON is the Herman Brown Professor of Political Science at Texas Christian University. He previously practiced law and served as a Judicial Fellow at the Supreme Court of the United States. Jackson's teaching and research interests include the protection of human rights in American domestic and international law. His most recent publications include *Presidential Policy Leadership and Civil Rights Policy* (co-editor with J. Riddlesperger), *Even the Children of Strangers: Equality Under the U.S. Constitution*, and *Comparative Judicial Review and Public Policy* (co-editor with N. Tate).

GISELLE DE BRUNO JAMISON is currently Coordinator for Academic Services for the College of Urban and Public Affairs at Florida International University. She earned her M.A. in international studies at Florida International University in Miami, Florida.

DONALD P. KOMMERS is the Joseph and Elizabeth Robbie Professor of Government and International Studies at the University of Notre Dame. He is also a member of the law school faculty. He has written extensively in the fields of German politics, American constitutional law, and comparative constitutionalism. The second edition of his book, *The Constitutional Jurisprudence of the Federal Republic of Germany*, will appear in 1996.

JACQUELINE LUCIENNE LAFON is a member of the Jean Monnet Faculty of Law at the University of Paris, XI. She has written *Les Deputes du Commerce et l'Órdonnance de mars 1673* and *Juges et Consuls: à la recherche d'un statut dans la France d'Ancien Regime* and co-authored *Judicial Selection: The Cross-Evolution of French and American Practices*. Lafon has published a number of articles and book chapters both in the United States and in France.

JOHN MCLAREN is the Lansdowne Professor of Law at the University of

Victoria, British Columbia, Canada. His research interests lie in Canadian legal history, and he has written on the history of vice law enforcement, racial and ethnic discrimination, and legal education. McLaren is co-editor of *Law for the Elephant, Law for the Beaver: Essays in the Legal History of the North American West* and *Essays in the History of Canadian Law: British Columbia and the Yukon.*

MARY JANE MOSSMAN is Professor of Law at Osgoode Hall Law School of York University. She teaches courses in Law and Gender, as well as in Family Law and Property Law. Mossman has undertaken research for a number of inquiries about women in the legal profession in Canada and has organized several conferences around these issues. She has also published a number of articles about women in the legal profession, and contributed to the academic symposium to honor former Justice Bertha Wilson at the time of her retirement as a member of the Supreme Court of Canada.

MASATSUGU NAYA is Professor of International Politics at Sophia University, Tokyo, Japan. He has written on security issues, arms control, and United Nations peacekeeping operations. Naya's current research is on nuclear weapons in the post–cold war era.

JEROME O'CALLAGHAN is Associate Professor of Political Science at the State University of New York at Cortland. He is the author of several law review articles and textbook chapters on American public law. O'Callaghan's current research focuses on the application of First Amendment principles to pornography.

VALERIE L. PATTERSON recently completed her Ph.D. in public administration at Florida International University. Her scholarly interests lie in the area of urban policy, and she is currently serving as Assistant Dean of the College of Urban and Public Affairs and Instructor in the School of Policy and Management at Florida International University.

CHERYL A. RUBENBERG is Associate Professor of Political Science at Florida International University, Miami, Florida. She is the author of *Israel and the American National Interest: A Critical Examination*, *The Palestine Liberation Organization: Its Institutional Infrastructure*, and numerous articles in scholarly journals and edited books.

REBECCA MAE SALOKAR is Associate Professor of Political Science at Florida International University. She is the author of *The Solicitor General: The Politics of Law* and has published articles on the congressional legal counsels, church politics in Florida, and on abortion and the Florida constitutional right to privacy. Salokar is currently working on a comparative analysis of state constitutional rights to privacy in the United States.

TERESA SCASSA is an Assistant Professor of Law at Dalhousie Law School, Nova Scotia, Canada. She teaches and writes in the area of public and administrative law. Her current research focuses on issues relating to the impact of law on language and culture, and she has published several articles in this area.

C. LYNN SMITH, Q.C., is Professor and Dean of Law at the University of British Columbia, Vancouver, Canada. She is the co-author of *Civil Jury Instructions* (with J. Bouck), editor-in-chief of *Righting the Balance: Canada's New Equality Rights*, and contributed a chapter (with W. Black) entitled "The Equality Rights," to the book *The Canadian Charter of Rights and Freedoms* (E. Mendes and G. Beaudoin, eds.). Smith has written in the areas of constitutional law and civil litigation, and is a founding director and former Chair of the Women's Legal Education and Action Fund. She is currently chair of the Board of Governors of the Law Foundation of British Columbia.

YOSHIHIDE SOEYA is Professor of Political Science at Keio University, Tokyo, Japan. He has written extensively on Japanese diplomacy in the Asia-Pacific and is the author of *Japanese Diplomacy and China, 1945–1972*. Soeya's current research focuses on Japan–Southeast Asia relations.

C. NEAL TATE is Regents Professor of Political Science at the University of North Texas. He has studied the Philippine judiciary since 1968, most recently under the auspices of a Fulbright-Hays Senior Research Fellowship. He is currently serving as Program Director for the Law and Social Sciences Program at the National Science Foundation.

CASSANDRA R. VENEY is Assistant Professor of Political Science at Illinois State University. She completed her doctoral degree at the University of Missouri–Columbia and submitted a dissertation that focused on the politics of refugee assistance in Kenya with a particular emphasis on women refugees.

MARY L. VOLCANSEK is Professor of Political Science at Florida International University. She has written *Judicial Politics in Europe*, *Judicial Impeachment*, and *Judicial Misconduct*, and co-authored *Judicial Selection*. Volcansek edited *Judicial Politics and Policy-Making in Western Europe* and has published a number of articles on aspects of judicial behavior, selection, and removal in Europe and in the United States.

GILBERT WARE is Professor of Political Science at Drexel University. He edited *From the Black Bar: Voices for Equal Justice* and wrote *William Hastie:*

*Grace Under Pressure*. His principal work-in-progress examines the political utility of prejudice, notably, and racism.

DAVID WESSELS is Professor of International Relations at Sophia University, Tokyo, Japan. He has written on international relations theory and international human rights. Wessels' current research is on human rights and forced migration.

MICHAEL WILSON is a graduate student in the Masters of Public Administration program at Florida International University in Miami, Florida.

SARAH WILSON is an attorney in the Civil Division of the Department of Justice in Washington, D.C. She served as a 1994–1995 Judicial Fellow at the Federal Judicial Center, where she conducted an oral history of women federal judges. She is currently working on a study of the appointment of women to the federal bench, and a history of gender equality law. Wilson received her J.D. from Columbia Law School and a Masters of Philosophy in American Studies from Yale University.

ZIPPORAH BATSHAW WISEMAN has been teaching commercial law and courses focusing on discrimination in law for over 20 years at the law schools at Northeastern University, Harvard, and the University of Texas. She has been married for 40 years to a film maker and is the mother of two sons. She is writing a biography of Soia Mentschikoff, who blazed the trail.

ISBN 0-313-29410-0

90000>

EAN

9 780313 294105

HARDCOVER BAR CODE